INTIMATE EMPIRE

INTIMATE **EMPIRE**

Collaboration and Colonial Modernity in Korea and Japan

NAYOUNG AIMEE KWON

Duke University Press   Durham and London   2015

Typeset in Arno Pro by Graphic Composition, Inc.,
Bogart, Georgia

Library of Congress Cataloging-in-Publication Data
Kwon, Nayoung Aimee.
Intimate empire : collaboration and colonial modernity in
Korea and Japan / Nayoung Aimee Kwon.
pages cm
Includes bibliographical references and index.
ISBN 978-0-8223-5910-4 (hardcover : alk. paper)
ISBN 978-0-8223-5925-8 (pbk. : alk. paper)
1. Japanese literature—Korean authors—History and criticism.
2. National characteristics, Korean. 3. Korea—History—
Japanese occupation, 1910–1945. I. Title.
PL725.2.K67K96 2015
895.609′9519 —dc23
2014046256
ISBN 978-0-8223-7540-1 (e-book)

Cover credit: Kim Saryang's postcard correspondence from
Tokyo to Korean author Ch'oe Chŏnghŭi, reprinted with
permission from Mr. Kim Jihoon of the estate of Ch'oe
Chŏnghŭi. Originally published in Kim Yŏngsik, ed., *Chakko
munin 48-in ŭi yukp'il sŏhanjip Pa'in Kim Tonghwan 100-chunyŏn
kinyŏm*. Minnyŏn, 2001.

For my parents,
Myung Hae Jun and Yong Sam Kwon

CONTENTS

ACKNOWLEDGMENTS

From conception to completion, this book has taken over a decade to write while in transit among three countries and stumbling across three languages. Along the way, I have been sustained by the generosity of many individuals, and I am indebted to the hospitality of those who have kindly opened up their homes, classrooms, libraries, collections, and conversations to this itinerant's many comings and goings.

First, my teachers at UCLA guided me from the beginning: Peter H. Lee, John B. Duncan, Namhee Lee, Seiji M. Lippit, Jinqi Ling, and the late Miriam Silverberg. This book could not have been conceived or realized without their intellectual rigor and generosity of spirit through the years. Friends from graduate school days supported me as fellow travelers and co-conspirators at various stages of the journey: Takushi Odagiri, Chiyoung Kim, Jennifer Shin, Mickey Hong, Seung-Ah Lee, Yingzi Stella Xu, Charles Kim, Sonja Kim, John Namjun Kim, Min-Suh Son, Hijoo Son, Ellie Choi, Todd Henry, Koichi Haga, Youngju Ryu, Chris Hanscom, and Jinsoo An. I thank Hyaeweol Choi for the opportunity to teach at Arizona State University and the wonderful colleagues there for their warm hospitality during my stay.

In Korea, I am grateful to Kwon Youngmin for welcoming me to Seoul National University. Kim Chul and Lee Kyounghoon kindly allowed me to join their seminars and collaboratives at Yonsei University. One of the most influential was Hanil munhak yŏnguhoe (aka Suyohoe), which became my home away from home in Seoul. Other teachers and friends I continue to learn from include Sin Hyŏng-gi, Seo Jae-kil, Cha Seung-ki, Baek Moonim, Kwŏn Myŏnga, Jung Jaewon, Tajima Tetsuo, Kim Yerim, Pak Hana, Yi Hwajin, Choe Yŏngsŏk, Chŏng Chonghyŏn, Kim Chaeyŏng, Makase Akiko, Hwang Hoduk, Yi Yŏngjae, Kim Chaeyong, and Chung Kŭnsik. I thank each of them for ongoing dialogues.

In Japan, I thank Hotei Toshihiro for kindly hosting me at Waseda University. In Tokyo, I have also been the beneficiary of the teaching and friendship of Ōmura Masuo, Sim Wŏnsŏp, Kim Ŭngyo, Nam Bujin, Kwak Hyoungduck, Pak Hŭibyŏng, Cho Kiŭn, and Fujiishi Takayo. I would like to thank Yonetani Masafumi and the graduate students at Gaidai, and Kawamura Minato and his graduate students at Hōsei University for making me feel welcome in their seminars. Watanabe Naoki and friends at Inmun P'yŏngnon Yŏnguhoe deserve special gratitude: this became yet another home away from home when in Tokyo.

Shirakawa Yutaka has been a thoughtful supporter of my work. I would like to especially thank him for graciously sharing ideas and resources, including rare photographs, and for introducing me to the Noguchi family who have so kindly made available their stories and personal collections to me. In Kyoto, I continue to be inspired by Mizuno Naoki for his intellectual generosity and rigor. I also thank Matsuda Toshihiko at Nichibunken for kindly sharing his expertise on colonial era police records.

At Duke, I could not have wished for a more supportive group of colleagues and friends to accompany me at the final stretch of this journey. I would like to thank the Franklin Humanities Institute for sponsoring my manuscript workshop and to all the participants for their rigorous and careful reading of the manuscript: David Ambaras, Leo Ching, Kyeong-Hee Choi, Eileen Chow, Hae-Young Kim, Reed Malcolm, Ellen McLarney, Walter Mignolo, and Naoki Sakai. I am especially grateful to Naoki Sakai, Kyeong-Hee Choi, and Reed Malcolm, for traveling from far away, and for their thoughtful comments, criticism, and encouragement at this crucial junction. Ellen and Eileen also deserve special mention for being the best writing team, cheering me toward the finish line. I thank miriam cooke, Shai Ginsburg, Gennifer Weisenfeld, Guo-Juin Hong, Carlos Rojas, Rey Chow, Hwansoo Kim, Eunyoung Kim, and Cheehyung Kim for their continued guidance and friendship. I am grateful to several people who have read all or parts of the manuscript and offered their insights at crucial stages: Takashi Fujitani, Jin-Kyung Lee, Theodore Hughes, and Jonathan Abel. I thank library specialists Kris Troost, Luo Zhuo, and Miree Ku for their research expertise. Special thanks to Elizabeth Brown for her careful and incisive editing and warm encouragement in preparing an early draft. J. Rappaport expertly added the final touches at the last stage of production.

The research, writing, and publication were generously supported through grants from Fulbright-Hays, the Fulbright IIE, the Korea Foundation, Duke University Arts and Sciences, the Andrew W. Mellon/Franklin Humanities Institute, the Asian Pacific Studies Institute, the Triangle Center for Japanese Studies, and the Office of the Dean of the Humanities.

Parts of chapters 1 and 2 appeared in an earlier version as "Colonial Modernity and the Conundrum of Representation: Korean Literature in the Japanese Empire," in *Postcolonial Studies* 13, no .4 (2010): 421–39. An earlier version of chapter 5 was published as "Conflicting Nostalgia: Performing *The Tale of Ch'unhyang* (春香傳) in the Japanese Empire," in *Journal of Asian Studies*, 73, no. 1 (February 2014): 113–41.

The following individuals and institutions were instrumental in securing images and permissions: Chung Wha Lee Iyengar, from the estate of Yi Kwangsu, and Hatano Setsuko for help acquiring rare photos of Yi Kwangsu; Liu Chih-Fu, from the estate of Long Yingzong, with special thanks to Wang Huei-Chen and Shin Ji-Young, for their help accessing a copy of a rare correspondence between Kim Saryang and Long Yingzong; Jihoon Kim from the estate of Ch'oe Chŏnghŭi for permission to reprint rare postcard correspondences. I would also like to acknowledge the archivists at Seoul National University Rare Book Archives; Waseda University Archives; Tsubouchi Shōyō Memorial Museum; Ōhara Institute for Social Research, Hōsei University; and Meiji Gakuin Archives of History.

At Duke University Press, I thank Ken Wissoker for having faith in the project and for his grace and expertise in shepherding it through the various hurdles, and Elizabeth Ault and Sara Leone for their professionalism and guidance in the final stages of the publication process.

Finally, my family is my anchor, and I cannot adequately express my appreciation for their constant love, encouragement, and patience. It is with boundless love and gratitude that I dedicate this book to my parents, Myung Hae Jun and Yong Sam Kwon, whose paths as teachers I myself have embarked upon, and whose lifelong love of books, I have inherited: 감사합니다.

Naming is a complex matter in colonial and postcolonial contexts. Many proper names can be read or rendered in multiple ways in Korean, Japanese, and variant hybrid forms. When we take into account pseudonyms, pen names, colonial name changes, and so forth, each name holds yet more multiplicities. For example, the author Chang Hyŏkchu is also known as Chō Kakuchū, Noguchi Kakuchū, Noguchi Minoru, and so on. Following one convention with consistency for all names would have been impossible in this book, and while variants are introduced at times, I have often chosen one rendering per author to reduce confusion.

Romanization of words from Korean, Japanese, and Chinese follow the McCune Reischauer, Hepburn, and Pinyin systems respectively. Exceptions were made when more commonly known conventions are available (e.g., Seoul or Tokyo), or in cases when authors have expressed alternative preferences. Japanese and Korean terms are sometimes given together with corresponding initials J and K respectively. Proper names for authors who publish primarily in Asian languages follow cultural conventions of given names following surnames. Unless otherwise indicated, all translations are my own.

ONE

COLONIAL MODERNITY AND THE
CONUNDRUM OF REPRESENTATION

In embarking on an examination of the contentious and divided modern histories of Korea and Japan, we might do worse than begin with the following: a small story just seven short pages, long forgotten but significant, of their once shared literary past. The Japanese-language short story "Aika" (Love?) appears with a byline of a colonial Korean author, Yi Pogyŏng, who is labeled as a "Korean exchange student" (Kankoku ryūgakusei). We now know that this story was penned on the eve of Japan's colonization of Korea by none other than Yi Kwangsu (1892–1950?)—the father of modern Korean literature. In the following decades, as Korea was becoming more deeply subsumed into Japan after being demoted to colonial status, Yi Kwangsu (Pogyŏng was his given name) would soon become one of the most prominent and contested colonial writers in the Japanese empire. Yi wrote "Aika" in Japanese as a student studying abroad in the imperial metropolitan center of Tokyo. His travels paralleled the journey toward "enlightenment," what Edward Said elsewhere calls the "voyage-in,"[1] of so many of his colonial counterparts from around the world into the heart of empire. Yi affectionately called "Aika" his "maiden work" (ch'ŏnyŏjak), a melancholy story about the unrequited homoerotic desire of a Korean schoolboy Bunkichi/Mungil for his Japanese classmate Misao.[2] The story was penned nervously in the formative years by the young boy who would quickly rise to

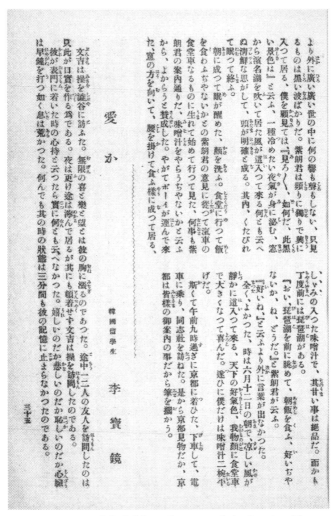

FIG. 1.1 Yi Kwangsu's "Aika" from *Shirogane gakuhō*. Reprinted from Meiji Gakuin Archives of History.

fame as the "father of modern Korean literature" and then seemingly just as quickly fall infamously as a traitorous colonial collaborator (even changing his name to the Japanese Kayama Mitsurō). This rise and fall of Yi Kwangsu or his journey toward becoming Kayama Mitsurō is still contested and little understood, and the story "Aika" takes us back to a primal scene of scandalous confluences in Korea and Japan's contested colonial encounter at the turn of the twentieth century.

After wavering impotently in the dark, hovering at the threshold of the

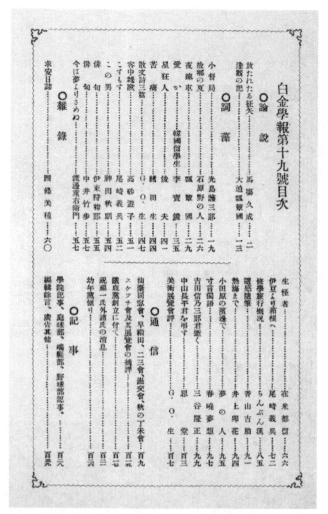

FIG. 1.2 Table of Contents for *Shirogane gakuhō* lists Yi as a "Korean Exchange Student." Reprinted with permission from Meiji Gakuin Archives of History.

guesthouse where Misao lodges, Bunkichi/Mungil wonders anxiously to himself whether Misao would reciprocate his affections:

> Bunkichi/Mungil went to visit Misao in Shibuya. Joy and pleasure and boundless hope filled his breast. Stopping along the way to visit one or two other friends had only been a pretext. Night was falling, and the street was becoming hard to see. But Bunkichi/Mungil was determined to make

FIG. 1.3 Students and teachers at Meiji Gakuin. Yi Kwangsu is standing in the last row to the far left. Reprinted with permission from the Meiji Gakuin Archives of History. Special thanks to Professor Hatano Setsuko for sharing a copy of this photo.

FIG. 1.4 Students and teachers at Meiji Gakuin. Yi Kwangsu is the third from the right in the second row from the top. Reprinted with permission from the Meiji Gakuin Archives of History. Special thanks to Professor Hatano Setsuko for sharing a copy of this photo.

his way to Misao. . . . He passed through the gate and walked toward the entrance. His heart was beating even faster and his body was shaking. The storm door was shut and everything was deathly quiet. Maybe he's asleep already. No, that can't be. It's only a little past nine. It's the middle of exams, there's no way he'd be in bed already. It must be that out here they lock up early. Should I knock? Someone's sure to come to the door if I do. . . . But Bunkichi/Mungil was unable to stir. He held his breath and just stood like a wooden statue. Why? Why did he come all this way only to find himself unable to make a move? It wasn't that he thought he'd get into trouble if he knocked, or that he stopped his raised fist at the last second; he simply did not have the courage. Right now Misao must be hitting the books hard for his exams. He would never dream that I am standing here now. There are only two thin walls between us, but our thoughts are a million miles apart. What should I do? All that expectation and joy melted like spring snow. Do I give up and just leave like this? Despair and pain tightened Bunkichi/Mungil's chest. He turned around and began to tiptoe away.[3]

The conflicted emotions contending within Bunkichi/Mungil's solitary soliloquy is noteworthy. After much agonizing, he remains stiff and "unable to stir," in an impasse to decide one way or another and "make a move." The thin wall renders his love so close, yet so far away (seemingly "a million miles away"), and exacerbates his impossible longing. Powerless to endure the silence from the absent object of his desire, Bunkichi/Mungil finally turns back, alone and dejected. The story ends with him laying himself down on train tracks, tearfully awaiting the train to speed by and put an end to his lonesome misery.

Despite its long absence from their literary histories, this story is remarkable for both modern Korean and Japanese literatures, in form and content, textually and meta-textually.[4] Loosely based on snippets of the writer's own life, it was written in the imperial language of Japanese in the metropolitan form of the "I-novel," a fictionalized, self-conscious, confessional narrative that would become *the* canonical form in modern Japanese literature.[5] It also prefigures important themes in the rise of modern Korean literature, not the least with Bunkichi/Mungil's final lament, "stars are heartless" (*hoshi wa mujō da*) which anticipates Yi's later masterpiece, *Mujŏng* (The heartless), which would inaugurate a national canon and be considered the first modern novel of Korea.[6]

Such confluences of cultures between Korea and Japan (especially but not limited to their literatures) have long been evaded in both *postcolonial* nation-states.[7] Although Yi would subsequently grow up to become one of the most prominent figures (not only in colonial Korea, but in the Japanese empire at large), this work—like other Japanese-language writings by former colonized subjects—was long forgotten after the abrupt collapse of the empire in 1945, in both Japan and Korea. Only in 1981 would it become available in Korean translation.[8] In Japan, it would not be published in an anthology on post-colonial literature until 1996, almost a century after it was first written.[9]

Intimate Empire examines the broader significance of such intimately shared but disavowed colonial pasts in the modern histories of Korea and Japan and their contested legacies in the Asia-Pacific. "Disavowal" here means the ambivalent and unstable play of recognition and denial.[10] While I begin with Freudian and Lacanian psychoanalytic senses of the concept, I am more interested in how it translates to the social context of imperialism. The secret desire for the colonial Other in this story hints at the unspeakable nature of such colonial intimacies that have yet to be fully recognized or reckoned with in the postcolonial aftermath. The imperial encounter as a discomforting scene of desire (coexisting, yet with repulsion) has become familiar from other glob-ally translated and documented colonial contexts, for instance, from Europe's empires. The works of those who have become luminaries of the postcolonial canon, such as Aimé Césaire, Frantz Fanon, Albert Memmi, Marguerite Duras, Jacques Derrida, Abdelkebir Khatibi, Salman Rushdie, and many others, are wrought with famous scenes of colonial miscegenation and the resulting anxieties. Although ubiquitous in narratives of Europe's encounters with its colonial Others, these contact zones of transcolonial misogyny still remain some of the most troubling and conceptually difficult aspects of colonization to address in postcolonial reckonings (I will return to this ubiquitous challenge in chapter 10).

The homoerotic tension in "Aika" further alludes to the particular complex-ity of the imperial history of Japan and the rigorous policies of assimilation (in language, culture, and political affiliation) of intimate Asian neighbors like Korea, with centuries of proximate and shared cultures and histories. Japan's ultimate goal was the formation of imperial subjects for wartime and imperial expansions into the "Rest" of Asia in what was couched as a mutual struggle against Western imperialism. In Korea (and to a lesser degree, in Taiwan), the goal was said to become one with Japan, as exemplified in the slogan *Naisen ittai* (内鮮一体, Japan and Korea, One Body).

However, such a Pan-Asianist impulse was always self-divided and self-contradictory. It involved the simultaneous production and consumption of the colonized as same and yet different. This contradiction undergirds all colonizing endeavors but took on a particular valence in the experience of colonizing proximate neighbors who were already closely affiliated—geographically, culturally, historically, and ethnically—long before the fact of colonial penetration. In such a case, the always already unstable divide between the colonizers and the colonized had to be managed closely. The production and consumption of colonial identification on the one hand and differentiation on the other wavered throughout the colonial period, depending on the empire's shifting needs and policies within constantly changing degrees of regional and global liaisons of affiliations.

In this context, many prominent colonial intellectuals, like Yi Kwangsu, were actively and rigorously mobilized for imperial agendas, and many even internalized the desire to "become Japanese" in order to overcome racial discrimination in the imperial hierarchy.[11] The story "Aika" anticipates the challenges raised by the life and works of Yi Kwangsu and many other prominent figures within modern Korean history and culture. It is difficult for Koreans to reconcile Yi's prominence as both a patriotic nationalist leader *and* a traitorous pro-Japanese collaborator. How does a postcolonial nation come to terms with the paradox of these seemingly incompatible and mutually exclusive, and yet intimately coexisting characteristics in someone who played such an influential role in the construction of modern Korean art and society? Yi went from penning *The Heartless*, the aforementioned first "modern Korean novel" about patriotic national reconstruction, and a draft of the declaration of independence demanding freedom from Japanese rule, to actively leading the way in espousing the assimilation of Korea into Japan (*Naisen ittai*) by the era's end. However, in postcolonial Japan, the artistic endeavors of colonized subjects like Yi, who had been pressured to stand before the public at the forefront of imperial policies, were completely erased from its history.[12] The story "Aika" and Yi's own life, along with the lives of countless other significant colonial-era figures from Korea, inscribed conflicting desires of the colonized in their collusion (voluntary or coerced) with the colonizers that neither side wanted to remember in the postcolonial aftermath.

At the height of the Japanese empire (1895–1945) and especially after the so-called Manchurian Incident of 1931,[13] colonial Koreans were rigorously assimilated and mobilized to cooperate with Japan's imperial expansions. The Korean language was increasingly censored and a rising number of colonial Korean intellectuals were educated in Japan, wrote in Japanese, and collaborated with the Japanese in order to produce cultural works and have their voices heard. Japanese-language writings and translations by colonized Koreans were at the forefront of cultural debates in both Japan and Korea. However, immediately following the empire's collapse in 1945, the writers and their works were put on trial (literally and figuratively) and their very existence was repressed in divided national discourses for over half a century.

This book examines the rise and repression of this controversial body of writings by colonized subjects at the contact zones of empire, and the ways in which these writings have reverberated since. The objects of inquiry are the writings of those who were on the front lines of cultural debates during one of the most contested and least understood moments of the colonial encounter between Korea and Japan, as well as the colonial and postcolonial debates surrounding them. Many of the works considered here have been defined within the rhetoric of colonial assimilation (*Naisen ittai*, Japan and Korea, One Body) during the colonial period and then in the postcolonial aftermath, as a literature of collaboration (*ch'inil munhak*, 親日文学), where *ch'inil* literally means "intimacy" or "collusion" with Japan. Rather than relying on such binary notions of assimilation versus differentiation (during the colonial period), or collaboration versus resistance (in later postcolonial assessments), this book proposes that we need to reframe the scandalous confluence of cultures under imperialism, as embodied by these texts, within a more historical term of intimacy. In this reformulation, the term "intimacy" is historically derived and translated from both the colonial-era rhetoric of *Naisen ittai* and the postcolonial rhetoric of ch'inil. This critical move allows us to cut across the impasses of imperial and nationalist binary rhetoric to redefine intimacy as an unstable play of affects informed by desire, longing, and affection—all of which coexisted with the better-known violence and coercion undergirding empire. This unstable play of affects was violently elided post-1945, when the rigid colonizer/colonized binary came to the fore as the organizing framework of re-membering colonial history on the Korean peninsula in Korea and Japan. Furthermore, redefining colonial collaboration as the uncanny coexistence of desire (or intimacy) along with coercion (and violence) at the scene of the colonial encounter also signifies broader impasses of the ambivalent experiences of colonial modernity.

In recent decades, pioneering scholars have begun an earnest examination of colonial modernity. In the case of East Asian studies, for example, Tani Barlow and a team of collaborators inaugurated one of today's most influential Anglophone journals on East Asian cultural productions by way of thinking through this problematic (*positions*, issue 1). This and other contributions, both coeval and subsequent, such as the later anthology *Formations of Colo-*

nial Modernity in East Asia, as well as *Colonial Modernity in Korea* (coedited by Gi-Wook Shin and Michael Robinson), stand at the forefront of a broad transnational outgrowth of scholarship wrestling with precisely what is meant by this suggestive but elusive term. For example, Shin and Robinson expressly declined to define colonial modernity at this early stage, leaving it open so as to encourage further transnational dialogue. Joining the ongoing conversation of many scholars who subsequently have been inspired by and have been building upon these important contributions, *Intimate Empire* proposes to reconsider this problem of colonial modernity as a "shared but disavowed" *conundrum* of modernity experienced in colonial subjection.

"Colonial modernity" is a paradoxical concept that is difficult to pin down. Komagome Takeshi points to the "ambiguity" of colonial modernity, its exact meaning often depending on the individual writer evoking the term.[14] This difficulty is further compounded because of its ironic resemblance to the imperial apologist rhetoric of colonial modernization (Ch'ŏn Chŏnghwa, Yonetani Masafumi, Yun Haedong, and others).[15] This book does not conceive that the condition of modernity in the non-West is a priori different from or alternative to that of the West in its empirical conditions. Instead, it takes as self-evident with many others (Fredric Jameson, Walter Mignolo, Arjun Appardurai, Gayatri Spivak, Leo Ching, Rey Chow, Yun Haedong) that modernity is a globally shared condition, coeval and ushered in by worldwide shifts wrought by the *uneven* global dispersion of capitalism.[16] It is, however, important to note that this unevenly shared predicament of modernity resulted in significant differences in the ways modernity was experienced by those who were defined *as if* they were in development and in need of catching up by external standards. Walter Mignolo has diagnosed the problem of coloniality as the constitutive "darker side of modernity," as its unacknowledged but intimate counterpart. Likewise, this book argues that the paradox of colonial modernity emerges not because there exists an internal contradiction between coloniality and modernity, but from the fact that such a contradiction was produced and imposed discursively and continues to undermine our understanding of the true intimacy between coloniality and modernity. What are actually constitutive and coeval (coloniality and modernity) have been discursively and hegemonically severed and forced into a contradictory relationship (psychically and politically) *as if* they were incompatible and not coeval. This rhetorical move had dire consequences for those lives most burdened by it; those experiences of the colonized that were relegated into a forever distant place and time in the hierarchy of the modern world order (see Fabian, *Time and the Other*).

In this book, I narrowly redefine colonial modernity as the experience of modernity in colonial subjection, whether through actual colonial domination or the hegemonic power and occupation of the West, both real and imagined (psychic, political, economic, militaristic, territorial, etc.). Colonial modernity is defined as a disavowed conundrum shared between the colonizer and the colonized in Korea and Japan, and more broadly shared throughout the non-West, with troubling implications for postcolonial legacies into the present. Reframing our understanding of colonial modernity thus further allows us to think through intimate yet unexamined connections between the paradox of colonial modernity and the paradox of postcoloniality, as will be further examined in chapter 10.

This book considers the devastating implications of such disavowed yet intimate histories for the lived experience of the colonial modern subject and their legacies. The refusal to recognize the modernity of his or her experience violently imposed impasses and antinomies deep into the fabric of that life. The fundamental contradiction or impasse that the colonial modern subject was forced to negotiate on various levels, bodily, psychically, linguistically, and politically, is characterized in this book as a "conundrum of representation." This conundrum of representation of the colonial modern subject will be examined using the case study of a body of imperial-language texts by colonized cultural producers. These texts reflect the condition of modernity lived in the shadows of both direct colonial rule (by Japan in the case of Korea) as well as the omnipresent threat of Western imperialism (for both Korea and Japan). These are in essence (both literally and metaphorically) translated or self-divided representations emerging out of the social context of colonial unevenness, in which colonial cultural producers—artists and writers, for example—necessarily and strategically were compelled to borrow the language of the hegemonic imperial Other in an attempt to voice themselves and to have the Self heard at the imperial discursive table in the language of that imperial Other.

The conundrum of representation via the imperial language of the colonial modern experience translates, mimics, and illuminates anew what has become a truism to characterize the modern experience at large as a "crisis of representation." This so-called universal crisis was said to arise from "the challenge of representing new content, the historical experiences of the modern world, in the context of changing social norms about the status of art and literature themselves." In practice, this is said to have produced works of art and literature that displayed formal characteristics such as fragmentation, stream of consciousness, anxiety, and atomization, and thus revealing a lack of faith in language to represent "reality as is."[17] However, such a characterization was never meant to recognize the experiences of the colonial modern subject who is often relegated to the status of a mere object in canonical texts. In response, there have been numerous important interventions to document the coevalness in the modernist forms produced by non-Western artists. For example, Seiji Lippit's *Topographies of Japanese Modernism* and the anthology *Modanizumu* (edited by William J. Tyler) have examined the case of Japanese modernism; Leo Ou-Fan Lee's *Shanghai Modern* and *Lure of the Modern* by Shu-mei Shih examine the Chinese case; and more recently Theodore Hughes's *Literature and Film in Cold War South Korea* and Christopher Hanscom's *The Real Modern* consider the case of Korea. Following such important endeavors, this book asks: how would characterizations of artistic content and form translate across the imperial divide when we put the politics of the imperial language and translation at the center of the colonial modern impasse?

In other words, what is meant by the conundrum of representation here is both inspired by and translates beyond this oft-cited truism in modernity studies at large which, because of their myopic tendency toward a Western-centric view of modernism, elaborate a universal "crisis of representation" that is more about the psycholinguistic reaction to representing the fractured existence of modern life than to the geopolitical circumstances that might have grounded such a fracture in the first place. There have been numerous deconstructive critiques from within studies of European modernisms and their inherent blind spots, following such pioneering contributions as Jean Rhys's *Wide Sargasso Sea*, Said's *Culture and Imperialism*, and Jameson's *Nationalism, Colonialism and Literature*. This book joins these discussions to consider the intersection of modernity studies with postcolonial studies toward another path for understanding representations arising out of the modern experience of the colonized, which are to be sure just as fragmented, atomized, and rife with anxious stream of consciousness as are the works of Western colonizers, but which necessarily take on specific and salient forms (form and content) for the colonial modern subject such as Korean writers and their Japanese counterparts at the colonial contact zones in the shadows of Western standards of value.

For the "Rest" who were modern but were denied full recognition *as such* in the hegemonic but all-too provincial logic that equated modernity with the West, modernity was a self-contradictory experience.[18] In this Eurocentric discourse, modernity itself was colonized and accepted as the purview of the West, and then "exported" to colonial Korea and semi-imperial Japan,[19] and elsewhere in the non-West. An instilled sense of the self as "belated" and "lacking" vis-à-vis a standard or value system set elsewhere—the self perceived and experienced as Other—is central to the colonial modern experience of the global majority, though never acknowledged as *authentically* modern in hegemonic discourses. This happens in degrees, infecting in concentric circles outward from imperial centers into the "non-West"; likewise, the "West" is not one. Dipesh Chakrabarty, in *Provincializing Europe*, for example, argues for the need to deconstruct Europe from within and without. Naoki Sakai's ongoing interventions interrogating essentialism in multiple languages have been important (*Translation and Subjectivity* and *Traces*). Roberto Dainotto in *Europe in Theory* has critiqued the internal dynamics behind the formations of Others within Europe. In the Japanese empire, this sense of belatedness or Otherness is shared by both the colonized (Korea) and the colonizer (Japan), aligning and complicating the colonial binary relationship, in ways dissimilar to dynamics more common in the dominant European empires.

The conundrum of representation for the colonial modern subject is manifold:

1. Conundrum of (modern) subjectivity: The subjectivity and agency of the colonized become paradoxical as the requisite membership to the bounded nation-state (with its privileges) is stripped away from the colonized subject. The conundrum consists foremost in being modern yet being denied, not only discursively but institutionally and systemically, the most fundamental "rights" of modern subjecthood. Since the modern subject is invariably linked to the nation-state form, for those living under the threat or actuality of colonization, or the related predicaments of occupation, exile, and so forth, the lack or the constant fear of losing this requisite nation-state status through colonial subjection causes tremendous anxiety, collectively and individually.

2. Conundrum of language: In addition to the universal inability to represent *reality* as is through language, the colonial modern experience is further burdened by the coercive lure of the normative universality of the imperial language. For the colonial modern subject, the mother tongue is always an Other. In *Monolingualism of the Other*, Jacques Derrida begins a powerfully personal indictment starting at the scene of coloniality from the position of a postcolonial subject; however, he regrettably ends his musings by subsuming the predicament of the m(other) tongue into an amorphously broad "Universal" condition. I would like to keep in mind

the earlier parts of his critique and extend its relevance to the colonial modern subject's constant need to translate the self as well as broader concepts into and from imperial cultures. Furthermore, the question of language is intimately connected to the question(s) of subjectivity and history.

3. Conundrum of history: For those relegated to the "waiting room of history" (those without history, according to Hegel), the question of who speaks for and passes down these histories has been wrought in controversy from the colonial to the postcolonial eras (Chakrabarty, *Provincializing Europe*). As unbelievable as it may seem, the modernity and the "timeliness" of the colonized and the formerly colonized, once deemed belated and lacking, are *still* being contested today.[20]

4. Conundrum of aesthetic representation of form and content: Violent metaphors of deracination, transplantation, and devouring inundate the anxiety of influence experienced by the colonized in their encounter with mighty empires. The pressure to translate native content into Western forms is tremendous and has continued long after the end of formal colonial rule. The tension between viewing art as an expression of the self or viewing it as a collective representative continues to haunt the artistic productions of the colonized and the formerly colonized. It is worth pointing out that such anxieties rarely plague those self-situated in civilizational centers. For example, the modernist artists and writers centering themselves within the West blithely *borrowed* "primitive" forms and content not only without anxiety but also without any qualms about whether to give credit where due. In the colonial modern experience, the questions of translating form and content become even more complex since the self is often perceived as Other. There is a deeply self-conscious sense of alienation that emerges from the problem of translating the self as Other for an imperial or world audience in the hegemonic language of the Other.

5. Conundrum of recognition: Philosophical, civilizational, ethical, and political questions are implicated in the failure to accord recognition to the colonial modern experience as representations of human effort on multiple levels. The history of the global failure to account for these experiences persists from the colonial to the postcolonial, although involving different degrees of disavowal.

In his essay "Representing the Colonized: Anthropology's Interlocutors," Edward Said critiques prior claims to universality and links the declining legitimacy of Eurocentric perspectives to what he in turn calls the "crisis of modernism."[21] He locates the origins of this crisis not in universal artistic formalism, but in the ethical, political, and historical failures of hegemonic Eurocentric narratives. Said argues that these narratives that have claimed to represent universal modern experiences have utterly failed to take into account the humanity of [Europe's] various Others. This glaring neglect, he charges, occurred over and over again, despite the fact that the "alterity and difference [which] are systematically associated with strangers, who, whether women, natives, or sexual eccentrics, erupt into vision . . . to challenge and resist settled metropolitan histories, forms, modes of thought."[22] Said critiques willful blindness of such metropolitan narratives as "paralyzed gestures of aestheticized powerlessness," which assume a "self-conscious contemplative passivity" and demonstrate the "formal irony of a culture unable to either say yes, we should give up control, or no, we shall hold on regardless."[23] The prevailing reluctance of imperial powers to let go of their empires, territorially and psychically, and the postcolonial implications will be examined in chapter 10.

Unlike many metropolitan canonical texts, in their self-assured (although misguided) certainty of their centrality, identity, and self-sameness, the imperial-language "representations of the colonized" never had the luxury of evading their constitutive imperial landscape, either on the textual or metatextual levels. The writings of colonized writers who aspired to address the imperial discursive space are painfully marked by the paradoxes and contradictions of empire on every level—from the context of being produced under imperial rule and being consumed across a colonial divide; it is this conundrum of representation that emerged in the barred or disavowed condition of the colonial modern encounter. It is an experience shared across the colonial divide between Japan and Korea as well as by the majority of the world's population but which has paradoxically been relegated to the devalued status of the particularity of the "minor," or the minority, that this book proposes to engage. It is a conundrum fully embedded in the violent history of imperial encounters, but one which has been historically marginalized (from local, regional, and global markets, as well as discursive spaces) and only seldom taken seriously as a model or representation of "human effort"—to borrow Said's phrasing—in the global modern experience.

Taking seriously Said's critique of collective failures of understanding global modern experiences thus far, this book asks: how then might the modern experience translate differently when refracted through the prism of the perspective of those who had to live through it in colonial subjection? In other words, how might our collectively inherited myopia be illumined otherwise when we actually take into account those Others who have long been absented in prior narratives of modernity, according to Said's critique? Also, how might familiar key terms from imperial encounters such as "collaboration" and "translation" take on new meanings when they are refracted through the parallax lens of the colonial modern encounter shared between the colonizer and the colonized and whose experiences were both deemed as translations of a *Western originary modernity*?

Deliberately translating and defamiliarizing universalist claims to modern experience at large, this book argues that the conundrum of representation in imperial-language writings penned by the colonized writer for imperial or metropolitan audiences necessarily arises from a different sort of "self-consciousness" or "aestheticized powerlessness"—one which includes and extends far beyond the issues of literary formalism noted by Said.

Furthermore, this book examines an altogether different type of failure and blindness of insight in the colonial encounter: the inordinate labor of translation of colonial writers, embodied in the unacknowledged efforts of the colonized to translate themselves into the imperial language in an attempt to participate in the imperial discursive space. The (naïve?) hopes of the colonized to be heard at the imperial discussion table face-to-face with their subjugators, where their fates were determined, without self-determination, were ultimately crushed in the hierarchical structures undergirding empire.

The book chapters are organized around select "translated encounters" of transcolonial collaborations between the colonizers and the colonized. The question of "collaboration" is taken away from the binary rhetoric of the empire and nation (*Naisen ittai* and ch'inil) to reexamine mutual implications at the various scenes of the colonial encounter: the production, consumption, and repression of the so-called literature of collaboration written by colonial Korean writers predominantly in the Japanese-language for imperial audiences; the negotiations of colonial writers in their roles as translators, native informants, or (self-)ethnographers; the examination of such transcolonial coproductions as theatrical performances and roundtable discussions (*zadankai*, Japanese [hereafter J]; *chwadamhoe*, Korean [hereafter K]) between the colonizers and the colonized; and the mass media curation and reproduction of translated colonial literature and culture as kitsch objects of colonial collections, or assimilated as sites of imperial "locality" (*chihō*) in the expanding empire. These various forms and forums of colonial collaborations between the colonizers and the colonized and the history of their rise and repression offer us an essential key to understanding anew broadly shared but disavowed histories and legacies of imperial relations in Japan and Korea, the Asia-Pacific, and beyond.

Ultimately, *Intimate Empire* pays attention to an archive of imperial-language writings by the colonized that have until now been marginalized in local and global theories and discourses on empire and modernity. Taking translation as both an object of inquiry and a tool of critical methodology, this book brings such translated texts into conversation with more familiar metropolitan terms.[24]

In other words, this case study of Korea's colonial encounter with Japan is offered not to provide a particular or aberrant example little known by its peripheral geographical location in obscurity and therefore in need of excavation or translation, but rather to reveal what was actively repressed to shed light back on and refract upon the blind spots of the center.[25] In paying attention to these hitherto disavowed efforts, this book will illuminate our collective failure to reckon with shared colonial pasts and will document how this failure not only devastated the individual authors and translators but also brought about detrimental national, regional, and global misunderstandings of empires past and present.

_____

TWO

TRANSLATING KOREAN LITERATURE

Munhak (文學) is a translation of the Western concept of literature.

YI KWANGSU

The Korean peninsula was being rigorously assimilated and increasingly integrated into the Japanese empire by the late-colonial period (*ilche malgi*). This periodization in Korean history typically refers to the late 1930s until the collapse of the Japanese empire in 1945, when assimilation policies intensified for the purposes of making Koreans into imperial subjects (hwangminhwa, K; *kōminka*, J) as the colony was mobilized for war, with the intensification of censorship of Korean-language media and the rise of Japanese-language texts by Koreans—although the watershed year shifts depending on the focus of scholarship.[1]

In this book, the late-colonial era is pushed back to the period from the Manchurian Incident of 1931 until 1945, when Japan was forced to relinquish its colonies in the *gaichi* (*oeji*, K, 外地, hinterlands).[2] While the political climate in colonial Korea certainly manifested a decisive shift in the late 1930s, my purpose in broadening the scope of inquiry is to highlight continuities in the run-up to the outbreak of all-out war in Asia, and to situate the particular experience of colonial Korea both in terms of its shifting relations with metropolitan Japan and also in terms of its regional status simultaneously menaced by Japanese and Western imperialism during the 1930s and beyond.

At this time, the Japanese empire itself appeared vigorous and boundless as it was expanding further into Manchuria and China, using Korea as a stepping stone or middleman along the way. In such a climate, the colony's culture, and especially its literature, was far from a detached or apolitical space to produce art. Works of art and literature, along with their producers, were actively mobilized by Japanese propaganda to reflect changing political trends in the empire. As Koreans' hopes of gaining political sovereignty seemed to become more and more remote, the question, what is Korean literature? (*Chosŏn munhak*, K; *Chōsen bungaku*, J) emerged with renewed spirit in the colony's cultural field.

This chapter examines colonial-era debates over the shifting location of Korean literature, debates that emerged in response to contradictory demands on colonial culture within the Japanese empire. It was a time when the keen desire for a modern Korean literature in the colony (which was deemed "belated" vis-à-vis hegemonic notions of temporality precisely because it seemed to lack such technologies and accoutrements of the modern) coincided with increasing censorship of the Korean language as well as a rising demand in the empire for colonized subjects to produce Japanese-language literature.[3] The specter of the absent nation is palpable in these and other cultural debates at this time, and rather than revert to a facile dismissal of the concept of the nation as an imagined community, this chapter interrogates inherited and constructed categories of the nation and its narration, and the tenacity of the desire for such bounded categories, as *precisely* the conundrum of the colonial modern condition. In the absence of Korea as a sovereign entity, the perceived lack of a modern national literature in the colony exemplified the paradoxes of the conundrum of representation in the imperial global order in paradigmatic ways. This is because the colonial modern subject was beset by impossible demands: the impossibility of writing in the vernacular, and the impossibility of writing in the imperial language. The impossible question of the national language speaks to broader issues regarding world standards of valuations of cultures according to imperial hierarchies. All these points came to the fore in the debates.

The debates about the shifting location of Korean culture, and particularly its literature, focused on the rising phenomena of Japanese-language literature penned by colonized Koreans who inhabited the colonial contact zones. Their writings caused deep anxieties across the borders of the empire at the time and also engendered troubled legacies. Such works have been embroiled in controversy from the time of their appearance and have long been relegated to the margins of the postcolonial national literary histories of both Koreas and Japan.[4]

In both postcolonial Koreas, these writings have been systematically and actively excluded or marginalized from literary histories for more than half a century. For example, Kwon Youngmin, a prominent literary scholar in South Korea, told me that he purposely avoided including these texts in his histories of Korean literature.[5] A North Korean collection of the writings by the bilingual writer Kim Saryang (who will be examined in chapters 3–5) likewise purposefully erased any traces of their Japanese origins.[6] The challenges to accessing these texts were myriad: significant hurdles include linguistic, spatial, and political barriers erected after the collapse of the Japanese empire between the subsequently partitioned Koreas and Japan. Scattered among major and minor colonial-era journals in both Japan and Korea, these writings have been gathering dust in rare collections and archives. Systematic compilations of some of them into scholarly anthologies did not begin in earnest until the late 1990s. The era in which many of them were penned—from the late 1930s until liberation in 1945—is commonly characterized as the "dark period" (amhŭkki) in Korean literary histories, following the famous coinage by the influential critic Paek Ch'ŏl in the immediate postcolonial aftermath.[7] After decades of complete silence shrouding this contentious issue, the significance of the publication of Im Chongguk's extensive compilation, Ch'inil munhak non (親日文学論, On literature of collaboration, 1966) cannot be understated, and it became an indispensable source in helping researchers navigate the murky terrain for the very first time.[8] Im's detective work was a solitary and even dangerous affair of laboriously combing through limited resources to compile evidence on meticulously hand-jotted note cards, braving political censure and censorship during the draconian Pak Chŏnghŭi dictatorship. It was in the year following the controversial normalization treaty between the governments of Japan and South Korea (1965) when sleuthing out colonial collaborators was deemed too close for comfort for the political establishment, with scandalous debts and legacies to Japan rumored to hark back to the colonial era (many such rumors have subsequently been exposed and confirmed, but not all). Im's magnum opus was impressive, encyclopedic in sheer scope, and its unveilings sent shock waves throughout South Korean society in its fearless exposés of some of its most prominent cultural and political figures, both historical and contemporary.

Although this work's significance in the modern history of the Koreas is in-

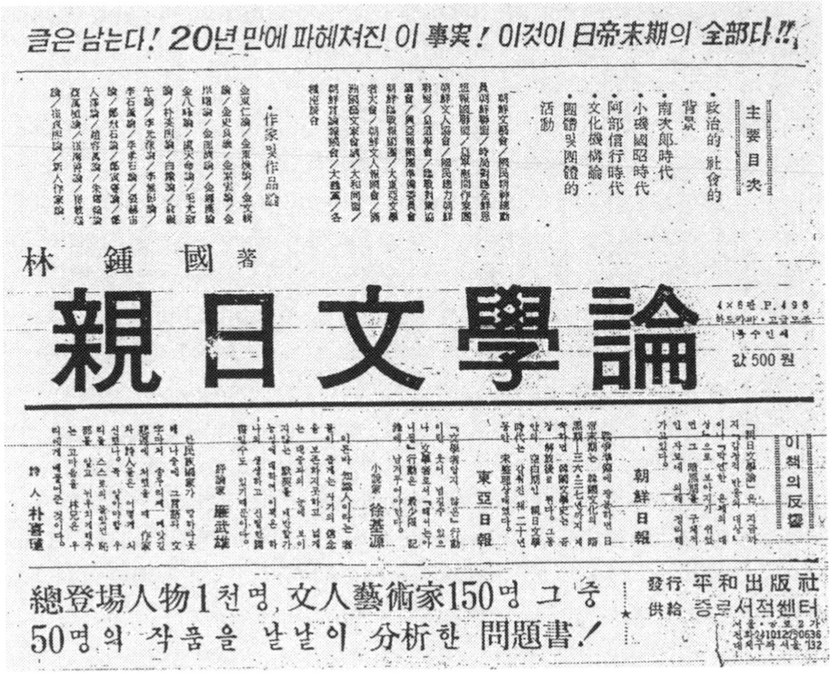
글은 남는다! 20년 만에 파헤쳐진 이 事実! 이것이 日帝末期의 全部다!!
主要目次
政治的 社會的 背景
南次郎時代
小磯國昭時代
阿部信行時代
文化機構論
團體및團體的 活動
作家및作品論
林 鍾 國 著
親日文學論
값 500 원
이책의反響
朝鮮日報
東亞日報
小說家 徐基源
評論家 廉武雄
詩人 朴喜璡
總登場人物1천명, 文人藝術家150명 그 중
50명의 작품을 낱낱이 分析한 問題書!
發行 平和出版社
供給 종로서적센터

FIG. 2.1 Newspaper advertisement announcing the publication of Im Chongguk's *Chinil Munhangnon* (Pro-Japanese literature).

disputable today, in its contribution to raising awareness and shedding light on the tabooed question of colonial collaboration, its very *form* of encyclopedic cataloguing rigidly fixed the parameters and categories under which these texts would be assessed. This work, more than any other, single-handedly defined the way in which these writings from the late-colonial era would be judged and discourses about them framed in subsequent decades. The operative word in the title ch'inil (親日), as we will recall from chapter 1, literally means "intimacy with Japan." But the term is inseparable from the stigma of traitorous collaboration, which would be married in fixed opposition to the opposing concept of "resistance" to delineate how the colonial past would be narrated and re-membered.

It is only in recent years, as late as the turn of the millennium, that the rigid binary of "resistance" versus "collaboration," implicit and explicit in Im's categorical judgment of writers and their texts, was finally challenged by scholars. These scholars are rethinking the binary opposition that had for so long been imposed upon postcolonial memories of the colonial past and continue to haunt the fates of not only those who appear in Im's volume but also others added in similar compilations by later endeavors. More nuanced and open dialogue, especially across the rigid borders between Korea and Japan, has been newly enabled but still remains limited because scholars fluent in both languages, who are also willing to scale the messy scholarly and political terrains, are still in the minority. Korean scholars of colonial history, for example, are adept in reading Japanese-language texts but few, even today, can converse freely in Japanese with their Japanese counterparts. The situation is even more dire the other way around, as knowledge of the language of the colonized was not a requisite for Japanese scholars of colonial history; and this bias largely persists even today, with few exceptions.[9] Furthermore, the overarching framework of binary opposition has far from disappeared even within dominant academic circles and is still prevalent in popular conceptions of the colonial past.

Since the late 1990s and early 2000s, a number of pioneering scholars have begun to take more nuanced and closer analytical examinations of the actual writings themselves. Kim Yunsik was the one exception, from a prior generation, who proved the rule. As a postcolonial scholar of the transitional generation, Kim himself had studied in the colonial education system and was thus fluent in Japanese, and had a long-held personal interest in this topic. The issue of Japanese-language writings was always a concern for Kim, but in his earlier works, it was primarily framed around other issues (proletariat literature, for example, as seen in his important work *Hanguk kŭndae munye pip'yŏngsa yŏngu* [On modern Korean literary criticism], 1973). It was only after Kim's retirement at the turn of the millennium that he began to publish prolifically and in a focused way on this issue, almost as if it had been repressed until then. (Since his retirement, Kim has published numerous volumes devoted to this topic and continues to remain prolific today.) We may recall from the previous chapter that Kim was the scholar who introduced Yi Kwangsu's "Aika" to South Korean readers in the 1980s. In his recent writings, he aligns the important but long neglected bilingual writer Kim Saryang (whose life and works will be examined in chapters 3, 4, and 5 in this book) to Lu Xun, the canonical author in Chinese literary history. For those familiar with both writers, the comparative gesture may come as a shockingly belated recognition of Kim Saryang's significance. Kim Yunsik's bold comparison, in fact, behooves us to think about the significance of the reasons behind why such an important writer had to be forgotten in the literary history of Korea throughout the greater part of the long twentieth century. Aside from Kim Saryang's controversial Japanese-language writings, he also "went north" (越北 *wŏlbuk*) during the Korean War, resulting in the banning of his writings from the South Korean literary field. Theodore Hughes makes the important connection between colonial and postcolonial disavowals in the making of a South Korean national canon.[10] In a preface to an important multivolume compilation of Kim's works recently released in Korean translation, the editors anticipate the day when "Kim's complete works can finally return to our bosom."[11] The scholarly endeavor to recuperate long-lost literary histories has not been easy. Kim Yunsik was indeed a pioneer in such efforts, but he was, as already mentioned, an exceptional figure, whose interest in this issue happened to coincide with his own linguistic background stretching into the colonial period. Generations subsequent to Kim Yunsik were actively discouraged from learning Japanese and were taught virulently anti-Japanese sentiments in the nationalist postcolonial education system. In fact, it is only in recent decades that Japanese programs have started to garner attention in Korean universities. We may recall that it was as late as 1998 when the legal bar against imports of Japanese cultural products was lifted in South Korea.[12]

The colonial generation, too, was actively encouraged to repress any remnants of the Japanese language that they had been forced or lured into learning, and which some had already deeply internalized as their own. With the abrupt collapse of the Japanese empire in 1945 and the new ideological and territorial divisions set in place in the postcolonial national milieu, each individual was left to reckon with the Japanese language within him- or herself on an individual basis and as a private matter, made to act *as if* they had never been exposed to Japanese at all. During a lecture, the critic Han Suyoung reminisced about his childhood horror at discovering his father's hidden fluency in Japanese when his father was drunk with his guard down. Han recalled that in his child's mind, he harbored a shameful secret that his own father might be a *ch'inilp'a* (親日派, pro-Japanese collaborator or faction). Han's important pioneering book on this topic further elaborates this issue.[13] With active, official suppression of the former imperial language firmly in place, conflated with the fact that opportunities for Koreans to study in Japan were severely limited, an effectual impasse prevented critical dialogue from occurring across the postcolonial divide. Hence, the controversial writings from the colonial past remained buried deep within obscure archives—cloaked under unquestioned assumptions about evidence of traitorous collaborations that had to be contained, and it appeared there was neither desire nor wherewithal to confirm or deny such assumptions.

Around the late 1990s, however, scholars began to access and read the contents of these texts, starting with a handful of Japanese exchange students studying in Korea, such as Hotei Toshihiro. Hotei told me that he was shocked by his realization of how little he and his countrymen knew of Japan's colonial relations with its Korean neighbor. He quit his corporate job and enrolled as an exchange student at Seoul National University. He began by compiling one of the pioneering catalogues introducing the broad scope of Japanese-language writings from colonial Korea as his MA thesis under the guidance of Kim Yunsik. Seoul National used to be the old Keijō Imperial University, and Hotei also had access to the vast collections of the Japanese-language holdings in the former imperial university archives that many Koreans by then had either forgotten about or were unable to read. He continued to contribute to scholarship in this area in substantial ways by compiling primary-source facsimile reprint compilations with Ōmura Masuo, another pioneer who left an earlier passion in Chinese literature to pursue scholarly work on Korean literature and had originally started this excavation work with the *zainichi* scholar Im Chŏnhye, among others. These scholars and other noteworthy pioneers like Shirakawa Yutaka made important headway into illuminating our understanding of this little understood colonial past.

Shirakawa wrote important critical analyses on Chang Hyŏkchu, a controversial and tabooed figure, examined in this book in chapters 6 and 7. (I myself am personally indebted to Shirakawa's pioneering scholarship; he also kindly introduced me to Chang Hyŏkchu's family when I was completing a translation of his pseudo-autobiographical literature.)[14] In addition, Shirakawa developed a new framework of *chinichi,* J; *chi'il,* K (知日, knowing Japan) beyond that of "pro-Japanese collaboration" by considering the unexpected similarities of bilingual writings shared among colonial-era intellectuals, even such canonical writers as Yŏm Sangsŏp along with Chang Hyŏkchu, and so on, in an attempt to get beyond the "scapegoating" logic of exceptionalizing ch'inil (親日, intimacy or collaboration with Japan) as a limited concern of just a few selectively branded writers.[15]

Exchange scholars from Japan were soon joined by their contemporaries from South Korea who also began to study abroad in Japan in greater numbers around this time. Lee Kyounghoon was one such scholar who went to Japan as an exchange student to do fieldwork for his doctoral dissertation, and his subsequent research in the archives of Japan enabled him to write one of the most influential rereadings of the works of Yi Kwangsu, including many of his Japanese-language works that had not, till then, been known in South Korea. As an exceptionally nuanced reader and critic of literary texts, he opened up a new critical space to engage with these texts closely. With exceptional linguistic talent, Lee also translated many of the more controversial texts that had not been available in Korean. While many of his contemporaries were focused on single-author studies, Chŏng Paeksu, another early postcolonial exchange student, penned an important book-length analysis (first published in Japanese and then in Korean translation) that considered several important writers, including Kim Saryang, in a nuanced comparative perspective, to map out a more complex terrain than had been available until then. He was also one of the first to engage with postcolonial studies perspectives in the comparison of Korean and Japanese modern literature through Japanese-language writings by colonized subjects. Others who have subsequently applied postcolonial and other theoretical paradigms are Yun Taesŏk and Hwang Hodŏk. Yun, for example, engages with Homi Bhabha's notion of mimicry and hybridity. Feminist perspectives such as those of Kyeong-Hee Choi, Myŏnga Kwŏn, Yi Haeryŏng, and Yi Sŏnok have expanded our understanding of how gender affected imperial-language writings.

Following these pioneering contributors, there have been numerous others working across the Korea-Japan divide. For example, Cho Kwanja put forth the provocative idea of "ch'inil nationalism" to consider the coexistence of seemingly oppositional traits in the writings of Yi Kwangsu and others.[16] Kim Chaeyong has made significant contributions, first through unearthing works previously unavailable. His and others' discoveries of Japanese-language writings by major canonical writers like Yi Kiyŏng and Han Sŏlya helped to expand the boundaries that literary history had to reckon with, beyond those few exceptional figures—or scapegoats—as earlier assumed. Kim Chaeyong, Kwŏn Bodurae, Kim Yunsik, Shirakawa Yutaka, and others have written about broader implications for modern Korean literature. Kim Chaeyong has also been active in promoting transnational scholarly networks connecting scholars from Korea and Japan with like-minded scholars working on Manchuria, Taiwan, mainland China, and Southeast Asia, and the United States to think critically and collectively about little-understood but historically significant connections.[17]

In Japan, postcolonial assessments of Japanese-language texts by colonial Koreans first came to prominence in the marginalized ethnic Korean minority communities. This community found itself suddenly and unceremoniously demoted from having been mobilized to active duty for the wartime empire, to ignored personae non gratae, effectively rendered stateless in a hostile postcolonial Japan where their very presence became unwanted reminders of traumatic war and imperial loss. Theirs was an important ethico-political mission to recuperate endangered histories that were being actively suppressed in postcolonial Japan. The recuperation of literary figures like Kim Saryang, Kim Talsu, and so on, were part and parcel of the efforts to construct a minor ethno-national canon, in the absence of recognition (in multiple senses) in the broader political and cultural fields in Japan.

Major pioneering contributions include those of the zainichi scholar Im Chŏnhye and other zainichi writers and scholars working closely with sympathetic Japanese scholars like Hayashi Kōji, in collecting and archiving the works as well as through writing critical analyses. This early generation succeeded in inaugurating a zainichi canon: on the one hand, they recuperated a much-needed genealogy of zainichi history that the mainstream society was deeply biased against; but on the other hand, they enacted their own exclusions through mythmaking and reductive, patriarchal retellings of select male authors who were said to have bravely resisted the Japanese colonial powers. While the desire to commemorate heroes for a deeply pained and excluded minority community may be understandable, other nuanced complexities of the zainichi history were excised from these early efforts as a result. Chang Hyŏkchu, the quintessential "traitorous collaborator" who married a Japanese woman and naturalized as a Japanese citizen after the colonial era (see chapters 5 and 6), is notably absent in these collections. Even today, zainichi authors such as Kim Sokpŏm rave about Kim Saryang but have little to say about Chang Hyŏkchu.[18]

These important contributions, however, remained on the margins of Japanese literary debates for decades. It is worth noting that only in 2006 were the first "complete works" of resident Korean literature (*zainichi bungaku*) finally compiled.[19] Kawamura Minato may be one of a few noteworthy exceptions, a scholar of Japanese literature and a specialist in the cultural productions from the Japanese empire who has been a prolific writer about colonial and postcolonial (including zainichi) literary output. Aside from Kawamura, scholars of modern Japanese literature have only recently come to take interest in colonial literature by the colonized themselves (as opposed to Japanese writers writing from the empire) and their legacies. Postcolonial zainichi literature did garner critical and public attention, especially as several zainichi authors were nominated or received the coveted Akutagawa Literary Prize. Chapter 3 discusses the colonial era precedence in the nomination of the colonial writer Kim Saryang and its relationship to how this ethnic minority group continues to remain categorically marginalized and relegated to an ethnic ghetto despite such exceptional moments of metropolitan recognition.

Some recent literary histories have also begun to deal with resident Korean literature in more substantial ways (as an important part of modern Japanese literary history).[20] However, the very use of the term "zainichi" gestures to a fundamental impasse, drawing attention to the status of these texts as marginal minority literature, set apart from mainstream "Japanese literature." In full awareness of this problem, critics such as Kim Sŏkpŏm and Komori Yōichi have challenged the very category of "Japanese literature," calling for the adoption of the term "Japanese-language literature" instead, as a means of moving beyond naturalized assumptions about the correspondence between nation, ethnicity, and language. The debate about just how far this category should extend, whether to minority or diasporic writers beyond the Japanese archipelago proper, resonates with similarly unresolved debates on the borders of Francophone and Anglophone literatures. Korean scholars specializing in Japanese literature, such as Nam Pujin, Ko Yŏngnan, Pak Yuha, and others have been active in the Japanese scholarly field as well.[21] The efforts of these scholars are now beginning to gain more recognition in mainstream Japanese scholarship as the discipline of postcolonial studies has become a major field of inquiry. Japanese scholars of Korean literature, such as Ōmura Masuo, Saegusa Toshikatsu, Hatano Setsuko, Hotei Toshihiro, Shirakawa Yutaka, Watanabe Naoki, Serikawa Tetsuya, and Fujiishi Takayo, have made important contributions by introducing Korean literature to Japanese audiences through translations, compendiums, and scholarly writings. Publishing houses committed to producing quality books (Yumani and Iwanami) have emerged to support such efforts. And more recently, there are Japanese scholars of Japanese literature (still a minority) who are considering the colonial relationship as an integral part of modern Japanese literature as well. Other scholars, like Watanabe Naoki and Hatano Setsuko (specialists on Im Hwa and Yi Kwangsu, respectively), have further contributed to bridging divides by promoting transnational collaborations and dialogue. For example, in addition to building an open environment and salon-style forums where international students and scholars can gather for intellectual exchange, they have spearheaded a transnational collaborative on thinking collectively and across nations about the question of "Japanophone" writings. Thanks to the tremendous contributions of these scholars, I believe the way has now been paved for the future, which lies with the next generation of postcolonial exchange students who are able to crisscross fluently in multiple languages and scholarly fields to truly map the complex terrain traversed by colonial writers, such as work done by Ch'oe

Chinsŏk, Hwang Hoduk, Ko Yŏngnan, Kwak Hyoungduck, Shin Jiyoung, Ryu Ch'unghee, and others.

Despite these important strides, a general divide persists in the scholarly and popular remembrance of the colonial pasts today, erupting into view with each contemporary political conflict. In chapter 10, I will revisit the ongoing implications of postcolonial disavowals between Korea and Japan and more broadly in the region. For the rest of this chapter, I would like to look closely at the era in which Korean literature was being subsumed into the Japanese empire and the anxieties triggered at the time of these transitions.

Transition (轉換期) and Crisis (危機)

The 1930s and 1940s were decades of political and economic tension across the globe; mass media descriptions of a time of "crisis" and "transition" were not unique to colonial Korea. Global anxieties were "coming together" on an unprecedented scale in the clash of war, from the metropoles to the colonies, and from East to West.[22] In the case of colonial Korea, the challenge of representation would become particularly marked after the so-called Manchurian Incident of 1931, when the colony was being assimilated and mobilized linguistically and politically for imperial expansion into China and beyond. During this period, a new generation of colonial writers with complex linguistic affiliations began to emerge. The majority of these prominent colonial intellectuals attained the requisite pedigree of a tour of study in Japan during their youth.[23] Japan served to mediate cultural imports from the West to the Rest of Asia. Colonial writers, whether or not they had physically journeyed to the heart of the imperial center, were learning the idiom and technology of literature from the West as it was translated through Japan and through the Japanese language.

It is in such a context that we may begin to understand why Yi Kwangsu, "the father of modern Korean literature," wrote his first literary piece "Aika" (Love?)—about the unrequited homoerotic love of a Korean exchange student called Bunkichi/Mungil for his Japanese friend Misao—in the Japanese language (see chapter 1).[24] This context also helps us to appreciate the agonized confession of another canonical literary figure, Kim Tongin (1900–1951), in which he describes his need to translate thoughts originally formed in Japanese as he began the painful process of writing in the Korean language.[25] There was a significant increase in the number of Japanese-language texts written by colonial Koreans from the late 1930s onward, a situation that arose from a combination of harsh censorship policies on Korean-language productions and an accompanying propaganda drive that *encouraged* the use of the Japanese language throughout the colony. It is for this reason that previous scholarship on these texts generally begins at this point.[26] Yet recent compilations of primary texts reveal that Japanese-language writings by colonial Koreans were produced throughout the early twentieth century too.[27] These writings did not suddenly appear, but emerged from a steadily intensifying context of assimilation and colonial unevenness. Furthermore, their rising significance into the decade of the 1940s must be situated within the larger backdrop of global imperialist struggles, culminating in World War II, a conflict increasingly couched in terms of the clash between East and West. (See John Dower about propaganda from the United States and Japan during this time.)

What Is Korean Literature?

At a time when the past seemed to be melting away—imperial borders were in flux, and the distances between the metropole and the colony appeared to be shrinking fast through technologies of imperial expansion and assimilation—cultural productions from the colony became notably contentious sites. The boundaries of Korean literature seemed anything but self-evident, and the question, "What is Korean literature?," was being posed with different registers of significance.

In the colony, the discourse of Chosŏn munhak embodied the urgent desire to construct a national literary canon amidst rising anxieties about the fluctuating borderlines of the assimilated colony and its (absent or exiled) nation.[28] In a new global order then fully abiding by the imperial logic of the nation-state, such flexible and porous borders provoked extreme anxiety in the colony, where the absence of a bounded nation-state and an established national literature was keenly felt as a colonial "lack" that needed immediate remedy.

In the metropole, meanwhile, Chōsen bungaku was becoming the object of imperial desires for "colonial kitsch." In this book, colonial kitsch refers to the devaluation and exoticization of elements of the colony's culture becoming mass-produced objects for indiscriminate imperial consumption. It is a type of sentimental desire common in colonial encounters, which, as Renato Rosaldo notes, is "a particular kind of nostalgia often found under imperialism in which people mourn the passing of what they themselves have transformed."[29] Nostalgia for colonial kitsch may appear as innocently genuine appreciation for colonial culture, but in fact veils collusion with its domination and destruction. Colonial objects that were circulated during the passing trend of the "Korea Boom" appeared to conflate far-flung fields: tourism, folk culture, food, fash-

FIG. 2.2 Chang Hyŏkchu's literary debut in the journal *Kaizō*. Reprinted with permission from Waseda University Archives.

ion, architecture, literature, and art. Each object, whether from highbrow or lowbrow culture, was significant only as a symbol of "Koreanness," arbitrary and exchangeable among a potentially infinite chain of possible signifiers.

In chapter 5, I discuss the basic incompatibility between these parallel nostalgic desires across the colonial divide: for a timeless national tradition on the one hand, and for a passing imperial trend on the other. My concern here, however, is with the anxieties of colonial cultural producers embodied in the

FIG. 2.3 *Representative Collection of Korean Fiction*. Reprinted with
permission from Waseda University Archives.

debates that converged around writings by colonial Koreans at the contact
zones.[30] More specifically, I am interested in exploring the significance of the
contest over colonial literature between Japan and Korea, notably how it was
demoted from national canonicity to colonial kitsch, and its precarious, multiple definition—as *gaichi bungaku* (literature of the hinterland or colony),
chihō bungaku (regional, local, or minor literature), or *kokumin bungaku* (imperial or national literature)—depending on how one understood Korea's
proximity to Japan.[31]

Debating Colonial, National, and World Literatures

A survey conducted among major Korean writers in the popular journal *Samch'ŏlli* (Three thousand leagues) in August 1936—one year before the informal war in China turned official in the empire—posed the urgent question of how Korean literature should be defined in these times of crisis.[32] The article begins thus:

> Strictly speaking, Korean literature should be literature that is A) written in the Korean language, B) written by a Korean, and C) written for a Korean readership. Only such [writings] should be considered as Korean literature in the full sense of the term. But we would like to raise the following paradoxical questions.
>
> A) *Yŏlha ilgi* by Pak Yŏnam or *Samguk yusa*,[33] which are written in literary Chinese, are they not Korean literature? Further, Tagore, Singe, Gregory, and Yeats wrote in English,[34] but Tagore's writings seem to be considered as part of Indian literature, and Yeats's as Irish literature. In such cases, how do we define the relationship between literature and language (*muncha*)?
>
> B) If the writer must be "Korean," then how about Nakanishi Inosuke [1887–1958] who wrote . . . about Korean sensibilities, should his writings be excluded from Korean literature?
>
> C) If [Korean literature] must be for a Korean readership, then what about Chang Hyŏkchu [1905–1997] writing for the Japanese literary establishment, and Kang Yonghŭl [1903?–1972], who wrote for Americans; works like *Grass Roof*, for example, are these not Korean literature? How about those masterpieces in Korean, such as *Dream of Nine Clouds* and *Lady Sa's Journey South*,[35] are they Korean literature? If you could each reply to these questions using such examples, with a view to coming up with a definition of "Korean literature," this will in effect be a great purifying process in these confusing times when our current chaotic literary field is encircled in an unpleasant atmosphere . . . so we urge your careful consideration. (82)

Thus, from the very outset of the survey, readers glimpse the sense of crisis that was prevalent during this period, and which pivoted around the urgent desire for a strict definition of Korean literature. This desire arose from a sense of anxiety about the fluid boundaries of Korean literature in such "unpleasant" and "chaotic" times, and from a perceived need for "purification," presumably from foreign infiltration. How to assess the defensive xenophobia of the colonized is a complex question that must be deferred to a later occasion. What is more pertinent to my concerns here is the fact that, despite the survey's expressed hopes to overcome the current chaos and purify the literary field, the opinions range widely, with no easy consensus proffered. Some of the participants who adhere to the strictest definitions are, quite intriguingly, those who would come to occupy the most controversial positions in the literary field for their own Japanese-language writings.

Yi Kwangsu, Yi T'aejun (1904–?), and Chang Hyŏkchu, for example, state that only literature written in the Korean language should be considered as Korean literature.[36] Yi Kwangsu claims that the citizenship (*kukchŏk*) of a literature is based not on the citizenship of the author, but of the language (83). He takes this standard so literally that texts written by Koreans in literary Chinese, the lingua franca of the past, are considered by him to be part of Chinese literature (*China munhak*),[37] and Chinese texts such as *The Water Margin*, once translated into Korean, then became Korean literature (83). Chang Hyŏkchu, meanwhile, adds one further criterion to those posed by the survey: Korean literature is not only "that which is written by Korean writers, in the Korean language, for a Korean readership" but it should also deal with "Korean subject matter" (86–87).

Many of the other respondents, however, attempt to face the complexity of the issue in more nuanced ways. For example, Yi Kungu responds that Korea is not unique in having been forced to borrow the language of a foreign culture in its past (90–92). He writes that the perceived need to borrow the language of another, presumably more advanced culture is a common condition in contexts of unevenness. He points out, however, that this condition is only a temporary stage that must be passed through within a limited time frame, since the ultimate goal is to import the tools necessary to develop one's own traditions of language and culture. "Hence, only after a period of total devotion over one or two generations in which [a culture's] own full and abundant language is built up, can a national literature enter into the second stage of developing [its own] traditions" (91). According to Yi, Korea is still struggling to develop its own language, and thus has been unable to escape infiltration by other cultures. He laments that such a dependency is discernible across all aspects of Korean culture, but is particularly conspicuous in its literature: "The fact that it could not free itself from the *écriture* of other cultures [*t'amuncha*] is the biggest sin not only for Korean culture, but for Korean literature. Thus, it is of primary urgency for us to construct our own literature after a certain level of importation and digestion of other cultures" (91).

It is important to note that Yi is far from questioning the logic of cultural hierarchies in the imperial context, but rather chastises Korea for its inferior position. An echo of Goethe's violent metaphor of devouring cultures through translations, part of his theory of world literature, can be heard here. Moving on to specific examples, Yi posits that authors who write about other cultures in their own language should be included in the national literature of their own country. Yet in the case of authors who write about their own country in the language of others, the problem becomes more "delicate." Admitting that the situation is complex in cases when one lacks the ability or the freedom to express oneself in one's own language, he writes: "These writings are in fact literary works that are lacking not only their family registries (*hojŏk*) but also their citizenship (*kukchŏk*)." The problems of such writings—for example, English-language works written by Korean authors—are further exacerbated by the fact that they struggle to attain "wholeness," writes Yi. Rather than being considered as literature, they are more likely to be viewed as mere "introductions" (*sogae*) or "reportage" (*pogo*) on the level of "social-science" (*sahoe sasangchŏk kyŏnji*) (91). Although Yi does not explicitly address the current colonial condition in Korea and is careful to use examples from other colonial contexts such as India and Ireland, it is significant that he links the emergence of such homeless literatures (which lack a family registry or citizenship) with contexts of cultural unevenness and global empires at large.

Other writers rely on examples from distant colonial contexts even more explicitly. For example, Im Hwa (1908–1953) writes that the establishment of a national literature in each nation has in fact occurred alongside the formation of modern democratic society, and that in the absence of a coherent national entity, the concept of a national literature is "shaken at its essence and is in fact impotent" (94). Furthermore, he writes that it is a well-known fact that the contemporary context is characterized by a general cultural shift, spearheaded by the publishing industry as well as by translations, from national literatures toward a world literature. In the case of Korea, however, this process was vanishing even before it had fully appeared, since the establishment of an independent and unique Korean literature was itself an impossibility. Im argues that the peak of Korean literature occurred during the transition period from the "late-Chosŏn dynasty (1392–1910) until around the last decade of the Taishō era [1912–1926]" (*Hanmallo put'ŏ Taejŏng 10-nyŏn chŏnhu*), and he laments that this "renaissance" suddenly ended with the class-based, internationalist proletariat literary movement (94–95). Since then, he writes, the question of Korean literature has been a fraught one: "In the here and now, when the literary situation is quite severe, one cannot claim a work as Korean literature just because one writes in Korean, or because it is written by a Korean writer, or because it was penned for a Korean readership" (94). Like Yi, Im links this paradoxical situation to the colonial context—though strategically transplanted to the cases of India and Ireland:

> It is a shameful fact [*yoktoen sasil*] that [the English writings of] Tagore, Singe, Gregory, and Yeats are considered as Indian or Irish literatures. Yet rather than being wholly Indian or wholly Irish, their works are Indian or Irish literature, in collusion with and defeated by British imperialism. In other words, they are not a vital Indian or Irish literature but merely symbols of defeat by an invader. True Indian and Irish literature will be revived again in the future. In form and in content, these works are too troubling to be considered simply as Indian or Irish literature. (95–96)

More explicitly than anyone else, therefore, Im Hwa draws a direct link between the conundrum of representation of writers writing in other languages and their constitutive imperial conditions. But Im Hwa's critique of imperialism is ambivalent at best. Far from problematizing empire's Darwinian logic of the "survival of the fittest" based on national strength, it seems that here and elsewhere (as discussed below), Im Hwa's focus of critique is the lack of a modern national literature in the colony itself. The position of lack and belatedness occupied by colonial Korea in comparison to the standards of world literature maintained by seemingly cohesive and independent nation-states is, for him, a "shameful fact," much like the case of Ireland and India. Im's statements may be construed as subversively revolutionary in that he is implicitly critiquing the colonial context; yet insofar as he does not question the hierarchical logic of colonialism, but only Korea's inferior place in it, his critique remains limited, trapped under the double bind of both Japanese and Western imperialism.

As stated earlier, the respondents of the *Samch'ŏlli* survey pose more questions about the definition of Korean literature than they solve. What does become clear from the exchanges, however, is the extreme urgency of these inquiries, and the intense anxieties that were stirred by the perceived lack of a clearly bounded national literature in the colony. After all, the world was fully revolving around the logic of the nation-state by this time; and in the absence of the nation-state, not only the present, but also the past and future of a culture appeared to be destabilized and under threat. In this sense, the urgency that we can perceive in these responses is, at base, an anxious awareness of the need to build a culture whose past, present, and future will be on a par, or coeval, with the standards of the world.[38] The pressing nature of this discourse of the colonized on Chosŏn munhak stands in stark contrast to its counterpart, the imperial discourse on Chōsen bungaku, which was emerging simultaneously in the metropole.

The discourse on Chōsen bungaku mirrors in some ways the discourse on Chosŏn munhak, yet it also reveals its untranslatability with the latter on several counts. First, the question of language which is of foremost concern in the Chosŏn munhak debate is utterly suspended in the imperial discourse. In fact, Japanese-language writings or translations by Koreans are assumed to be seamlessly equivalent with Korean literature. Thus Itagaki Naoko (1896–1977), a metropolitan critic, assumes that she is qualified to critique the general inferiority of Korean literature based on her limited readings, which are mediated entirely through Japanese translation. In a similar vein, I will examine more closely in chapter 8 the way in which translations of literary works from Korea were being advertised and published for Japanese readers in the regional editions (chihō-ban, 地方版) of metropolitan newspapers, with the act of translation itself significantly elided in the process. The equating of Japanese-language translations with Korean literature disregards the colonial condition in which Koreans were writing and finesses the fact that it was colonial censorship and assimilation policies that forced these authors to use the imperial language instead of writing in their mother tongue.

The discourses of Chosŏn munhak and Chōsen bungaku often converged on the same object of concern. For example, the writer Chang Hyŏkchu became popular fare in both of these discourses, but he evokes significantly disparate assessments from each. In Korea, Chang's Japanese-language writings are, for the most part, excised from the body of Chosŏn munhak. Indeed, Yi Kungu, as noted above, wondered if writings in a foreign language for foreign readers could be classified as literature at all and dubbed them a kind of "reportage." In the imperial discourse of Chōsen bungaku, however, the Japanese-language texts of colonial writers such as Chang Hyŏkchu were consumed voraciously and unreflexively as representative texts of Korean literature. Interestingly enough, metropolitan critics also commented frequently on the "reportage" aspects of Chang's writings. They, too, suggested that these aspects revealed the shortcomings of Chang's work as literature, a point made in critiques of his short story "Gakidō" (Realm of hungry ghosts, 1932).[39] Nevertheless, this story still managed to win him a nomination for an imperial literary prize; and Chang's translated works, together with those of other writers, were circulated widely in Korean literature specials.

Part of the reason why Chang Hyŏkchu's texts were consumed so eagerly in the metropolitan literary establishment as reportage was precisely because they were seen as exposés that revealed the reality of colonial Korea to imperial readers. In fact, Japanese critic Hirotsu Kazuo (1891–1968) even chastises Chang for being too literary and conjectures that overly fictional elements, such as the opening scene of "Realm of Hungry Ghosts," which features the sound of detonating dynamite, may not have been effective for Japanese readers; if the work had sustained a reportage style throughout, it might have been easier for these audiences to understand.[40] Korean literature in the metropole was gaining attention because it offered a taste of the exotic reality of "Koreanness," suitably stripped of any awareness of the dilemmas facing Korean writers who were called upon to represent some presumably collective colonial reality to cater to consuming imperial tastes. For writers such as Chang, it seems that this pressure came from both external and internal sources: the metropolitan demand for representations of Koreanness on the one hand, and on the other, his own personal desire to offset the dominant image of Koreans that had been circulating in the Japanese media up until that point. For example, he writes in "Boku no bungaku" (My literature):

> A country of bald mountains, a country of red soil, and so on; when I read the travel writings of those who have visited Korea, this is what they usually write. Such images represent poverty, they represent decline. When these tourists see Korean peasants with long pipes walking along in languid strides, they assume that these are a lazy people. Even now, in the regional editions [chihō-ban] of Japanese newspapers, there are sections entitled "Lazy Scenes of Early Summer" shown with photo sketches, which always seem to include a laborer taking a nap by the roadside. It would appear that the man deplores work and is leisurely napping under the shade of a tree. . . . I want to get to the bottom of why these peasants and laborers came to appear this way. I know for certain that it is not that they have stopped working because they are lazy, and they are not loitering around for pleasure's sake.[41]

Here, we can see a glimpse of the conundrum faced by a colonial writer such as Chang Hyŏkchu, who wishes to address metropolitan audiences on behalf of the Korean people in order to change racialized perceptions of the colonized that were pervasive at the time. He himself senses that a deeper logic may lie behind metropolitan tourists' first impressions of a lazy ethnic group. Yet Chang's efforts are met with dissatisfaction by readers in the colony on the grounds of their "inauthenticity"; and he ironically ends up in the service of metropolitan consumer desires as a writer who provides reportage of Koreanness translated into the imperial language, encouraged to deploy a narrative mode resembling a guided tour which was clearly privileged—by his Japanese audience—over other forms of Korean literature.

So far, we have seen the fluctuating position of Korean literature at the interface of contending discourses across the empire. In the metropole, Chōsen bungaku was consumed as objects of "colonial kitsch" to serve imperial desires for exotic Koreanness. On the other hand, the status of Chosŏn munhak was being compared by colonial intellectuals to world standards dictated by the monolingual logic of the nation-state, in which the absence of a clearly defined national literature signified a shameful colonial lack. The urgency, complexity, and contradictions of defining and constructing a timeless tradition of Korean literature in the colony at this time can only be understood when contending debates across the colonial divide are brought together in mutual relief.

Constructing a History of Korean Literature

It may be no coincidence that the 1930s, a time when intensifying assimilation policies were subsuming Korean culture into the Japanese empire, witnessed a marked rise in attempts to record the history of Korean literature. One significant milestone in the writing of Korean literary history was *A History of Korean Fiction* (*Chosŏn sosŏlsa*, written in 1930, published in 1933) by Kim T'aejun (1905–1949), which articulates the pressing nature of the need for accounts of literary history in the colonial context. In a related essay in the inaugural issue of *Sahoe kongnon* (Public discourse), entitled *"Sosŏl ŭi chŏngŭi"* (Defining *sosŏl*),[42] Kim T'aejun addresses the problem of whether Western notions of the novel can be applied to the vernacular fictional narrative form of *sosŏl*.[43] According to Kim, the novel was ushered in to set a new standard for Korean literature. The problem was that Korea's sosŏl appeared to be lacking in comparison to its Western counterparts. Kim is quick to point out, however, that the sosŏl in Korea had a rich heritage of its own that could be traced back to various vernacular genres, as well as to its origins in the Chinese classics. Furthermore, the concept of the sosŏl, writes Kim, was not a stagnant term but one that has evolved through history, not unlike the Western novel. What is significantly different is that the Western novel came to assume a hegemonic place in the world literary order, backed by other technologies of imperialism—so much so, in fact, that it has imparted its standards as "universal" throughout the globe, and relegated other forms of fiction from less powerful cultures to positions of lack and inferiority.[44]

What I want to emphasize here is that Kim's attempt to defend a hoary

Korean literary heritage reveals the pervasive sense of a lack that must be explained away. The attempt to apply the standards of the Western novel to the Korean context is seen as deeply dubious because the concept of the novel itself was constantly evolving in the local contexts (mainly the imperial metropoles of Britain and France) in which it emerged. Although there may not have been fictional works equivalent to the Western novel in Korea, Kim argues that Korean literature is neither belated nor lacking because the concept of sosŏl itself had been evolving throughout history, ever since its earliest known references in the writings of the Chinese historian Ban Gu (AD 32–92).

Im Hwa also began writing his own version of Korean literary history around the same time as Kim, and his study reveals similar anxieties.[45] In the serialized literary history that he wrote in the 1930s and 1940s, Im Hwa makes the controversial claim that has ended up plaguing all subsequent literary histories of modern Korea: "The modern literary history of Asia is, in fact, the history of the importation and transplantation of Western literature. So why do we take as our subject a modern literary history which has been imported and transplanted from the outside? . . . The reason is that the literature which we have inherited can in no way be considered a modern literature."[46] Im Hwa then outlines the process whereby Western standards came to take precedence over Korea's literary heritage and explains the near impossibility of writing a history of modern Korean literature (sin munhaksa) in these circumstances. Im Hwa laments that a process that took several centuries to develop in the West, and almost one hundred years for Japan to take on board, has been imported in thirty short years by Korea.

Furthermore, the thirty years that spanned the totality of the history of modern Korean literature were inseparable from the infiltration of Western culture into the "locality" (chibang, K; chihō, J) of Asia, which lay on the "periphery" of the cultural world order.[47] During this period, transformations in Western cultural thought that had evolved over many centuries were experienced all at once; and in this sense, the shock of the modern was doubly intensified in the East. Another key factor that made it difficult for Korea to counter such complexities head-on was the tremendous shift occurring in its own geopolitical condition. The thirty years spanning the history of modern Korean literature saw a profoundly unsettling transition in Korea, from a China-centered world order to a Western-centric one led locally by Japan. Such problems made it impossible simply to "cook up"—as Im Hwa puts it—a modern literary history that was only a few decades old, yet could somehow encompass all the complexities of an era on the wane and another on the rise.

Im Hwa further explains the difficulty of defining what constitutes a modern Korean literature and refers specifically to the inadequacy of the monolingual definition espoused by Yi Kwangsu in the above-mentioned *Samch'ŏlli* survey, as well as in an article entitled "Chosŏn munhak ŭi kaenyŏm" (The concept of Korean literature) which appeared in *Sahoe kongnon*.[48] Yi Kwangsu's response in the *Samch'ŏlli* survey repeats verbatim many of the points and examples from his essay in *Sahoe kongnon*, which is a more extensive treatment of the topic. In the same issue, he also wrote another critical essay, entitled "Chosŏn sosŏlsa" (History of Korean fiction),[49] in which he repeats the premise that "Korean literature must be a literature written in Korean" and proceeds to construct a literary history that begins with the *idu* scripts from the Silla dynasty and then traces a genealogy of vernacular literature all the way to the *sin sosŏl* (new sosŏl). What is significant here is that Yi explicitly excludes minor writers such as Kang Yonghŭl, who wrote *Grass Roof* in English, and also "those who are writing in the Japanese language," without citing any of the latter category by name. This gesture opens up the possibility of considering the issue of Japanese-language writings within the larger frame of the Korean literary field, most of whose practitioners, including Yi Kwangsu himself, had necessarily learned to write via Japanese translations brought in from the imperial centers. Such an interpretive possibility is minimized in the *Samch'ŏlli* survey, which singles out only Chang Hyŏkchu for exclusion.[50]

Im Hwa opines that Korea's complex situation is shared by other Asian nations that must face the onslaught of Western hegemony, but notes that the case of Korea is complicated still further by its forced transition from a Sino-centric regional order to a Western-centric world order, spearheaded locally by Japan. It is difficult to ignore Im Hwa's uncritical acceptance of a developmentalist history rooted in the West as standard, an acceptance underscoring his theory of a "literature of transplantation." Yet it is essential that we pay due attention to the sense of urgency informing his text and those of other colonized writers who were active in the discourse on Chosŏn munhak. The "belated consciousness" seen here was a widely shared affect, not only in Korea but across Asia and throughout the non-Western world.[51] If we approach Im Hwa's views from the vantage point of the contemporary critique of Eurocentric modernity, they can be easily dismissed as false consciousness; yet it is essential to give due attention to the way in which experiences of modernity in Korea were perceived at the time: as life lived in the shadows of Japan and the West. However problematic such views may be, they deserve exploration for what they tell us about these lived experiences. The pained writings of Im Hwa and other colonized authors reveal that the condition of dislocation that is arguably universal to modernity was further exacerbated in the non-West by the urgent sense that modernity signified a series of standards that had to be imported from elsewhere. The brutal and ironic consequence of chasing after these imported standards was a perception in the colony that the past—and even the self—had to be discarded.[52] In the case of Korea, this well-understood colonial predicament was hopelessly complicated by its incorporation into the Japanese empire. On the one hand, Korea shared status with its Japanese colonizers vis-à-vis Western imperialism, but on the other it had to endure the predicament of being doubly subjected, by both Japanese and Western imperialisms. Moreover, this triangulation is far from over in Korea, and persists in the overdetermined conditions of postcoloniality and Cold War geopolitics (this will be examined further in chapter 10).

Whether they are opposing or agreeing, what all these various voices have in common is their articulation of a sense of lack and belatedness that is (self-) imposed on the basis of histories of development conceived elsewhere. And all these writers tried to overcome this diagnosis of the inferior state of Korean literature and culture, either by pointing to the dynamic history of Korean culture to show that there was no lack, or by urging on a transformation of the present situation in order to meet the standards set by the West and followed efficiently by Japan.

The conundrum of imperial-language writings by colonized subjects exemplify some of the contradictory opportunities presented by colonial subjection: namely, the necessity of acquiring the technologies of the Other in order to translate the self into that Other within the new modern world order. These texts were the result of a labor of translation that was never acknowledged as such, neither in the colonial era in which they emerged, nor in the postcolonial aftermath when they were, for all intents and purposes, erased by the pressure of postwar geopolitics. In this sense, these texts manifest the dislocations felt by Korean writers who experienced modernity in translation. The next chapter examines the case of Kim Saryang/Kin Shiryō (1914–1950?), a minor writer who negotiated the boundaries between Japan and Korean literary fields at this time.

THREE

A MINOR WRITER

The problem of the I-novel is never limited to questions of
literature. Instead, it is related to the nature of the modernity
[*kindai*] of our country.

TAKEUCHI RYŌCHI

Literary critics both in Japan and in the West have characterized
the Japanese "I-novel," the *watakushi shōsetsu* or *shi-sōsetsu*, as the
most salient and unique form of modern Japanese literature.

TOMI SUZUKI

Beneath the announcement was Satō Haruo's comment: [Kim's
is] an I-novel with the entire people squeezed into it. Is this right?
Is it right? I must now write what is true.

KIM SARYANG/KIN SHIRYŌ

P'yŏngyang, winter 1940. Kim Saryang [Kin Shiryō, J] receives
a telegram announcing the nomination of his Japanese-language
short story "Into the Light" (*Hikari no naka ni*) for the prestigious
Akutagawa Literary Prize in Japan. He's on the verge of greatness. He
boards the southbound train, and then the ferry, for the long journey from his home in northern Korea to attend the dazzling awards
ceremony in Tokyo, the empire's capital. The journey signifies Kim's
celebrated debut into the limelight of the Bundan, Japan's literary
establishment; for most writers, this could be the breakthrough that

ensures their literary career, but the trip is recalled with ambivalence in Kim's "Letter to Mother" (*Haha e no tegame*):

> Dear beloved mother . . . on the platform of the train station in Heijō [P'yŏngyang, K] on that bone-chilling windy day in February, I remember how concerned you were about the brewing cold infecting my body as you hurried me onto the morning express, Nozomi [Hope], for my journey. . . . As I pulled myself onto the violently shaking train, my head was filled with so many thoughts. Thinking about the remote possibility of writing in Tokyo, I felt terrified [*osoroshii ki ga suru no desu*]. . . . On the third-class ferry across the Dark Seas, I was suffering from a severe fever, and in the train from Shimonoseki, I was practically comatose. But I told myself over and over again, from now, I must write what is really true.[1]

"Letter to Mother" is overlaid in a montage of memories and holds a complex spectrum of emotions, from hope and excitement, to anxiety and fear. This letter, pregnant with conflict, offers essential clues in our attempt to glimpse the "third class" minor writer's literary voyage upstream into the imperial city.

The letter textually and metatextually embodies the linguistic conundrum of a colonized writer on the threshold of imperial recognition. It is written in Japanese, which at first glance may seem neither surprising nor noteworthy, considering that at the time of its writing in 1940, Japanese was already the official "paper language" throughout the colony. A closer reading reveals a surprising revelation. Here is the ending: "Isn't Sister coming home soon from the capital city for summer vacation? Would you please ask her to translate this from the Japanese [*Naichigo*] into Korean [*Chōsengo*] so that you can read it?" The letter in the end curiously undoes itself, revealing its own self-divided impossibility to communicate with its intended recipient. It self-consciously confesses its fundamental impasse: the impossibility of communication and the linguistic incommensurability between the sender and the receiver within the imperial encounter.

The chasm between mother and son is unbridgeable. The opportunities promised Kim (and other Korean male intellectuals in the new colonial world) distance him further from his own mother and from his mother tongue. Here the imperial language, rather than working as a tool of mediating and enabling communication, instead bars it, standing between sender and receiver. The cumbersome linguistic exchange draws attention to an awkward ventriloquism that threatens the very integrity of the epistle, making a travesty of the epistolary genre itself as it denies its most fundamental raison d'être: as intimate

FIG. 3.1 Kim Saryang as a student at Saga High School in Kyūshū. Kim is in his school cap with arms crossed in the middle. Reprinted with permission from Professor Shirakawa Yutaka.

liaison between sender and receiver. Here the imperial language, rather than facilitating communication in the colony, exposes its divisive nature: it severs the people in the colony by generation, class, and gender. And an unanswerable question lingers long after we finish reading it: why on earth was Kim writing to his own mother in Japanese?

This chapter examines the significance of a moment when the literary histories of Korea and Japan converged on an individual writer from colonial Korea, and on his Japanese-language writings. It is a moment that is noteworthy as much for the fanfare surrounding it in the Japanese empire as for its immediate forgetting in the postcolonial aftermath in both Japan and Korea. At the center of the limelight was a young writer from colonial Korea by the name of Kim Saryang (1914–1950?). The "voyage-in" of Kim and his Japanese-language texts to the metropolitan literary establishment (Bundan) caused deep anxieties within the writer and his Japanese and Korean critics about the unsavory contamination of cultures across the colonial borderline. These anxieties, though felt for different reasons, offer insights into the ways in which both a minor writer and his text remain perpetually in transit between the colony and the metropole, never belonging unequivocally to either.

FIG. 3.2 Kim Saryang as a student at Saga High School in Kyūshū. Kim is sitting, second from the right. Reprinted with permission from Professor Shirakawa Yutaka.

The concept of the "minor writer" is from Gilles Deleuze and Félix Guattari's discussion of "minor literature" in their important study of Franz Kafka. In their conceptualization, "minor literature" is a literature written by a minority writer in a major context, and in the *major* language. It is a literature written from a position of exclusion that gives it a coefficient or level of "deterritorialization," that is, revolutionary potential. It is necessary to translate Deleuze and Guattari's definition, which was formulated from a specific context, in order to expand its usefulness to the context at hand. For the purposes of this book, minor literature will apply to Japanese-language writings by colonized Koreans in particular, as well as to a broader concept including literature written by a marginalized writer produced in any major context of uneven power relations in *any* language. I shall be using the categories of the "colonized" and the "minor" interchangeably in this book, but the concept of the "minor" is useful in particular to discuss common ground in the shared plights of the colonized with that of other subjectivities relegated to subaltern status in uneven global contexts with continuities from the colonial to the postcolonial. It is important to keep in mind that these experiences are by no means interchangeable; some inequities are starker than others. Their continuities and discontinuities will be explored throughout the book, especially in chapter 10.[2]

Linguistic Homelessness

The internal linguistic division (or foreignness within) expressed in Kim's letter is not an isolated act of playful formalism designed for the imperial gaze, and it is repeated throughout Kim's writings. For the minor writer, the imperial divide is internalized and irreversible. Kim confesses this impasse, an uneasiness in both languages, in a correspondence sent to a fellow writer in Korea:

> My Japanese is still awkward, and I am ashamed to admit that my Korean is also awkward. I do not know whether you have had a chance to read it, but I am now struggling with my language problem as I write the serial *Setting Sun* in [the journal] *Chogwang*. If only I could reach a level of writing a good work in Korean, I could hope for nothing more.[3]

For a bilingual writer and translator whose claim to fame in the colonial contact zone was precisely his agility to bridge linguistic gaps and colonial divides, this confession of internal linguistic division is quite startling. Thus these epistolary exchanges offer us rare glimpses into the colonized writer's linguistic turmoil and the impossibility of severing the personal (private) and political (public) nature of his writing act.[4] After all, Kim, as much as any other writer of that time, was lauded throughout the empire as a sort of poster child of colonial success in the metropole, proof that if the colonized worked hard enough, they, too, could achieve the imperial dream.

Kim was traveling into Japan at the time of its imperial expansion into China; mobilization for war infiltrated the everyday lives of colonizers and colonized, although unequally. In order to harness support in colonial Korea for the Japanese war machine, imperial policies had shifted from a conflicted logic of differentiation (*ika*) coexisting with policies of assimilation (*dōka*), toward what was intended to be a more streamlined form of co-optation of imperialization (*kōminka*) or, ultimately, the forging of colonial difference into unified oneness in the empire. Such efforts to fashion imperial subjects from colonial Koreans were exemplified in the ubiquitous slogan: *Naisen ittai*— Japan and Korea, One Body.[5]

However, even at the height of kōminka policies, the contradictions of empire and hierarchies based on ethno-racial discrimination refused to completely eradicate markers of colonial difference. Not coincidentally, an imperial desire for objects of colonial exotica saw an unprecedented resurgence in the consumer trend of the "Korea Boom" (*Chōsen būmū*) at this time.[6] In the literary field, the dual demands of empire became manifest in the increase in critical

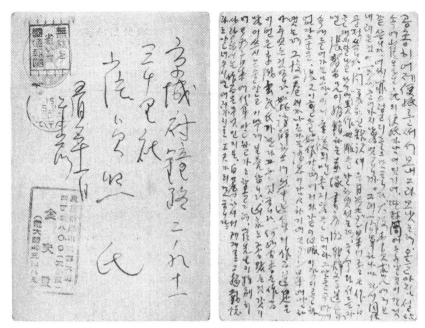

FIG. 3.3 Postcard from Kim Saryang to author Ch'oe Chŏnghŭi. Reprinted with permission from Mr. Kim Jihoon from the estate of Ch'oe Chŏnghŭi.

and popular attention paid to bilingual writers and translators from the colonies (Korea, Taiwan, Manchuria, Mongolia) who could write, or translate into, Japanese. A sudden increase in the appearance of colonial Korean writers in the Bundan occurred in tandem with the rapid decline in the mass media and literary market for Korean-language works. Japanese was the official language of empire, coded as a homogenizing "national language" (*kokugo*) throughout the newly imagined imperial community, and the Korean language—having lost its national affiliation, being a language without a country—was increasingly marked as undesirable. Relegated to a marginal status, the Korean language was actively repressed and censored, not only in public, but also in private spheres, even within the colony itself.[7]

The minor writer Kim Saryang and his texts examined here reveal a painful conundrum imminent to the process of their co-optation by the empire. In the face of contradictory demands of assimilation and differentiation, Kim was seeking both recognition and affirmation by the metropolitan literary establishment while simultaneously attempting to negotiate the integrity of a collective Korean national culture as well as his own singular identity as an individual artist. He wanted his culture and his writing to be viewed as more

FIG. 3.4 Advertisement of *Modern Japan—Colonial Korea Special Issue*. Reprinted with permission from Waseda University Archives.

than mere objects of colonial exotica. Here I am interested in tracing the complex nature of Kim's responses in the face of the impossible circumstances into which he was thrown, a complexity that was never fully acknowledged at the time and that has been actively silenced in the postcolonial aftermath.

The Akutagawa Literary Prize is one of the most prestigious awards that an aspiring writer can win in Japan, even today. Established in 1935 by *Bungei shunjū*, one of the foremost literary journals, the judges of the prize were prominent writers and critics of the time, among them: Kawabata Yasunari (1899–1972); Kume Masao (1891–1952); Satō Haruo (1892–1962); and Yokomitsu Riichi (1898–1947). The award was given biannually, with the finalists invited to the awards ceremony where the winner was announced with fanfare, and the winning story published in *Bungei shunjū Akutagawa Prize special edition*. It boasts a pedigree of many who have subsequently become literary giants, and the prize has played an important role in the production of the canon of modern Japanese literature.[8]

The critic Kawamura Minato has written about the Japanese imperial project and the Akutagawa Literary Prize. Kawamura's concern is limited to the representation of the colonies by "Japanese" writers, distinguished from

FIGS 3.5. AND 3.6 *Bungei shunjū Akutagawa Prize special edition.* Reprinted with permission from Waseda University Archives.

colonized subjects, and does not make the link between literary productions by colonized writers and the formation of the modern Japanese literary canon, which occurred through their systematic exclusion.[9] While Kawamura primarily focused on the role the empire played in the literary imaginaries of ethnic Japanese writers from Japan proper (paralleling the contributions of Edward Said in the case of European writers in *Orientalism* and *Culture and Imperialism*, for example), here I would like to highlight the secondary yet significant role

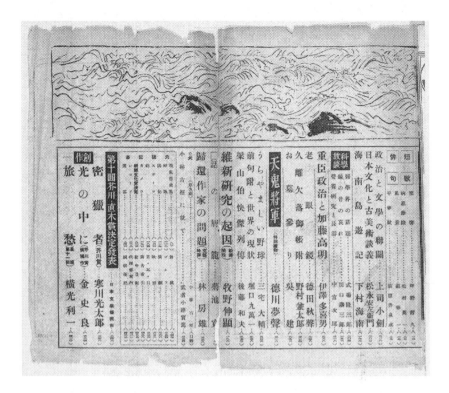

played by writers from Japan's colonies during the foundational moment of literary prizes in modern Japan and examine how those writers redrew the very boundaries of the metropolitan literary establishment and, in fact, pushed the borders of the canon of modern Japanese literature at that time.

Japanese-language writings by colonized writers were being actively mobilized and given substantial attention in the Bundan, but not without having their colonial difference noted, and then being symbolically relegated to marginal positions. In fact, it was common practice to award colonized writers' works "second place" or "honorable mention" in literary competitions, thus symbolically mirroring imperial hierarchies, whether intentional or not.[10]

The Akutagawa Literary Prize of 1940

The competition in March 1940 seems to have been especially exciting, as overheard in comments by one of the judges, Kume Masao, editor in chief of *Bungei shunjū*: "The Akutagawa Prize finalists this time were of excellent caliber which has not been paralleled recently and all have received the praise of the entire judging committee, a rare feat."[11] According to the comments of the judges, which were published along with the winning story, this seems to have caused them quite a conflict and for reasons significantly other than the high literary quality of the nominations.[12]

There were seven finalists, and according to Kawabata Yasunari, the judges in the last instance wavered intently on whether to award the prize to Samukawa Kōtarō (1908–1977) or to Kim Saryang.[13] Many of the comments of individual judges echo this quandary and give special mention to Kim and their reason for not choosing him. They explain that the decision finally came down to either offering the award to Kim along with Samukawa, or giving Kim special mention as a finalist. In the end, they decided to give Kim recognition for second place because, according to Kume Masao, "of the rule not to award simultaneous winners this time."[14] No explanation is given as to why this rule was decided on, nor was there mention that this rule had been broken before; in fact, two winners were awarded in the previous period.[15]

I will quote at length from Kume Masao's commentary because it encapsulates the tenor of the rest of the commentaries:

> The overall excellence of the works nominated for the Akutagawa Prize this time gives tremendous delight to all the judges for the first time in a very long time. A new era has been inaugurated. Reading the winning work "Poacher" [Mitsuryōsha] reminded me of twenty-five years ago when Akutagawa Ryūnosuke (himself) submitted "Nose" to Natsume Sōseki. Of course I am not comparing myself to Mr. Sōseki, but considering the passage of time and the generational change, readers may grin, and grant that history may be repeating itself.
>
> Anyway, in some sense, this work reminded me of Tanizaki Junichiro's "Tattoo," Shiga Naoya's "Razor," and brought to mind Satomi Ton's "Hiemon Gate," Kikuchi's "Record of Sir Tadanao," and Satō's "Pastoral Melancholy." The degree of excitement stirred up by this work surpassed that of the first Akutagawa Prize winner, "Sōmin," and went beyond "The Record of Koshamain" . . . and if we get past our own borders, we might venture to say . . . it may even beat out Kipling's seafaring adventure stories. It also brings to mind Poe . . . and Mallarmé.
>
> At the very least, if we translate this one piece and send it out to the world market, it will have first-order marketability. . . . *In contrast*, the second runner-up "Into the Light" was, in fact, close[r] to my own tastes, and I felt an intimacy with it. Moreover, it deals with the "Korean problem" [*Chōsenjin mondai*], which may indicate a significance of national import;

so I especially thought it was worthy of the prize. I myself felt that both of the works, *each for a different reason*, deserved to be nominated. But unfortunately, this moving work was overpowered by the strength of "Poacher." Besides, it fell out of competition based on the rule [*tatemae*] that, if possible, only one winner should be chosen. (emphasis added)

What can be overheard in Kume's comments, which is also uncannily repeated throughout the other judges' remarks, is the distinction between a *universalism* (equated with the West) accorded to Samukawa's work versus an emphasis on the *particularity* in Kim's works. Samukawa's "Poacher" is placed in a genealogy of not only Japanese literary luminaries such as Sōseki and Akutagawa (the latter in whose honor the prize itself had been established), but those of "world literature," which here signifies the literature of the West, such as the works of Edgar Allan Poe and Stéphane Mallarmé.

Through a star-studded montage of literary genealogies, a self-conscious equivalence is established between the canons of Japanese literature and world (Western) literature. The assumption throughout their commentaries is that Samukawa and "Poacher" have met an imagined standard that was seen as equivalent to the universal value of "world literature" and, by extension, the world literary market. Furthermore, the judges focus primarily on the formal aspects of the work, of literary and authorial style: Taki Kōsaku, for example, remarks on Samukawa's work: "It is similar to the short story technique [*shuhō*] used by France's Mallarmé, and has the wit and brilliance [*saiki*]) reminiscent of yet another Akutagawa." Kojima Seijirō writes of "Poacher": "The Japanese language is powerful and beautiful. The writer's voice came through in his efforts to bring out the simplicity and beauty of his descriptions."[16]

In contrast, the discussion on Kim's "Into the Light" is almost entirely limited to the particularity of the content of what is perceived to be the ethnic alterity of the story and its writer; for example, Taki Kōsaku comments: "I was pleased that such a talented writer came out of Korea. . . . The topic of Kim Saryang's 'Into the Light' is the ethnic psychology of the Korean people [*Chōsenno hito no minzoku shinkei*]. . . . It is a significant theme in today's context [*kyō no shisei*]." Uno Kōji says, "Kim's 'Into the Light' embodies the peculiar ambiance of Koreans [*Hantōjin no irikunda bimyō na kimochi*]."

What is noteworthy throughout the commentaries as a collective (not just in one or two isolated cases) is that in contrast to what is assumed to be the universalist and "timeless" artistic genius of Samukawa as an individual author and artist and of the literary *form* of his writing style, the focus entirely shifts to the particularity and "timeliness" of the *content* of Kim's writing: most importantly, to its embodiment of what is perceived as its colonial ethnic alterity—what was called the "Korean problem" at the time.[17]

Whereas one author has been nominated for the prestigious prize because his *individual* artistic talent is seen to be on par with the canons of Japanese and "world literature," the literature of the colonized is exotic and untranslatable beyond the particular and "timely" role it is playing in the *collective* national politics of a particular moment.

In the final analysis, the judges all seem to be in agreement that Samukawa was the superior candidate, but they collectively and apologetically dwell on the final decision for quite some time. Kawabata, for example, writes: "A feeling of sadness after selecting out [*sengai*] Kim Saryang lasted for a long time afterwards." In fact, for Kawabata, it was precisely his "humane inclinations" toward Kim's ethnicity that made him want to nominate him in the first place, despite what he sensed the work lacked (*tarinu tokoro*) in comparison to that of Samukawa. (His exact words were "sakka ga Chōsenjin dearu tameni suisen shitai to iu ninjō.") Here we see the critics struggling with their "humane" sympathetic desires to embrace the colonial writer despite his lack, contending with their fixation on his ethnic difference. The inordinate amount of attention given to the colonial alterity of the text and its writer differentiates both as Other, even while the nomination for the metropolitan Akutagawa Prize suggests their assimilation. The transcription of the comments of the Akutagawa Prize judges offers us a glimpse into the ambivalence of the critics themselves in the face of the colonized text at the "Dragon Gate" (*tōryūmon*), the symbolic entryway of the metropolitan literary establishment of the Bundan.

The awards ceremony itself becomes another apologetic enactment of the ambivalent expression of inclusion and exclusion of the colonized writer by metropolitan critics. Realizing that he was not the actual winner, Kim takes a peripheral seat in the banquet room, but a grand gesture is made to move his seat to share the limelight with the winner. Kume Masao, the master of ceremonies and one of the judges, is said to have joked that it was his strong opposition to giving the award to Kim that resulted in the final decision, but that looking at Kim sitting next to Samukawa, he now felt the urge to give him something after all.[18]

In the end, despite their best intentions, the judges unwittingly reveal their ambivalence toward the minor writer and his text at the threshold of Japanese literature. So, too, they share deep anxieties and contradictions in the face of colonial contamination and the need to keep the texts of the Other in their proper place in the imperial hierarchy.

The comparison of Samukawa to Rudyard Kipling here is also noteworthy. As Kawamura Minato has shown, the Akutagawa Prize at the time made a point of paying special homage to Japanese writers who were writing in and about the "frontiers" of Japan's imperial expansions. Whether these works can all be read as supporting such imperial policies or as subversive (or ambivalent) is open to readers' interpretations and continues to be contested; but what is clear is the symbolic significance of the Japanese imperial project in the development of Japan's modern literary field in this new era (*shin jidai*).[19]

What I would like to note here is that while the Japanese imperial discourse exhibits familiar binary oppositions also seen in many other imperial contexts, between universalism and particularlism, form and content, pure literature and political literature, these assumptions also expose the precarious place or impasse of Japan itself, tottering between the West and the Rest. While the assimilated works of minor writers like Kim Saryang gave credence to the image of Japan's rise as a world-class empire, on par with Western imperial powers, they also caused deep anxieties about Japan's intimate links to its closest cultural neighbors who had to be incorporated and repudiated at the same time. While the Akutagawa Prize judges positioned themselves as magnanimous purveyors of recognition (based on metropolitan and therefore presumably world standards) of the literary product from the colony, a close reading of their judgments shows that there is simply no "objective" standard of "world literature" that existed independently of the logic of empire that would overlook the colonized status of the writer and his text.[20]

In fact, sweeping generalizations on the inferiority of colonial literature broadly, not limited to Korea alone, were commonly heard in the metropolitan literary field at the time of Japan's imperial expansions. For example, in *Jihenka no bungaku* (Literature in these times of crisis), in a chapter entitled "Colonial Literature: The Emergence of Korean and Manchurian Writers," critic Itagaki Naoko explicitly refers to Kim Saryang and the Akutagawa Prize as she writes about the Korean literature special edition of the journal *Bungei*, which introduces Korean literature in Japanese translation to imperial audiences:

> I comment on [these texts] here even when they are not very good because I want to expose the current state of Korean literature. . . . They show no depth, new perspectives, or individuality. . . . In this aspect, only Kim Saryang is different. In his work, there is something more than a description

of reality. Here is a sharp interiority, a modern eye that does not exist in the others. Of all the new writers, he is the most noteworthy and to me personally, of particular interest. . . . In Kim there is a strong fixation on the various particularities of and the fate of the Korean people [*Chōsen minzoku*]. His work also has something je ne sais quoi which is effective in a dark and wretched sort of way.[21]

Itagaki's "compliments" go on to make sweeping generalizations about the lack of development in Manchurian literature as well (which she's read in Japanese translation). In comparison, she writes, "Kim Saryang's works are almost on par with the level of the Japanese. If I were to compare the average levels in Korean and Manchurian literature, I would say that the former is just one day more "grown up" (*ichinichi dake otona de aru*). Today, rather than just considering the location of Korean literature at this time, it is necessary to cast a broad perspective on Korean literature and reprimand (*tataku*) its immaturity."[22]

Itagaki's comments echo those of the Akutagawa judges in more focused terms, suggesting that for the colonized subject to attain modern subjectivity, it must necessarily be supplemented by that of the collective. Here, too, Kim is being called to perform the uncertain role of an "exceptional representative" among the rest of the inferior writers of Korea (and even throughout the other colonies). It is significant that such sweeping assumptions on the inferiority of Korean literature in general (albeit "one day" more mature in comparison to the literature from other colonies) are based on the critical misrecognition of literature written by Koreans in, or those translated into, the imperial language (Japanese) as representative texts of "Korean literature." Such self-proclaimed positions of expertise on the inferior state of colonial literatures in toto based on limited readings of translated works reveal the colonizer's monolingual conceit and failure to understand the broader imperial context in which colonized writers were being called to write so-called representative and self-exoticizing texts in the colonizer's language for the colonizer's taste and consumption.[23]

Colonized I-Novel

How was the minor writer Kim Saryang perceiving his own position in the midst of this flurry of imperial (mis)recognition? Let us return to "Letter to Mother," to a section in which he recalls a newspaper advertisement announcing the nomination: "Below the advertisement for my story was the following critique by the writer Satō Haruo: 'A work that is an I-novel which has the tragic fate of an entire people [*minzoku*] squeezed into it.' 'Is this right? Is it right?' I asked myself. . . . Even though it is my own work, there is something about 'Into the Light' that I couldn't quite make satisfactory [*sukkiri dekinai mono ga arimashita*]. It's a lie. I'm still telling lies, I told myself, even while writing it."[24] Here we glimpse the deep anxiety the writer feels toward the disjuncture between his own writing, which he sees as lies, and the pressure to represent the truth. This burden of truth or authenticity and the writer's self-perceived failure to represent it is at the heart of the minor writer's conundrum. The pressure seems to come from multiple sources, not the least from an internalized self-critique, as seen here. To try to understand this conundrum of the writer, let us take a closer look at what seems to have triggered such anxieties: the metropolitan critic Satō Haruo's characterization of "Into the Light" as an "I-novel" containing the tragic fate of an entire people. Perhaps we can try to approach the larger implications of this statement by examining the genre of the "I-novel" itself.

Written either in the first person or third person point of view, the I-novel has been read to be confessional in nature and is often said to reveal the truth of the writer's own personal life. In orthodox Japanese literary history, the "I-novel" (*watakushi shōsetsu* or *shi-shōsetsu*) has come to be considered *the* quintessential modern Japanese literary form. As Tomi Suzuki argues, this dominant view came to see that "the Japanese modern novel, in attempting to follow the 'true' realism of Europe, produced a 'uniquely Japanese' form called the I-novel, which was deeply rooted in Japanese society and 'tradition.' This genealogy of the I-novel was created in the late Taishō period [1912–1926], was fully developed by Kobayashi Hideo, Itō Sei, and Nakamura Mitsuo, and then subsequently adopted by all literary histories in one form or another."[25]

Whether the major critics of modern Japanese literature defined the Japanese I-novel as inferior or superior to its Western counterparts, it is evident that for many of them, the point of reference was always the West as a standard that either needed to be caught up with or which Japanese literature was in the process of, or already had succeeded in, overcoming. Suzuki points out that in this context, the orthodox view of the I-novel was constructed through the history of modern Japanese literature by way of what she calls an "I-novel discourse" whose development itself paralleled the vicissitudes of modern Japan's conflicted confrontation with Western modernity in general and with Western or world literature in particular. Suzuki concludes: "This genealogy, which supplied the main narrative for the 'history of modern Japanese literature,' also represented an autobiographical moment in which the Japanese literary and cultural tradition was retroactively constructed in the intense debate over the meaning of modernity, westernization, Japanese identity, and the self. There is no transcendental position to frame this I-novel discourse, which still persists."[26] In such landmark essays as "On the I-novel" and "The Literature of Homelessness," both considered as the most influential literary criticisms on modern Japanese literature, Kobayashi Hideo reveals the ongoing conundrum of Japanese modern literature vis-à-vis the West. In "On the I-novel," Kobayashi laments the lack of development of the Japanese I-novel in comparison to Western counterparts while he simultaneously posits a potential equivalence in which Japan in fact had developed over the years to attain more and more in common with the West. Such an assessment of a rising equivalence with the West is remarked on with ambivalence, however. Kobayashi laments Japan's alienation, "homelessness," or "dislocation" from its own past and traditions in its race to catch up with the West; at the same time, he also seems smugly proud of Japan's purported achievement and "arrival" at a "universal standard" equated with the West (before any of its own neighbors or any other non-West nation).

Such ambivalence can be heard clearly in one of the most oft-quoted passages from Kobayashi's "Literature of Homelessness": "This style . . . [in Western literature and film] elicits a sense of intimacy, so that we feel closer to the Moroccan desert we have never seen than to the landscape of Ginza before our eyes."[27]

The ideological implications of the "I-novel" discourse take on yet another layer of complexity when translated to the colonized texts of Japan. Satō's characterization of Kim's story as an "I-novel with the entire nation squeezed into it" marks the ethnic alterity of Kim's text as what I call a "colonized I-novel."

Satō's comments seem to suggest that while the "I-novel" is said to be a repository of the interiority and authenticity of an "I" of a universal modern subject translated to a native Japanese form, it needs to be supplemented by a collective "we" when translated to the colonized text and context. If the discourse on the I-novel in Japan highlighted the *individuality* of a single author as an artist, or the artist as a universal modern subjectivity as represented through his writing, the "colonized I," in contrast, must supplement and represent the *collective* "I" or "we" of the gemeinschaft of the ethnic collective of the colony. Kim's text is being lauded for translating the entire colony into the quintessential Japanese "I-novel." In other words, the "colonized I-novel" is an "I-novel," but not quite.

In fact, the irony of the judges' claim that Kim Saryang's "Into the Light" can be read as a representation of the collective spirit of the Korean people surfaces when we take a closer look at the story itself against the grain of such metropolitan critical assessments. "Into the Light" is not about the "Korean problem," nor is it about a unified collective Korean people. It is about characters living in the slums of Tokyo—a child of Korean and Japanese intermarriage and a teacher from Korea, both of whom try to "pass" as Japanese. In chapter 4, I read the "I" of the story, not as a unified symbol of a coherent ethno-national whole, but rather as multiple, fragmented, and schizoid. Each character in the story can be diagnosed as shattered and broken, both psychologically and bodily, suffering a crisis of the wounded self, manifested in self-loathing and self-denial. In this reading, the "I" is far from being a symbol of a unified ethnic collective, representing a mythical wholeness of the colony, as assumed by Satō and the other judges. If anything, rather than being about the Korea problem, the story may be about the "Japanese problem"—about the inequalities, contradictions, and unsavory interethnic intimacies of empire.

The conundrum of the "colonized I-novel" is a "Japanese problem" on yet another register. It uneasily mirrors Japan's own position relative to the West. In an effort to distinguish Japanese literature from a Western standard and counterpart and to claim a sense of authenticity, the predicament persists of reducing Japan to a collective essence and particularity in relation to the universal modern Western subject. While Japan's experience of modernity has historically been a struggle to differentiate itself from Asia (Datsu-A-Ron) and attain equivalence with the West, the ultimate irony is that the shared conundrum of Japan with the very Asian neighbors it colonized erupts to the surface in these ambivalent exchanges.

Hubris of Pure Literature

Another important aspect of the "I-novel" discourse is the construction of the genre as a quintessentially "pure" *l'art pour l'art* form uncontaminated by political impurity. The "colonized I-novel," however, is not allowed even this semblance of so-called purity but is said to be about a collective experience that is always already politicized. For the colonized writer, the personal is always political, and he or she must represent the entire (absent) nation and all the colonized people.

This reading conjures up American critic Fredric Jameson's now oft-cited declaration that "all third world texts are necessarily . . . national allegories . . . where the telling of the individual story and the individual experience *cannot but* ultimately involve the whole laborious telling of the experience of the collectivity itself" (emphasis added).[28] There is an echo of the Akutagawa judges in Jameson's reading, in which he tries to "praise and valorize positively" the "third world text," while claiming the position of a sympathetic reader.[29]

Jameson's argument has been cogently critiqued elsewhere,[30] but the critique bears repeating here because the age-old predilection still persists all around us. Furthermore, by juxtaposing the parallel logic in critical productions across the East/West and colonial/postcolonial divides, we must point out the pervasiveness of the myopia of metropolitan critics that is repeatedly reproduced in various contexts in the face of the minor writer, whether defined as the colonized or the "third world" or other forms of subalternity.

It is necessary to emphasize here that Deleuze and Guattari, whose concept of "minor literature" informs this project, make the same assumptions when they claim that the minor literature is a literature that is necessarily political and of a collective nature. What I do find useful for my purposes is their exposition of the distinct power dynamics at work in the minor writer's act of appropriating the major language. In general, Deleuze and Guattari's conceptualization is useful as a starting point, offering a common language in which to begin to discuss the particularities of minor literary acts in all their different manifestations from a multiplicity of contexts. Having said this, I think it is important to be reminded that these particularities by no means abide by one overarching generic definition.

We metropolitan critics not only fail to consider the repressive roles of our own privileged positions vis-à-vis the minor text, but we also reproduce the same old dynamics because it is not in our interest to change or relinquish our power and therefore we do not want to give up such positions of privilege.[31] If the minor text *cannot but* be read as a national allegory, as the Akutagawa Prize judges and the first world critic Jameson argued, it is because these texts *cannot but* be read in this way in the metropolitan critical encounter.

The further irony in this encounter is that the minor writer or translator in fact has access to valuable knowledge to which the metropolitan critic must be indebted. If the minor writer is accorded a seat of equal rank at the discursive table and access to the technologies of knowledge production, and is not merely relegated to the secondary position of a native informant or translator, the danger persists that he or she will rise to make the metropolitan critic's role irrelevant and obsolete. Without the curtain of hubris (backed by economic and military might), the emptiness upon which the hierarchy is built will be exposed. The illegitimacy of power positions based on actual ignorance rather than knowledge will become visible to all.[32]

As seen in the previous chapter, Kim Saryang wrote "Into the Light" in the imperial language—Japanese—for consumption by the metropolitan literary establishment at a time when colonial Korea was being rigorously assimilated for imperial agendas.[1] In view of contradictory demands placed on the colonized writer by the metropolitan literary field, it may not be surprising that his literary work embodied deep anxieties about the colonial encounter. Each character in Kim's "Into the Light," including the narrating I, is marked by bodily and psychic fragmentations that not only evoke questions about the unification of the I and the generic categorization of the story as an "I-novel" (by the metropolitan critic), but also raise doubts about the selfsameness of identity in the colonial modern experience.

Textually and metatextually, the story embodies the complex process of imperial co-optation. On its own, the story is ambivalent and open-ended, lending itself to multiple rereadings, even those that are ideologically mutually exclusive. By rereading the textual failure to fit the generic form of the "I-novel" in opposition to the claims by the metropolitan critic, we can be mindful of the text's disconcerting subjectivities (the narrating/narrated and the colonizer/colonized, for example). We shall see that the text's multiple breakdowns, on the formal level and in the narrative content, gesture toward the conundrum of representation and the discontent caused by assimilation of colonial modern subjects in the uneven context of empire.

Epistolary Exchange

Let us turn briefly to another epistolary correspondence between Kim Saryang and fellow colonized writer Long Yingzong (Ryū Eisō, 1911–1999), from Taiwan; this letter reveals the anxieties of shared predicaments by colonized writers across vast distances of the empire. This virtual meeting (the two never met in person) can be glimpsed through a letter written by Kim in response to a letter Long wrote to Kim in which he critiqued Kim's "Into the Light."[2] Long's letter was written after the publication of his own Japanese-language short story "Yoitsuki" (Twilight moon) in the same journal,[3] and Kim, writing in Japanese, seems eager to reciprocate: "I am grateful to have received your letter this morning. We are born of distant and disparate places, but our circumstances of writing in a foreign language have allowed us to become new friends, and this more than anything else, delights me (210)."

This meeting of two colonized writers through the written medium has been enabled by what seems at a glance to be the cosmopolitan fluidity of empire, through their shared imperial language and mutual debut into the Japanese literary field. But as will become evident, the letter shows a deeply ironic response toward opportunities enabled through colonial subjection. Writes Kim: "Reading your story 'Twilight Moon,' I felt it was very close to my own heart. I shudder at the realization that the circumstances of your location and my own are not much different. Of course, that work is not in any way a debunking of the present situation, and in fact, it is written in a matter-of-fact tone. But in your writing, I sensed your trembling hand. Maybe I am being presumptuous or sentimental. If so, won't you reprimand me! Reprimand me!" (211) Thus, deeply identifying with a fellow writer from a distant colony, the letter reveals the shared plight of displacement and the desire for solidarity between colonized writers in the expanding empire. The painful writing act is embodied in Kim's evocation of "trembling hands" and the "shudder" coursing through his body in recognition of their mirrored circumstances. Kim's anxieties about their uncertain positions as colonized writers in the metropole can also be sensed in his masochistic pleading for reprimanding. In this ambivalent letter entwined with delight and melancholy, it is clear that Kim is moved by the meeting of two souls in their mutual anxiety, more so than by the celebration of their success in the metropolitan literary field. It is also significant that despite his recognition of their similarities, Kim does not assume equivalence of their disparate experiences subsumed in terms of his own limited point of view.[4]

After asking Long to join him in solidarity, encouraging and supporting one another in their continued literary efforts, Kim turns to Long's critical comments on "Into the Light." "Your critique of 'Into the Light' is right of course. With all my heart I too am eagerly waiting for the day when I may be able to revise it. It is not a piece that I myself like. It was written for the Japanese reader. I know this well. Because I know this all too well, it frightens me" (211–12). Here Kim interestingly admits his own dissatisfaction with and even partially repudiates the story that has brought him so much fame and recognition throughout the empire. He regrets that it was written self-consciously for the gaze of the Japanese reader, and this fact troubles him deeply, to the point of filling him with fear.[5] He also suggests that the intended audience and other external circumstances may have had a direct effect on his inability to write a story that was fully satisfactory to him. Further, in expressing hope for a day when he would be able to revise the text, Kim's is a melancholic, future-oriented gesture, deeply dissatisfied with the present but forward-looking, toward a time in which he will live in circumstances different from those surrounding him, a time when his writings may one day be able to follow his vision.

The paradoxes of the colonial situation are brought out in this brief exchange; traversing spatial and linguistic distances, these two writers encounter one another in a literary exchange of mutual recognition and friendship by the very context of empire that has relegated them as colonized subjects to different rungs on the imperial hierarchy, as the empire was expanding into China. Such ironies and the ambivalence of the minor writer in the face of his own writing seep into the very textual level of the story they so passionately discussed; it is to this story to which we now turn.

"Into the Light"

Let us examine the story that caused such angst in the writer and received much critical attention throughout the empire. Contrary to the metropolitan critic's categorical pronouncements, "Into the Light" goes against the conventions of the "I-novel." It is not a story of a unified and selfsame I, nor of the I as a symbolic collective of a colonized people. Rather, each narrated subjectivity (including the narrating I) is more than one (multiple) and schizoid (fragmented). In the story, identities defy ontological wholeness not only in their

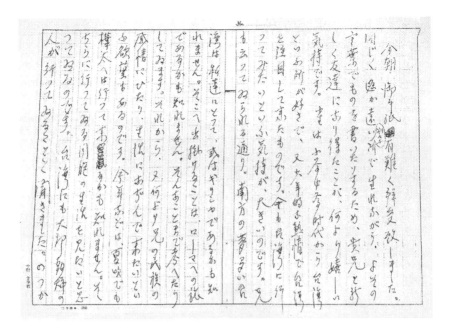

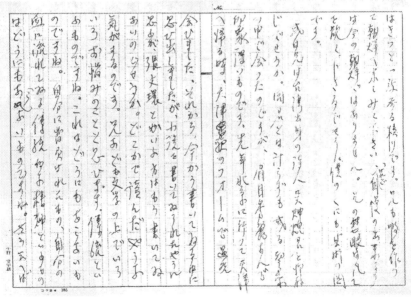

FIGS. 4.1., 4.2., 4.3., 4.4., 4.5., AND 4.6 Letter from Kim Saryang to Long Yingzong. Reprinted with permission from Mr. Liu Chih-Fu, from the estate of Long Yingzong. Special thanks to Professor Huei-Chen Wang and Dr. Ji-Young Shin for help retrieving a copy of this rare letter.

結局お事あるのでせうか。それを意識めにも
振んでゐなからうか。それを考へるにものしが
ら、此の、自分の文章を行ことる◯べでせ
うね。僕のども御魂ゆに感じてゐるやうです。
やはり貴兄は文壇人の大きさをやつてゐる
し、又やる、やるし、僕は動揺してゐところを
うってゐるし、又やるべきことゐてゐるのです。
なり二行のこ、のだけれど、大事あくてる
せるね。貴兄の省とを読んで僕は何事
に身近かあそを感じました。やはり皆さん

ーーー

うところも僕のそうも現実のはおほまし
おりやうで擁立としますよ。あの作者は
勿論従来器露のものよく、攻めてもあ
風は第からうとおさうに作品もひますが、僕はも
の中に貴兄のふるくてゐる生とみさうで
す。武自僕の独断かも知れるよん、風。僕
も知れるよん、あつしてこうよ、少こしてても

貴兄はあの事者とか書く作気をどい
恐ひます。さう僕ゐた作気ひはそれかも知れな
さい。

十二月二五日

ーーー

が、語かにいい作れのでせうか。あ途は深
はぬさあ方かこう。彼り侍かうんじす。貴んど
それほど僕も必として、名を訪めさし、
してドこいいやとうゐのろこあつてゐ、れ
かも知れるよん、僕、皆日のやうにもつれ
はお作事をしてをこより作り古かる
りじす、僕も堪られ、いい作者を書くさん
のじす、あそらず、健産に、して行く後
せう。えもとしいしいい化事をして下
さい。やれび順すしゆけ念ひまうよう、な
の中にの美の御魂評充も代とよひます。
僕もいつのはかえるんあの化行し僕さか
かまることを思いつ待つてゐるのです。
好さんからひは御料思めせん。
自分ひも僕ゐはつまつてゐるので
評りはつまつ分つてゐるので、さういいつるか

二月八日

芥川龍之介

漢宇兄 几下

山添のこの紙に氏にとあとうてて
いやうです。御辞ひしてもらて下さい。

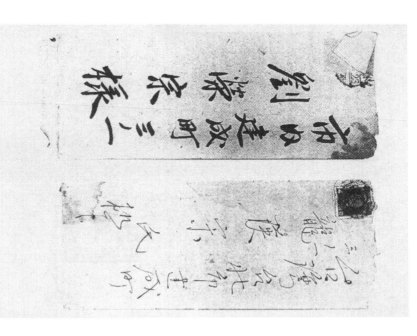

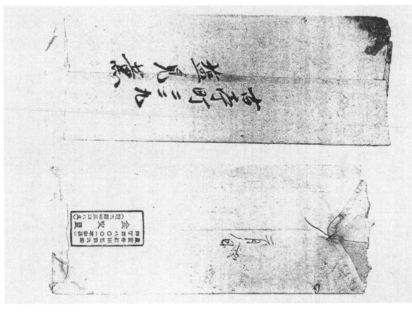

fractured states but in their performative and relational dependency vis-à-vis one another.[6] It seems significant that the text interweaves multiple stories of "borderline" characters, each of whom blurs the line between the colonizer and the colonized, set in their dilapidated habitations in the margins of metropolitan Tokyo. The narrative begins like this:

> The boy I'm going to tell you about, Yamada Haruo, was a strange child indeed. He didn't play with the other children and just circled around them as if afraid. Sometimes, the other children would bully him, and then he would turn around and try to bully one of the girls or the smaller children. And when someone happened to trip up, he made a big ruckus as if he had been anticipating it. Haruo didn't try to love anyone nor was he loved by the others. He had a thin head of hair and big protruding ears, and the prominent whites of his eyes gave him a strange appearance. Among all the other children, he was the most unkempt and dirty, and although it was already late autumn, he was still wearing thin ragged clothes that were clearly out of season. Maybe that's what gave him an even more gloomy and creepy air. (2)

Thus, we are introduced to a misfit and melancholy boy, who defies easy characterization or identification, a boy whom the narrator tells us is neither lovable nor able to love. Already clear from this beginning is that the story the narrator is about to embark on is not a story about himself, a unified narrating I. It turns out, in fact, to be a tale of the relationship between two characters, Yamada Haruo, and the narrating I, and neither of them, we find out, is a unified subjectivity.

The narrating I is not a reliable one, and he delays introducing himself until several pages into the story, as if he has something to hide. In fact, we soon find out that he does. In the beginning, we are offered only glimpses of his identity: a student at the imperial university and a resident at the S commune. He teaches English at the commune a few nights a week to the day laborers in the neighborhood. He does not readily reveal his name, and we must wait to overhear it through children calling out to him:

"Mr. Minami! Mr. Minami!"

Thus identified, "Minami" finally attempts to explain himself:

> Come to think of it, before I knew it, I was being referred to as "Minami" [南] at the commune. As you know, my last name should be read "Nam"

but for various reasons, it was being called in the Japanese way. It was my colleagues who first began to call me that, and at first, the name did grate on my nerves. But gradually, I began to think it might be for the best. I mean, in order to play freely with these innocent children. And I told myself over and over again that this did not make me a hypocrite or a coward. I earnestly convinced myself that if there had been even one Korean child in the commune, I would of course have insisted that everyone call me "Nam [南]." (4)

Thus, several pages into the story, we finally get a delayed glimpse of the identity of the narrating I, whose fragmentation is marked immediately by the doubled name "Minami/Nam." Like Haruo, Minami/Nam, too, is uncanny, split from himself and somewhat too eager in trying to convince himself and the reader (whom he addresses directly and too intimately here: "as you know," when we didn't know) of why he is passing as a Japanese by going by the Japanese pronunciation of his name. But before he has a chance to convince the reader, Minami/Nam is forced to "come out" as his internal identity crisis is violently exposed by an angry, young Korean man named Yi, who accuses Minami/Nam in front of the children of cowering behind his Japanese name: "Why is it that even someone like you tries to hide your name?" I was speechless. . . . Yi was so impassioned that he began to stutter. Why was he so worked up? (5). Both Yi and Minami/Nam seem unable to continue the conversation in this emotional moment of recognition. Such bodily impairments, the failure of speech and sight, are repeated tropes throughout the story, marking each character's conundrum of identity and the (in)ability to identify one another. Minami/Nam manages to let out a weak moan as he struggles to defend himself:

"I agree with you. . . . But I wasn't trying to hide the fact that I'm Korean. Other people started calling me that. And I didn't think it was necessary to go around shouting out that I'm Korean. But if I gave you the wrong impression, I have no excuses." Just then, one of the children peeking in through the cracked door began to scream: "See, I knew it! The teacher is Korean!" It was Haruo. (5–6)

As the narrative continues, we begin to see that Minami/Nam's fragmented identity is intimately linked to this boy, Yamada Haruo. In fact, the narrative itself develops through the interweaving stories of the two characters, whose identities mirror one another and are formed in the story through their mutual relationship, in a series of recognitions and misrecognitions. We find in the narrative that each fragmented narrated subject is dependent on the other and cannot stand apart from that relationship to the other.

In one subsequent scene, Haruo begins to chase after a girl, yelling, "Chō-senjin *chabare chabare!*"[7] The narrator explains:

> "Chabare" means "to grab" in Korean, a phrase often used by Japanese migrants in Korea. Of course the girl was not Korean. He was harassing her in order for me to hear. I ran to Yamada, and grabbing his collar, started slapping his cheeks mercilessly.
>
> "What the hell do you think you're doing?"
>
> Yamada became quiet and didn't let out a word. He just stood frozen like an animal. He didn't even cry. He merely stared up at me with rounded eyes, exhaling roughly. . . . Suddenly a teardrop squeezed out of his eye. But as if trying to swallow back the tear, he barked in a low voice, "Idiot Chōsenjin!" (7)

Here, in the face of Minami/Nam's violent blows, words fail Haruo until he can barely squeeze out a racist epithet to hide his own emotions. "Chōsenjin" (Korean) is the derogatory interpellation of colonized subjects, and *chabare* is in fact the pidgin pronunciation of "chabara," which is the imperative form of the verb *chapta* (to grab or to seize); thus the phrase can be roughly translated as "Get that gook!" The pidgin phrase introduced here as that commonly used by Japanese migrants in Korea exposes not only the violence of the colonizer's racism against the colonized but also the infiltration of the colonizer's speech by the language of the colonized. The colonial encounter thus is exposed as deeply infecting both sides of the colonial divide. The uncanny contamination of the colonizer and the colonized by one an(other) becomes more evident as we keep reading.

Marking the failure of sight, Minami/Nam continues to misrecognize Haruo as he watches him in these scenes. Relying on the binary logic of colonizer and colonized, he assumes that Haruo must be a Japanese migrant who had grown up in colonial Korea. How else would one explain Haruo's twisted sense of racist superiority over colonized Koreans?

But several pages later, in a belated moment of recognition, we realize that this scene of Haruo's *acting* up, filled with affects common in cultural clashes (violence, hatred, vulnerability, and racial slurs) is not simply a binary encounter between the racist colonizer and the discriminated colonized, as it first appears. The fact that Haruo attacks a Japanese girl and projects onto her a Korean identity already disturbs this clear distinction. That something is amiss is further foreshadowed in the confusing power dynamics when the child Haruo, the apparent colonizer, is being punished by the grown-up Minami/Nam, the colonized. In the scene, however, Minami/Nam and the reader are not yet able to *see* the actual significance of this face-to-face encounter with Haruo. Only later, through a gradually developing relationship with the boy, do we find out that the two have more in common than meets the eye.

The moment of mutual recognition finally comes in a scene mirroring Minami/Nam's "outing," when Haruo's identity, too, is violently exposed by Yi. Despite Haruo's asocial racist behavior, Minami/Nam finds himself somehow drawn to the strange boy and makes efforts to befriend him. He seems to have made some progress, when one day, as the two are spending time together at the commune, a commotion breaks out and a wounded woman is carried into the commune hospital by Yi.

> The woman was leaning back with her head covered in blood. Trembling, Haruo tried to approach her, but catching sight of me, he suddenly stopped in his tracks. (10)

Yi explains to Minami/Nam that she is a Korean woman whose husband, a Japanese man, had stabbed her in a fit of rage because she had been visiting with Yi's mother, whose ethnicity is visibly marked by her Korean dress. Then, catching sight of Haruo, who has been cowering in the background as if trying to disappear, Yi pounces on him, shouting:

> "It's him! It's his father!" (10)

Thus, we see that Haruo, like Minami/Nam, has been performing all along, trying to pass as a Japanese. As a hybrid offspring from a Japanese-Korean intermarriage, Haruo has been performing what has been associated with his father's "Japaneseness" at the expense of total repudiation of what has been marked as the "Koreanness" of his mother. In this scene, he cannot even approach his severely wounded mother, afraid of exposing his racial impurity. Haruo's mother herself tries to hide the fact that Haruo is her own son to protect him from the discrimination she has suffered as a Korean. She even tries to "pass" by refusing to speak Korean although her accented Japanese and foreign name give her away.

What is significant here is that racist assumptions of pure and natural identities held by the colonizers have seeped deep into the psyche of the colonized as well. The mother's denial of herself and Haruo's hyperexaggerated embodiment of "Japaneseness" and his denial of his/mother's "Koreanness follow the same logic of racial purity that sustains the imperial project on both sides of the racial divide. Such racist attitudes have seeped into the character Yi as well, who, on the surface, seems to be most adamantly revolting against colonial discriminatory logic. In fact, it is ironic that Yi mimics the logic of empire in his inability to see beyond Haruo's contaminated Japanese blood, and Yi's violent discrimination of the boy is based on his assumptions about Haruo's selfsame Japanese identity. By conflating and repudiating Haruo with Haruo's father, as the symbol of unitary Japaneseness, Yi can safely protect his own sense of selfsame identity as a Korean. Such a neat division between the Japanese colonizers and the Korean colonized would be disturbed by the presence of hybrids like Haruo, or perhaps even more so, Minami/Nam, who can pass in and out of both worlds. The contamination of the colonizers and the colonized by one another, and the impossibility of telling one another apart, are their shared anxieties in the colonial encounter. This anxiety was unlike Western imperialism, which commonly colonized racially visible Others, whereas the Japanese and the Koreans were, as far as the eye could see, indistinguishable.[8]

The impossibility of sustaining the colonial binary and the anxieties thus triggered are brought to the fore in a scene in which Yi accosts Minami/Nam for sympathizing and identifying with Haruo, who should be kept at a safe distance as an Other. Afraid to visit his mother in the hospital because his love for her is tainted by his hatred of what he identifies as his/mother's Koreanness, Haruo has spent the night in Minami/Nam's room. Discovering this, Yi loses his temper and yells at Minami/Nam: "Even after he calls you 'Chōsenjin,' you still insist on protecting him!" The conversation continues:

> Nam: Yamada's come to see me through this rainstorm. Even if he wanted to go back home, he has no place to return.
> Yi: Who is the one with nowhere to return? That poor woman is the one who has no place to go. That kid can go back to his father. Damn it, go to hell, you bastard! (15)

In this exchange, it is unclear whom Yi is damning to hell, Haruo or Haruo's father. Yi's inability to distinguish Haruo/Haruo's father shows Yi's own blindness, conflating their complex identities as a symbol of the unified Japanese colonizer. Just as colonial racist depictions of colonized subjects often failed to distinguish individuals from their collectivity, Yi's reaction shows a similar blind affliction of the colonized, psychically wounded by the imperial racist system and unable to see differences among the Japanese as a collective whole. From Yi's perspective, it seems, even a drop of Japanese blood automatically and naturally marks someone as "Japanese," to be repudiated as an Other, defying any possibility of identification. Such racist attitudes refuse to recognize borderline characters such as Haruo and Minami/Nam.

Although it is necessary to be aware of and to interrogate illegitimate privileges endowed to the colonizers in the Manichean system constructed by colonialism, to respond to this constructed binary with the same divided logic merely replicates the circle of violence with no possible exit from the impasse.[9] Following the above exchange between Yi and Minami/Nam, this scene illustrates the complete unraveling of Minami/Nam in his psychic breakdown as he literally turns to face and to speak to himself as Other.

> Suddenly I screamed as if possessed. I thought I was going mad. . . . Of course I understood naïve Yi because I too had passed through such a phase. But then, in the next moment, the full impact of the realization that I was being called "Minami" was ringing like a bell through my five organs. Taken aback, I tried to find excuses as I always did. But it was useless.
> "Hypocrite, you're turning into a hypocrite again."
> I heard a voice next to me.
> "I suppose you've finally lost your grounding and become a coward, heh?"
> Shocked, I tried to ignore the voice and said,
> "Why must I keep yelling out, 'No, I will not be a coward!' Doesn't that in fact push me deeper into the swamp of cowardliness?"
> I had believed I was an adult. I wasn't twisted like a child, and I didn't xx[10] madly like a young man. But wasn't I lying down comfortably on my belly like a coward? I turned to myself, you said you didn't want to create a gap between yourself and those innocent children. But what is the difference between you and the Korean man who frequents a bar in order to hide himself? In protest, I accosted myself. What is the difference between yourself and the man who yells out in a moment of sentimentality, "I'm a Korean, I'm a Korean!" There was fundamentally nothing different from Yamada Haruo, yelling that he was not a Korean. . . . I was fed up with my useless one-man act. (15–16)

In this schizophrenic moment of complete breakdown of subjectivity, Minami/Nam (mis)recognizes him/self and begins to address him/self in the second-person Other, "you." In the scene, Minami/Nam splits once more as "I/You" and is caught in an accusatory impasse with him/self. Tired of his identity performance, he cannot deny being a Korean, but likewise cannot claim himself to be a Korean either. Both are merely two sides of the same coin, trapped in the politics of identity. In this dilemma, neither assimilation nor differentiation offers satisfactory answers to the colonized subject who is already contaminated by the colonial system and has "nowhere to go." Further, Minami/Nam realizes that he can neither shed nor wear the burden of identity that is pressing upon him from multiple contradictory demands within the colonial system. The character nearly goes mad in the impasse.

It seems significant that this moment of complete breakdown of the narrative I is also the moment of most clarity, when he seems most honest or true to him/self. It is also the moment of I's identification with the other abjected and fragmented characters, Haruo, Yi, and even the imagined everyman in the bar. In the absence of a coherent, unified I, the fragmented I seeks to form connections with other divided selves by virtue of the shared sense of pain from their exilic conditions. The text does not offer an easy solution to their conundrums, but this relational subjectivity, one that is able to find meaning in one another, commiserating in the pain of others, gestures toward a new conception of identity that is neither the selfsame nor of an ontological collectivity based on an unquestioned pure ethnic bond. Perhaps a similar bond with the Other that is broadly defined (linked across vast distances) yet individual (singular through the affect of experience) as suggested here is echoed in Kim Saryang's letter to Long Yingzong, in which Kim shared his anxieties in the metropolitan limelight with a fellow colonized writer from Taiwan.

In fact, in the act of turning toward him/self in an address to an Other, I reveals the split within the self and the presence of the Other within the I. The predicament of the foreign within the self is one that is shared by each of the characters in the story—Minami/Nam, Haruo, Haruo's mother, and, as we are about to discover, Haruo's father. Even Yi and Yi's mother, who at first sight appear to represent unified Koreanness, rather reveal in their exaggerated masquerades (Yi's mother flaunts her Korean dress and Yi wears a chip on his shoulder, exploding in violent and indiscriminate anger toward anyone Japanese) that what may appear to be a unified subjectivity exposes a defense mechanism; and this defensiveness tries to compensate through a hyperperformance of the wholeness of identity in the face of the colonizer's violent repudiation of the colonized. Even these seemingly unified subjectivities are in fact relational in this sense, ironically indebted to the Other, which, on the surface, is adamantly repudiated.

Minami/Nam's moment of truth, his moment of self *recognition*, occurs when we see his own subjectivity coming undone, at its most vulnerable. There is no selfsameness here, and Minami/Nam's subjectivity is clearly split and wounded, but he recognizes him/self only when he is able to identify with others who themselves are exposed as fragmented and abjected in their own singular ways, through their shared exilic experiences. Subjectivity here is not unified and ontological, but relational and deeply embedded in the relationship with the Other.

Unhomely Home

Thus far, we have examined the fragmentation of subjectivity in the story by focusing mainly on Kim Saryang's two characters Yamada Haruo and Minami/ Nam. We have seen how the narrative formations of these fragmented identities occur through a series of recognitions/misrecognitions in encounters among the characters, and how subjectivities in the story are relational, vis-à-vis the foreign Other within as well as with the foreignness of other abject characters in the story. This reading of subjectivity as multiple, split, and embodying the foreign within not only rejects the myth of self-contained identity but also opens up spaces where identifications and relationships with the Other are not only possible but always already embedded in subjective formations.[11]

In this section, I shall examine the ways in which the fragmentation of subjectivity in the story is intimately linked to the textual representation of spatial breakdowns, particularly in the slums of the metropolitan city-space and the uncanny lived space of domesticity. In the beginning of the story, from the moment we are introduced to Haruo, the narrative links his mysterious identity to the question of "where he is from":

> It was quite strange, but [Haruo] refused to tell people where he lived. On the way from the university to S commune, I ran into him several times in front of Oshiage Station. I saw the direction he was walking from, and it seemed he lived somewhere in the swampy area behind the station. So one day I happened to ask him,
> "So you live behind the station?"
> But he quickly shook his head.
> "No. My house is next to the commune."
> Of course this was an outright lie. (3)

The question of "where one is from" is often posed to the apparent foreigner among us as a way to mark that foreigner, not necessarily as a way to "identify with" her as a subject but as a way to differentiate and define her as an object of knowledge and control. For Haruo, the answer to the question, "where are you from?" is dangerously close to exposing the foreignness within him/self that he has been desperately trying to repudiate.

The swampy area behind the station is marked historically as a ghetto inhabited by foreigners, particularly the Korean migrant community in Tokyo.[12] This ghetto space, socially marked by poverty and the foreignness of the colonized abject community, causes Haruo to do whatever he can to try to dissociate himself from it. In his desperate desire to pass as Japanese and to protect his secret, he makes a daily detour on his way to and from home. The psychology behind this repudiation in his everyday life is not difficult to understand as we have already seen its more drastic manifestation in Haruo's denial of his wounded mother.

For young Haruo, the home is a place of repudiation not only for its location in the slums of the metropolitan city, and thus for its external mark of ethnic and economic Otherness, but also for its uncanny contamination by foreignness within. Paranoia toward the foreign within is so pervasive that it has contaminated all aspects of the family, rending apart the domestic unit as well as each individual psyche. Such discord is most obviously manifest in the father's physical attack on the mother. This domestic violence mirrors each family member's internal struggle with his/her own foreignness within.

The home, as a space of disharmony, is broken asunder, seemingly from the clash between Father and Mother and what they represent: Japan and Korea, respectively. However, the actual problem is more complicated, arising not from the clear opposition between Father/Japan and Mother/Korea but from the impossibility of distinguishing Japan and Korea, which are internal to and embodied by each member.

The performative nature of identity that we have been tracing throughout the story climaxes when we discover yet one more character who has been passing all along: Haruo's father. Haruo's father's name, Hanbei, grates on Minami/Nam's ear in its strange aural déjà vu until he recalls that the two had actually crossed paths in the past, in another marginal space, a prison cell in the colony. In this scene of belated recognition, Haruo's father, who has been wreaking havoc on the family in the "Name of the (Imperial) Father," is himself outed as contaminated by the colony. In the confidence of the prison cell, he had come out to Minami/Nam that he was born in Korea of a Korean mother, but once out in the metropolitan city-space, he seems to have kept his own hybridity well under cover and has even passed on his identity crisis to the rest of his family.

This inability to "see" and to distinguish the colonized and the colonizer within the self contends with the external pressures of the logic of colonialism that is predicated on differentiating and marking of difference for the imperial world order. Such a discord lies at the heart of the anxiety of this family, both among the members as well as within each individual psyche. Even the mother, a "pure" Korean by birth, is contaminated by the internalized racist values of the colonizer, passing on her inferiority complex to Haruo, who must reject his own mother by this same logic. However, as seen above, Haruo's repudiation of Mother/Korea is deeply ambivalent, mixed with love and attachment. When neither Haruo nor his mother seems to be able to express such complex emotions in words, it is Minami/Nam, a complete outsider to the family, who best captures this predicament, identifying with the experience based on his own identity crisis:

> I thought about the tragedy of one boy and his internal split, a disharmony inherited from the blood of the Japanese and the blood of the Koreans. Unconditional acceptance of all things related to Father and a blind rejection of all things related to Mother, these two sides were constantly in opposition to one another. No doubt that for someone who has been mired in the depths of poverty, he was barred from the affectionate world of his own mother. He couldn't openly embrace his mother. But I knew that behind that blind rejection of all things related to Mother, he was filled with warm breath, heaving for that same Mother. (14)

Thus repeating the tropes of blindness and sight, we see Haruo's identity fragmented along multiple divisions, the self between Father and Mother and between his public and private selves. In concentric circles, the unevenness and disharmony between the colonizers and the colonized that began on the level of empire have trickled down to the heterotopic slum space of the metropolitan city inhabited by this tainted family. The uncanny family structure in turn embodies uneven hierarchies, which finally seep into the fragmented psyches of each individual member.

Here I would like to pause to point out that this reading does not simply reduce the entire story to an allegory of a collective experience, which can be a common pitfall of metropolitan readings of the minor text as we have seen. By highlighting the pain of singular lived experiences of individuals within the family, I would like to suggest that the story is not just an allegory of the "imperial family" on the sublimated level of a symbol. In fact, as I have tried to point out, the focus of the story is not on the level of binary collectives, such as the colonizer versus the colonized, but on pain inscribed on individual identities and their relationships with one another, triggered by the ideologies and hierarchies of colonialism. In other words, Kim Saryang's story tells us not just of the collective experience of life under colonial subjugation, but also how that subjugation affects the inner psyche of each character. While the story refuses to reduce individual experiences to that of a collective, it is open to be read as a larger social commentary on racism triggered by imperial hierarchies and their detrimental effects on the individual psyche.

By focusing on the pained and broken moments of singular experiences, the story performs the breakdown of the slogan of collective imperial harmony. It goes further to accuse the violent contradictions of discriminatory racist structures embedded within the imperial system that have bound the colonizers and the colonized in a vexingly uneven marriage. By examining the psychic breakdowns of individual characters within this "imperial family," the story also shows the instability of the system of imperialism itself, which is never far from the danger of being split asunder by the discontent of those who were forcibly subsumed within its internal contradictions.

Thus, we see that the uncanny Yamada family drama is brought to a shocking climax through the discovery that Haruo's father, who has been condemned as the symbol of "Japaneseness," is himself already tainted bodily and psychically by the colony. This marking of Father/Japan by colonial contamination destabilizes the myth of a selfsame, stable I of the colonizer, segregated from the colonized, and further destabilizes the myth of racial purity that lies at the heart of the uneven structure of the imperial project itself. The paradox of empire is that while it is simultaneously making contradictory demands of assimilation and differentiation upon its subjects, as the borders between its expanding territories are opening up on unprecedented scales, the imperial center itself is also becoming vulnerable to the influx of colonized Others. As this story shows, the anxiety that infects both the colonizer and the colonized in regards to the increasing difficulty of recognizing differences, particularly at the contact zones of miscegenating borderlines, also threatens the divisive logic of empire itself.

Distintegrating Form

Our reading thus far, which began with the representation of the fragmentation of identities in a story by a colonized writer on the threshold of the metropolitan literary field, has brought the dilemma of subjectivity to the very heart of the metropole. On the textual level, this story shows the conundrum of identity seeping in beyond the psyche and body of the colonized subjects to infiltrate the colonizer, triggering deep anxieties about the inability to distinguish identities for both sides. This breakdown of subjectivity in the colonial context is further linked to the metatextual level of the politics of cultural representation in colonial literary encounters. Here, I examine the predicament of subjectivity through the conundrum of representation on the formal level of the colonized writer in the empire.

I have already touched upon the symbolic import of the categorization and incorporation of "Into the Light," as an I-novel in the cultural field of the empire in chapter 3. In a similar vein, I would like to examine the significance of the way the text performs an internal breakdown of form on the level of representation, which defies such simple categorizations as an I-novel. It is not my goal to argue against a straw man representing the genre of the I-novel, which has already been deconstructed by others, as an effect of the discourse surrounding it more so than as a coherent genre in and of itself. However, in the context of imperial assimilation of colonized texts, the gesture of inclusion into the imperial literary canon (which itself was under formation through newly established institutions like the Akutagawa Prize) is deeply significant to the colonized writer. This was revealed in Kim's response to Satō Haruo's generic designation of Kim's "Into the Light" being an I-novel "with an entire people squeezed into it" (see chapter 3).

On the one hand, seeming to invite the colonized text to partake in the formation of the modern Japanese literary canon, Satō's commentary was in fact oxymoronic. This designation of the minor text as a quintessential Japanese modern literary genre is based on certain assumptions. By being so named, the text supposedly meets the metropolitan critic's expectations for the colonized text: on the one hand, by supplying an authentic account of the colonial subject and the colony as a whole, and on the other hand, by showing its harmonious assimilation into the larger empire. The gap between the differentiated colonized subject and the assimilated imperial subject of these two simultaneous yet contradictory demands must remain suspended in this imperial logic.

We can easily detect aspects of the story that indeed overlap with the personal experiences of the writer Kim Saryang, a colonized intellectual in Tokyo who also attended the imperial university. However, the story as we have examined it is not about a selfsame narrating I but about the breakdown of multiple I's through the infiltration of the foreign Other. This schizoid I, both narrated and narrating, is emblematic of the painful colonial affect experienced by colonial subjects in the face of contradictory assimilationist demands.

In the case of Kim's minor literary act, the infiltration of the foreign also occurs on the level of inscription itself. The narrative is mediated through the imperial language, refusing the myth of a direct, unmediated narrative experience that is said to define the metropolitan I-novel. The fact that the story was written in the foreign language of empire, as well as the unbridgeable gap between the language of inscription and the writer's "mother tongue," further problematizes the text's simple categorization.

In fact, for the colonized minor subject, the issue of a "mother tongue" is itself complicated, already tainted by the foreign. Educated in the colonial education system both in the colonial periphery as well as in the metropolitan center, the linguistic conundrum of minor writers is no longer that of the binary between the "mother tongue" and "foreign imperial écriture," but the impossibility of keeping the two safely apart.

Kim Saryang was keenly aware of his "contamination" by his long habitation in the metropole. In a letter to another bilingual Korean writer, Ch'oe Chŏng-hŭi, Kim reveals his anxiety toward the Korean language as well when he asks her to scrutinize his Korean-language writing for any mistakes. This letter is noteworthy in that it shows Kim's relationship to his "mother tongue," Korean, mirrored similar anxieties he felt with the Japanese language.

Kim's uneasy narrative of the fragmented I contaminated by coloniality, mediated through the écriture of empire, raises questions regarding the myth of an unmediated, authentic writing experience in general. It also points to the blindness of metropolitan critical assessments regarding the success of assimilation of the minor literary text into the canonical genre of modern Japanese literature and, in turn, the abject position of minor literature in relation to metropolitan literature.

Indeterminate End

The conundrum of representation on the formal level is particularly evident in the story's ending, which refuses a neat closure. After a suspenseful development of the psychic drama of the characters, it suddenly comes to an end before a satisfactory denouement.

The trope of recognition/mis-recognition of performative identities repeats unabated until the end. In the final scene, Haruo is still unable to join the other children, so Minami/Nam takes him out on an excursion into the metropolitan city-space. After shopping at the Matsuzakaya department store, the two head out to Ueno Park. In this scene among the crowds, the two have effectively moved out of the ghettos into the symbolic center of the metropolitan city, bustling with people and the signs of imperial capitalist opulence. However, their wanderings in the city streets do not signify full participation or assimilation into this imperial space. Their negotiation of the new space is still full of self-consciousness, and their gazes are not being returned by the crowds who do not recognize them. They are in effect still "passing" in the crowds as their economic and ethnic alterity remains invisible to those around them.

In a private conversation, Minami/Nam offers to supervise Haruo's solitary hobby of dancing in the dark. In a society that refuses to recognize and accept him as he is, Haruo habitually severs himself from this society and dances with lights off, alone and away from the judgmental gaze of others. In a literal bodily performance of multiple identities, he plays a ventriloquist, creating a make-believe cast of characters to keep him company. For someone who has spent his life self-consciously performing identities for the unwelcoming gaze of an outside world, it is significant that he has chosen to create a world of his own where he can express him/self freely in private. He has been leading multiple lives, with his private and public selves split, where, as we have seen, he must deny not only himself but the intimate links to his own mother in public.

In the last scene, Minami/Nam promises Haruo that he will dance with Haruo, assuring him that he is no longer alone. The two are bonded through their mutual recognition and shared pain. They have made a pact to recognize one another's alterity, exemplified when Haruo turns around and says, "I know your name. It's Mr. Nam!" (29). The crowd may not yet be ready to accept them as they are, but through their recognition of one another (which mirrors the personal epistolary encounter between Kim and Long, away from the limelight of the literary field), they are free, at least in private, of the burden of their identities.

Kim Saryang wrote "Into the Light" at a time when writings by colonized writers were being subsumed, while also being marked as different, vis-à-vis the canon of imperial literature, which was itself coming into formation through the contradictory logic of inclusion and exclusion of its colonized Others. The story's fragmentations on multiple levels, textual and metatextual, gesture toward the deep pain and anxiety about its own uncertain location in the cultural politics of representation in the empire. As seen in Kim's epistolary encounter with Long, the text embodies the shared dilemmas and the deep ambivalence of the bilingual writing act for colonized writers. The crisis of representation, which has been designated an emblematic predicament of modern times, is here exposed in its complexity through the prism of the colonized, in the ambivalent act of self-representation in the language of empire for consumption by the imperial audience. The text's multiple fragmentations and its inability to close itself into a unified self-contained entity are suggestive of a deeply melancholic conundrum marked by the wounds of an unspoken loss, and though perhaps not satisfactory to writer and reader, "Into the Light" leaves itself open toward another future.[13]

FIVE

COLONIAL ABJECT

By winter 1940, the war was in full swing after the Manchurian Incident of 1931, culminating in Japan's invasion of China by 1937. It was a time of "total war" which was infiltrating all aspects of life in Japan and its colonies. For the battlefront, men were being mobilized as soldiers, and women as the "comfort brigade"; and on the home front, women were called on to make sacrifices in their daily consumption habits and to play the role of "imperial mothers" by sending their sons off to serve in the "holy war."[1] Cultural figures, particularly authors, in Japan as well as its colonies, were mobilized as propaganda tools for the war effort.[2]

Along with Japan's crackdown on the Korean language, the field of Korean-language writing was rapidly shrinking. This began with the shutdown of major newspapers in the colony, *Tonga ilbo* and *Chosŏn ilbo*, and by the infiltration of a Japanese-language page in the remaining *Maeil sinbo* in 1939. Quickly afterward came the closing down of the literary journal *Munjang* (Composition), and the reconstruction of *Inmun p'yŏngnon* (Humanities criticism) as *Kokumin bungaku* (Imperial literature).[3] At first *Kokumin bungaku* intended to publish alternate issues between Japanese and Korean; but the magazine quickly published exclusively in Japanese.[4]

Furthermore, it was in such a milieu that special editions on Korean literature, written in Japanese, were cropping up all over major journals and newspapers in the metropole, of which *Bungei* (July

FIG. 5.1 *Modern Japan—Colonial Korea Special Issue*

1940), *Chōkan asahi* (May 1941), and two special Korea issues of *Modan Nippon* (November 1939 and February 1940) are a few prominent examples. Tremendous efforts arose to translate Korean-language literary texts into Japanese, many of which were compiled into collections and anthologies.[5] This *special* recognition and the production of a new colonial culture further required the active participation of bilingual writers and translators from the colony.

The nomination of Kim Saryang for the Akutagawa Prize as well as the establishment of the Korean literary and art prizes, and so forth, were all part and parcel of the Korea Boom (as discussed in previous chapters) that must be

FIG. 5.2 Yi Kwangsu wins the first Korean Arts Award. Reprinted with permission from Waseda University Archives.

contextualized within the broader tendency toward the incorporation of the colonies into the Japanese empire, and the subsumption of colonial literatures and cultures into the makings of a new Japanese imperial literature.

Furthermore, such recognitions of the colonial writer and colonial literature in the metropolitan literary field at this time, far from celebrating the value or talent of authors as individual artists, interpellated and relegated them to new secondary roles as ethnic translators or native informants. Their newly assigned task was to write exotic self-ethnographies in translation for the consuming

朝鮮國民文學集

朝鮮文人協會編

FIG. 5.3 *Colonial Korean Imperial Literature Anthology*. Reprinted with permission from Waseda University Archives.

passions of the metropolitan audience.[6] The broader significance of the rise of numerous "colonial collections" throughout the empire will be addressed in chapter 6. This chapter builds on the discussions from chapters 3 and 4 to consider other implications of the paradox of imperial recognition for the colonized cultural producer.

In particular, I consider the *abject* position of bilingual colonized writers relegated to translators and self-ethnographers, in transit between two literary fields—in the metropole (Bundan), and in the colony (Mundan). The notion of the abject has been defined by Julia Kristeva as a "threat . . . that disturbs identity, system, order [which] does not respect borders, positions, rules . . . the in-between, the ambiguous, the composite."[7] This concept may be useful for us to understand the liminal position of bilingual colonized writers not only in relation to the metropolitan Japanese Bundan, but also to the cultural fields of the colony and the subsequently divided postcolonial context. In Kristeva's delineation, the abject is rooted in the unconscious and seeps into the psychological and bodily being.[8] It is an essential part of identity and language formation processes in which boundaries are necessary for meaning and order to occur. Through the demarcation of differences in these processes, order is created and maintained for the subject.[9]

Kristeva suggests that this psychic phenonemon can translate to the societal level, where the abject may refer to those who are socially liminal to a community's marked boundaries. The examples she gives include "the traitor, the liar, the criminal, the rapist, the killer."[10] The abject ultimately "persists as exclusion,"[11] as that which does not belong within imagined or real boundaries, hegemonically formed and maintained by the collective. The abject is "neither subject nor object"; it is neither completely subsumed in the Self nor does it remain external to it. The abject is not an Other that can be named and thus controlled. In the social context, the abject is the intolerable, that which must be "expelled," yet stubbornly persists to reveal the fractures within the Law, that is, any unquestioned authority that undergirds social formations. The Law futilely attempts to cast aside that which is deemed "the irregular, anomalous, or unnatural" through such means as rituals and sacrifices.[12] However, the abject is in its essence ambiguity[13] and refuses to be purified.[14]

Kim Saryang exposes his own self-awareness of the unstable ground he treads as a writer of two tongues, and he carefully negotiates between the variously contradictory demands of the Bundan and the Mundan in his critical essay "Chōsen bunka tsūshin" (Dispatches on Korean culture).[15] Here, Kim directly addresses this dilemma, his very own, which he shared with other writers from the colonies: that of the abject writing subject precariously tottering between multiple audiences in the colonial divide.[16]

The essay itself self-consciously performs the very act of translation (in the Japanese language) while self-reflexively referencing the colonial writer's own deep conundrum in the impasse between the paper language of empire and his m(other) tongue, which as we saw in chapter 3, was just as alien to him in the structural colonial divide. The essay was written in direct response to rigorous censorship policies on Korean-language cultural productions and the rising demand for colonized writers to write in Japanese. Kim carefully delineates the reasons why it is necessary to allow Koreans to continue to write in Korean even in this time of extreme assimilation. He claims that this would ultimately benefit not only the future of Korean culture but also Japanese and even world culture.

Here, Kim's primary motive appears to be to speak out against the complete disappearance of the Korean language by implicitly claiming the mutual debt all cultures have on one another, and the negative implications of the disappearance of a culture on world cultures at large. In this sensitive political milieu, Kim calls for a more complex understanding of the shifting linguistic terrain of the colony. In order to negotiate the seemingly insatiable demand in the metropole for consuming Korean cultural material, Kim proposes to establish an official translation bureau. The essay performs a subtle feat of negotiating multiple and opposing interests: imperial policymakers who demand Korean authors write exclusively in Japanese, and cultural nationalists from the colony who accuse all Japanese-language writers as traitors to the Korean language and absent nation; and abject bilingual writers (cum translators) like himself who were caught in between and at the forefront of these opposing sides. Kim writes:

> Essentially, Korean literature should be written by Korean writers in the Korean language, and this should of course be made the foremost priority. If we consider the situation from the practical perspectives of the writers themselves beyond mere theorizing, we see that when Korean writers write in Japanese, it involves so many obstacles and challenges that it may easily cause a breakdown of their motivation to write. Let's just be frank about the current situation in the Korean literary field. Writers are simply up to their ears trying to produce good works in their own language for Korean readers. Their foremost priority at the moment is to follow their passion to make Korean literature flourish, and they simply do not have the time to entertain the idea of writing in Japanese. These of course are highly subjective reasons, but perhaps precisely because of this, it isn't going to be effective to demand that they stop writing in Korean because it won't put food on the table, and [instead] to start writing in Japanese.[17]

In response to the call from the metropolitan literary field and to the strict imperial censorship of the colonial language, Kim claims that requiring Korean writers to write exclusively in Japanese is simply impractical. He further describes the situation of those who were able and did decide to write in Japanese:

I believe it is essential to understand the situation of those who are writing in or are considering writing in Japanese. Why? Because we must be aware that in order for writers to be writing in Japanese, in order for them to make the tremendous sacrifice, to give up their own language and their audience [in the colony] they should be addressing, there must be some keen psychic motive driving them. (29)

What are these motivations that trigger a writer to give up so much? Writes Kim:

The motivation to communicate Korean culture, lifestyles, and sentiments to a wider audience in Japan, or in another sense, the motivation to spread Korean culture to Japan, to Asia, and to the world at large, to have the honor of being a mediator between cultures, these may be some of their motives. And of course, this more than anything is being called for by these times. And this in fact is probably why the Japanese literary field is calling out to Korean writers right now. (29)

Writing in Japanese for colonial subjects, Kim contends, is in essence a sacrificial act. He points to the circumstances of empire that call for such sacrifices: hierarchies inherent in the colonial encounter that call on (or provide the motivation) for some writers who are able to make the sacrifice and play the role of a mediator, or translator, to take up the pen in Japanese. Characterized in this way, Kim does not seem to be idealizing the position of those writers called to be mediators or native informants in such circumstances. This assessment manifests most clearly in his references to the way in which the metropole critically misrecognized his own Japanese-language story "Pegasus" (Tenma, 1940), by conflating the author and all bilingual writers of the colony with the story's protagonist, thus failing to distinguish among individual colonized subjects.

However, Kim suggests that it is despite or perhaps precisely because of these misunderstandings commonly arising from the severe representational gaps extant in all realms—cultural, political, and economic—that *some* colonized writers need to continue their efforts to communicate in Japanese with the metropole. According to Kim's essay, the role of the colonial translator should be taken up by a few (self-)chosen writers with the linguistic capability and the desire to make this sacrifice. Kim stresses that such a burden should not be forced upon all writers in the colony equally. By offering up a few "sacrificial lambs" (himself included), Kim attempted to negotiate the political demand of the age (*jidai no yōkyū*) in order to salvage the Korean language from total imperial censorship while carving out a space for colonized writers to continue to engage the metropolitan center of discourse.

However, such attempts at direct engagement or dialogue with the metropole by the colony's cultural producers were always in danger of being reduced to mere representation of colonial exoticism or as an authentic account of a fixed colonial reality by native informants. Conversely, a similar demand by Japanese critics for an authentic account of a collective colonial reality—though for political purposes at odds with Korean colonial subjects—haunted the minor writer through the ghostly presence of the audiences of the colony that the writer could not but fail to address in his Japanese writings. Simply put, the Korean writer couldn't write for two audiences at the same time; and as he or she began to write in Japanese, it was clear which audience was left behind.[18] Caught between the various demands of competing gazes from the metropole and the colony, the colonized minor writer also finds himself under the ambivalent self-conscious scrutiny of his own critical gaze. For the writer situated at the front lines of the colonial divide, the split gaze of the audience refuses a one-to-one correspondence between the writing subject, the text, and the addressee. In the traffic between the gaze of an internalized native demand (from the colony) to represent the colonial reality of the plight of a colonized people and the call of the metropolitan audience for an exotically authentic version for imperial consumption (by the colonizer), a breakdown inevitably occurs. The desires of the writing subject consist in competing with, while attempting to answer, the contradictory demands of the various audiences he was simultaneously addressing—to different degrees of failure.

This impasse undergirding the question of audience—for whose gaze is he writing?—lies at the heart of the abject colonized writer's conundrum of representation. The colonized minor writer is pulled in various opposing directions: the contradictory demands from the metropole for colonial difference and exoticism of *Koreanness* versus the colony's demand for the representation of authentic colonial reality of *Koreanness* as a collective experience. These demands further the writer's anxieties about answering such calls and mix with his own personal desires to simply produce a good work of literature that will be valued and will resonate beyond his immediate surroundings.

The predicament of Kim and other colonial writers writing in Japanese may remind us of the old Hegelian opposition of whether and how the master's tools can indeed be used to break down the master's house. Some, as Kim suggests, may have desired to challenge the imperial status quo from within the system itself, similar to the goals of the Gramscian organic intellectual.[19]

However, in the colonial context, the heroic representative or spokesperson for a people is reduced to the liminal and abject figure of the anthropological native informant qua traitorous translator between cultures,[20] whose writings become instrumental to serve mutually opposing ideological purposes. Whatever the true intentions of the colonized minor writer may have been, the very act of representing the plight of the colonized for metropolitan audiences made his writings vulnerable to the possibility of being co-opted and utilized by the colonizers as a source of exotic self-ethnographic account for purposes of further control, differentiation, and discrimination. Perhaps Kim Saryang more than many of his contemporaries may have been keenly aware of the abject role he himself was playing in this context as reflected in his writings.

(Self-)Reflexive Parody

The iconic modern boy (*mobo*),[21] like his counterpart modern girl (*moga*), was a ubiquitous figure on the streets of colonial modern cities throughout East Asia and elsewhere during this era.[22] In Kim Saryang's short story "Pegasus" (Tenma),[23] which he referenced in the above essay on the predicament of the colonial translator, the colonial modern boy (*mo-yobo*) appears as a figure of self-parody.[24] The story shows the colonial writer Genryū/Hyŏllyong's desperately slapstick and ultimately thwarted desire to enter the Japanese Bundan.[25] It opens with him roaming around lost in the labyrinth of the colonial city Keijō (Kyŏngsŏng, K),[26] seeking an audience with metropolitan literary luminaries who are rumored to have stopped over briefly in the colony on their way to Manchuria and Northern China.

"Pegasus" reflects the situation of the contemporary colonial cultural field as it was being subsumed into the metropolitan counterpart. For example, major writers of the Japanese literary establishment were being sent off to the war front, including Manchuria. Soon writers of the colonies would be called to follow suit. Kim Saryang himself recalls meeting and entertaining Japanese writers who stopped at P'yŏngyang (Heijō, J), his hometown, on their way to Manchuria.[27] It was published in Japanese in the major Japanese journal *Bungei shunjū* in 1940, just a few months after Kim Saryang's nomination for the Akutagawa Prize catapulted him into the limelight of the Japanese literary world; and the story's production and circulation in Japan were contemporaneous with Kim's own voyage from the colony into the metropolitan literary field. The story itself depicts a colonial writer's abject location in limbo between the Japanese and Korean literary fields. These multiple border crossings textually and metatextually defy easy characterization. Like Kim's other writings, the gazes of the writing subject, the subjects and objects represented within the text, and those multiple readerships simultaneously addressed crisscross and overlap in complex and indeterminate ways.

Linda Hutcheon's characterization of modern parody as a "form of repetition with ironic critical distance,"[28] that is, repetition that includes difference, usefully expands our understanding of parody beyond the realm of mere ridicule and satire. According to Hutcheon, parody is a genre or an anti-genre that continuously transforms itself; as such, "parody changes with the culture" (xi). Furthermore, parody's "double-directed irony seems to have been substituted for the traditional mockery or ridicule of the 'target text'" (31–32). Parody is complex in its ideological ambivalence, at once ridiculing and paying homage to the target text. Hutcheon writes, "Like irony, parody is a form of indirect as well as a double-voiced discourse, but it is not parasitic in any way" (xiv). Although Hutcheon admits that parody can change substantially "transcontextually," she nonetheless insists on the formal and textual level of parodic play, which she attempts to delineate, while acknowledging the difficulty of a clear distinction, from satire's targeting of "social reality."

Building on these insights, this chapter considers the ways parody might translate in new ways in the colonial modern encounter. In "Pegasus," we see parody's double-directed and double-voiced nature further rerouted simultaneously toward the self and Other, through a complex traffic of self-conscious and self-reflexive gazes. Taking account of the "social reality" of the uneven colonial encounter, I expand Hutcheon's definition to read "Pegasus" as a self-reflexive parody of actual historical figures of the author Kim Saryang's own social context.

Colonial Modern Boy (*Mo-Yobo*)

"Pegasus" is at once comic and tragic. It embodies the entangled relationship of the author to the protagonist and main object of his parody, the colonial bilingual writer Genryū/Hyŏllyong. The subject and object of parody here reflect the lives and experiences of actual literary figures of the period,[29] including the author Kim Saryang himself, linking the textual and metatextual conundrum of the colonial translator. The character of Genryū/Hyŏllyong is simultaneously the ridiculed object of parody as well as sympathetic identification. The author's ambivalent ties to the object of his representation foreclose the reading of the main character as simply an external Other. Rather than being seen as an object of unmediated contempt accused as a traitor to the nation,[30] the puzzling protagonist serves as the nexus of textual and metatextual intercourse that highlight the abject predicament of the bilingual colonized writer as occupying both the subject and object positions as colonial literature was undergoing a self-ethnographic turn.[31]

The story opens with Genryū/Hyŏllyong lost and disoriented in the labyrinth of the streets of Honmachi, a segregated Japanese section of the colonial city: "the most prosperous Japanese street in Keijō,"[32] "stretching out from East to West."[33] Honmachi is a fashionable district within the colonial city, marked by opulent signs of the colonizer's prosperity: Western-style buildings such as the Mitsukoshi department store, the Bank of Chōsen, and the Chōsen Hotel.[34] This area offers the ever-new spectacle of the ever-changing city-space of the colony, a place where Koreans went to loiter amid imported modern infrastructures, but only as a distant phantasmagoria, not a place where they resided or felt "at home."[35] On special occasions, some might get dressed up in the latest fashions, masquerading as a *modan kkôr* (moga) or a *modan ppoi* (mobo) to "mimic" the hybrid styles of modernity's eclecticism.

Honmachi appears in many stories of the colonial period, a metonymic Other place, a spectacle to be desired but not possessed. In fact, loitering in this area and window-shopping in particular became a spectator event, a phenomenon known as Honbura, in homage to the metropolitan pastime of Ginbura, or walking around the fashionable district of Ginza in Tokyo.[36] What was important was the performance of visuality, to see and to be seen, and such colonial *flânerie*, strolling in the Japanese section of the segregated city-space, became a dress-up show, a collective fantasy of the colonized.

However, today Genryū/Hyŏllyong is not in Honmachi for a leisurely afternoon stroll. He has a clear mission: to verify rumors that "Tanaka, the writer of the Japanese Bundan, has stopped over in Keijō on the way to Manchuria and is staying at the Chōsen Hotel."[37]

Let's return to the description of the city:

> The main thoroughfare of Honmachi, from the Meiji Bakery all the way to the other end, is always alive with people, even in the early morning hours. The Japanese [Naichijin] are hurrying along, clacking their wooden clogs [*geta*], and country bumpkins stare into the shop windows with mouths agape. Old women are bewildered by blinking dolls displayed in the shop windows, and the Naichi wives are out shopping. The servant boy races by on his bicycle, ringing his bell loudly. The laborer with an A-frame is squabbling over a mere ten *sen*. Genryū/ Hyŏllyong broke past the waves of people and hurried out of the street, coming to a halt in the

large square in front of the Bank of Chōsen. Electric trams were gliding back and forth nonstop, and cars raced by in a mass, toward the rotaries. Genryū/Hyŏllyong rushed awkwardly across the open square and slid into the quiet Hasegawa Street across the way. After a while, there suddenly appeared to the right side an old style wall and a large gate. When you entered through that gate, there was a grand Western-style building that had been some country's embassy from the turn of the century. Genryū/Hyŏllyong arrived there in a confused state, and with his heart beating hard, he pushed through the revolving door as if he were being chased. "Get me through to Tanaka-kun!"[38]

The scene is punctuated by the loud sounds and sights of colonial modernity. Genryū/Hyŏllyong's quick glance panning across the scene establishes for the reader the stark contrast between the Koreans and the Japanese here. For example, the country bumpkin standing with his mouth open in astonishment, the poor porter with an A-frame quibbling over small change, and the errand boy rushing past are all Korean. They seem displaced and untimely in their environment. In contrast, the Japanese are shown to be the new masters of the Korean city, like the fashionable Japanese woman clicking along in her Japanese *geta*, going about her business. The Manichean divide in the colonial modern city is merely enumerated as a naturalized part of the everyday landscape, setting the stage for the antics of our antihero.

Genryū/Hyŏllyong, despite his contemptuous regard toward the country-bumpkin Koreans he passes on the streets and the loud pretentions associated with the metropole (referring to them in familiar terms Tanaka-*kun*), is also quickly exposed to be beyond his element here. After running around lost in the mazes of the city streets, he scrambles out of breath and flounders like a fish out of water, in his effort to reach the magnificent Chōsen Hotel.[39]

He attempts to make a grand entrance, barking loudly for the famous Japanese writer. But the hotel clerk manning the front desk merely offers him a bored stare. The narrative explains: "The fact was, when anyone of name from the Japanese literary establishment arrived, there were pathetic waves of those from the Korean literary circles who came declaring themselves as *the* representative Korean writer, so the boys were rather bored of it."[40] But our antihero Genryū/Hyŏllyong will not be so easily discouraged.

He knew that the lobby was quite useful for waiting for people to put on airs of "look at how sophisticated I am." He swaggered his shoulders and walked with deliberate strides toward the lobby. Now that he thought about it, there appeared without fail, a hotel, a lobby, a dance hall, or a salon with some high-class madam or a negro chauffeur in every one of his stories.[41]

The scene humorously pokes fun at the pretentions of writers like Genryū/ Hyŏllyong chasing after those of the Japanese literary establishment, as well as the latest literary trend imported from elsewhere, in his superficial references to modernist tropes and accoutrements, fetishizing the images of the West mediated through the Japanese literary field. Beneath this comic exterior, however, is the sad reality of asymmetric power dynamics between the metropole as the site of knowledge production and the colony. In the imperial logic of global capital, the culture of the former—the metropole—is symbolically constructed as the norm or legitimate, that which the latter—the colonized—as "lack" must try to perform or mimic.

Genryū/Hyŏllyong's colonial belatedness or lack in relation to the metropolitan standard he so desperately desires is evident in his rushed and agitated meanderings in the city, chasing after Tanaka-kun. His dislocation and untimeliness—literally running after metropolitan cultural "names"—are evident in this scene in which he seems to be a stranger even in the colony, juxtaposed against the visitors from Japan, who are treated like royalty on their short stopover at the colony. The privileged position of the Japanese guests cannot be understood simply by the hospitality extended by their Korean hosts, but is a symptom of the colonial logic of metropolitan cultural legitimacy accompanied by the colonizers' arrogance in their right to occupy the territory.

After a long nap, Genryū/Hyŏllyong decides to try his luck elsewhere and sets out for the bars and cafés of the Korean district, convinced that the Japanese visitors would of course want the taste of "authentic Koreanness" on their visit to Korea. They are on a whirlwind tour of the colony on their way to Manchuria for an exotic "continental experience" that cannot be obtained on the mainland (Naichi).[42] Once Genryū/Hyŏllyong finally locates them, the writers from Japan pretend to include him in their circle, but the gesture is forced and awkward. He tries to ingratiate himself to them by alluding to the colonial assimilationist ideology of *Naisen ittai* through the metaphor of marriage between masculine Japan and feminine Korea in which Korea will "rise to the level" of Japan through the union. The Japanese writers seem to agree heartily and appear to be momentarily moved by the earnestness of Genryū/ Hyŏllyong whom they consider a "representative" Korean writer. However, as Genryū/Hyŏllyong's recollections of his ridiculous and failed attempts at an intercolonial romance with a Japanese woman reveal, this "marriage" of the colony to the metropole may be sustained metaphorically but is not without conflict in reality. The arrogance of the colonizer is seen in the metropolitan writers' assumption that they will "know" Korea through such a speedy tour in order to write about "the Korean situation" for consumption by their awaiting audience in Japan, eager for news of the colonial possession.

We find Genryū/Hyŏllyong chasing after an object of desire that by imperial logic must remain spatially and temporally just beyond his reach. Confused in the heady atmosphere of the ever-new and ever-changing colonial modern city, such a rejection is devastating. This colonized modern boy, mo-yobo, is a melancholy shadow of the iconic modern flaneur, leisurely strolling the boulevards of Paris, what was considered "the capital of Europe." In this story, the alienation in the colonial city in the face of Western commodities imported through Tokyo is marked by the fetish of metropolitan culture as the object of unrequited desire. The alienation of the colonial subject is simultaneously mirrored in the self represented as Other, which is fetishized and relegated to a "relic" of colonial belatedness. This impasse exacerbates the experience of the colonial modern boy (mo-yobo) as seen in Genryū/Hyŏllyong's increasingly deteriorating mental state.[43]

Genryū/Hyŏllyong is painfully aware of the unbridgeable gap between his belated or abjected self within the logic of metropolitan progress and standards. However, he is much too preoccupied with the chase to understand the structural imbalance upon which colonialism and global capital are predicated and sustained, thus making his floundering attempts at catching up ridiculous and ultimately futile. Although he does recognize that the reason for his alienation is precisely because of his identity as a colonized Korean, he is blinded by the desperate desire to dis-identify himself as this object of discrimination. The critique of the asymmetric relationship to which the protagonist himself is utterly blind occurs through the parody mode of storytelling.

The segregation that marks the colonial cityscape mirrors the position of Genryū/Hyŏllyong and that of colonized writers in general in relation to the literary establishment. Similar to the city-space, which seems to promise access yet only partially, colonized writers are lured by the promise of equality as members of the Japanese Bundan and the empire at large; but in actuality, full equality is constantly deferred. Genryū/Hyŏllyong's ultimate abjection is foreshadowed in his inability to make it past the threshold space of the lobby of the Chōsen Hotel.[44]

When taking account of the actual conditions of the intimate yet asymmetric relationship of the colonial encounter in the literary field, in which the colonized text is "necessarily politicized" at the level of critical consumption, the crossing of the line between fiction and reality in the story "Pegasus" is not without significance. Both in Japan and in Korea, at that time, although still true to an extent today, writers and critics occupied a small and closely knit coterie of intimacy. In this context, locales of seemingly casual encounters like cafés, once they became known as being frequented by the members of the Bundan, became spaces encoded with commonly shared values and power structures. Even personal relationships—seemingly casual or intimate, developed through networking in these closed and encoded spaces, as well as through introductory letters written by established writers on behalf of aspiring writers—hide their inherent power hierarchies and performative structures in the guise of civility.

The confounding of the line between fictional characters and the author, and between Kim Saryang and his own contemporaries in the literary field, draws attention to the intimacy between the personal and the political in the highly charged context of cultural unevenness. By removing the boundaries between the world of the text and the world of the actual literary field, the text makes a self-reflexive gesture regarding the conundrum of the colonized writer, whose writing act was exposed to appropriation by various (often contending) ideological interests. Further, the story "Pegasus" specifically draws out the intimate relations (albeit asymmetrical) between the two literary fields at this time. This link is sustained intra-textually as well.

Tanaka Hidemitsu (1913–1949), who is believed to be the real-life model for the character Tanaka the metropolitan writer in "Pegasus," apparently wrote his own version of the story later in which he foregrounds his own doppelganger as the protagonist. Characters that appear in "Pegasus" who are parodies of actual literary figures of the time make encore appearances in Tanaka's story, which again tells of the colonial literary encounter, this time from the perspective of the Japanese writer. In this context, the boundaries of the Bundan spilling out into various locales of the colonial city, though seemingly fluid, can become sites of extreme anxiety and ambivalence, particularly in the colonial context.

Colonial Modern Girl

The story of the conundrum of the colonial modern writer is predominantly told as the story of the modern boy, and in the case of colonial Korea, the intellectual elite male with the wherewithal to cross the border to the metropole and back. The modern girl, on the other hand, is rarely permitted such peregrinations. The poet No Chŏnmyŏng is a noteworthy exception. A colonial modern girl, she appears thinly disguised in "Pegasus" as the peripheral character Mun So-ok, and in an even more obvious manifestation in Tanaka's story as No Ch'ŏnsim.

Mun's character, like Genryū/Hyŏllyong, is based on an actual figure and embodies the abject conundrum of the colonized writer to represent "colonial reality," and similarly is at once an object of parody and sympathy in the story. It is said that Kim Saryang himself knew No personally; and because of her close ties to the Japanese Bundan, she is often included in lists of "pro-Japanese" writers in South Korea.[45]

Mun, like Genryū/Hyŏllyong, is portrayed as a dilettante imitating Western modernist tropes, readily identifying herself with French poets like Rimbaud and Baudelaire. However, her desire for translated Western literary modernism and thus Western modernity is further complicated in that they signify for her a means of escape from the male-dominance of past customs:[46]

> She could be seen as yet another tragic woman born of Korea. After she finished at the woman's school, shouting out passionately for the destruction of the old feudal customs, she broke away from this "marriage story" and went off to Tokyo as an exchange student. . . . Even if she tried to get married now, she couldn't find any young man who was not already married because of the early marriage custom of the time. Unfortunately, she couldn't do anything about the passions of youth and by and by she attracted men and fell into the path of immorality. She believed without doubt that she was a pioneer who was opening up the road to free love and revolting against antiquated institutions, and so she welcomed opportunities to draw men near. Genryū/Hyŏllyong was one of them.[47]

Although in this scene Mun is more the object of parody than sympathy, there is an element of truth in the production of desires that the discourse of the modern offered to colonial women. The problematic logic of such promises is exposed in new forms of subjugation under the rhetoric of modernity, but such contradictions were not always evident. Likewise, "pro-Japanese" writings by women writers supporting the war effort were sometimes opportunities for them to come out of their homes, to become politicized.[48] Thus, these two characters reveal their desires arising from their perceived lack that drives such choices.

Genryū/Hyŏllyong recognizes Mun as his counterpart, as a sympathetic listener, someone who would understand his disillusion with the state of Korea and his need to turn to Japan for something new and better: Genryū/

Hyŏllyong boasts of being invited to write for a Japanese journal: "I was just writing a manuscript to send to Tokyo. It's a work that the top journal 'D' has been pushing me about for the last three months. . . . I'm tired of writing in Korean. Korean is mere trash. That's right. It's a talisman for downfall. I want to make a comeback in the Japanese Bundan. All the men of letters in Tokyo are advising that as well."[49] Despite the lady poet's obvious appreciation of this moment of self-aggrandizement, the reader by this stage in the story knows all too well of Genryū/Hyŏllyong's liminal position vis-à-vis the Bundan. He is at best on the low rung of the ladder of the literary establishment and is pitifully unsuccessful in trying to burrow inside. When we recalibrate the focus of the story's critique, we may glimpse that behind Genryū/Hyŏllyong's abject position lies the emptiness of colonial ideology itself. On one hand, imperial slogans lured colonial writers to write in Japanese with promises of personal fame and political equality, yet on the other hand relegated the language and the culture of the colonized to a place of lack and inferiority. In the reality behind alluring imperial signage, colonized writers in the Bundan like Kim Saryang himself faced a glass ceiling, as second-class writers, banished to an abject place of translators and native informants in the margins of empire.

Roundtable: Reconstructing National Literature

The call from the metropolitan Bundan pressing colonial writers to write in Japanese was matched by a simultaneous and equally strong opposing pressure from within Korea to resist it.[50] Although most writers wrote in Japanese during this time, many were condemned by other Koreans for doing so and also were encouraged to break their pens and burrow into silence. In "Pegasus," Genryū/Hyŏllyong attempts to attend a meeting of the Korean Mundan; but because he has earned himself a terrible reputation for writing in Japanese, he is expelled from the gathering. This textual event also reflects many round-table discussions actually staged at the time of Kim Saryang's writing, and Kim himself also participated in them. One noteworthy event was in 1946 immediately after liberation, as part of an effort toward constructing a new national literature in the postcolony.

With Japan's loss, the colony was swiftly occupied by the Soviets in the North and the United States in the South, and the Mundan was divided into leftist and rightist factions, with debates becoming polemical.[51] In the discussion entitled "Writers' Self-reflection,"[52] the debate turned to the issue of writing in Japanese during the colonial period. In response to Yi T'aejun's accusation that Korean writers writing in Japanese were nothing less than "traitors to the people," and that writers should have kept silent rather than succumb to writing in Japanese, Kim responds that for him "it is more important what one writes. I disagree with the view that it is the role of the writer to hide away, sitting with one's arms crossed because the situation has become difficult or because one can no longer make a living with writing."[53] In the context, condemning all Japanese writings by Koreans is "extreme linguistic chauvinism." These same sentiments are inserted in the story "Pegasus" as well, through the voice of a Korean writer with more credibility than Genryū/Hyŏllyong.[54] It is clear that Genryū/Hyŏllyong is thwarted by both the Korean and the Japanese literary circles. The object of critique is no longer simply the colonizer but the multiple imbrications of power relationships and censorship at work in the colony.

As the story pans out with Genryū/Hyŏllyong desperately trying to ingratiate himself to the Japanese writers and their repeated evasions, it becomes clear how ridiculous it is for a Korean writer like him to expect to be fully accepted as an equal member of the Japanese Bundan. The story ends with Genryū/Hyŏllyong spending all night chasing after and being thwarted by the members of the Bundan, alone and literally "left out in the rain" in the meandering labyrinth of the streets of Keijō. In the final scene, Genryū/Hyŏllyong stops in his tracks when he hears frogs ribbiting in a pond, which he hears as the colonizer's racist interpellation of Koreans: "yobo, yobo." He yells out in denial, like a madman, "I'm not a *yobo*! I'm not a *yobo*.... I'm a Naichijin."[55] The story ends with the tragic-comedic scene of Genryū/Hyŏllyong trying to deny his identity as a colonized and to identify instead with the colonizer. However, his futile efforts to be accepted in the Japanese Bundan show the hopelessness of such desires. He has been lured by the empty promises of the metropole and—now caught in a place of abjection, neither here nor there— finds himself in a melancholy position of perpetually desiring that which is thwarting him.

One rarely finds heroes in Kim Saryang's stories. Genryū/Hyŏllyong is far from the heroic character that postliberation literary histories have demanded in re-membering the painful colonial past. Instead, the text's ambivalent place in the literary histories of both the metropole and the colony, during and after the colonial period, seems to emerge from the external form and context in which it was written as well as the difficult subject matter of its content. On the surface, the text written in Japanese at the very moment when such writings were demanded of colonial writers by the metropolitan literary field appears to be seamlessly aligned with imperialist motives. However, the self-consciousness of the text (and writer) that turns to this dilemma as the very subject matter through the writing act opens up a space within the text that may be read as a self-reflexive gesture toward revealing the exterior and interior contradictions under which the text itself was produced. The text, through multiple crossings of boundaries—between the writer, narrator, and protagonist; between the textual narrative and the metatextual external circumstances of its production and consumption; between fact and fiction; and between comedy and tragedy—performs a multilayered metadiscourse on the challenges of bilingual colonial writers and their texts, perhaps *in spite* of itself. "Pegasus" through self-reflexive parody exhibits the conundrum of the minor literary act: abjected between multiple gazes, negotiating between silence and utterance, hovering between the language of the colonized and that of the colonizer, stymied by the impossibility of writing and the impossibility of not writing.

SIX

PERFORMING COLONIAL KITSCH

When Kim Saryang found himself suddenly propelled into the lime-light of the metropolitan literary field (Bundan) as a finalist for the Akutagawa Prize in 1940 (see chapter 3), he found himself joining the company of other bilingual colonial writers who had already "arrived" before him. Chang Hyŏkchu was Kim's senior (*senpai*, J; *sŏnbae*, K), who had himself debuted into the Bundan back in 1932 with his own "second prize" Japanese-language short story, "Gakidō," in the leftist journal *Kaizō*. Despite their parallel predicaments during this time, Kim and Chang in later postcolonial literary assessments are often placed in polar opposition to one another. Each of the divided postcolonial Korean literary fields, the zainichi ethnic minority community in Japan, and North and South Koreas, has separately claimed Kim as its own (some immediately and others eventually after some delay), while Chang is excised or marginalized in them. The forgetting of Chang from the divided postcolonial Korean literary histories stands in stark contrast to the actual prominence he had achieved during the late-colonial era. In fact, of all the bilingual writers from the colonies, Chang truly was the poster child, better known than any other.

Writers from other colonies like Taiwan and Manchuria were ambivalently watching Chang's imperial recognition with both admiration and concern. Lü Heruo (呂赫若, 1914–1947), an important writer from Taiwan was inspired by Chang's success and famously took the character 赫 (pronounced, hyǒk, K, kaku, J, he, C) from Chang's name in his penname. When Yang Kui (1905–1985) from Taiwan debuted in the Bundan with his award-winning story "Newspaper Boy" an oft-cited reader response in the journal *Literary Review* (*Bungaku hyōron*) refers to Chang's success:

> After countless struggles, one year after a Korean, our Taiwanese writer finally enters the Japanese literary establishment. My heart was filled with joy when I saw my friend and rival Yang Kui's name in *Literary Review*. First let us celebrate this new development of Taiwanese literature. Of course, we Taiwanese writers are not satisfied just simply to be recognized as Japanese writers. As a new work, one cannot deny that "Newspaper Boy" is immature. The creative style is childish and certainly not up to the level of Chō Kakuchū 張赫宙 [a Korean writer]. But Chō's work does not deal with the historical reality of the colonies as authentically as Yang's. It is precisely in this realism that the value of "Newspaper Boy" lies. We must observe the island with proletariat eyes, dig deeper, and continue to achieve high-quality artistic works.[1]

A collection of writings from Taiwan and Korea originally written in Japanese and translated into Chinese by the Taiwanese writer Hu Feng (1902–1985), prominently features two of Chang's works including the eponymous story "Mountain Spirits."[2] While there has been a welcome rise in recent years in scholarship considering the cultural encounters between the metropole and colony, further research remains to be done in examining the complex intra-colonial camaraderie and rivalry among writers from the colonies. The long absence of this much-needed intra-colonial cognitive mapping from the past is related to the contemporary call for a postcolonial inter-Asian dialogue (see chapter 10).

Furthermore, the glaring difference in the way the two writers, Kim and Chang, from colonial Korea would be re-membered in divided postcolonial national histories, is based on the degrees to which their writing is perceived to embody signs of collaboration (ch'inil and *Naisen ittai*) with the colonizer.[3]

While Kim's writings have been read as ambivalent and even subversive to the imperial order, Chang's are seen as having traitorously and unequivocally collaborated with Japan. This assessment is based on Chang's writings such as *Iwamoto Shiganhei* (Volunteer soldier Iwamoto) which urged Korean youths to fight for the imperial military and *Kaikon* (Reclamation) about the migration of Koreans into Manchuria as the front line of Japan's imperial expansions. This

FIG. 6.1 Staging the Japanese-language play *Shunkōden*, J; *Ch'unhyangjŏn*, K. Reprinted with permission from the Tsubouchi Shōyō Memorial Museum.

judgment was finally clinched with Chang's later decision to remain in Japan, marry a Japanese woman, and naturalize as a Japanese national. Kim Saryang's writings are seen to be much more nuanced and subversive, despite attempts to co-opt him into the Japanese literary field (see chapter 3). Joining recent scholarship that has been complicating such neat readings of binary resistance (Kim Saryang) versus collaboration (Chang Hyŏkchu), this chapter examines Chang's own precarious place between the literary fields across the colonial divide by considering his role as a translator and native informant of colonial culture for metropolitan audiences.

Part and parcel of the Japanese metropolitan consumer trend of the Korea Boom, which embodied an imperialistic fascination with colonial culture as exotica, the highly anticipated Japanese-language theatrical adaptation of Korean folktale *Ch'unhyang chon* (*Shunkōden*, J, The tale of Ch'unhyang) opened to rave reviews in major cities throughout Japan.[4]

The story is about a handsome young aristocrat who is smitten at first sight by a beautiful girl of questionable origin (her mother is a *kisaeng*, a hereditary low-status female entertainer, and her father is an aristocrat). The two exchange promises of eternal love and conjugal bond, and the ensuing love affair is passionate but all too brief. The lovers are cruelly separated by familial and societal opposition, and their love is tested through heart-wrenching trials,

春 香 傳

張 赫 宙 著

FIG. 6.2 Cover of *Ch'unhyangjŏn* by Chang Hyŏkchu. Cover art by
Murayama Tomoyoshi. Reprinted with permission from Waseda University
Archives.

which Ch'unhyang overcomes through steadfast adherence to her "chastity,"
or loyalty to her husband, before a happy ending of cathartic revenge and a
dramatic reunion.[5]

The popularity of the play ignited an encore run later the same year
throughout colonial Korea, and the significance of the transcolonial traveling
performance became the object of heated discussions throughout the empire.
The play was commissioned by Murayama Tomoyoshi (1901–1977), the Japa-

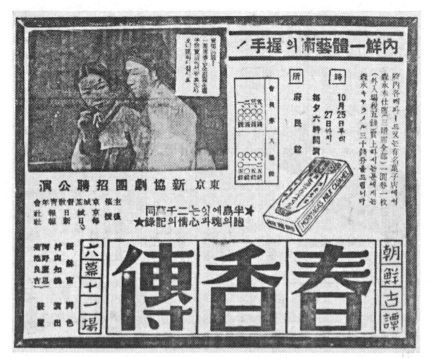

FIG. 6.3 Newspaper advertisement of the play as "the handshake of the art of *Naisen ittai*" (*Naesŏn ilch'e yesul ŭi aksu*).

nese modernist playwright and artist, and was staged by his Shinkyō Theater Troupe. The script was penned in Japanese by Chang at a time when Japanese was the official language in the colony and Korean-language and cultural productions were being subjected to increasing censorship.

This chapter considers a long-forgotten moment of colonial cultural collaboration between Korea and Japan when their literary histories converged in a much-publicized spectacle performance in the Japanese-language Kabuki rendition of a *p'ansori* tale that was, and still is, considered the epitome of Korean "tradition."[6] By paying attention to tensions between the reproduction and consumption of the tale as trendy commodity of "colonial kitsch" in imperial Japan, and as timeless art of "national tradition" in colonial Korea, and by focusing also on the conflicting desires of cultural producers between Korea and Japan, I suggest that the event may be read against the grain of its commissioned purpose—not as the embodiment of harmonious assimilation of Korea into Japan, as touted by pundits and in advertisements and reviews at the time,[7] but rather as performing the anxieties and breakdown of imperial ideologies.

Colonial kitsch refers to the devaluation and exoticization of the colony's culture circulated as mass-produced commodities to fulfill imperial consuming desires. Renato Rosaldo has elsewhere likened such imperial nostalgia to a murderer mourning the death of his victim.[8] The imperial desire for colonial kitsch may appear as innocently genuine appreciation for colonial culture, but in fact veils collusion with its domination and destruction. Colonial objects that were circulated during the passing trend of the Korea Boom appeared to conflate far-flung fields: tourism, folk culture, food, fashion, architecture, literature, and art. Each object, whether from highbrow or lowbrow culture, was significant only as a commodity symbolizing *Koreanness*, and as such was, for its Japanese consumer, arbitrary and exchangeable among a potentially infinite chain of consumable signifiers.

What I am interested in exploring is the particular significance of the contest over colonial Korean literature, notably its demotion from national canonicity to colonial kitsch in the encounter between Japan and Korea. Conflicting nostalgic desires between the colonizers and the colonized (for colonial kitsch and for national tradition respectively) may converge on the same object but for different purposes. I suggest that this moment of convergence may offer us productive insight into the failed collaboration and translation of colonial culture in the unequal context of empire as well as point out the significance of its forgotten legacy in the postcolonial era.

Retelling The Tale of Ch'unhyang (Ch'unhyangjŏn, K, Shunkōden, J, 春香傳)

In an era of imperial wars on a global scale and worldwide economic instability, a general sense of unease was pervasive in Japan and, by extension, in its colony of Korea. This period was often characterized in the mass media as an era of "crisis" or "transition," and urgent debates sprouted up throughout the wartime expansionist empire on how best to respond to the onslaught of an epistemic shift of "world historical" import. The putative West was said to be in the throes of decline, and what once seemed to be universalist assumptions of the supremacy of the Western world order were being questioned in Asia, with Japan as a self-declared leader.[9] In such a context, Japan's imperialist expansion into Asia was justified by the rhetoric of a shared "Asian tradition" on the basis of which Asia was to unite against the imminent threat of Western imperialism. Japan assumed the privileged role of leader among "fellow Asians" it had colonized for what was considered the common plight of the East in the contest against the West. Overlooking the irony that Japan justified its leadership role in part based on the merits of having been the first non-Western country to have acquired modern trappings and technological acumen from the West, Japan nonetheless called for a spiritual unity of the East against the infiltrations of the materialist West. Such debates culminated in the famous "Overcoming Modernity" discourses of the early 1940s when the threat of the West began to take concrete form as an actual wartime enemy. The sense of urgency ushered in at this time may have been unprecedented, but the discourse of an East/ West binary, and the call for a "Return to Asian Traditions," harked back to a long history of Japan's ambivalent modern experience, self-consciously situated between the West and the Rest.[10]

Japan's unstable position between competing universals of East and West would further complicate the perspective of its colonial periphery of Korea.[11] The pursuit of "tradition" in colonial Korea at this time accompanied a nationalist sense of urgency, an attempt to preserve cultural assets that were increasingly under threat from both direct Japanese domination and the pervasive and ominous shadow of Western imperialism. By the mid-1930s, as Japan's assimilationist policies in Korea intensified, an increasingly constricted and claustrophobic political sphere resulted in the cultural realm taking on rising symbolic import as a metonym for the identity of the absent nation and its lack of political sovereignty.

A discourse of "Revival of Traditions" began to garner popularity in the colony, which called for the compilation and cataloguing of past cultural artifacts to be preserved for posterity in the face of pressures to assimilate into the image of the imperialist cultures of the West and Japan.[12] Such a nostalgic turn toward a lost or vanishing past, however, could not but be ambivalent in a culture relegated to colonial status in the modern era. The very logic of colonialism justified Korea's subjugation based on the assumed "stagnancy" and "pastness" of the colony's culture. Furthermore, the very desire for the construction of a national genealogy from the colony's imagined, hoary past was in fact of rather recent vintage, as it relied on modern structures of feeling of imperialist nationalism as well as on technologies learned from the colonizers themselves for excavating, cataloguing, and evaluating these relics according to new global standards set and promulgated from the imperial centers.

Likewise, the invention of tradition would be an ambivalent gesture in Korea, a colony of Japan, a fellow Asian state itself lurking in the shadows of Western imperialism. This desire to construct and preserve a national tradition embodied the colony's need to affirm its coevalness with global standards of value and to ameliorate its sense of lack in the modern imperialist world order that was fully abiding by the logic of the nation-state. However, highlighting the uniqueness of colonial culture under the threat of imperial assimilation would ironically bring these very "traditions" under the desiring attention of the imperial gaze. In the metropole, the same colonial traditions doubled as objects of imperialist nostalgia, and that nostalgia simultaneously subsumed their regional particularities into a so-called universal Asian tradition. In turn, this subsumption devalued these Korean traditions as exotic objects of colonial kitsch, while highlighting their particular commodification of "local color" and denying coevalness by casting the colonized culture to the realm of a quaint and distant temporality.

Between Colonial and Imperial Nostalgia

The sentiment of nostalgia was fixated on the same object—relics from colonial Korea's past—and was shared by the Koreans and the Japanese. However, a perceived and real difference in spatial and temporal relationships to that same object of desire renders the nostalgia of the colonizer and that of the colonized untranslatable across the colonial divide—a divide wider than the sea that separates them. Nostalgia, defined as a sentimental longing for a place, especially a past home, akin to homesickness, or as a longing for a period of the past, assumes a familiarity with the lost object that is now distant in either space or time, from the standpoint of the subject's present perspective.[13]

In the case of Japan's imperialist nostalgia for colonial kitsch, this assumed familiarity to the "lost" object is in fact an illegitimate and imaginary relationship to Korea's bygone days based not on an actual memory but on the present colonizing desire to subsume even a past *prior* to colonization. Conversely, Korea's nostalgic desire for a national tradition is similarly a projection of present anxieties onto a past constructed as an ideal time and place uncontaminated by current imperial incursions.

In her seminal work *The Future of Nostalgia*, Svetlana Boym's reminder that "while the longing is universal, nostalgia can be divisive" seems pertinent, particularly when contemplating contending nostalgia arising from the unevenness of colonial encounters and the contested significance accorded to the same object across the colonial divide.[14] In this chapter, I would like to pay attention to the significance of such divisiveness, and in particular, to the *untranslatability* of these parallel nostalgic desires in the modern colonial encounter between Korea and Japan in the era of late colonialism. I shall also look at the dialectics of forgetting and remembering the encounter itself in the postcolonial era.[15]

Ch'unhyang as National Tradition

It is widely claimed that *Ch'unhyang* is Korea's most popular and most widely recognized story. How did the oral narrative *Ch'unhyang* rise to national prominence? Why was there so much fascination over this story about Ch'unhyang? In both Koreas (North and South), *Ch'unhyang*'s place in the literary canon is undisputed. For years many have asked how the simple love story has charmed so many over time and what qualities might be the story's most endearing.

Various reasons have been suggested to explain why this tale is an ideal text to be passed on as *the* representative "tradition" of Korea.[16] It is often deemed the single most "representative" text of classical Korean literature, with numerous extant versions, either in vernacular Korean or in literary Chinese (the lingua franca of the educated), passed down from the premodern period.[17] From the late nineteenth to the early twentieth centuries, with the emergence of the modern era in Korea, the tradition of *Ch'unhyang* experienced a renaissance. Even the strict colonial censorship of that time did not seem to affect the popularity of *Ch'unhyang*. In fact, in this dynamic period of colonial modernity, *Ch'unhyang* emerged anew in various novel manifestations. New forms of mass entertainment and the arts—such as theater and "motion pictures" (*hwaltong sajin*)—appropriated *Ch'unhyang* as a popular subject for experimental adaptation. The significance accorded *Ch'unhyang* in the colonial modern era is evident as it became the subject of Korea's first talkie.[18] Thus reinvented through a ritual of repetition as the most popular subject matter for these newly emerging mass cultural forms, *Ch'unhyang* found its place as the premier modern tradition of Korea undisputed by the 1930s.[19]

Conventionally, the concept of "tradition" has been understood in two overlapping yet opposing ways: that which precedes the modern, as a changeless, timeless relic of the past, and as a continuously transmitted cultural trace—spanning past, present, and future.[20] Reevaluating such assumptions, many scholars have pointed to the formation and legacy of tradition as involving a selective process indicative more of present desires than signifying some unaltered and continuous transmission from the past to the present.[21] Here, I would like to not only keep in mind the ideological effects of such inventions as false consciousness or contrivance,[22] but also remember the imaginative desires at odds in the struggle to reproduce traditions in the colonial modern context.[23] Rather than dismiss the fixation on an invented tradition simply as the product of shortsighted, colonized natives blinded by an ideological trap that might seem obvious to the more perceptive (presumably contemporary critics), I would like to remain mindful of the historicity of such an ambivalent and melancholy nostalgic turn in the colony toward a perceived and actual loss of its culture, and to a desire to construct symbols of a national tradition as a fetishistic placeholder for the absent nation.

Ch'unhyangjŏn/Shunkōden as Colonial Kitsch

This fascination for *Ch'unhyang* in colonial Korea was part and parcel of the contemporaneous discourse on "Revival of Traditions." Such nostalgic attempts by Korean cultural nationalists to define and invent their traditions, seen to be under threat from modern imperial incursions, were not without internal conflicts. A heated quarrel ensued about the significance of the very meanings of tradition and modern, and on the implications of these definitions for the future of a colonized society.[24] But the same objects of the past were simultaneously being reproduced to serve a parallel yet competing desire of imperialist nostalgia in Japan. If the "Revival of Traditions" in Korea focused on the transformative role of such traditions in constructing an autonomous cultural sphere and imagining a different future for the colony's absent nation, the fad of the "Korea Boom" in the metropole was merely a passing trend for instant gratification of imperial desires in the here and now.[25] The colony as a whole was fetishized as colonial kitsch, as a reified and devalued object of quick contemplation and indiscriminate consumption, and its traditions were being appropriated and exoticized as objects of a popular consumer trend sweeping through the empire, in mass reproductions of everything from alluring destinations in the tourist industry, to kisaeng in the pleasure quarters, to translated books in the literary market.[26]

The demand for exotic "Korean objects" (*Chōsentekina mono*) seemed insatiable.[27] The inordinate attention paid to Korean objects as exotic colonial kitsch stands in complete opposition to the assimilation policies imposed throughout the colony to erase Korean difference.[28] Korean language journals and newspapers were being censored and banned on an unprecedented scale, and the usage of the Korean language itself was prohibited in schools and in other official realms. This was also the time when Koreans were called to give up their Korean names and take on Japanese-style names, and to serve the Japanese imperial agendas of war and expansion in a shifting world arena. What seem to be two contradictory trajectories—on one hand, highlighting and preserving objects of Korean traditions, while on the other hand attempting to repress its particularities—may be understood within the inherently dual logic of imperialism itself: the simultaneous need to differentiate colonized subjects (in order to justify colonial subjugation) and assimilate them based on the ideology of shared Asian traditions (in order to mobilize support for imperial expansion and war efforts against the imperial West).

Various colonial nationalists were attempting to reinvent and recuperate their national legacies and to construct an identification with such traditions, in a nostalgic turn toward a lost past, to prove the dynamic depth and living continuities in their culture and, in turn, their right to exist as a people into the future. Meanwhile, in the metropole, these very same cultural artifacts came to signify colonial difference, as objects of imperial nostalgia for colonial bricolage, "exotic" and "primordial" relics of an ancient past that needed to be excavated and preserved (with the help of modern archeology and discerning imperial eyes). The consumption of colonial kitsch objects of the colonized past occurred in visual Technicolor, through the vexing marriage of imperialism with cutting-edge technology, relying on visualism as an important tool of domination through colonial knowledge. Travel guides, films, postcards, journals, and advertising that exoticized the colonies for consuming passions in Japan proliferated.[29] These objects were also to be displayed in museums or in colonial expos and would become metonyms for Korea itself, as an exotic place to visit, objectified as a quaint anachronism, revived in ever-new forms of mass culture to satisfy imperial desires.

The "Korea Boom" expressed forked imperialist desires: to assimilate and to differentiate the colony. While imperial expansions may have been justified under the name of a common tradition of Asia, these same traditions were also being marketed for their difference, as kitsch objects of imperial desire for the exotic colony. The irony of such imperial discourses becomes obvious when we compare the logic behind the Korea Boom with the Japanese debates on Overcoming Modernity and on Return to Tradition. While all of these discourses embody the desire to return to the spirit of Asian traditions against the threat of the materialist West, they also reified Asia as a primordial past, following the logic of Western Orientalism while simultaneously essentializing the West as Other. The commodification and consumption of colonial kitsch in Japan mirrored the same materialist imperialism of the West that Japanese imperialism had claimed to repudiate. The ultimate irony of Japanese Orientalism is that it unwittingly reflected an objectifying gaze toward itself as it schizophrenically sought to identify with, yet distinguish itself from, its Asian neighbors vis-à-vis the West.[30]

FIGS. 6.4. AND 6.5 "A Day in the Life of a *Kisaeng*" from *Modern Japan—Colonial Korea Special Issue.*

生妓の

① まぶしい陽光
を欄窓にさしこんで
來たので、眼をさめのま
した。こんなに眠ればあ
れるやうだと床の中にい
どまる

③ 妓生は寢間の時計を自分で楽しみにす。
寢ざめの衣服を脱いで寝に、かゝります。

FIG. 6.6 Poster advertising the dance performance of Ch'oe Sŭnghŭi [Sai Shokki, J] in Tokyo.

Murayama Tomoyoshi and Chang Hyŏkchu

The performance of the Shinkyō Theater Troupe under the guidance of Murayama Tomoyoshi was staged first in Japan, in the metropolitan city centers of Tokyo, Kyoto, and Osaka. It was widely touted as a "harmonious exchange between two merging cultures" (*yūgō shita futatsu no bunka no kōryū*) in reviews, and advertisements, as well as through carefully staged promotional roundtable discussions.[31] *Ch'unhyang* became the locus of various converging debates in the metropole and in the colony as the first Korean play to be performed in the Japanese language by Japanese actors, with the historical import of the cultural exchange between Korea and Japan being pointed out by pundits on both sides.[32] For all appearances, it seemed to be a timely and poster-perfect symbol of the harmonious merging of Korea and Japan, particularly at a time when the colony was being called to play a more active role in the expanding Japanese empire. But on closer examination of the tensions embedded in its production and reception, we can read the performance rather as a strange hybrid that simultaneously embodies and rejects the logic of assimilation inherent in the violent colonial encounter.[33]

Chang Hyŏkchu/Chō Kakuchū's role as the translator caught in the midst of these contending debates offers us insight into his precarious position between the colony and the metropole, and reveals the pain of a colonized writer in the borderlines of empire. Like many intellectuals in various colonial contexts, Chang was educated in the colonial system, acquiring the requisite language of the colonizer, which was privileged over his own mother tongue.[34] Embracing aspirations as a writer, Chang, like so many of his peers, voyaged-in to the metropole that offered more opportunities to write and to publish than Korea.[35] What set Chang apart from his peers was his growing success in the Bundan, even winning the nomination for a prestigious literary prize sponsored by the prominent journal *Kaizō*. In fact, his meteoric rise in the Bundan was beyond anyone's expectations, especially since Chang was a second-class colonized writer who was still somewhat awkward at wielding the language of the colonizer.

After his initial success in Japan, Chang continued to write in both Japanese and Korean, but he found more success with his Japanese-language writings. During this time, he was often criticized in the Korean literary field as a "traitor" for his role in the Japanese Bundan, and eventually, he began to write exclusively in Japanese. In the postcolonial period, he chose to remain in Japan, adopted his Japanese wife's surname, and became Noguchi Minoru, a naturalized Japanese with a hybrid penname, Noguchi Kakuchū. It is worth noting that Chang's success began to decline in postcolonial Japan when he tried to write as a "Japanese" writer. His writing had once been in demand because of his ability to provide authentic "local color" as a colonized writer and because it was used to support the imperialist agenda of assimilation. There was no demand for a colonized writer passing as a Japanese after the empire's collapse.[36]

Chang's relationships to Korea and Japan were always of complex ambivalence rather than a simple alignment on one side or another as has often been portrayed, particularly in Korean discourses that dismiss him as a quintessential "pro-Japanese" or collaborationist writer. Chang was always peripheral, trying to find his place but never succeeding. Despite a prolific writing career and the prominent role he played in the early literary histories of modern Korea and Japan, and his wide recognition throughout the empire, he has been virtually forgotten in the postcolonial aftermath in all contexts.

In the colonial era, the colonized writer's conundrum lay in his need to authenticate and introduce colonial culture, to bring imperial attention to it at a moment when the colony was being assimilated and devalued. Likewise, Chang's privileged position between the colony and the metropole—which seemed to make him the ideal translator, able to move fluidly between two cultures—simultaneously tainted his "authenticity" as a Korean native informant. Further, his social awareness of the need to "represent" the endangered, disappearing culture of the colony conflicted with his personal ambition to cultivate a singular point of view as an individual artist and writer, beyond serving as a translator or native informant for imperial ethnographic desires.

Translating "Koreanness"

Regardless of Chang's personal dilemmas as an individual writer, the drama he penned soon took on a life of its own in the broader context of empire. Murayama Tomoyoshi, the leftist, avant-garde playwright who commissioned the play, was keenly aware of the historical import of staging a "Korean" performance for imperial consumption at this particular historical juncture. For Murayama, the desire to pioneer a performance of "something Korean" (*Chōsentekina mono*) seemed pressing, above all other concerns, and the inconvenient fact of his own lack of knowledge about Korean culture would not dampen his determination. In a newspaper article, he describes the backstory of the project's beginnings: "I had wanted to introduce Korean arts and culture to Japan for a long time. I asked Chang Hyŏkchu to write something with a 'Korean theme,' and he came up with *Ch'unhyang*. . . . Chang told me that his version was his own adaptation, which was different from the 'traditional' version of *Ch'unhyang*, and I wanted to retain this flavor, too."[37] Murayama's foremost concern was to pioneer the first Korean drama to be performed by a Japanese cast in Japan, though he was keenly aware of the "great influence" (*ōkina eikyō*) such a precedent would have on the exchange between the theatrical worlds (*engekiteki kōryū*) of Japan and Korea.[38] Elsewhere he writes, "This was the first time that Japanese players are putting on a Korean drama in Japan, so I absolutely wanted to make it a success."[39]

Overshadowed by Murayama's "historical" vision (which, ironically, seemed blind to the power dynamics inherent in the colonial setting of which he himself was a privileged participant), Chang, the original writer, was then relegated to a peripheral role and reduced to providing ethnic data of "Korean authenticity" as one among many (exchangeable) informants with whom Murayama surrounded himself during the production.

What is even more ironic is that Murayama, the one in charge of shaping the performance and introducing the colonial culture, readily admitted he did not "know" Korea. According to newspaper articles of the period, Murayama went to Korea for the first time and took a speedy tour for a taste of an "authentic" experience in preparation for the upcoming play. On this whirlwind tour, he famously inquired of his tour guides: "If I want to *know* Korea, where should I go? Please show me around."[40]

In order to quickly make up for his lack of knowledge about Korea, Murayama consulted Chang and many other colonized intellectuals,[41] and made significant adjustments to the script, even grafting entire sections from another version of *Ch'unhyang* by a different writer, and thus substantially altering the final script.[42] Contrary to Murayama's previous remark about wanting to retain the "flavor" of Chang's creation, he later writes, "The script was not just what Chang Hyŏkchu had written in the beginning, but I incorporated [playwright] Yu Ch'ijin's input and I myself added my own pen to it."[43] Yu Ch'ijin himself later recollects the conflicted feelings he had watching the performance at the Kŭkyŏnjwa Theater in Korea, which included an entire scene lifted from his own version.[44]

Under power dynamics inherent in the colonial setting, it seems Chang, in the end, had little control over the fate of the play. Murayama's concerns were about making an impact on the Japan-Korea historical exchange, not on the nuanced interpretation that an individual writer like Chang may have envisioned.

The speed with which Murayama was able to acquire sufficient colonial knowledge to realize his grand vision is remarkable. Here is Murayama's recollection of subsequent plans to produce a film version of *Ch'unhyang*. He mentions his first trip to Korea back in February 1938, in preparation for the Tokyo performance of *Ch'unhyang* to open in March. "February was my first time [in Korea] . . . and it was only for eight days, and I only went to Keijō. But now that there was talk about making the movie version of 'Ch'unhyang chŏn,' I thought, for that I needed to know more about Korea, so I took twenty days, and during my stay in Korea, I traveled and walked around as much as possible."[45] We may rightly wonder just how much of Korea this colonialist flâneur

FIGS. 6.7. AND 6.8 Photo album from Murayama Tomoyoshi's Seoul travels.

〜リアの旅

朝鮮での私　村山知義

私はカメラを持つてゆかないし、写真をうつすことも
できない。これは自分でも言明するところで、私の
特長とも言へ、カメラを切り離せないところであるの
に、どうしたことか撮せない。それゆえ、このアル
バムは、私のうつした「旅のアルバム」ではなくて、
素人のうつして呉れた私のアルバムである。このアル
バムは、一行と終始、三行行った。これらの写真がそ
の旅の死だつたか、基礎には分つてゐない、ただ
そのうち、1、2、3が朝鮮の旅のものであることは
確かだ。
私は異境の郷愁感の時、初めての写真に資いて
場所は異境の郷愁感を思ふ、それらの写真がその
旅路への通宵にかかまれて、たともうホッとしてゐ
る私である。うつしたのは朝鮮演戯式会社のカメラ。

＊＊は朝鮮の通信が私のために軍きまきつて送られると
2はその一瞬のうち、私のお客の人は歌の海思村を送るのである。
＊は私の背の高い人と事作家で演出家で演出家である。8は
大学の育作家の一瞬作である、私は特別に証言を死してゐる。
要するその一瞬の一。3は
要を次の旅路とに旅路し私はその頃朝鮮戯の新演劇
君は遠路で最切なりれと、そのころ朝鮮戯の新演劇
は遠路の前で、歌劇物切のときつけると思ふ、神
劇創組拠付の指圧道であつた。
4、5、6、7、は話題が時代に行つたとき、歌
劇の服を着てアーて、仁川交過に朝鮮戯劇
ふると今はどにでも起、基礎には道路への「作合」
佛を朝鮮旅に持つて行く友人、仁川交過から送路を
するしたのは川川川から送路朝鮮戯劇への「作合」
ラツシュを見せつに致る貴婦人。＼

FIG. 6.9 Actress Akaki Ranko cross-dressed as male hero Mongnyong. Reprinted with permission from the Tsubouchi Shōyō Memorial Museum.

got to "know" during his speedy tour. What we do know is that the result was the production of the grand spectacle of *Ch'unhyang*, which traveled around major cities in Japan, and after much pomp and circumstance, and anticipation in the mass media throughout the empire, the play crossed the sea to major cities throughout Korea.

Murayama imagined a daringly experimental play beyond generic and cultural boundaries and hitherto unprecedented across the colonial divide. He envisioned and realized a hybrid transcolonial *Ch'unhyang* that transgressed temporal, generic, gender, and cultural borders. Murayama's *Ch'unhyang* was pan-Asiatic: "Korean," "Japanese," and "Oriental." It was genre bending: Kabuki, p'ansori, and modern theater. And it was gender bending: the role of the hero Mongnyong was played by a cross-dressed actress, Akaki Ranko.

Was Murayama an avant-garde genius ahead of his time? Probably, but my immediate concern here is not to assess the value of Murayama's artistic contributions toward upending conventions in theater, literature, film, and visual culture. What I am interested in is closely examining the troubling logic underlying Murayama's apparently revolutionary artistic experiments when refracted through the lens of the uneven colonial encounter.

The performances in Japan (Tokyo, Osaka, Kyoto) received rave reviews and were widely praised for their total success,[46] and no time was lost in preparation for the play's travel to Korea. Months before the Korea shows, the mass media announced the coming attraction, building up anticipation through newspaper articles, previews, interviews, roundtables, musings, discussions, and grand advertisements. An article by Murayama in the May 31, 1938 issue of the *Keijō nippō*, entitled "*Shunkōden* yodan: Keijō demo jōen shitai" (Shoptalk on *Ch'unhyang*: I want to show it in Keijō too), is prefaced by the announcement of his arrival in Keijō (Kyŏngsŏng, K) via Akatsuki (Dawn)—the shiny new limited-express train linking the port city of Pusan (Fusan, J) to the colonial capital. This was the aforementioned trip in which Murayama went to Keijō for the second time to get to "know" Korea better. His primary goal was to prepare for the film version of *Ch'unhyang*, but he also expresses eagerness to realize a tour of the performance throughout Korea.[47] Here Murayama offers his own assessment of the play's success in Japan:

> *Ch'unhyang* performed by the Shinkyō Theater Troupe introduced Korean customs, sentiments [ninjō], and cultural traditions, and as the first Oriental Classic to have been performed by Shinkyō as a historical drama, it was met with an extremely favorable critical response by many. I borrowed the form of Kabuki and actually received acting instructions from Zenshinza [Kabuki troupe]. To this we mixed in Korean traditions and colors, and then added the sensibility of modern theater to envision an altogether new form of theater. Some criticized it as a merely beautiful and romantic scroll painting [egakimono], a simple spectacle [supekutakuru], but . . . it was met with an extremely positive critical response by the majority [daihō].[48]

In his review of the performance, it is noteworthy that Murayama's assessment of its success is based on what he perceives as a significant separation between form and content. Murayama distinguishes his own contribution of experimental stylistic innovations from what he characterizes as the play's fixed "Korean" elements. According to Murayama's binary assessment, Korean customs and sentiments embody the historical drama of a "timeless Oriental classic," while his adaptation of Kabuki raises this ancient "tradition" of Japan to the level of modern experimental theater. The eclectic blending of traditional and modern *form* is predicated upon the separation of the *content* of Korean customs and colors as essences signifying tradition in contrast to what is coded as Murayama's own modern stylistic and formal inventiveness. His insistence on the separation of content (Korean) and form (Japanese) assumes a visual segregation between the content of Koreanness as symbols of fixed authenticity and old tradition, in the sense of pastness, as provided by Chang and others, and the distinct formal experiments envisioned by Murayama (blending styles of Kabuki and modern theater) as symbolizing the new and modern.

In a later roundtable discussion, Murayama similarly repeats this symbolic act of severing an essentialized and stagnant notion of Koreanness as content from the dynamic formal level of modern Japan (symbolized by Kabuki mixed with modern theater). Refuting those who criticize the lightness of the overall atmosphere as a "silly romance" (*itazura ren'ai*) unlike the usual Shinkyō performances, Murayama insists that one of the major accomplishments of this performance was that it broke with old assumptions that the Shinkyō troupe could perform only dark and depressing dramas. The performance of *Ch'unhyang* showed instead that the troupe could tap a wide range of styles to produce something beautiful.

Murayama laments, "These critics have a fixed sense of what modern theater should be. They don't understand that modern theater is not such a narrow concept. Besides, they don't seem to see the significance of introducing Korean culture to those who didn't know it already."[49]

Here, Murayama sees two major and distinct accomplishments of the play: one, pushing the stylistic limits of modern theater, and two, introducing Koreanness. The division of these two elements in Murayama's assessment of the performance seems significant, but even more significant is the implication behind such a separation of the modern experimental form of the performance (including the incorporation of Kabuki as method) from the content of its Korean subject matter. While insisting on stylistic innovations to make this performance new and dynamic, he views Koreanness as a static object to be introduced *as is* to the audience. Here it is worth pointing out that the form of Kabuki is not conflated with an essential Japaneseness or with Japanese tradition, or even with Oriental tradition. Kabuki is associated with its dynamic potential to trespass the generic limits of modern theater itself. What seems to be a radical experiment that reaches beyond rigid boundaries in the *form* of modern theater is based on rather narrow assumptions of the essence of the *content* of an Other culture.

Another experimental aspect of Murayama's performance was to cast a woman for the role of the male hero, Mongnyong. Cross-dressing and gender performance play important roles in the history of theater not only in Japan but in Korea and elsewhere. Here, the Kabuki form of *onna-gata* (males in female roles) is reversed to surpass limits of conventional expectations. However, the

FIG. 6.10 Servant Pangja squats and pouts. Reprinted with permission from the Tsubouchi Shōyō Memorial Museum.

reasoning behind Murayama's decision warrants pause: Murayama explains that none of the Japanese actors in his troupe could truly capture what he essentializes as "Korean suppleness and grace" (*Chōsentekina jūnanseiga*).[50] Therefore, such characteristic Koreanness of the male hero would be better captured if performed by a Japanese woman. What first appears to be a revolutionary experiment in queering gender constructions is tinged with racialist views that hark back to the imperial ideology of the time. Murayama idealizes what he presumes as "suppleness and grace," essentially characterizing a Korean man that could only be performed by a Japanese actress who would better approximate what her male counterpart does not naturally inhabit. What needs to be artificially staged here is not gender as constructed, but rather colonized race as gendered—the Korean male as effeminized.[51] This view not only mirrors the colonial relationship often depicted in gendered hierarchies, but ironically presupposes a radical *un*-translatability of racial difference, unwittingly revealing a contradiction to the slogan *Naisen ittai* (Japan and Korea, One Body) which the play was purportedly staging.

Colonial Language and (Un)translatability

When critics pose questions about the translatability of the language of *Ch'unhyang*, Murayama offers a revealing comment: "I don't know the Korean language at all, but I have been told by An Yŏngil, the assistant director, that there are indeed certain unique elements of the language of *Ch'unhyang* [*tokuina yunikuna kotoba dearu to kikimashita*]. During the performance in Japan, I used coughing, sighs, *ne*—[yes] and *aigo*! [exclamation] in Korean style [*Chōsenfūni yarimashita*]. When in Keijō, please observe the real thing [*jitsubutsu o mite itadakitai*]."[52] Here, the interviewer is referring to the lyrical and literary language of *Ch'unhyang*, but Murayama defensively exposes his lack of knowledge of the Korean language and misses the tenor of the question by turning to what he considered as Korean sounds that he claims can be captured based on anthropological observations of the "real thing" (*jitsubutsu*). The performance as a whole was assimilated into the Japanese language, but we see here that Murayama attempted to represent Korean colonial difference through bodily expulsions such as coughing and sighs and simple utterances, as if to say such noises were easily recognizable as marking Koreanness even to those like Murayama himself who were unfamiliar with the language. Again, it is clear that while on the formal level Murayama seemed to have envisioned an eclectic blending of styles that crossed rigid boundaries, when it came to representing the content of colonial culture, he relied on essentialist assumptions of Koreanness, thus perpetuating rather than debunking age-old colonial stereotypes.

While Murayama seems eager to point out the significance of pioneering the first Japanese-language performance of a Korean drama in the cultural exchange between Korea and Japan at that particular historical moment, he does not seem to recognize the very power dynamics of empire that gave a cultural monolingual carte blanche to travel throughout the colony to appropriate just enough from his native informants and translators to produce a play about the colony for imperial consumption. Nor does he see the obvious

FIG. 6.11 Drunken evil magistrate heckles Ch'unhyang while cross-dressed guards snicker. Reprinted with permission from the Tsubouchi Shōyō Memorial Museum.

connection between the production of a Japanese-language *Ch'unhyang* with the assimilationist imperialist policies that paralleled the censorship of the Korean language and other coercive measures of forming and fashioning "imperial subjects" in the colony. Perhaps the possibility that he himself unintentionally may have helped perpetuate the ideology of imperialism would have been too much to bear for a social progressive like Murayama who saw himself aligned with the underprivileged.[53] However, in the context of the late 1930s when new assimilationist laws and slogans were ubiquitous in the colony, it is difficult to deny that the performance, in its primacy of the Japanese language and the relegation of the Korean language to a secondary position, wittingly or not, embodied the hierarchical logic of empire.

The play was vigorously promoted as a *performance* of harmonious cultural exchange of *Naisen ittai* by, in fact, evading the *actual* unevenness of the relationship in the colonial context. Murayama's focus on transgressing borders of artistic form and his own peregrinations back and forth between the metropole and the colony further highlight a seemingly fluid and even spatial continuum across the empire. The colonizer's unimpeded movements across the borderlines of the empire seem to be misrecognized as the absence of borders when, in fact, they merely highlight the colonial license to trespass into territories

FIG. 6.12 Poster advertising the play. Reprinted with permission from Ohara Institute for Social Research, Hōsei University.

seized as imperial possessions. The ease with which Murayama seems to move across imperial borders, allowing him to take center stage in envisioning and realizing a transnational and transcolonial production of *Ch'unhyang*, despite his lack of knowledge of the language and customs of the culture he is purportedly "representing," is nonetheless at odds with the uneasy, peripheral role played by Chang Hyŏkchu who was relegated to a mere native informant, despite his fully bilingual and bicultural background as a colonized writer active in the metropolitan literary field. The fluidity of Murayama's travels around the colony stand in stark relief to Chang's own semi-autobiographical reflections on being policed at every turn in his travels to and from Japan.[54] Furthermore, the performance and the controversy it ignited among Korean intellectuals eventually ousted Chang from the Korean literary field altogether, marking a point of no return for the migrant writer.[55]

Roundtable in Colonial Korea

Now, I would like to turn to one of the many roundtable discussions surrounding the performance of *Ch'unhyang*. Most of these roundtable discussions were carefully staged performances themselves, enacted to promote the appearance of harmonious exchange by bringing Koreans and Japanese to the discussion table. Here, I want to consider a gathering among Korean cultural figures to discuss the performance in the colonial city of Keijō. Numerous promotional roundtables that gathered together Koreans and Japanese cultural figures, some of whom were directly involved with the production and others not, were published in major newspapers and journals; these focused on the overwhelming success and the historical significance of the traveling performance of *Ch'unhyang* in the empire. Here, however, I would like to focus on a little-known roundtable that I discovered in an obscure leftist journal in Korea which exists now only in rare collections in Korea. This roundtable is noteworthy in that there is no pretension toward performing a harmonious exchange between Koreans and Japanese. In fact, it excluded Japanese participants altogether, as well as anyone directly involved in the production of *Ch'unhyang*. From start to finish, the roundtable participants had no qualms about criticizing and poking fun at Murayama and Chang's staging of *Ch'unhyang*.

This roundtable discussion assembled on the occasion of the Keijō performance begins with the expression of skepticism about the play's putative success in Japan: "It is said the reception in Japan was quite good, but that does not mean the performance was indeed a success because what can the Japanese know or understand about *Ch'unhyang* in the first place?"[56] With the tone thus set, the floodgates of the respondents' discontent are opened, and they point out one flaw after another, exposing the play's "inauthenticity."

A substantial amount of time is spent poking fun at the performance, from the details of costume (Ch'unhyang's dress is too fancy, the color scheme is wrong, and her hairstyle is inappropriate), to inconsistencies in cultural references. For example, Mongnyong is called "wakasama" (young master) in Japanese, whereas the servant Pangja is called "Pangja" in Korean. The mannerisms are inappropriate: Mongnyong does not behave as a proper Chosŏn aristocrat; it is absurd that he would drink with his servant. While granting that the evil magistrate is indeed smitten with Ch'unhyang, his overtly lascivious attitude seems more fitting of a low-born drunkard than someone from elite society. The audacity of Ch'unhyang boldly prancing over to Mongnyong reminds one participant of a sketch lifted from a "rendezvous [*rangdebu*] between a modern girl [*modan gŏr*] and modern boy [*modan ppoi*]" rather than an authentic scene from the Chosŏn dynasty. ("Even today's modern girls would not be so bold and flirtatious. And the way she flung herself around to change her costume right before the audience!")[57]

Underlying the laughter and the jokes, however, the disapproval felt by the colonized critics is revealed in the way they confront the monstrously disturbing text of *Ch'unhyang*. Their anxiety is most evident when they jokingly compare the dirty, primitive depiction of Korea in the play to the South Pacific during the discussion over Ch'unhyang's costume: one critic comments on the scarf veiling Ch'unhyang's head and asks whether Murayama may have mistaken Korea for a place in the South Pacific.

While pointing out the ridiculousness of equating Korea to the "barbaric" South Pacific islands' "natives" (*t'oin*), readers detect a nervous recognition of the parallel location occupied by both in the imperial hierarchy of Asia. Colonized Korean nationalists were not immune to exoticizing and disdaining others, within the empire, whom they considered inferior to themselves. One lingering issue in Korean colonial studies is the tendency to critique Japan for colonizing Korea, but not to question the greater logic of colonization. Many Korean intellectuals, like their Japanese counterparts, internalized the ideology of social Darwinism and the discourse of civilization and enlightenment. They accepted the structuring of the world in hierarchies; the problem was Korea's low place in it.[58] However, the roundtable reveals a moment of anxious recognition that the analogy between Korea and the South Pacific may not be so far-fetched in the imperial world scheme. The critics are offended by the equation, but the reality was that in the broader global context, there was merely a small degree of difference that distinguished their situation from that of Japan's other colonies in the South Pacific.[59]

Some of the roundtable criticism on the issue of authenticity seems rather petty, focusing on the body of Ch'unhyang: what she was wearing, her actions, and such. In the larger discourses on modernity and tradition, however, aspects of the quotidian—hairstyles, courtship, and clothing, which filled the pages of popular journals and newspapers—took on larger implications as they portended the imminent and forced disappearance of a familiar way of life and the world order as they knew it. Likewise, the seemingly petty debates over Ch'unhyang's body—what she was wearing; where she was allowed to walk; what she was permitted to say—held larger symbolic import for the anxious male critics who were trying to hide such tensions behind silly jokes and nervous laughter.

From our perspective, we can interpret the laughter as the site not only of the anxieties of the colonized intellectual, but also of the disturbance to imperial ideology.[60] The object of their jokes was Murayama, the cultural illiterate in this case, clueless of Korean customs, though able to stage a grandiose spectacle of a transnational *Ch'unhyang*. The Korean critics dismissed the performance, treating it with irreverence, as mere slapstick comedy. Perhaps it is better characterized as a tragicomedy from the perspective of these colonized intellectuals who had to be relegated to making backhanded remarks and jokes in their critiques, unable to effectively prevent the damage that was already being done while the much-publicized Japanese *Ch'unhyang* was touring throughout their beloved Korea.

Korean critics were idealizing Korea, much as Murayama had done, but for different ends. Their assumption is that *Ch'unhyang* as a quintessential Korean text would be impossible for a Japanese (or any non-Korean) to truly understand or appreciate. Such essentialist views in the defensive mode show well the conundrum of colonized nationalists: their blindness toward how they were perpetuating the same logic of the colonizer in their critique of that colonizer.[61]

Murayama became the object of the Korean critics' taunts and jokes, but the harshest critique was reserved for Chang Hyŏkchu, the "traitorous" translator of Korean culture for imperial consumption. First, Chang's fame is dismissed as illegitimate as he is relegated to being seen as an undeserved crony of the Japanese. The critics accuse Chang of having "made it" only with the backing of a Japanese drama troupe and for having what they consider to be a lack of concern about the question of authenticity. One participant of the round-table discussion admits that he has not actually seen the play, but that doesn't prevent him from claiming the right to criticize it because the assumption is that, as an ethnic Korean, he is more than qualified to make pronouncements on *Ch'unhyang*.

The critique of Chang often results from the participants' equating of Chang with Murayama, and thus both are accused of being ignorant of Korean culture. By conflating Chang and Murayama, and both of their "inauthentic" relationships to Korea, as well as their ignorance of Korean customs, the critics more harshly implicate Chang by their essentialist logic: as an ethnic Korean, Chang has no excuse for his ignorance, but Murayama, as a Japanese, is expected to be ignorant.

The critics make no attempt to understand the power relationship between Chang and Murayama in the making of the play. Chang's complex position as a translator between colonial cultures and his attempts to negotiate an autonomous space of creative expression—despite the strong hand of Murayama—is simplified and dismissed. Chang is further chastised as lacking the self-awareness of his true position as merely a puppet and traitor in the service of empire.

Because *Ch'unhyang* in this context has been coded as a metonym for the lost nation itself while remaining a national tradition to be protected from the infiltration of the foreign, the attempt to modernize it—especially at a time when modernity was often seen as synonymous with imperial Japan and the West—was met with strong opposition as an "inauthentic betrayal." The ambivalence of the Korean critics toward the modern adaptation of *Ch'unhyang* reveals the anxieties of cultural nationalists in the colonial modern era.

It is not without significance that such gestures of simultaneous essentialization and exoticization of colonized Korea are contested over the female body of Ch'unhyang. Paralleling the fate of the eponymous tale itself, Ch'unhyang, its heroine, has been appropriated for nationalist and imperialist desires. The body of Ch'unhyang becomes the locus of contradictory contentions for these critics.[62]

The Japanese-language *Ch'unhyang*, arising out of the "collaboration" between Chang Hyŏkchu and Murayama Tomoyoshi, was assessed in Korea as a monstrous grafting of Kabuki and Korean elements and was seen as "impure." The performance emerged in the context of imperial assimilation policies, but with the end of empire, it became a text too disturbing to be remembered. The lively debates, photo ops, advertisements, and other forms of fixation on Chang and Murayama's *Ch'unhyang* were matched by the depth of silence that followed, resulting in an almost complete erasure from collective memories of both Korea and Japan in the formation of national literary canons. In Korea, Chang and Murayama's *Ch'unhyang* is a painful reminder of a history of "collaboration." The fact that a Korean-born writer rewrote the story in Japanese may have been seen as a sign of betrayal. However, because the issues of "collaboration" blur the line between the colonizer and the colonized and have not yet been worked through, they continue to haunt the politics and history of Korea, as seen in the formation of a president's committee of historians to "cleanse" the collaborationist history sixty years after the end of colonial occupation. A similar erasure and forgetting have been enacted in Japan as well. For all the fetishization and fixation on colonized writers during the Korea Boom years, when many Korean writers were invited to share the limelight at the center

FIG. 6.13 Hero Mongnyong weeps in the farewell scene with
Ch'unhyang. Reprinted with permission from the Tsubouchi Shōyō
Memorial Museum.

of the Bundan, their sudden rise to fame was matched by an equally abrupt
forgetting of their very existence.

The Question of "Homecoming"

I have discussed the ambivalence of transcolonial nostalgia in the empire on
multiple levels, and I would like to conclude with some musings on the issue
of "homecoming" of the bilingual translator. One metropolitan critic, Akita
Ujaku, expressed his hope that this performance would be received warmly as
a "son returning home" to Korea. He was referring to the performance itself
and not to Chang specifically, but this issue is an interesting one to ponder in

the case of Chang's personal experience of homecoming along with the performance of *Ch'unhyang*. For Chang, this was a literal homecoming; however, the hostile reception rendered this homecoming an ambivalent one at best. Just as *Ch'unhyang* was appropriated by contending ideologies at the time, this statement, which on the surface explicitly promotes the imperial project of *Naisen yūwa* (Harmony between Japan and Korea), can also be appropriated as a trace of, albeit unintended, the irony and ambivalence of individuals' experience across the borderlines of empire. Ironically, imperialist desires for colonial kitsch and nationalist desires for a national tradition converged on the same object of desire for contending purposes. Likewise, the dilemma of a bilingual writer caught between the contradictions of a nationalist demand for authenticity and the imperialists' demand for exoticization highlights his conflicted allegiance in the uneven colonial exchange. Here, I considered a moment of "collaboration" between the colonized and the colonizers when conflicting nostalgic desires came to a head within the uneven context of empire. It was a moment that gives us a glimpse of the scandalous convergence of the literary histories of Korea and Japan before they divided into their own separate nation-centered master narratives in the postcolonial era.

SEVEN

OVERHEARING TRANSCOLONIAL
ROUNDTABLES

Colonial Korean authors like Kim Saryang/Kin Shiryō and Chang Hyŏkchu/Chō Kakuchū negotiated the contradictory logic of the Korea Boom, that trend of metropolitan consumer fetishism in Japan for Korean exotica translated into easily digestible language and form. Enabled by the increasing consumptive habits of the Japanese—embodying both the desire and the repulsion of the colonial Other—the trend mirrored the forked nature of the imperial project at large for the colony's assimilation and differentiation.

Paralleling the Korea Boom in the colonial cultural field, another popular discursive phenomenon emerged. Transcolonial roundtables (座談会 zadankai, J; chwadamhoe, K) brought colonizers and colonized together, seemingly in a series of intimate gatherings to share mutual concerns. However, contrary to appearances, these roundtables were, in fact, carefully staged performances to propagate imperial ideologies. This chapter considers the rise of these staged, transcolonial roundtables and examines just how successful they were in opening up communication between the colonizers and the colonized. However, a careful reading of an important roundtable offers a case study to expose tensions and failures arising from fundamentally differing visions about the future of the colony. By way of reading between the lines of two censored versions of the roundtable simultaneously, one published in Korea and the other in Japan, this chapter considers the significance of the *failure* of such transcolonial collaborations between the colonizers and the colonized in the unequal context of empire. Through a self-reflexive methodological strategy of "overhearing"[1]—by which I mean both to eavesdrop and to hear again—this chapter further suggests the need for a more critically nuanced assessment of the roundtable form of discourse in general. This points also to the need for an awareness of the overdetermined nature of any postcolonial encounter with contentious colonial pasts, which necessitates continual re-readings and overhearings in the ruinous aftermath.

Emergence of the Roundtable (Zadankai) in Japan

An article published in 2006 by Yamazaki Yoshimitsu on the rise of the roundtable format of discourse in contemporary Japan begins by observing the uniquely prominent place taken by the roundtable in Japanese journals.[2] Although it is arguable whether this type of discourse is indeed particular to Japan, its ubiquity from television to newspapers to journals does seem to be noteworthy as has been pointed out by others.[3]

This article seems in part to be a response to prior ahistorical and negative assumptions about the roundtable format in Japan. Tracing the roundtable's precursors back to the Meiji period, Yamazaki locates the rapid rise in the roundtable format during the transition between the Taishō (1912–1926) and the Shōwa (1926–1989) eras, sometime between the Great Kantō Earthquake (1923) and the Manchurian Incident (1931), a time of great societal upheaval and uncertainty.

Yamazaki suggests three major reasons for the emergent popularity of the roundtable in Japan at this particular historical juncture. One, the rise of competition among increasing numbers of journals which caused some like *Bungei shunjū* and *Shinchō*, in an effort to reach more readers, to seek ways to differentiate themselves from other journals such as *Chūō kōron* and *Kaizō*, which tended to focus on criticism and polemic (*ronsō, hyōron*). Two, the rise of a mass readership in Japan, a popular audience that demanded quick, succinct, and easy-to-digest forms of information, and the emerging interest in broad theme-oriented discussions no longer limited to literature, as was the primary focus of earlier versions of the roundtable, such as the *gappyōkai* (collective reviews). And three, as a direct response to the call of the times (*jidai no yōsei*) at a moment when multiple and opposing voices in the literary field were vying for attention, and a vibrant new public discursive space was opening up in an increasingly diversified and competitive market of the mass media.[4]

Yamazaki concludes:

The roundtable is built on the premise that a few select members come together to discuss the day's issues in a relaxed conversation in an intimate setting. It is a stage in which a horizon is opened for shared concerns and problems. Of course, in a short conversation, there is the chance that the participants's comments could become fragmented. However, by showing *as is* the back and forth and scattered exchange of multiple points of view, including antagonisms, or by showing a harmonious conversation, the roundtable *objectively displays* a casual exchange of every perspective.[5] (emphasis added)

Yamazaki's article offers a useful point of departure for this chapter. First, it seems any discussion of the shifting role of the roundtable form must situate it in the historical context of its emergence and reemergence, and secondly, this chapter, in some ways, begins where Yamazaki's article ends. I focus on the era immediately following the period of the so-called Taishō Democracy (1912–1926) introduced here, but more importantly, it begins by interrogating the very assumptions of the article's conclusion. It seems to me that rather than take at face value the atmosphere of intimacy and casualness, and the appearance of presentation *as is* of a multiplicity of opinions evoked by the roundtable format, we need to turn a more critical eye toward the ways in which the roundtable deliberately produces such an ambience. The need to reassess the ideological effects of the roundtable's atmosphere may become particularly obvious when we turn to the ways this forum was appropriated for propaganda purposes by the late 1930s throughout the empire.

Critics have expressed misgivings about the roundtable's penchant for propaganda from quite early on. For example, Kawabata Yasunari offers one such critique in an article entitled "Current Criticism and Creation—after the Monthly Reviews," published in the popular journal *Shinchō* in 1923. He is referring to "collective reviews," an earlier version of the roundtable, staged for the purposes of breathing new life into what was seen as a stagnant world of criticism. Kawabata writes that while the format of collective reviews is exactly what the times called for, bringing together prominent figures and thereby creating an air of "authority" (*ken'i*) heretofore seen as lacking in criticisms; but he also warns that such authoritativeness evoked by the roundtable format, while garnering the much sought-after popularity with the masses, is precisely what should give one pause:

In a collective review, a kind of "serve the great" mentality occurs by the very nature of the gathering itself, which tends to attract general attention and trust. There are many positive aspects of gaining such trust, but just as in the past, the *geppyō* [monthly reviews] were on the whole believed to have held no authority; it is very dangerous if the collective reviews come to be entrusted in toto. It would behoove us, the youth of the contemporary Bundan, to prepare ourselves to receive not only grace but also poison from the form of the collective review.[6]

In other words, the gathering of prominent and established figures itself— creating an aura of authority sorely lacking in the previous format of the monthly review—may lead to a situation where readers learn to take such "authority" for granted, and may even obstruct the development of new and emerging ideas. Kawabata's ambivalence regarding this forked potential of the roundtable seems prescient when we consider the way the format would soon be actively mobilized for propaganda purposes in the wartime empire.

Others remarking on the popularity of the roundtable have pointed to some reasons why the format may be so attractive, not only with audiences but for those on the production side as well: for editors and producers, and for invited participants alike, the roundtable venue offers a quick and easy way to come together to discuss any issue at hand without much preparation from either side. The format offers an instant, ready-made air of authority and an aura of expertise by way of the prominence of the participants' roster. It is easy to convince participants to join, as they are virtually guaranteed wide exposure and enhanced status by sitting beside other luminaries in the field. Its almost sure commercial success makes it alluring for everyone involved. These factors helped propel the roundtable into a seemingly permanent fixture in the Japanese mass media.

I now turn to a roundtable staged in 1992, and for different purposes. Several scholars based in U.S. academia came together to discuss some of the problematic characteristics of the roundtable forum itself in a roundtable discussion of their own—a sort of metacritique of the forum's ideological effects. Based on the star-studded lineup of some of the most prominent scholars writing from American academia then, including Harry Harootunian, Masao Miyoshi, Fredric Jameson, Najita Tetsuo, and Naoki Sakai, this roundtable was conducted in English. However, we do not have a note on such "origins" as the version here was published in the October 1992 issue of the progressive journal *Sekai* in Japan in Japanese. In the absence of the original transcript, I will attempt to retranslate the encounter from the published Japanese version back to English here.

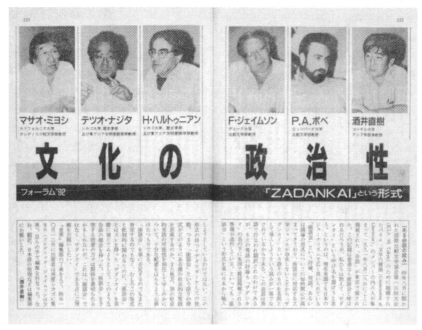

FIG. 7.1 Roundtable (Zadankai) from left to right: Masao Miyoshi, Tetsuo Najita, Harry Harootunian, Fredric Jameson, P. A. Bové, and Naoki Sakai. Reprinted with permission from Waseda University Archives.

While it is debatable whether these scholars were successful in accomplishing something wholly different from the typical roundtable they were assembled to critique, they did raise many important questions about the ideology undergirding its format. Their criticisms include targeting the roundtable's construction and performance of a ready-made consensus, by a gathering of celebrities, at the exclusion of topics that may incite uncomfortable conflicts (Harry Harootunian); the overall lack of well-thought-out discussion (Masao Miyoshi); lack of in-depth discussion and opportunities to express true disagreements (Fredric Jameson); and the absence of complex ideas, which are delivered broken up into easily digestible ready-made and packaged sound bites (Naoki Sakai).

While disagreeing on some points, these critics nonetheless seem to come to a consensus in their diagnosis of a general decline in the quality of the mass media culture of Japan.[7] Their critique is focused on contemporary society, and the ideological use of the roundtable as symptomatic of an overall degradation of the mass media, particularly after the postwar era—specifically in the context of globalization and postwar industrial and late-capitalist hyper-developments (*kōdō seichō*). Harking back nostalgically to past versions of the roundtable, Harootunian, for example, lauds the roundtable on "kindai no chōkoku" (overcoming modernity) and "Subjectivity" (*shutaisei*) and so forth, as exemplary of true dialogues and exchanges of ideas at their best, and laments how such potential declined in the depraved cultural context of postwar Japan.[8]

I would like to propose here, as suggested in Kawabata's statement earlier, that we need to be mindful of the potential for propaganda (both negative and productive censorship) latent in the roundtable format itself, which can be appropriated in different social contexts for varying purposes. It is unfortunate that the above metacritique of the roundtable is limited to a focus on the postwar period onward, diagnosing the roundtable's problematic role in Japanese society as a symptom of hyper-modernization or late (post)modernity. By examining the rise of transcolonial roundtables that emerged in the nexus of Japan and Korea in the prewar and wartime era, I would like to perform an anachronistic translation of their critique to read the roundtable of an earlier time and situate the critique fully within the colonial modern context to help us illuminate continuities from the colonial to the postcolonial eras.[9]

Overhearing the Roundtable

It is important to keep the above critiques in mind, as we now turn to wartime roundtables that emerged from the contact zones between colonial Korea and metropolitan Japan. The sheer number of such roundtables that were staged, with cultural figures gathered between Japan and Korea from the late 1930s to the early 1940s, is staggering and sharply contrasts with their virtual disappearance from the discursive space of Japan and Korea post–1945.[10]

In the earlier roundtable published in *Sekai*, Fredric Jameson offers a provocative insight. He writes that what may be a particular trait of the roundtable format (as opposed to other dialogic forms like the television talk show) lies in what he calls "chōshū no fuzai" (absence of an audience),[11] and that our encounter with the roundtable is characterized more aptly as an experience of "hearing" rather than that of "reading."[12]

This play between "reading" and "hearing" offers us a fruitful way to reconsider our own encounter with the transcolonial roundtable staged and passed down from a contested colonial past. Further, our own "absence" from the immediate event that we are interrogating makes our "reading/hearing" a necessarily mediated and distant experience from the actual site of the event of the roundtable itself, which is always already an ephemeral performance. Translating Jameson's important insight, I argue that the necessarily distant and mediated experience of our own postcolonial encounter with the transcolonial roundtable may in fact be closer to the experience of *overhearing*. Reframing postcolonial readings of absent or absented colonial pasts as an overhearing helps us to remember the distanced perspective of our own encounter with the original roundtable performance, which is available to us only as a flimsy residue buried under layers of conflicts that have divided colonial histories and postcolonial memories.

The theoretical methodology of overhearing offers us insights into the very limits as well as the possibilities of our overdetermined encounter with the texts of the past. This postcolonial position of overhearing situates us in a space of in-between-ness, neither fully inside nor outside the originary site of enunciation. On the one hand, the roundtable format appears to offer its audience the position of insider, a privileged location from which to eavesdrop on a conversation among an intimate coterie. On the other hand, the position of the roundtable's audience is also simultaneously a place of the "outsider," relegated to a position just beyond the inner circle of speakers. This ambivalent, borderline place, whose distance from the site of discursive production is a space of both limited and closed access, simultaneously opens up yet another space, full of other potential and critical possibilities. The very uncertainty of our positionality may also help us to be aware of the multiply limited nature of our access to the text at hand. The roundtable event that has occurred in the past has been passed down to us, in mere fragments of written records through the imperial language, which was subjected to multiple layers of censorship from the colonial to the postcolonial eras.

In "Understanding as Over-hearing: Towards a Dialogics of Voice," Richard Aczel proposes to rethink reading experiences in general as overhearing and calls for the development of a "historically situated, reader-oriented approach to over-hearing."[13] There is a play on words in what Aczel means by "over," signifying at least four different meanings: "It is at once the complex over of overdetermination; the temporal, historical over of something repeated, done over again; the incomplete, falling short over of overlooking; and the combination of fortuitousness and intention that informs the over of the more usual sense of over-hearing."[14]

Drawing on Derrida, Heidegger, Hans-Georg Gadamer, and Mikhail Bakhtin, Aczel proposes a reader-oriented theory or "reading as overhearing" and proposes that the "seeing of reading is always at once a hearing" of multiple voices within a text that are already overdetermined by the historical situatedness of the reader.[15] In other words, the act of reading is a dialogic process that involves a multiplicity of voices of the historical situatedness of the inherited text as well as the position of the reader whose own overhearing entails all prior historical hearings.[16] Aczel's insightful conclusion seems to bear repeating in our context: "It is of course the fundamental difference of the historically situated reader's horizon—from that of the text and from that of other historically situated readers—that constitutes the hearing (and letting speak) of voices in the text as a historical over-hearing, a hearing anew, in an overdetermined and dialogically projected encounter between self and other."[17]

I find Azcel's intervention to think about reading as an overhearing of voices, as an encounter between the self and Other, to be a productive way to reconsider our own experience of encountering the transcolonial roundtable, staged and then passed down (only in fragments) to us from a contested era. While we attempt to overhear the failure of such transcolonial encounters of roundtables assembled between Koreans and Japanese across various gaps (spatial and otherwise) dividing the colony and the metropole in the unequal imperial context, we must be aware of the temporal gap manifest in the post-colonial overhearing. It is essential to be self-reflective of our own limited access to these conflicted pasts, overdetermined by colonial and postcolonial legacies. Nonetheless, or perhaps precisely because of this vexed relationship to our shared but contested pasts, we must read and reread, hear and overhear, these texts without falling into narrow assumptions about our privileged access based on our own ethno-national affiliations to a once and definitive reading.

Roundtable "Future of Korean Culture"

Now we will attempt to "read/overhear" the transcolonial roundtable. Such roundtables became prevalent as the Japanese wartime empire was expanding into new territories, and Korea's role was accordingly shifted via rigorous assimilation and mobilization for the war effort. A perusal of the roundtables of transcolonial encounters published in just one major journal, *Kokumin bungaku*, which was itself produced in the contact zones of Japan and Korea, for example, yields a startling number of examples.[18] They were prominent in other journals and newspapers as well.[19] Such a boom in transcolonial roundtables must be understood in the context of the shifting role of the colony in the expanding wartime empire. An overhearing of an important case study will show that rather than embodying the success of such assimilation policies and the harmonious interactions of the colonizers and the colonized, these mass-produced, transcolonial roundtables unwittingly expose significant anxieties and conflicting desires.

It may not be surprising to find out that Japanese colonial officials made a concerted effort to propagate imperial ideologies through transcolonial round-tables.[20] What is so vexing about these roundtables, particularly in the colonial context, is that the format itself, which stages a semblance of intimacy and casualness, and the appearance of presentation of facts "as is," stamped with the authority of celebrity cachet, leads one to believe that the colonizers and colonized were indeed coming together for open exchange and dialogue in these uncertain times. However, this "boom" in the roundtable between Koreans and Japanese paralleled the Korea Boom, not only temporally, but also in their common objectification and commodification of Korean culture translated and commodified for imperial desires, mediated through the mass media, at the expense of true engagement and encounter with colonial Koreans as cultural producers. In short, the roundtables still left the Korean writers voiceless.

The transcolonial roundtable to which we turn now is a significant example of how the two wartime mass media phenomena mutually enhanced one another in the context of empire. Both the translated performance of *Ch'un-hyang* and the roundtable gathered to discuss its successful translation for imperial consumption were products of colonial collaboration between Japanese and Korean cultural producers. Both events attempted to stage the harmonious assimilation of Korea into the Japanese empire and were for the most part received as such by contemporaries. However, a rereading strategy of overhearing will take us to an entirely different conclusion, one that paradox-ically, albeit unwittingly, reveals the very breakdown of such imperial slogans of transcolonial harmony.

On the eve of the *Ch'unhyang* performance in Keijō, a roundtable discussion assembling an impressive array of literary luminaries from Japan and Korea gathered in the colonial city to discuss the future of Korean culture.[21] Hayashi Fusao (1903–1972), the master of ceremonies, opens the roundtable by recall-ing the following heartwarming anecdote about the importance of colonial knowledge. He tells the group his insight came to him on a recent train journey cutting through Korea on the way to Manchuria and Northern China, while he had been casually flipping through a collection of lectures by Governor General Ugaki:

> In today's roundtable, we would like to discuss the future and present of Ko-rean culture, or whither the road to *Naisen ittai*. My goal was to see Manchu-ria and Northern China, and I had left Japan expecting to just pass through Korea. But I happened to share a compartment with an elderly man on the

FIG. 7.2 The roundtable's first installment with subtitle "Suffering Peninsular Authors: Shrinking Publication Venues Make Life Difficult."

ferry ride between Shimonoseki and Fusan (Pusan, K), and he told me, "It seems you, too, are thinking of overlooking Korea with only Manchuria and Northern China filling your head, but that is a big mistake." . . . Then I came to Keijō and met various people from the Governor General's Office as well as youths from Korea. And tonight, with all of you gathered here, I finally realize that Korea is Japan's closest neighbor, and it doesn't seem right to suddenly try to know faraway places like Manchuria and Northern China without knowing one's closest neighbor.[22]

Thus, we see from its beginnings that this transcolonial roundtable, rather than being a casual and intimate space of gathering, is firmly embedded in the political context of Japanese imperial expansions into China and Manchuria and the changing role allotted to colonial Korea amid these endeavors. This becomes evident through Hayashi's passing comment about the railways he was traveling on having been strategically laid for optimal mobility of military supplies, and his reference to the former Governor General Ugaki's lectures on Korea as his preferred reading material on the journey. The utility of wartime mobilization of Korea, and not a utopian *humanistic* gesture toward equality as espoused by pundits, was the actual underlying premise behind this event as well as the slogan of *Naisen ittai* under whose banner it was staged.

Korea's role in the expanding empire was shifting at the time, and in this context, the catchy and seemingly flexible slogan of *Naisen ittai* was appealing precisely because it was open to various interpretations.[23] For imperial ideologues, we now know in hindsight, the slogan worked primarily as a ruse to lure Koreans to cooperate in the war effort,[24] whereas for many Koreans, it was interpreted as an opportunity to shed their secondary status as abjected colonized subjects. The contradiction marked on the words of the slogan itself may seem obvious in postcolonial hindsight, with Japan occupying the privileged primary position; and Governor General Minami's gruesome bodily metaphor of hearts, blood, and flesh mixing together now seems clearly to foreshadow the violent and painful (mostly unilateral) sacrifices that would be required of Koreans in this harmonious new relationship. However, in the midst of this tumultuous time, such contradictions either went unnoticed or were strategically downplayed by even some of the colonized who preferred to take a more utopian view and focus on the slogan's potential for an opportunity to shape a new future on more equal terms.[25] After the violent repressions and failures of various attempts at independence exemplified by the March 1 Movement of 1919, and in the context of Japan's expanding presence in the world theater (seemingly unchecked, much to the shock of many nationalist idealists who thought Woodrow Wilson's declaration for the right to self-determination might actually extend to the colonized of the non-West), perhaps it is no longer surprising that many Korean intellectuals were desperate for a new solution to their conundrum as colonized subjects.

However, the slogan's slipperiness, which initially may have given it its utopian potential in theory, was accompanied by shifting and contradictory policies and laws that, in practice, continually deferred giving true equality to the colonized—despite all the sacrifices demanded of them by these same laws as steps toward realizing such dreams.

Here, I focus on one roundtable discussion that brought together major cultural figures from Korea and Japan in a grand gesture to discuss the "future of Korean culture." However, rather than being a venue to engage diverse opinions toward shaping a new future together through open dialogue, the roundtable seems to have predetermined the future of Korea from the outset, and the participants seem to have purchased (perhaps unwittingly) a nontransferable, one-way ticket on the "road toward *Naisen ittai*" as Hayashi Fusao suggested.

The roundtable was staged in October 1938 and serialized in six installments in *Keijō nippō*, the Japanese-language newspaper of the Governor General, first in the colony, and then republished a few months later in the influential literary journal *Bungakukai* in the metropole. In order to bridge the temporal and spatial lag between the two versions, I will read them simultaneously and focus on the significance of the censor's alterations made between them.

Let's begin with the changed title: in *Keijō nippō*, the roundtable is entitled "The Future *and Present* of Korean Culture" (emphasis added) whereas in

Bungakukai, the title is "The Future of Korean Culture."[26] One might imagine myriad reasons behind the absence of the "Present" in the *Bungakukai* title, and it is not my interest to conjecture about a conscious act of conspiracy behind the deletion.[27] Rather, the absence of the "Present" in the title is useful as an entrée into considering the significance of the differing desires between the metropolitan critics' focus on the "Past" of Korean culture and the colonized participants' repeated attempts to reroute the conversation toward their "Present" circumstances, a contrast that becomes starkly evident in the very content of the discussion.

While everyone present at the roundtable seems to be in agreement that there is something amiss in the state of affairs in the Korean cultural field of the "Present," and of the urgent need to fix this problem in order to head toward a better future, we can hear fundamental differences of opinions about the underlying causes of such problems, and thus very different solutions for the future. Let us eavesdrop on the conversation:

After Hayashi's aforementioned personal anecdote sets the stage for the roundtable, he wryly confesses his total ignorance about Korea and asks the Koreans to act as native informants and start with a brief introduction on the state of the Korean literary field. He asks them to begin with the basics — the names of the journals — because "Japanese writers do not know anything about Korea."[28]

After listing the names of some of the influential journals and newspapers in the colony, Yu Chino (1906–1987) wastes no time in registering his lament on the state of the publishing field: "Korean writers can't make a living by writing." This bleak assessment of the present situation is highlighted in the section subtitled in the *Keijō nippō* version: "Suffering Writers of the Peninsula: Few Publication Venues and Straightened Lives."[29]

Horrified by this new information, Hayashi asks: "So what do writers do?" Im Hwa replies, "There is not a single person who makes a living as a writer, so they all do something else. Those who don't have other work eat when they can and don't when they can't."[30]

While everyone seems to agree that there is certainly a problem here, fundamental differences arise in their interpretation of what might be the culprit underlying such a "lack." The emphasis for the official Japanese side is clearly on the remnants of what they see as "backward" Chinese and Confucian influences. This assessment is evident, for example, in the subtitle to one section: "The Current Condition of the Korean Literary Field: Bad Influences of Confucian Dominance and the Preponderance of Chinese Studies."[31]

Under this heading, Koreans are again asked to play native informants and to provide information about the status of Korean culture, particularly on the situation of the dramatic arts. Yu Ch'ijin, the expert on drama, raises the lack of support for theatrical arts and drama in Korea, particularly since the Chosŏn dynasty, and blames the low status of this genre on the Confucian designation of theatrical arts as "vulgar," as a "low" folk art in the hierarchy of literary genres. Murayama responds, "Korean culture must emphasize this aspect or it will not develop. As far as literature is concerned, we need to discuss what we should do about this situation."[32]

The Korean critics' criticism of the low status and lack of attention given to the dramatic arts in the Chosŏn dynasty is here used to criticize what is perceived as the lack of development of Korean culture in toto. However, this is a common phenomenon in many cultures in the East and West—for example, Shakespeare in Elizabethan England and Kabuki theater in Tokugawa Japan struggled to garner social status and were only subsequently elevated to the highest of the two national literary canons. This broadly cast interpretation is made even clearer in the alterations to Murayama's comments made in the *Bungakukai* version: "As far as the future of Korean culture is concerned, we need to emphasize this, the very reasons why it is in such a state, and why it will never develop. We'll talk specifically about literature later, but now, we must address this point."[33] Through strategic censorship and a leap in interpretation by those admitting "total lack of knowledge" about the colony, the discussion about one particular genre has been extended to the deplorable state of Korean culture in general. Moreover, this is seen as directly resulting from the remnants of the past: specifically, the influence of Confucianism and Chinese culture. The implication here is that Korean culture has been stagnant since the Chosŏn dynasty and that a solution to this situation can be found with the help of Japanese modern sensibilities, through benevolent discussions toward a solution such as the present roundtable. This was a commonly heard imperialist argument in the colony at the time, in various fields ranging from economics to essentialist generalizations about national characteristics.

In contrast to this diagnosis, Korean critics suggest that it may not be necessary to hark back to such a distant past to locate the roots of the present problems. Kim Munjip begins his assessment on the present lackluster state of the Korean cultural field by pointing directly to the issue of colonial censorship:

Before, there were various journals, but these days, there are only a few. Dailies have stopped publication due to the famous photograph incident of

Son Kijŏng, namely the Japanese flag incident. And eventually, *Tonga ilbo* was permitted to publish again since last June or July, but *Chungang ilbo* has disappeared, and aside from *Maeil sinbo*, there is the *Chosŏn ilbo*. There used to be quite a few journals as well, but with the rise of the price of paper, and with the Governor General's shifting preferences as well, they gradually decreased, and the variety of dishes on our tables have also decreased as a result.[34]

Rather than laying the blame on remnants of the past or assuming a state of stagnation in the Korean cultural field since the Chosŏn dynasty, Kim makes it clear that the drastic turn for the worse occurred quite recently. Rather than looking to the ancient Chinese past for the roots of the problem, he points to the effects of the modern technologies of censorship and disciplinary control, in the contemporary mass media of Japanese imperial policies. The reference to the still sensitive case of the Korean marathoner, Son Kijŏng (1912–2002), who won the gold medal wearing the Japanese flag at the 1936 Berlin Olympics, and the sly editorial erasure of the Japanese flag on the newspaper photograph, drives this point home.

Thus, even when faced with the same empirical conditions in the colony's cultural field, the two sides arrive at utterly contradicting diagnoses of the situation resulting from the differences in their standpoints and their unequal positions in the empire. While the Japanese side, which must defend the cultural policies of the colonial regime, strategically evades the issues of censorship in the present, and turns an eye toward the past in order to diagnose the problem, the Koreans are pointing directly toward the context of Japanese imperial policies in the present.

This is not the only place in which the Japanese focus on the past and the Korean focus on the present prevent the two from seeing eye to eye on issues. The problem of lack of publication venues in Korea and the writers' conundrum of being unable to make a living are directly linked to the issue of language policies in the colony. On this essential matter, the two sides again cannot reach an agreement about the best solution, because their understanding of the fundamental issue is on different levels.

It is significant to point out that such clashes of opinions do not manifest themselves when the conversation dances around cultural productions of bygone days: the past seems to be a safe topic of conversation, filled with nostalgic happy memories for both sides. A long pleasant chat ensues about various folk arts of Korea's past, such as mask dances, puppet plays, and such, which seem to get the Japanese critics very excited, particularly Murayama, who apparently has acquired quite a collection of his own Korean artifacts. Hayashi generously offers that the colonizer might have been influenced by the colonized, that [even] some Japanese dramas were influenced by Korean culture.

However, when the Koreans (perhaps tired of beating around the bush this way) try to steer the talk toward issues that are most urgent to them, in the present moment, specifically to the fate of the Korean language in the empire, there is a sudden change in the atmosphere and one can almost sense the tension in the air. Let's look at the exchange in some detail:

> YI T'AEJUN: I'd like to ask Mr. Akita. You mentioned just now that it would be fine to write in either Korean or in kokugo [national or imperial language, Japanese]. Since this is a crucial issue for us, I'll ask my question even if it departs somewhat from the main focus here. Do our seniors in Japan hope from the bottom of their hearts that we Korean writers write in Korean, or do you prefer that we write in Japanese?[35]

> IM HWA: Would it be better for Koreans to write in Japanese, or in Korean?

> AKITA: As far as our hopes as writers, and the hopes of the general public [are concerned], in other words, as writers who are writing for the general public, Japanese is best.[36]

> MURAYAMA: That is to say, in order to have more people read about Korean culture, if you want responses from the Japanese people, since Japanese cannot read Korean, they will not be able to respond to writings in Korean. And in fact, since the national language (kokugo) has been propagated throughout Korea by now, if you actually want your works understood, then because Japanese will be more widely read, it would be best to write in Japanese.

> AKITA: It would be good to write in Japanese to have a wide readership, and then translate some of that into Korean.

> CHŎNG: I think it's best to write in both.[37]

Here we see in the transcription the Japanese critics parroting each other, almost as if their talking points had been synchronized (whether onsite or in postproduction is indeterminate), in contrast to the utter lack of communication with their Korean counterparts. In this exchange, Chŏng's comments sound to us as almost like a comical non sequitur after the repeated mono-logic utterances of the others. Despite these attempts by the Korean writers to engage this difficult issue, and contrary to the initial appearance of the willingness on the side of the colonizers to engage with the desires of the Koreans, the issue is not, as it soon becomes obvious, open for negotiation. There is a limit to the benevolence allowed the colonized, it seems. Let us keep reading:

> HAYASHI: Now the question of national language has surfaced, and this is a very serious issue. As far as we are concerned, I would like to tell all of you Korean writers that we would like you to write all works in Japanese.

> AKITA: And you can translate them.

> IM HWA: This is a major problem.[38]

Again, we cannot but notice a major disjuncture in the dialogue.

> MURAYAMA: If there are particular aspects of the Korean language that can be expressed only in Korean but are lost when expressed in Japanese, then that is a deep tragedy, but as long as this is not the case, and as long as the current state of affairs has come as far as this, as a matter of immediate concern, it doesn't seem there are major hindrances to writing in Japanese. And therefore, there seems to be no real reason why one absolutely must write in Korean.[39]

Here, Murayama's statement is contradictory and tautological. Otherwise, the reasons offered by these "Japanese seniors" seem quite pragmatic and reasonable, and the advice is couched in the language of generous gifts bestowed for the sake of their juniors who appear to be "too stubborn" and "narrow-minded" to know what is best for themselves. The lack of venues to publish in Korean, which has limited the writers' ability to make a living, and the lack of a wider audience in Korea are pragmatic reasons why Koreans should accept the fact that it would not be economical or reasonable to insist on writing in Korean. Thus, Japanese as the preferred and official "national language" is imposed not at all subtly on the colonized writers who have no choice in the matter but to accept this rational "choice" willingly and gratefully. The fundamental issue of censorship of Japanese imperial policy, which lies at the heart of such a lack as pointed to by the Korean critics, is conveniently left unaddressed by their Japanese counterparts, producing yet another level of censorship at the site of the roundtable itself.

Despite these seemingly rational, top-down injunctions, the Korean participants repeatedly attempt to negotiate with the colonizers to convince them of their desires to write in Korean. They explain that although they are happy to provide translations into Japanese as much as possible, there are certain aspects such as poetry and the flavor of the language that are lost in translation. Hayashi replies, "That's merely the theory of the impossibility of translation. There is a specific purpose for translations, you know."[40]

It is interesting to note that Hayashi's comment pointing to the absurdity of the Koreans' lack of logic is absent in the earlier *Keijō nippō* version and was subsequently added to the *Bungakukai* version. This addition seems to bolster the argument to impose kokugo in the colony, to make the reasoning seem much more theoretically rigorous rather than merely tautological as in the earlier versions. This also works to repress further contestation. Also noteworthy is that the Korean side is not extended the same editing courtesy; in fact, their arguments are curtailed in the *Bungakukai* version, making them appear petulant and illogical. In the face of imperial arguments based on rational theories of the modern technologies of economics and translation in the "borderless" empire, the Koreans are reduced to being chastised like ignorant children for their "stubbornness" and narrow-mindedness.[41]

This discussion on the issues of language and translation in the empire itself ironically reveals the utter untranslatability, or incommensurability, between the desires and discourses of the colonizers and the colonized. They are talking on differing levels that are seemingly unbridgeable: one on the superstructural level of cultural productions and preservation and the other, that of the substructural level of utilitarian economics and the logical conditions of the marketplace. The possibility that these two levels of cultural productions and economics are intimately linked in the colonial modern context cannot be entertained in this conflicted dialogue.

Thus, the Koreans' legitimate attempts to salvage their language, which was being banned and censored in practice and affecting their very livelihood, is sublimated to the level of theory, and dismissed and silenced as irrational essentialism of colonial nationalism. If their arguments at times do indeed fall into essentialist tendencies, seeming to dismiss the act of translation *tout court*, it must be contextualized in a situation in which translations into Japanese, the national language of empire, are overwhelmingly privileged over writings in the Korean language. This discussion must be further contextualized in these writers' attempts to negotiate multiple levels of censorship.

In turning back to the Korean folktale *Ch'unhyang*, it becomes clear that the translation into Japanese of this quintessential symbol of Korean tradition signifies quite different meanings for the two sides involved. The Japanese side sees the *Ch'unhyang* performance as a staging of a quaint relic of pastness. Murayama and others assure the Koreans that Korean culture will not disappear because such cultural products of the past will be carefully preserved. Im Hwa is quick to point out, however, that the real issue at hand is not about the preservation of past relics, but about cultural productions of the present: "I'm not talking about such museum pieces."[42] Despite the fact that the roundtable is conducted in the privileged language of the empire, Japanese, there is a limit to the translatability of the conflicting desires expressed.

The Japanese critics argue against the Koreans that the *essence* of *Ch'unhyang* was sufficiently communicated in translation to the Japanese, as revealed, according to Hayashi by the shared tears (and laughter, as added to the *Bungakukai* version) of the Japanese and Korean members of the audience.[43] Although Im Hwa points out that the reason for the Japanese public's interest in *Ch'unhyang* can be located in the contemporary "political context" (*jikyoku no kankei*),[44] the Japanese critics have a different view. When asked what aspect of *Ch'unhyang* moved the Japanese audience, there seems to be an interesting convergence.

Murayama says, "Ch'unhyang's chastity [*teisetsu*] was what was so welcomed,"[45] and Hayashi agrees: "Ch'unhyang's willingness to sacrifice herself and protect her chastity for Mongnyong, which is a trait that should be universally admired by all women."[46] Thus, according to Hayashi, what allows *Ch'unhyang* to be translated across cultures and gives it its universal value is located in what some by this time may interpret as an outdated ideology of female chastity. Hayashi seems completely unaware that this "universal" quality has in fact been the object of contestation in a dynamic discourse on gender, marriage, and free love that Koreans (not unlike their counterparts in Japan and elsewhere) have been grappling with for decades.[47] By pointing to this notion as a quality that he nostalgically admires in Ch'unhyang, Hayashi reveals not only his lack of knowledge about the dynamic contemporary discourses on gender in Korea but also his nostalgic predilection for outdated gender hierarchies, which he fantasizes through Ch'unhyang to have been preserved in the quaintly backward colony.[48]

Hayashi and other Japanese critics, who from the onset of the roundtable have admitted their lack of any deep knowledge about Korea, could only engage *Ch'unhyang* as a quaint relic of the unchanging past. They were not concerned with the significance of *Ch'unhyang* in the contemporary discourses in Korea that reproduce it as part and parcel of current debates on modernity. Here again, we see a total lack of awareness of Korea's "present" by the colonizers.

Chang's complex role as translator perched between the colony and the metropole is simply elided here. Chang is aligned unequivocally on the Japanese side, particularly in the later *Bungakukai* version, in which a thick bar literally is added to separate the participants into Korean and Japanese sides, with Chang positioned unequivocally right in the middle of the Japanese side.[49]

In a similar vein, the divide between Chang and the Korean critics is made deeper on the printed page through significant alterations to the content of the exchange between them from *Keijō nippō* to the *Bungakukai*. It is useful to juxtapose the two versions as the conversation turns to the topic of Chang's translation of *Ch'unhyang*:

Keijō nippō

IM HWA: That translation is good, and *Ch'unhyang* has been sufficiently translated, but I think it is tremendously difficult to translate the flavor of the language.

CHANG HYŎKCHU: My aim was to introduce Korean culture of the past which can be intimately linked to the future, that is, to introduce these two aspects of Korean culture in Tokyo in the Japanese language. In the present moment, since Korean-language drama troupes cannot perform in Tokyo, I agreed to write a Japanese version of *Ch'unhyang* for the time being.

YU CHINO: Now, that's what's so difficult.

———

Bungakukai

IM HWA: Is that translation good? Was *Ch'unhyang* sufficiently translated? I think it is tremendously difficult to translate the flavor of the language.

CHANG HYŎKCHU: To perform a play that deals with Korea's past and present in the world of Japanese theater and furthermore, to translate or adapt Korean writings into Japanese and to introduce them to Japanese. These are the two things that we absolutely must do. It's fine to stage a

Korean-language performance in Japan, but the effect it will have will be severely limited, and this is why I wrote the Japanese-language version of *Ch'unhyang*. And I think the result was quite a success.

YU CHINO: Now, that's what's so difficult.

In *Keijō nippō*, Im Hwa's comments are focused more on the limits of the role of translation in the empire, rather than on Chang's translation specifically. In fact, he admits that Chang's translation in and of itself is good enough, but that there are still aspects that are difficult to communicate in translation. Chang himself agrees with this assessment of the limits of a full rendering in the Japanese. In the *Bungakukai* version, however, this exchange is recast into a much more direct confrontation. In this altered version, through the addition of punctuation marks, Im Hwa's comments have been turned into a series of doubt-filled questions, and cannot be read as anything but a direct challenge to Chang's translation specifically. Also, Chang's response appears quite arrogant and defensive in his confidence in the success of the translation, and Yu's comment directly following can only be read as a direct challenge to this arrogance, whereas in the previous version, the antecedent to which Yu's comment refers is open for debate. In *Bungakukai*, through manipulations of punctuation and other seemingly minor alterations, the larger issue of the role of translation in the context of empire, increasing censorship, and repression of cultural productions has been translated into a petty quarrel among colonized individuals personally attacking each other.

Further, in *Keijō nippō*, Chang appears to share more in common with the other Koreans in his concerns about the language situation at hand than would appear in the later *Bungakukai* version. His explanation behind his reason to write a Japanese-language version in *Keijō nippō* is as follows: "At a time when Korean-language plays cannot be performed in Tokyo, I decided to translate it into Japanese, for the time being." This has been significantly changed in *Bungakukai*: "It would have been OK to stage a Korean-language performance in Tokyo, but because I knew that this would not be as influential, I chose to translate it into Japanese." In this latter version, any trace of the colonized writer's conflicts involved in his decision to write in Japanese has been erased. In the first version, one can still sense the dilemma behind Chang's decision to write in Japanese in a context in which a Korean version was not permitted. In *Bungakukai*, it appears he faced two equally viable options, and he made an opportunistic (convenient and pragmatic) choice to write in Japanese, although he could have just as easily done so in Korean.

Through the removal of any references to the limitations placed upon the colonized writer, the roundtable constructs the semblance of the colonized writer as having equality and the freedom of choice and thereby stages the spectacle of the harmony of *Naisen ittai*. However, by reading the misrepresentations behind the manipulated texts, we can begin to imagine a more complex nature of power imbalance and censorship, both external and internal, which were manifest at the time, when we read across the spatial and temporal distances between the two versions.[50] After a heated exchange between the Koreans and the Japanese about the issue of language in which the Japanese side increasingly refuses to entertain the very idea of writing in Korean, Hayashi suddenly suggests that the Governor General be asked to allow Korean writers to take propaganda tours to the war front. Yu Chino says he heartily agrees with this suggestion. In the *Bungakukai* version, his comment is then followed by the addition of a round of applause, punctuating the Korean writers' eagerness to head to the warfront.[51]

Censoring the Colonial Other

The roundtable significantly comes to an abrupt end when the discussion turns directly to the topic of censorship. In an apparently benevolent gesture toward open exchange, a censor from the Governor General's publication bureau, Furukawa, has joined them, apparently to answer whatever questions the colonized writers might have about the censorship process, "even complaints regarding the present situation" as generously offered by Hayashi.[52] However, the limits of this seemingly open invitation are revealed as soon as the conversation develops.

First, it is worth noting that the questions of the colonized writers reveal that they have been provided with no guidelines about the criteria thus far used for censorship. When asked about this directly, Furukawa remarks vaguely, "Well, obviously, anti-social and anti-Japanese matter will be censored."[53] This brief exchange reveals that what seems "obvious" and commonsensical to the censoring authority is anything but to those whose very livelihood is dependent on such rules (or lack thereof).

Yu Chino remarks that, at times, the censors seem to expunge works without even reading them in their entirety.[54] Furukawa then replies, "If you go on about communism throughout the work and in the last five or six lines add something like 'now, that's why this is bad,' then of course, even if the conclusion happens to be good, we'd censor it [because it could have propaganda value]."[55]

Yu insists, "I think even if the writing might appear bad at certain stages, as long as the conclusion is fine, it should be permitted,"[56] to which Furukawa replies: "Untrue. As I said, even if it's bad in parts . . ."[57] However, the conversation and the roundtable itself are abruptly interrupted by Hayashi: "OK, that's enough of that."[58]

In the *Keijō nippō* version, Terada, who has been silent the entire time, steps in with, "Well thank you all very much!" bringing the roundtable to an awkward ending. In the *Bungakukai* version, the abruptness has been smoothed out: Hayashi's sudden interruption is softened with the following addition to his statement: "We can continue this conversation over drinks. This roundtable will be published in *Bungakukai* so that it can be available to Japanese readers. (Applause). Then we will wrap it up here. Thank you very much!"[59] Juxtaposing the two endings becomes meaningful on multiple levels as in montage they reveal some of the contradictions embodied by the roundtable itself that may go unnoticed if only one version is read. Initially, the seemingly generous gesture toward open communication—by inviting the colonized to join the colonizers at the discussion table, and encouraging them to raise their concerns ("even complaints") with the censor Furukawa—appears to be a true example of the harmony of *Naisen ittai*. However, as soon as the colonized take up this offer, the conversation is abruptly silenced and we see that this "openness" extends only as far as the invisible boundaries drawn by the colonizers.

Censorship works on the level of publication as well, in which Hayashi's original abrupt ending has been enhanced to appear less awkward and hostile and to construct the appearance of a friendly and natural ending on equal terms, thus suggesting that the conversation was not violently silenced but will continue on at another venue. The addition of the self-referential line about *Bungakukai* in the *Bunkakukai* version further works to erase the existence of the roundtable's other publication in the pages of *Keijō nippō*, and this last statement is punctuated by the addition of eager applause which links everyone in what appears to be a harmonious transcolonial community in the end.

By way of overhearing the two versions of the roundtable together, we ironically arrive at a different reading of the event from what may have been intended. Rather than showing the harmony and intimacy of *Naisen ittai*, with emphasis on the benevolence of the colonizers who have generously permitted such a venue for open dialogue, our reading exposes rather the impossibility of communication in this context. The failure of communication occurs on multiple levels, as revealed in the expression of conflicting desires and visions between the colonizers and the colonized during the event itself, as well as on the pages of the mass-produced print-media transcriptions in which these conflicts have been reproduced and repressed. By reading between the lines of the two versions, we might conclude that this roundtable may be overheard as evidence of the power imbalance between the colonizers and the colonized, foreclosing any semblance of a community built upon open dialogue and freedom of expression to meaningfully engage one another on the way toward a utopian future. However, even such a tentative conclusion must remain inconclusive in our multiply mediated encounter with the *reality* of the colonial past.

EIGHT

TURNING LOCAL

The transcolonial roundtable on "The Future of Korean Culture" among Japanese and Korean cultural figures, which was examined in chapter 7, opened with Hayashi Fusao's recent memories of his train travels into Manchuria via the Korean peninsula. He expressed remorse at his prior tendency—common in Japan at the time—to disregard the significance of Korea in the midst of the heated "Manchuria craze." However, a conversation with his travel companion helped him to realize how truly significant Korea was to the larger imperial endeavor. Hayashi's cautionary tale appealed to the readers of the roundtable about the danger of "overlooking" Korea, Japan's closest neighbor, in their pursuit of new colonial frontiers in Manchuria and Northern China.

Hayashi's allusion to the popular Manchurian craze overtaking the empire at the time through official policies and popular initiatives suggests the importance of considering the intimate links between the various regions in the ever-expanding empire. Many scholars such as Yamamuro Shin'ichi and others have pointed to the entanglements among imperial policies of Korea and Manchuria rather than merely considering binary relations between the metropole and one colony.[1]

Hayashi's impulse was in thinking about how to mobilize Korea through slogans such as *Naisen ittai*; but for further imperial expansions (into Manchuria, etc.), taking account of the complex triangulations across geopolitical divides will help us see relationalities that have subsequently been downplayed or actively forgotten or erased. This chapter examines such triangulations by considering Korea's shifting location in light of the empire's expansions into Manchuria. The role of Korea was anything but fixed as the changing significance of one strategic interest caused anxieties about the loss of significance (and related resources) accorded elsewhere. The question of colonial culture and the role of cultural producers became especially fraught as they were mobilized actively to propagate imperial and wartime expansions. Rather than lying back, as passive objects of representation by imperial cultural producers, cultural producers were to take on active roles showing their support. However, the question of participatory agency of the colonial cultural producer in the unequal imperial discursive space is always a wrought one. In the context of the Japanese empire, this problem must further confront the lure of the discourse of Pan-Asianism in which contiguous neighbors were colonized in the name of mutual collaboration for the common goal of overcoming "Western imperialism."[2]

From Colony (植民地) to Chihō (地方)

With Japan's expansions into the Asian continent, colonial Korean culture in general, and literature in particular, came to take on important roles as both object and agent of such imperial expansions and embodied unstable colonial hierarchies in the region. However, these unsavory relations have since then disappeared from postcolonial cognitive mappings of colonial pasts in the region. This chapter reexamines the colonizer and colonized binary by contextualizing the rise of translated texts packaged as ethnographic "colonial collections" from contact zones within triangulated geopolitical relations in the region. These complex interrelations subsequently resulted in uneasy alignments in the Asia-Pacific in the postcolonial aftermath (see chapter 10).

After the Manchurian Incident (1931), there was a significant expansion of the spatial mapping of the colonies reimagined as "chihō" (peripheral localities, regions, or countrysides within a nation's territory in opposition to its metropolitan centers, such as Tokyo or Seoul)[3] that symbolized the incorporation of the colonies as an extension of the archipelago of Japan proper. This newly imagined and refashioned "imperial community" anticipates new forms of empires that emerged among late-imperial powers, which would obfuscate imperial power relations through strategically inclusive methods.[4] Takashi

Fujitani has compellingly argued that these attempts at inclusion *in practice* embodied the ambivalence and contradictions that arose on both sides of the colonial divide. The gap between the colony and the metropole on the one hand appeared to be shrinking, thanks to imperial assimilation policies and technologies; but on the other hand, a closer look exposes deeper fissures resulting from the need to retain colonial differences in order to maintain imperial hierarchies even as these differences were being disavowed.[5]

In particular, this chapter historicizes the *ethnographic turn* relegated to colonial culture by examining the rise of "colonial collections" as yet another manifestation of mass-produced objects of colonial kitsch. In turn, the complex position of the colonial artist and writer cum (self-)ethnographer situated in between the colony and the metropole embodies yet another contact zone as the artist and work of art become reified as objects of imperial consumer fetishism. In the colonial encounter, the artist as producer and the art object of his or her labor meld into indistinguishable and interchangeable forms as commodities of kitsch. In such relations of colonial alienation, cultural producers struggled to map out spaces as agents of artistic expression, while agency for the colonized artist often meant further alienation through self-ethnography or through mimicry of the colonizer's forms and discourses of racializing colonial subjects as Others.

These important transitions in the location of the colonial artist or writer were occurring in relation to the backdrop of the new frontier of Manchuria, which was opening up new imperialist imaginaries, uneasily and unequally shared by Korea and Japan. These various challenges of representation in the unstable borderlines of the colonial modern encounter had repercussions in the Asia-Pacific that would last long after the collapse of the Japanese empire.

The shifting position of Korean literature (and culture at large) in the Japanese empire toward an ethnographic turn can be traced by examining the ways colonial texts were produced, curated, and consumed for broader markets across the empire's expanding borders. Let us consider, for example, the circulation of Japanese-language newspapers throughout the vast chihō of the empire, expanding from Okinawa to Fukuyama to Taiwan and Manchuria, and the particular ways in which Korean literature in Japanese-language translations was packaged, promoted, and circulated as part and parcel of the trendy Korea Boom. A series of "colonial Korean collections," including the works of Korean migrant writers in Manchuria, that emerged after the Manchurian Incident, and that packaged colonial literature for mass-market consumption throughout the empire, illuminate these colonial modern triangulations.

Korea between Empires

Andre Schmid's description of Korea between empires is an apt one that symbolizes the conundrum of Korea caught in the crossroads of multiple empires, past and present, and the uneasy questions of complicity and collaboration.[6] After Japan established the puppet regime of Manchukuo in the lands contiguous to Korea's northern border, Japan withdrew from the League of Nations as a result of global condemnation of its imperial ambitions and found itself in need of realignment with its colonized fellow Asian subjects. This move complicated colonial Korea's location in the empire. Latecomers to the imperial banquet such as Japan, Russia, and the United States were under tremendous pressure from shifting winds around the globe to couch their imperial ambitions in guises other than brute territorial aggrandizement.

By the time of the Manchurian Incident of 1931, which indicates the shift in Japan's expansionist (and concomitant ethnographic) gaze toward the Asian continent, Korea was already a veteran colony, and a general sense of despair and decadence was pervasive in the air with little hope for independence in the face of increasingly repressive policies of wartime imperial expansions.[7] Shifting imperial policies within Korea by this time were occurring in tandem with Japan's expansions into the Asian continent and beyond, and any attempt at understanding the complexity of experiences in colonial Korea (beyond simplistic binaries of resistance and collaboration) must take into account Japan's invading presence in China and, in particular, in the northeastern regions known as Manchuria. Likewise, China and Manchuria were more than mere backdrops or landscapes to imperial policies unfolding within Korea, but came to take on a significant presence, both real and imagined, in realms ranging from the economic, the political, and the cultural, thus implicating colonial Korea in the next stage of Japan's policies of wartime imperial expansion.

By the 1930s, imperial policies in colonial Korea were fluctuating between assimilation and differentiation toward the making of imperial subjects. Korea's place in the imperial hierarchy was precarious, as an external colony (gaichi) that was simultaneously being subsumed and consumed as a chihō, locality or region, of Japan proper.[8] Korea was being mobilized into the imperial body politic to support Japan's expansions into China and Manchuria through repressive policies of mass migration and war.

As the colony was rigorously incorporated into the discursive space of empire, the spread of modern imperial technologies in education, transportation, and the mass media appeared to link the vast areas of the empire into an imagined community of a broader scale and more complex affiliations than theorized by Benedict Anderson.[9] By this time, Korea was no longer a clearly defined Other but would take on an abject status (see chapter 5), neither clearly inside nor outside the fluctuating boundaries of empire, depending on how Japan itself (as imperial leader or as a fellow Asian brother, for example) was defined. The logic of cultural proximity implicit in imperial slogans such as *Naisen ittai* hailed the harmonious oneness of the colony and metropole, and Japanese-language mass media frequently referred to Koreans as *dōhō* (our brethren), especially in regards to Koreans at the forefront of imperial migration policies into China and Manchuria.[10] While Korea was being yoked to metropolitan Japan through assimilation, it was also being differentiated and aligned to the new frontiers of Manchuria as exemplified in slogans such as *Senman ichinyō* (Korea-Manchuria as one) as well as through renewed interest in what was called Mansenshi (Manchurian-Korean History).

Despite imperial slogans touting the "oneness of Asia," Japan was at the head of this Asian community with the self-appointed role of leading the Rest, which were relegated to peripheral positions aligned in hierarchical concentric circles in relation to one another according to their apparent proximity (spatially, linguistically, racially, for example) to the metropolitan center. Below the surface of the image of the harmonious imperial family roiled dysfunctional relations among these localities in relation to one another, as well as between provincial localities and the metropolitan center.[11]

A hierarchy of concentric circles that seemed to privilege colonial Koreans immediately below Japan but above the rest (Chinese, Manchurians, Mongolians, etc.) in fact exacerbated Korea's precarious position in relation to other colonized subjects. Imperial strategies of divide-and-conquer often foreclosed opportunities for colonies to align themselves, and instead pitted them against one another. Colonial Koreans were often seen as and actually became the front-runners of imperial Japanese aggressions into other territories. They occupied unsavory roles as simultaneous victims and perpetrators of fluctuating and unpredictable imperial policies.

Imperial Mass Media and Circulating Chihō

The circulation of the *chihō-ban* (local or regional edition) of the metropolitan newspaper *Osaka mainichi*, which appeared daily across the vast territories of the Japanese empire, created a spectacle of an imagined imperial community that, by the 1930s, appeared to link the metropolitan center of Tokyo to the peripheries of the Naichi proper: from Kyūshū, Wakayama, Hokkaidō, and

Okinawa all the way to the gaichi hinterlands of Karafuto, Taiwan, Korea, and Manchuria.[12] A series of "Korean Culture Specials" appeared in *Osaka mainichi's* "Korea local edition" (hereafter *Chōsen chihō-ban*) alongside headlines claiming that the ever-shrinking distances between Japan, Korea, and China could be attributed to imperial economic and technological advancements. This juxtaposition on the newspaper's pages visually highlights the link between the imperial consumer trend of the Korea Boom and Japan's Pan-Asianist expansion policies into China and Manchuria, both of which incorporated dual gestures of assimilating and differentiating Korea in the growing empire.

The incorporation of the colony into a chihō—a specific locality—of Japan embodies a conundrum of representation in colonial modernity that paralleled the logic of imperialist nostalgia of colonial kitsch and the Korea Boom examined in chapter 6. Chihō was a nostalgic imaginary space in Japan, both a repository of Japaneseness and of pristine wholeness untainted by foreign infiltrations. Temporally, it also signified a quaint and stagnant *pastness* set apart from the modernity of the rapidly transforming metropolitan center.[13] This dual image of chihō, when it travels outward to the colony (the gaichi), translates in complex ways. On the one hand, the designation of the colonies as chihō seems to assimilate them into a spatial continuum with the metropole, linking the center of empire to its peripheries in a harmonious communal circle. On the other, it relegates the colonies to a position of difference, of perpetual provincialism, always relative and secondary to the standards set in the metropolitan center. Here, I shall examine the implications of the provincialization of Korean culture and of Korean literature specifically as the colony was being incorporated as chihō in the late-colonial period.

The Korea Boom reached the height of its popularity in the late 1930s and the early 1940s when imperial desires for colonial kitsch from Korea seemed insatiable. Previous chapters have discussed the implications behind the consumption of exotic Korea translated for imperial tastes, and the particular conundrum this caused for cultural producers from the colony. What I would like to focus on in this chapter is the intimate link between the inordinate attention paid to such translated cultural products from colonial Korea and Korea's newly supporting role as an in-between location as chihō of empire at a time when Japan's territorial gaze was shifting toward Manchuria and China.

At this time, a new *image* of Korea was being curated and circulated in the imperial mass media; this image paralleled Korea's changing place in the expanding empire post–Manchurian Incident. The increasing attention paid to "the new future of Korea"[14] for the purposes of furthering Japan's imperial expansion into (and war with) China was accompanied by a shift in the cultural realm of the Korea Boom, highlighting exotic and quaint colonial kitsch objects; this shift served to distract imperial audiences from the otherwise increasingly repressive conditions of wartime. The rising numbers of Koreans writing in Japanese and propagating imperialist causes such as war and migration into China were directly linked to Japan's policies of expansion and war in China and Manchuria of the 1930s. Likewise, the Korea Boom, a trend highlighting the duality of both the incorporation and exoticization of Korean culture, began in the early 1930s and rose to the heights of popularity by the late 1930s and early 1940s as Korea's role as middleman was becoming more and more important.

A noteworthy moment in the literary field showing this convergence with the geopolitical changes of the times was Chang Hyŏkchu's debut in the Japanese Bundan. Chang became the first colonial writer to emerge in the Japanese literary field, and he did it with great fanfare in April 1932, just one month after the official foundation of the puppet regime of Manchukuo on March 1 of the same year.[15] Chang first made his mark in the Bundan in 1932 with the nomination of his Japanese-language story "Realm of Hungry Ghosts" for the literary competition sponsored by the major metropolitan journal *Kaizō*.[16] The April issue of *Kaizō*, which announced his nomination (for second place) and published the story,[17] devoted the issue to celebrating the "Manchurian Incident" (1931) and the establishment of Manchukuo (1932). The journal opens with a multipage sepia photo extravaganza fresh from the Manchurian frontier: images and captions narrating the happy coexistence of various ethnic groups (in their exotic native regalia), living in rich fertile lands in the newest localities targeted for imperial expansions. One photograph that depicts the prosperity of Korean migrant farmers in Jiandao does not fail to mention that Koreans outnumber the Chinese in this northeastern chihō of Manchuria. This caption conveniently segues into our own narrative linking Japan's imperialist expansions into China via Manchuria to its policies of imperialization within Korea.

The new role of Korea in the expanding empire was evident throughout the 1930s from mass-migration policies that mobilized Korean migrants into Manchuria in numbers surpassing those of Japanese migration. It was no coincidence that the Korea Boom and the "Manchurian Migration Boom" became simultaneous and parallel imperial trends that marked the shifting position of late-colonial Korea. Scholars have pointed out the strategic role Korean migrants played in the region as extraterritorials under Japanese jurisdiction in the service of Japan's claim to these territories.[18] Japan's imperialist ideologues

FIGS. 8.1. AND 8.2 *Kaizō* issue featuring Chang Hyŏkchu's literary debut opens with a multipage photo op celebrating the first anniversary of the establishment of the puppet regime Manchukuo. Reprinted with permission from Waseda University Archives.

took advantage of this situation and used the presence of Koreans as Japan's imperial subjects to justify territorial infiltration in the name of "protecting our Korean brethren." Many of these Korean migrants may have trickled into Chinese territories when their own lands were confiscated in the wake of forced land reforms and the migration of Japanese settlers into Korea that far surpassed the numbers of European settler colonialism elsewhere;[19] but there was no denying that from the perspective of the Chinese and Manchurians displaced by them, little distinguished the Koreans from Japanese imperialists. One of the most controversial events was the Wanbaoshan Incident in which clashes between the Chinese and the Koreans occurred over water rights near the borders. Japanese officials intervened on behalf of the Koreans, resulting in further violence and resentment across ethnic lines.

In hindsight, the intimate link between imperial policies in Korea and those in China and Manchuria in the 1930s may not be surprising when we consider that policy makers in Japan had their gaze set simultaneously on these areas from early on. As Yamamuro Shin'ichi reminds us, "the Korean peninsula and the terrain of Manchuria and Mongolia beyond it have been compared to a dagger thrust into the side of the body of the Japanese archipelago," and Japan had already fought two wars, with China (1894–1895) and with Russia (1904–1905) for domination in Korea and Manchuria.[20] It was no coincidence that images of Korea began to appear in Japanese popular and official discourses around this time,[21] lending credence to the view that the Korea Boom in Japan arose periodically at significant historical moments in the relations between Japan and Korea.[22]

By the 1930s, however, Japanese imperial ideologies were spearheading further infiltrations into the Asian continent while simultaneously emphasizing the oneness of Asia. Imperial slogans like *Naisen ittai*, *Mansen ichi'nyo* (Harmony of Manchuria and Korea), *Gozoku kyōwa* (Harmony of Five Races), and *Nichimanshi* (Japan-Manchuria-China) inundated the mass media and called for Asians to unite against the common enemy of Western imperialists.[23] That Japan's own imperialist expansions into Asia resembled the imperialism of the West was an inconvenient and irreconcilable irony for many Pan-Asianists in Japan.[24] Assimilationist policies in Korea, including the censorship of the Korean language and the promotion of writers writing in the Japanese language, were part and parcel of this larger context of the empire's ambivalent agenda of violent territorial infiltrations into Asia in the name of uniting Asians within one community. Likewise, such assimilation policies in the colony were never straightforward, as they continued to promote differentiation, even in the name of equality.[25] Such was the backdrop of the predicament of Korean cultural producers who were being promoted and consumed; as part of the Korea Boom, their assimilated Japanese-language writings were simultaneously lauded for their exotic Koreanness and their provincial "local color."

Let us now turn to the pages of the chihō editions of the *Osaka mainichi* that played a significant role in the circulation of the dual logic of assimilation (incorporation) and exoticization (differentiation) throughout the vast regions of empire. By the 1930s, the *Osaka mainichi* was being circulated daily throughout the regions of the Naichi and gaichi, seemingly linking these areas into a spatial continuum of an imagined imperial community of an "empty homogenous time," reminiscent of what Benedict Anderson theorized on the scale of the nation-state. For example, on June 6, 1936,[26] every reader of the *Osaka mainichi* from the vast areas of empire—spanning from the Naichi such as Yamaguchi, Miyazaki, and Kagoshima/Okinawa to the gaichi of Manchuria, Korea, and Taiwan—awoke to see the same front-page layout of their imperial-language newspaper: the pages mirrored one another in their identical layout with the *Osaka mainichi* logo on the top right-hand corner next to the headline of the day, in the same bold font, with the bottom of the page splashed with the identical quarter-page advertisement of Fagōru, a metropolitan medication used for curing infections and available throughout the empire.[27]

The *Osaka mainichi local editions* and other major mass media outlets were selling more than consumer products that symbolized metropolitan advancements throughout the empire. The image of Japan itself as a modern (*modan*), advanced (*shinka*), and scientific (*kagakuteki*) force linking the vast regions of the empire into a harmonious community through technological innovation was being promoted not only through such advertisements but also through the headlines.[28]

For example, the headline on the same day in the *Korea local edition* read: "Completion of oceanic-continental transport corps connecting Japan-Korea-Manchuria,"[29] and in the *Tottori local edition* on the same day, the headline was "Building Resumes on Airport [Connecting] Japan-Manchuria-Korea: Budget Set at 150,000 Yen."[30] In the *Manchuria local edition*, one can see the headline: "Japan-Manchuria—One Mind, One Heart—Medical Examinations Dispatched from the Heart,"[31] celebrating the dispatch of Japanese voluntary medical examiners to Manchuria. Another headline in the same paper reads "From Taiwan to Manchuria—with Just One Ticket,"[32] reporting the opening of better connecting routes to make travel between Taiwan, Manchuria, and Korea much smoother.

FIG. 8.3 Ajinomoto corporate advertisement announces branch stores in
Korea, Dalian, Osaka, and other places. The copy reads "Ajinomoto Team
Services ALL *of Japan*" (*ō-ru Nippon*). Reprinted from Seoul National
University Rare Books Archives.

The overwhelming impression garnered through the pages of the imperial
daily *Osaka mainichi* was that of the empire linked into a smooth continuum
through modern imperial technologies and economic prosperity. For the
readers of the *Osaka mainichi* throughout the ever-expanding empire, the
borderlines of empire seemed to be opening up for the benefit of all.

Advertisements in the newspaper repeatedly promoted a message of economic progress and prosperity enabled by transcolonial commodity and capital. For example, the *Osaka mainichi* on January 3, 1935, was splashed with a full-page advertisement of Ajinomoto, artificial seasoning salt, with a photomontage to juxtapose various imposing Western-style buildings of Ajinomoto branch offices scattered throughout the empire, including Keijō, Dalian, Taiwan, Fengtian, among others. The giant copy shouts: "Ajinomoto Team Services ALL of Japan."[33]

The image of this prosperous and borderless empire was being advertised to the readers of the *Osaka mainichi* through other means as well. Coverage of "'Brilliant Japan' Great Expo" (*Kagayaku Nippon daihakurankai*), for example, was extensive and lasted for weeks in the pages of the *Osaka mainichi* from the Naichi to the gaichi, highlighting the economic prosperity of Japan. A full-page advertisement with a large Japanese flag in bright red stands out on the otherwise muted page, announcing the upcoming event, followed by detailed coverage (including extensive photo ops) throughout the following days.[34] The overwhelming message is of a technologically advanced and modern Japan with exhibits representing economic prosperity.[35] Some highlights were colonial exhibitions, such as the Korea exhibit and the Manchuria exhibit which apparently drew a large crowd.[36] The Korea exhibit displayed exotic objects of *Koreanness* such as kisaeng entertainers and ginseng, as well as information booths with guides for travel and investment opportunities for the entrepreneurial adventurer.[37] The image of Korea as a stagnant object for the pleasure of imperial consumption and visualism is at odds with the image of Japan as rigorously active, economically vibrant, and technologically progressive.

By the 1930s, Japan already had decades of experience promoting its image as one among the colonial powers on the world stage, through active participation in world expos. The expos were competition grounds for imperial powers to display their own advancements and acquisitions vis-à-vis one another, as well as in relation to their colonial possessions which often were displayed as primitive and lacking, in striking juxtaposition to the dynamic, forward-moving image of the colonizing powers.[38] We can see that these deliberate displays of imperial prowess were promoted within Japan proper as well as throughout its empire as propaganda to sell the image of an advanced Japan— from the Naichi to the gaichi.

When flipping through the pages of the *Osaka mainichi local editions*, from the Naichi to the gaichi, the overwhelming message was of a prosperous and transcolonial empire, with fluid borderlines traversed by technological and economic expansion. Through such images linking the vast regions of the empire, *Osaka mainichi* did its part in promoting the image of Japan as advancing into and incorporating unbounded territories, while at the same time commodifying those colonies as exotic Other lands.[39]

Colonial Collection

Here we turn again to an exchange from the "Roundtable on the Future of Korean Culture" (1938):

> MURAYAMA TOMOYOSHI: I agree that we need to preserve Japan's particularities such as Kabuki and puppet theater. We must preserve objects from the past that have uniqueness in the larger world context. Likewise, the traditional arts of Korea must also continue to exist. The government must preserve such objects.
>
> IM HWA: We're not talking about such museum pieces.[40]

The above exchange reveals not only the miscommunication between the colonizer and the colonized, but also the tension between an imperialist nostalgia to collect and preserve antique objects of colonial culture and the colonized writer's attempt to reroute the conversation to the present condition of cultural production in the colony. In the following, I would like to consider the significance of how colonial literature in particular was being collected and curated as mass-produced objects of colonial kitsch for consumption in the empire.

A seemingly endless series of features on various topics of Korean culture began to appear in the local edition of the *Osaka mainichi* in the mid-1930s. Just some examples included a "Collection of Korean Women Writers" following the series on "Collection of Korean Ingénues" (*Hantō shinjinshū*), a serialized essay entitled "On the Future of Korean culture" (*Chōsen bunka no shōrai ni tsuite*), "Collection of Best Works by Korean writers" (*Chōsen sakka kessakushū*), a serial on "Eight Scenic Landscapes of Korea" (*Chōsen hakkei hasshō*), and "Collection of True Stories from Korea" (*Chōsen jitsuwa ban*), as well as a series of photomontages of the Korean landscape. These series were often anticipated by advertisements and gimmicks to draw readers' attention to such upcoming attractions. For example, the series on "Eight Scenic Landscapes of Korea" was published after an ongoing reader poll that lasted for several weeks, in which readers voted for their favorite scenic location in Korea. A running tally of top picks was published on a regular basis, with more and more space on the newspaper's pages dedicated to the gimmick and building up to the anticipated deadline of the final tally.

The purpose of the serials as claimed in advertisements was to introduce Korean culture to Japanese readers. The advertisement announcing the "Collection of Korean Ingénues" proudly claimed the serial as an *epochal* moment, since never before were Koreans given the *opportunity* to represent themselves to Japanese readers because "until now, those who wrote about Korea and Koreans, particularly in Japanese-language newspapers, were mostly the Japanese." The advertisement continues:

> True understanding lies in open communication [*hanashiai*] which this paper will reflect. We have "picked up" [*piku appu*] and commissioned thirty-some scholars, intellectuals, well-known writers, artists, etc., among contemporary Koreans who are truly representative of this culture, and asked each to write, in a few installments, short articles which would not burden them too much. We have entitled it the "Collection of Korean Ingénues" and will have it serialized in the *Korea local edition* of this paper. The contributors are . . . a lineup of almost all of today's young Koreans . . . and we have mapped out here a truly complete shrine of peninsular culture. . . . For Japanese readers, this offers a good resource to gain appreciation for and a chance to rediscover [Korean culture], and for Korean readers, this will not only offer good reading material—literature—by Koreans in the Japanese language to distract from the summer heat, but will without doubt contribute to the development in its culture through research and self-reflection. Each contributor was very cooperative [*hijōni sansei*] in contributing to this paper . . . and eagerly submitted installment after installment. . . . Keep your eyes on this paper. Coming soon, starting July 1![41]

Even keeping in mind the generally hyperbolic nature of advertisement copy, the *Osaka mainichi*'s claims to have collected a "complete shrine of Korean culture" seems to reveal hubris of an imperial scale. However, when considering the breadth and extent of the serial's coverage, the advertisement may not have been exaggerating all that much. The serial planned by the paper seemed to have made every effort in its attempt to offer a ready-made collection of "Korean culture" for easy consumption by its readers. With a wide range of topics—Korean literature, Korean film, trends around the colonial city of Keijō, scientific classification of Korean insects, the trials and tribulations of the life of a kisaeng, musings of a Korean collector of ancient arts, sexual perversions particular to the Koreans—Korea seemed to be captured from all angles.

Susan Stewart's insightful study of "narrative, exaggeration, scale, and significance" may give us helpful clues in assessing the rise of such colonial collections in the empire.[42] The collection, Stewart writes, "is often about containment on the level of its content and on the level of the series [as well as] in a more abstract sense. . . . Those great civic collections, the library and the museum, seek to represent experience within a mode of control and confinement" (161).

Likewise, the colonial collection, like the *Osaka mainichi* series on Korean culture, attempts to display colonial culture in toto through assigning order and classification. Like the museum, the "central metaphor of the collection," the series "strives for authenticity and for closure of all space and temporality within the context at hand" (162). The context at hand is the context of the collection itself, which is privileged while the location of production itself is decontextualized. The context of the production of each contribution and the identity of the individual contributors are stripped of significance, with precedence given to the broad overview of colonial culture as a whole assembled by the series over its individual parts. Each of the contributors is assigned a special field of which he or she becomes a representative native informant. As Stewart writes, "The collection as a whole implies a value—aesthetic or otherwise—independent of the simple sum of its individual members" (166).

An advertisement anticipating a "Collection of Korean Women Writers" places this particular series in a genealogical continuum with all the other Korean culture specials, and echoes the claim of bringing Korean culture to the readers of the *Osaka mainichi*—this time through a total mobilization (*sōdōin*) of women writers in Korea:

> Beginning with the "Collection of Korean Ingénues," "On the Future of Korean Culture," and "Best Works by Korean Writers," as well as the poll on "Eight Scenic Landscapes in Korea," "True Stories from Korea" so on and so forth, the Keijō branch of our company has exerted our utmost efforts, to mutually communicate, through one work of art after another and through discussions with ingénues, to contribute to the advancement of Korean culture by introducing the reality [*jitsujō*] and landscapes [*fūbutsu*] of our peninsula [*waga hantō*] near and far. . . . Now, for the first time ever, the much anticipated "Collection of Korean Women Writers" will begin serialization from April 15. Nine women writers active in the Korean literary circles today have been totally mobilized [*sōdōin*]. From short stories, to poetry, to essays . . . each writer is now throwing herself into producing a true gem . . . which we eagerly await.[43]

FIG. 8.4 Colonial Korean Women Writers Collection. Reprinted with permission from Seoul National University Rare Books Archives.

Here, too, the collective as a whole takes precedence over the identity of individual contributors. In fact, the advertisement itself features photographs of nine writers but the actual series featured only seven with no explanation about why the serial claiming "total mobilization" was curtailed after the seventh story, Kang Kyŏngae's "Changsan Bay."

The two advertisements introduced above proudly claim to have made pioneering contributions in bringing "our Korea" (including its landscape and its customs) directly to the readers of the *Osaka mainichi*. Such an epochal feat was purportedly accomplished through open discussions or exchanges with the Korean contributors who were apparently each and every one eager and busy at their pens, even as the advertisements were going to press. Both advertisements highlight the significance that such contributions would no doubt make to the "advancement of Korean culture."

What seems significant is that such exaggerated claims were made possible only through total disregard for the actual context and circumstances of production behind each individual contribution. The historical context in which Korean writers were "encouraged" to represent themselves in the Japanese language—at a time when Korean-language productions were increasingly repressed under censorship—may not have been seen as either "opportunities" or as "open exchanges" by some of the colonized writers. What Stewart describes as the collection's tendency toward "reframing of objects" through a "manipulation of context," which decontextualizes the circumstances of production, might be relevant here.

The erasure of the labor of translation involved in publishing this series in the imperial language is especially worth noting. Most, if not all, of the contributions to the "Collection of Korean Women Writers" were first written in the Korean language and published previously in Korean-language journals. The burden of translation was on the colonized writers to offer up Korean cultural products to Japanese readers who merely sat back and consumed them effortlessly in their own language. However, the burden and labor of translation are nowhere evident in the series, making it appear as if the stories were originally written naturally and effortlessly in Japanese by the writers themselves. Here we can recall Stewart's observation on the collection from a faraway yet comparable context: "Objects are naturalized into the landscape of the collection itself . . . made cultural by classification . . . naturalized by the erasure of labor and the erasure of context of production" (156). The image of colonial writers eagerly writing in Japanese, apparently in real time, here and now, even as the advertisement was going to press, and being excited about the opportunity to truly represent themselves in the Japanese language, is produced through a misrepresentation of the actual circumstances of the original production of each story in the Korean language, and also through the erasure of the subsequent labor of translation that enabled such "open communication" in the empire. When we keep in mind that the vast majority of the population in the colony, and in particular women, were severely limited in their access to the "paper language" of empire, the language of officialdom and power, it becomes clear that a harmonious linguistic community of empire is an illusion. In fact, only a few of the featured women writers published other Japanese-language literary works, making it highly unlikely that most of these women writers were even capable of writing literary works in Japanese. The image of open communication and cultural exchange, purported by the advertisement, has been constructed through selective blindness toward the uneven linguistic context in which colonized writers had to appeal to metropolitan readers in the language of empire. The fact that these translated encounters were overwhelmingly one-sided, with the burden of representation on the shoulders of the colonized, is not recognized.

Far from creating spaces of open exchange and communication, the series were carefully planned propaganda not to contribute to the "development of Korean culture" as they claimed, but rather to subsume Korean culture in the Japanese language for the consuming passions of Japanese readers. In other words, the Japanese mass media curated an appearance of a united and harmonious community throughout the empire by erasing the actual violence of the agenda of assimilation from its pages. From the perspectives of the colonized, particularly those who could not read or write in Japanese, the privileging of Japanese-language media only meant further alienation from the sites of cultural production, knowledge, and communication.

In this light, the advertisement that boasted of making an epochal contribution to the advancement of Korean culture by benevolently offering colonial writers a stage seems not only overly self-important but utterly misplaced. Such articulations privileging the very subject that has assembled such a collection replaces the "narrative of production" by the "narrative of the collection" and replaces the "narrative of history" with the "narrative of the individual subject—that is, the collector himself" (Stewart, *On Longing*, 156). In our particular case, the point of view of the *Osaka mainichi* takes precedence as the subject in charge of curating and introducing Korean culture, whose producers themselves are not accorded individual subjectivity but are merely displayed, much like their cultural productions, like stagnant museum pieces for metropolitan audiences.

In the context of discussion, Im Hwa's remark at a transcolonial roundtable about "The Future of Korean Culture," from which I quoted earlier, seems to take on added significance. It is worth recalling here that when metropolitan critics tried to assuage the concerns of the colonized writers about the devaluation and disappearance of Korean culture by pointing to Japan's commitment to preserve Korean relics, Im Hwa retorts, "We're not talking about such museum pieces."[44] It appears that what mattered for colonized writers was the freedom to continue to pursue and develop cultural productions for the present and future, while metropolitan concerns were limited to the illusion of "knowing" *Korea* stagnant and "as is," captured and fixed in the collection.[45]

The decontextualization of the conditions of production in which Korean writers were writing in or being translated into Japanese, then, erases the

FIG. 8.5 Cover of *Asahi gurafu* featuring a colonial Korea exhibition.
Special thanks to Jonathan Abel.

social relations of colonial unevenness. This eradication includes the very
imperial condition in which individual cultural producers and their products
were simultaneously being reified into collections of colonial kitsch, or exotic
objects, fetishized to represent colonial culture in toto, regardless of different
individual histories.[46]

The imperial rhetoric in which the colony was to "become One" with the
metropole was silently predicated on the alienation of the colonial cultural
producer, as both the producer and his or her product were becoming one as
colonial kitsch objects of imperial consumption. Each contributor was signifi-

cant only insofar as he or she was representing an element of Korean culture, the whole of which was being curated for imperial audiences. In the logic of the colonial collection, differences in individual histories were irrelevant; thus, writers like Kang Kyŏngae from a peasant background, with severely limited access to the metropolitan center, were placed in a position of equivalence to other writers of more privileged conditions, constructing an illusion of colonized individuals reified to represent merely a piece of the larger colonial collection of Korean culture.

I would like to conclude the chapter by linking Stewart's provocative suggestion about the collection as offering a metaphor of production not as "the earned" but as "the captured" to the context of the reification of colonial culture under discussion here (164). Stewart writes that unlike the souvenir to which we must go, "the collection comes to us. The collection says that the world is given; we are inheritors, not producers, of value" (164). The imperial hubris with which the colonizers tried to see and ascertain the whole picture of the colony, through collecting, curating, measuring, rearranging, manipu-lating, and finally even by forcing the colonized to "represent themselves" for imperial consumption ironically made them blind to the excruciating labor of production under which the colonized writer was working. It was in such a context of apparently open borders and fluid movements in which colonized producers were left *free* to search for a stage from which to voice themselves, even if it was more and more being restricted to translations into the imperial language and market, and only in mass circulation as trendy commodities for the imperial gaze.

NINE

FORGETTING MANCHURIAN
MEMORIES

As seen in previous chapters, Korea's shifting location in the Japanese empire was intimately linked to geopolitical changes occurring in Northern China and Manchuria. In fact, as many scholars have pointed out, these triangulations in the region among Japan, Korea, and China/Manchuria were extant long before Japan's colonial invasions into the peninsula and the rest of the continent. However, regional connections remained obfuscated for decades as a result of postcolonial and Cold War divides imposed with the abrupt collapse of the Japanese empire in 1945. This chapter joins recent developments in scholarship to reframe the history of the region beyond ongoing divides.

The life and works of Kang Kyŏngae, a colonial-era writer from Korea who migrated to Manchuria, offers us an important vantage point from which to think about the intersections in the region and their divided legacies into the postcolonial present. The complexities of Kang Kyŏngae's corpus and its fate in the literary canons of the divided postcolonial Koreas will be read to consider the significance of what is *left out* in a simple binary reading of nationalist resistance and pro-Japanese collaboration.

The Korea Boom we have been examining throughout the book included the rise of Manchurian frontier literature by colonized Koreans who migrated during the late-colonial era. This body of works defies the binary logic of national resistance and colonial collaboration that became the dominant way that the colonial past was re-membered in the postcolonial aftermath. Furthermore, such binaries have mapped the boundaries of inclusion and exclusion of the canon of postcolonial literatures divided by nationality.

By rereading the location of Kang Kyŏngae and her Manchurian frontier writings and their precarious relationship to the national literary canon, this chapter argues that such binary thinking is woefully inadequate in taking account of colonial Korea's complex entanglements with the rest of Asia, Japan, and the West. Furthermore, this chapter examines the ways postcolonial re-ification of authentic representations of colonial reality (*singminji ŭi silsang*), primarily of the colonial peasantry (to signify national resistance to Japanese imperialism), ironically and unwittingly mimics the imperial demand for reified colonial authenticity from these same texts and subjects during the colonial era. I would like to examine the significance of the ironic similarities between what I call the postcolonial regime of realism, a politicized demand for the representation of colonial reality (which often means an exposé of colo-nial exploitation by Japan and colonial resistance by Korea), and the demand for colonial authenticity that was placed on these same texts in the context of their production and consumption in the empire during the Korea Boom, by reading Kang as a seemingly unlikely, yet exemplary, case in point.

Kang Kyŏngae is considered one of the most representative writers of the colonial period, one of the few who were canonized in North and South Ko-rean national literary histories. For example, in order to commemorate the one hundredth anniversary of Kang's birth, scholars from North and South Korea came together to publish a compendium in her honor. The cover of the book reads as follows: "Kang Kyŏngae rose above the perspective of a lower-class woman, and through her acute ability to see colonial reality as no other writer of her times, came to take her place in the modern literary history lauded as a paramount author of realism from both North and South Korea."[1]

Further, as a woman writer of peasant background, it is unlikely that she had the opportunity to go to the metropole or learn to write literary works in Japanese. In fact, her limited access to the metropolitan center of imperial cul-ture and in turn from its contamination helped to raise her in the postcolonial aftermath to the level of a national symbol of authentic colonial literature of heroic resistance, at a time when most elite male writers revealed an unsavory desire for the metropolitan center in some form or another.[2] In fact, with recent attention turned to Japanese-language writings by colonial Koreans, one of the most disturbing aspects from the perspectives of nationalist literary history is the discovery of Japanese-language texts by some of the most revered writers of the national canon; this triggers the need to reassess these writers along the binary of resistance and collaboration all over again, with the line merely redrawn. My purpose is to reread Kang's works, not to relocate sites of collaboration, but in order to interrogate the inadequacy of the binary logic of resistance and collaboration which nonetheless still dominates the study of colonial literature and hinders our understanding of it.

Kang Kyŏngae's place in the national canon was not always self-evident as it seems today. For example, Kang and her stories, like all writers who came to be affiliated with the North, were banned in South Korea until 1988. Most of these banned North Korean writers had actually gone north (and they make up a new genre of *wŏlbuk chakka*—writers who went north, in South Korea) around the time of the partition and during the tumultuous liberation period. But Kang Kyŏngae, who died in 1944 before liberation, was censored along with them by association to her husband, who became a major figure in North Korea in the postliberation era.

In fact, as a woman writer, Kang's relationship to the patriarchal literary field in colonial Korea was often mediated through her relationships to the men in her life. As a woman writer from a poor peasant background, she was removed from the institution of literature, not only in the metropole but in the colony as well. After Kang's father passed away, her mother married a well-to-do elderly man and essentially labored as his servant. Kang's biography often includes the fact that she learned to read by picking up books discarded by other people; she had severely limited access to education.[3] She was able to go to school for a few years on the charity of her stepsister's husband (21–24). Another famous episode is that Kang approached Yang Chudong (1903–1977), a famous literary figure in colonial Korea after he'd given a moving speech, and learned to write while living with him in Seoul (35).[4] Her first published work was in the journal *Kŭmsŏng*, which was edited by Yang Chudong himself.

Despite Japan's increasingly severe assimilationist promotion of the Japanese language through colonial education, at a time when "80 percent of the population was still illiterate in their mother tongue" as Kim Saryang wrote as late as 1940,[5] for a woman of Kang's background, even access to imperial propaganda of assimilation was severely curtailed. It was highly unlikely that Kang had access to the imperial language to the extent of being able to write fluidly in it.[6] While it is common knowledge that many Korean intellectuals from the colonial era studied abroad in Japan, it is important to keep in mind that most of them were men. The women who became writers or notable cultural figures otherwise at the time were usually from elite backgrounds, and some of them did study abroad in Japan, although they were so exceptional that they would make headlines or society gossip columns.[7]

Nowhere in her biography does it indicate that Kang had the opportunity to go to Japan; and in fact, she migrated in the other direction, north to Manchuria. It is interesting that her abject status as a peasant woman with limited access to colonial education actually helped solidify her now-undisputed canonical status as a national writer, untainted by collaboration with Japan. Particularly by the late-colonial period, when more and more Koreans of elite backgrounds, including the majority of male writers, were being mobilized for and being implicated in the imperial process, Kang had the makings to become a symbol of national authenticity (and resistance).[8] One by one, canonical Korean male writers were being thrown into question: the last shock being beloved and revered Yi Kiyŏng.[9] In the case of the majority of the male writers who studied abroad in Japan, there is always the anxiety from the perspective of the national literary canon that a new pro-Japanese source will be discovered to implicate them as collaborators.

Kang Kyŏngae wrote from the perspective of dispossessed peasants and women, and the struggles of her subjects against exploitation were easily sublimated to symbolize the collective struggle of the nation against Japanese imperialism in the postliberation canons. As can be seen in the subtitle of the South Korea section of the North and South Korea Centennial Compendium, which reads "Consistency of the People's [*minjung*] Solidarity and Anti-Japanese Resistance," one of the hegemonic readings of Kang is as a representation of the solidarity of the people standing in opposition to imperialism.[10]

Another factor that helps Kang's canonical status is the spatial imaginary of Manchuria that pervades her writings, most of which were penned as a migrant in that region. Manchuria occupies a deeply contested space in the Korean nationalist imaginary: on one hand, it is idealized as a repository of a once-glorious Korean heritage. Particularly during the colonial period, when heroes were desperately lacking, the brave and strong imperial history of the ancient kingdoms of Puyŏ and Koguryŏ, which stretched deep into the continent, were glorified synchronically as a nostalgic past before the decline into ruin that culminated in colonization in the historicist view.[11] Manchuria, by the colonial period, also symbolized a space of colonial resistance of nationalist guerrilla fighters, often in alliance with Chinese communists. The most famous was Kim

Il-Sung [Ilsŏng] (1912–1994) himself who would later take the leadership of the DPRK largely based on such heroic credentials.[12]

Thus, Manchuria, as a geographic imaginary in colonial Korea in general, and in Kang's texts in particular, has been thus far imagined largely as a site of Korean resistance to Japanese imperialism, and a place to which Korean peasants migrated to escape exploitative imperial policies. Stories of their harsh living conditions, as described in Kang's texts, exposed in a realistic manner the victimization of Korean peasants displaced by imperial policies from their homes into severe, uncharted frontiers.

But on the other hand, there remains another less savory aspect that has only recently been tapped into by scholars.[13] Recent scholarship on Manchuria has tried to complicate the position of Koreans in the region, which cannot easily be comprehended through a simplistic binary of resistance versus collaboration. In fact, imperial migration policies transplanted thousands of peasants in line with Japan's expansionist agenda. For Korean peasants whose livelihoods were severely exploited through imperial policies, Manchuria became a land of opportunity—kingly paradise (*wangdo nakt'o*), and a new heaven and earth (*sin ch'ŏnji*)—a territory inscribed as a clean slate.[14] For Chinese peasants displaced by imperial migration policies, however, there was little distinguishing the Koreans from the Japanese imperialists. In fact, Japanese imperial ideologues strategized about the role Korean migrants would play as frontrunners of Japanese imperialist expansions, and often intervened in ethnic conflicts on the side of the Koreans in the name of representing and advocating for imperial subjects when the underlying motive was to expand Japanese influence in the region.[15] Considering this broader context now available through new scholarship, it is necessary to reread Kang Kyŏngae's texts beyond the limits of nation-centered readings. The popularity of her story "Changsan Bay" (Chōzangan J; Changsankot, K), which was reproduced repeatedly as part and parcel of the Korea Boom, offers us one important site to examine the complexities of Kang's oeuvre when contextualized among multiple borderlines.

Paradoxes of Colonial Reality

The three stories I will examine closely here are "Salt" (Sogŭm),[16] "Opium" (Mayak),[17] and "Changsan Cape," which all reveal the anxieties of imperial borderline encounters and raise complex questions about the triangulated position of Korea in between Japan and China, rather than a simple binary of nationalist resistance versus collaboration as has been commonly assumed.

"SALT"

"Salt" was serialized in the women's journal *Sin kajŏng* (New home), from May to October 1934, with the ending inked out by the colonial censor's heavy strokes. The ink marks remain brooding evidence of the violent censorship to which Kang's and others' texts were subjected during the colonial period. It also produces various speculations about what may have invited the disapproval of the censor's eyes to deserve such a banishing judgment. Korean literary history of the colonial period has to be constructed out of such fragments of texts passed down—embodying the vast onslaught of colonial censorship. In the face of such "wounded" texts, critics turned their keen eyes toward the project of looking for traces of heroism and resistance at a time when heroes were sorely lacking.

Kang Kyŏngae's texts like "Salt," already decorated with the badge of censorship, written in the Korean language when everyone else seemed to be writing in Japanese, were natural sites to look for such evidence of resistance to be raised to the level of the new postliberation national canon. Let's take a closer look at the story:

Pushed to the limits of existence—losing her husband and son to the confusing political strife in Manchuria, and losing her daughters to poverty-inflicted disease—the protagonist, Pongyŏm's Mother,[18] turns to smuggling salt across the border of Korea and China. Salt is a controlled substance in the empire, under the jurisdiction of the Governor General Monopoly Bureau in the empire.[19]

What was abundant and available for easy consumption in Korea, migrants in Manchuria discover, is now tightly controlled by the empire's economic policies across newly defined imperial borders, and they barely have enough salt to flavor their daily dishes. The fact that she could not provide satisfactory meals for her family is a concern that continues to haunt Pongyŏm's Mother after everyone dies. Suffering from political strife and economic hardship, she finds work as a servant in the house of a wealthy Chinese landlord who exploits her labor power, then rapes and impregnates her before expelling her from his house. Thus the story describes the precarious position of Korean migrants in Manchuria, including their conflicts with the Chinese and the Japanese.

Pongyŏm's Mother suffers tragic losses in her family due to the turbulent, shifting power relations in the empire. As a colonized woman migrant, she is multiply alienated from the actual ideological forces behind such global movements, but nonetheless, her life is affected on every level. After one personal tragedy after another, she decides to take matters into her own hands, however limited, to smuggle salt across the border for the sake of survival. When the line of smugglers she is following is suddenly stopped by a band of unidentified ideologues, Pongyŏm's Mother is only concerned about the fate of her contraband goods and her economic well-being:

> "Who's there? Hands in the air and freeze, or I'll shoot!" With this scream, blinding blue lights flashed on their faces. The glare of the light felt like a stabbing blade or a firing squad, and their arms lifted up automatically.
>
> Now they'll steal our salt! Each smuggler had the same thought. They were resigned to their fate, but they wondered if these were communists or bandits. They hoped they were one or the other because communists and bandits, if you begged them, sometimes didn't steal your salt.[20]

As can be seen, the smugglers are not concerned with the ideologies that are merely hindrances in their struggle for basic survival. Their utmost concern is to return safely to their homes and to deliver their goods without confiscation. The content of the speech does not seem to matter much either. In fact, after the initial call: "Everyone! Do you know why you are forced to lose sleep and carry these burdens of salt?" (391), the rest of the speech is drowned out as the thoughts of the smugglers take over:

> They're communists, they thought. They won't take our salt. [The smugglers] thought about how to plead their case. The voice still flowed out from afar. The longer the time passed, the more they kept wishing they would hurry and shut up and let them go. There was a watchtower either below this slope or just beyond, so they were anxious about getting caught listening to the speech of the communists. Listening to the speech, Pongyŏm's Mother suddenly recalled the day she lived in Sandeguo, when she had followed Pongyŏm to school and listened to the teacher's speech. This voice was similar to that teacher's. She lifted her head suddenly and stared over beyond. Only pitch darkness held them in and she could only hear the voice. She wondered if her [son] Pongsik might be among them, but she shook the thought off. She told herself, no, Pongsik is not like the average kid, he's too smart to get involved with the likes of them. She felt better about Pongsik but kept thinking that this was all a ploy to steal their salt, and she started to fear that they might kill them after the speech. (391)

Here it is clear that Pongyŏm's Mother's mind is preoccupied with whether these voices in the dark will let them pass with their salt bundles, rather than paying attention to the content of the ideological message. Like the other smugglers, Pongyŏm's Mother has been merely concerned with her everyday reality. She is driven to a criminal act, trespassing imperial borders under the circumstances, and is not attempting to subvert the law for ideological reasons. These ideologues in the woods let them go after the speech, and Pongyŏm's Mother returns to her home safely. In the ironic ending, we find that her home itself is not safe from the intrusion of imperial policies.

> Two suits had taken out the sacks of salt and were glaring down at her. She knew in a lightning instant that they were policemen, and she trembled like a leaf.
> "Hand over your salt license!" There was a salt license written up by the officials [kwannyŏm]. She felt suffocated and everything went black. And she noticed her senses were heightened just like the time she was struggling with all her might not to spill her sacks of salt into the Tumen River. The navigator had grabbed her hand then but Ah! Who would dare pounce on these men wielding guns and sabers to save her now? "Wench! You've been smuggling unlicensed salt [sanyŏm], haven't you? Get up this minute!" (393)

Here, we see that Pongyŏm's Mother has broken the imperial law, disregarding the distinction between "licensed salt" controlled by the Governor General and sanctioned by the empire, and "unlicensed salt" illegally smuggled by individuals. The difference is between legitimate international trade in the name of empire, and illegitimate smuggling for private profit. However, such distinctions, like the other political ideological distinctions that have taken the lives of her husband and son (each seeming ironically to fight for opposing sides in the shifting tides of the times) are blurry, confusing, and thus rendered meaningless for someone like her, who is multiply alienated and removed from the production of such laws.

For Pongyŏm's Mother, her concerns are on the level of the everyday; she is simply aware of the lack of a daily necessity and of her need to survive. There is demand and she is desperate enough to take the necessary risks to fill it. For her, it is simply a matter of survival and basic economics of supply and demand, but her actions have unknowingly crossed into the complex realm of transcolonial trade laws of the empire's monopolistic capitalism.

The intrusion of the public/official in the private mirrors the doubleness of the seemingly fluid borders opened up in the context of empire which is simultaneously strictly policed and under surveillance through modern technologies. The story ends with the following:

> The police knew right away that this was not officially sanctioned salt. That's why they were screaming at her and grabbing at her hands. Suddenly her body burned and last night xx at the xxxxx no, the annoying speech xxxxxxx xxxxxxxxxxxxxxxxxxxxxxxxxxxxxxxxxxxxxxxxxxxxxxxxxxxxxxxxxxxxxxx xxxxxxxxxxxxxxxxxxxxxxxxxxxxxxxxxxxxxxxxxxxxxxxxxxxxxxxxxxxxxxxx xxxxxxxxxxxxxxxxxxxxxxxxxxxxxxxxxxxx in the darknessx xxxxxxxxxxxxxx xxxxxxxxxxxxxxxxxxxxxxxxxxxxxxxxxx could fight. No xxxxxxxxxxxxxxx xxxxxxxxxxxxxxxxxxxxxxxxxxxxxxxxxxxxxxxxx xxxxxxxxxxxxxxxxxx climbed. She jumped up.[21] (393–94)

As we can see, the ending of the story is unreadable, erased by the violent marks of colonial censorship. If this story is a representation of colonial reality as has been lauded, the censor's ink strokes hint at the fact that this is a reality to which we have severely restricted access from textual and metatextual limitations. On the textual level, the story is bounded by the narrow perspective of Pongyŏm's Mother. What is significant is that this perspective, which the story repeatedly hints at, is severely curtailed. A woman of limited means, she simply does not have access to the various contending ideologies at work around her. The story is more about the utter lack of access to this reality which nevertheless affects the lives of such subaltern characters in the most intimate ways.

The story, while depicting such "impairments" (Choi Kyeong-hee), further embodies other limitations. Pongyŏm's Mother is the only realistic character in the story, and the rest are relegated to stereotypes. The wealthy Chinese man and the imperial policemen, the voices in the woods, are all in effect faceless entities playing supporting roles in the melodrama of Pongyŏm's Mother's trials and tribulations. The text completely elides the complex role of Korean migrants in Manchuria at the time, when imperial migration policies were actively transplanting Koreans into China as a way to make room for the incoming Japanese presence into Korea as well as the Koreans' role as Japan's forerunners into China.

The raising of Kang's story in the national literary canon as a representation of colonial reality follows the demands of what I call the postcolonial regime of colonial realism. This dominant postcolonial rereading of the colonial past was enabled through a selective myopia that privileged the nationalist perspective and sublimated characters like Pongyŏm's Mother as symbolic representations of Korean national suffering over a more complex understanding of the imperial context in which Koreans were not simply victims. Such an image of colonial reality equated to the representation of national victimhood in Kang's texts and her position in the national literary canon have been enhanced through selective readings and censorship. In both North and South Korea, Kang's texts were notably altered by "editors" who reconstructed them to appear more nationalistic and "resistant" than what Kang herself wrote. Conversations and words in Japanese were "translated" into Korean, freely erasing the bilingual nature of the original.[22] It is ironic that another layer of censorship occurred yet again in postcolonial nationalist attempts at reconstructing the parts erased by colonial censors.[23] For example, in a North Korean version, the ending is restored to read as follows:

> As Pongyŏm's Mother was being dragged away by the policeman, suddenly the thought of the speech she had listened to absent-mindedly on the mountain the other day came to her. She felt she finally realized the workings of the world.
>
> And she knew that the propaganda of the Japs about the evils of Communists were all lies, and she knew without doubt that the rumor that Pongsik had been killed by the Communists was also a big lie. What Pandung [Chinese landowner] had told her about Pongsik having been arrested by the regional patrols was an unbelievable trick, and she knew that Pongsik had become part of the Communists and was fighting along with them in the mountains. She knew all this because Pongsik was an intelligent and brave young man! No longer with fear nor sorrow, Pongyŏm's Mother stood with head held high and walked on ahead.[24]

In this new version, we see a much more politicized woman, certain of who were the good guys and the villains of the empire. This version unmistakably posits the "Japs" and the Chinese landowner as the unscrupulous ones who were responsible for her misery and the Communists as the true heroes with whom the story's sympathies lie. Such rewriting was not an isolated incident. In fact, the position of Kang as an undisputed writer of colonial reality and resistance has been made possible by several postliberation redactions to her stories.[25] Such postcolonial constructions not only add another layer of censorship to the texts, censorship which elides the complexities that the texts originally embody, but also ironically reduce the reality effect by fabricating a semblance of coherent nationalist ideology where there was none, and even unwittingly ameliorate the damaging extent of colonial censorship by appearing to have mended the fragments into a semblance of a whole story.

"OPIUM"

"Opium" is another story that confounds the inherited reading of Kang Kyŏn-gae's corpus as representations of colonial reality along the binary of national resistance and colonial collaboration. It begins with Podŏk's Mother, following her husband in the dark woods, not knowing where he is leading her. She had followed him out reluctantly, too afraid of him to even ask where they were heading.[26] It is a long, difficult, and "blind" journey in the dark in which her vision is impaired,[27] and in the absence of sight, her imagination runs wild about what lies ahead. Podŏk's Mother's bodily impairments (inability to speak and lack of vision and clarity about where her husband is leading her) allude to the lack of access and control over what her future holds, and as will soon become apparent, lack of control over her own body.[28]

The reader finds out with Podŏk's Mother the true horror of the situation: her husband, an opium addict, has sold her off to a Chinese shop owner. The horrific scene of recognition of her trafficked fate as an object of exchange in the unsavory economic contract between the two colonized men in the empire comes with the disappearance of her husband and the appearance of the Chinese shop owner to take his place.

Podŏk's Mother attempts a desperate escape after a night in which she endures violent rape and torture by the Chinese shop owner.[29] But the wounds inflicted on her body in the violent encounter prove to be fatal. However, even as she is dying, she seems to be concerned with sacrificing her body for her child and is filled with worry about her husband's fate under imperial law. This ending is linked to how the story began, with the husband being kicked around and arrested by an imperial policeman after the death of Podŏk's Mother. The husband tries to explain that he has registered as an opium addict, but the policeman shouts, "The law will not forgive the likes of you, you woman killer!" (221).

TRAFFICKING OPIUM

The irony of the situation in "Opium," in which justice for the dead colonized woman seems to come clothed in the uniform of empire, becomes further significant when we consider the double-sided opium policies in the empire. According to researchers, opium was strategically grown in Korea for export to the other colonies.[30] Farmers in Korea were encouraged to grow it for the expanding imperial markets, and numerous Koreans overseas were involved in drug trafficking between the borders. The role of Korean migrants in opium trafficking is a shady part of transnational histories that has been little researched.[31]

The Japanese empire's role in this exchange is no less savory. Opium was strictly controlled in the empire, under the jurisdiction of the top governing organizations including the Home Ministry (Naimushō) and through various offices of the Governor General, in an established imperial monopoly.[32] However, those who became addicted in this context of rampant opium farming and trafficking were severely disciplined and prosecuted by the same laws. The overall doubled structure of imperial opium policies actively encouraged its production and sales under policies of a clandestine imperial monopoly on the one hand, and on the other, of strictly controlled illegal traffickers and addicts as the very culprits of resulting social ills. The prevalence of opium as a mounting societal problem in colonial Korea can be seen in the appearance of opium-addicted characters in many literary works of the time.[33] The double standards of imperial opium policies resulted in a rise in the presence of opium to unprecedented proportions.[34]

In such a context, many Koreans as traffickers were in effect simultaneously both perpetrators and victims of the system, and such ambivalent roles complicated their positions in the imperial economy, perched between China and Japan, particularly as the empire expanded further into China. It is important to note that while border crossings in the empire were enabled (albeit unequally) by the imperial economy linked to the colonies, this also brought about the circumstances in which different nationalities could intermix in a cosmopolitan context. At the same time, the situation gave rise to the clashes among these groups in these very encounters. Such clashes are evident in many literary works of the time—for example, through beastly depictions of the Chinese in this and in other stories, through which we get a glimpse of less than humane or harmonious interactions in the context of empire. Racist depictions of the Chinese in stories by colonial Korean writers reveal the actual unbridgeable distances that still existed between different groups of people, distances that were based on age-old race conflicts as well as those newly provoked and enabled by the realignment of imperial hierarchies and systematic discriminatory policies.

Such ambivalence in the position of the colonized in relation to imperial law in this "Opium" story is further complicated when refracted through the spectrum of gendered hierarchies. In the story, it is clear from the beginning that problems for the family began when the husband became addicted to opium after he lost his job.[35] Emasculated thus due to an unexplained shift in the economy at large, the husband is clearly a victim of an unpredictable social and political climate, and after failed attempts at suicide in his despair, he has turned to opium. While the point of view of the storyteller sympathizes with his plight, he is also shown to be a perpetrator who turns his emasculated victimhood against his own wife in order to feed his addiction, and finally is shown as being persecuted by imperial law.

This story also shows the doubled nature of the ways imperial law and economic policies infiltrate the lives of the characters on the level of storytelling. The story is somewhat reminiscent of the conventions of suspense fiction, holding back information in the beginning, keeping the reader and the character "in the dark" and using flashbacks. We find out early on that opium is the initial cause of the breakdown in the family; this sets the stage for the family discord to come. The end is linked to the very beginning of the story in which the husband is being kicked around and arrested by the imperial policeman, shouting, "But I am registered!"—though unable to "register" the fact that he is being arrested not for his opium addiction but for causing the death of his wife.

However, unlike a satisfactory suspense story, this one refuses a neat ending. Perhaps not unrelated to censorship at work at the time, direct references to the imperial opium policies are avoided. The significance of some of the allusions, such as the registration of opium addicts in the colony, remains suspended if the reader is not aware of the policies that required addicts to register their names for the surveillance of the imperial government. Further, the irony that justice for the dead mother comes clothed in the uniform of the empire is easily missed if one is not aware that policies of the same empire have actively promoted opium harvesting in the colony which, as the story points out, was the true cause of the economic downturn and breakdown of the family in the first place.

Once the reader is made aware of the double-sided nature of imperial laws, the story refuses to be read simply as imperial justice coming to save the day by accusing the criminal—the brutal, colonized husband. This story rather hints at the in-between position of Koreans in the empire as both victims and perpetrators of imperial policies. In particular, the significance of the victim-turned-perpetrator in the character of the husband, and the logic of domestic violence in the realm of the intimacy of the home, are directly linked to and mirror social inequalities in the context of the official ideology of the family system of the empire in disharmony rather than harmony as espoused in imperial slogans. Caught in the unsavory homosocial contract among the male characters, each representing a cog in the imperial economic bloc, the female body becomes the sacrificial site where their violent power struggles converge. This reading (from the point of view of Podŏk's Mother) refuses the simple binary of resistance and collaboration altogether, but raises more questions about the shifting roles of colonial subjects in the expanding empire.

"CHANGSAN CAPE"

When the Japanese-language story "Changsan Cape" by Kang was discovered posthumously, one might have expected a debate about how it may fit into the nationalist canon with the rest of Kang's corpus. However, the text was quickly translated into Korean and introduced to readers in Korea as follows: "This work, set in a small fishing-farming village in Hwanghae Province dominated by Japanese monopoly capital, realized the theme of solidarity between Korean and Japanese proletariats [minjung] by overcoming racial prejudice."[36]

The story, set in the poor fishing village of Monggŭmp'o and surrounded by the slopes of Mt. Chang, begins with Hyŏngsam, a poor Korean fisherman who has recently lost his wife and is left with the burden of two starving little girls, heading listlessly toward the fishing cooperative in the hopes of begging for his job back. He had been laid off by Yoshio, the Japanese leader of the co-op, after Hyŏngsam and his friend Shimura got caught in a typhoon and ended up ruining their fishing net. Since then Shimura has been drafted to fight in the war in Manchuria, and with his only Japanese friend gone, there is little hope for Hyŏngsam to regain his old job; he has no other means to make a living. The area has been taken over by the Japanese conglomerate Mitsui, and it seems that even the fish and the trees now have owners.[37] Hyŏngsam is hopeful he would be rehired now that the economy has gotten better with the newly established "mass-scale export of fish to Manshūkoku" that required more and more fishers.[38] But before he can conjure up the courage to approach the door of the co-op, Hyŏngsam happens to overhear Yoshio and his Japanese friends talking about Shimura's family:

"His older brother? Yes, he has one, but he's in the slammer."

"Slammer? Go figure. So, will the older one come out and take care of the old lady?"

"Humpf, think the likes of them give a damn about the mother? If the sons were half decent, there would be at least some compassion, but as is, who'll give them the time of day? Look at the way that little one talked back to me. Kicking back all day long then coming around with a bunch of lies about some storm. Drafting the likes of him won't do the country any good. They're all rotten to the core and that's why they spend all their time with the *yobo*."

Hyŏngsam's head was spinning and he felt hollow.[39]

The conversation continues as Hyŏngsam eavesdrops:

"The old woman said she felt sorry for Hyŏngsam, so I told her why not go live among the *yobos* then, and she jumped up in anger and said she'll have nothing to do with them."

"Hahahahaha."

"Hohohohoho."[40]

Thus Hyŏngsam is shocked at the extent of the racial prejudice of the other Japanese at the co-op not only toward him, but even toward his Japanese friend, Shimura, by association. He also realizes the reason that Shimura's mother has been so distant of late is because of the discrimination she has received from her neighbors for befriending Koreans (derogatorily called yobos in this exchange). Contrary to the postcolonial Korean critic's reading, I would suggest that this scene lays bare the actual impossibility of solidarity in this case due to imperial hierarchies and ethnic discrimination. The fact that Hyŏngsam is left literally outside the intimate gathering of Yoshio and his Japanese friends, forced to eavesdrop rather than allowed to partake as an equal in the conversation, suggests his colonial alienation. Imperial racial hierarchies have been exported along with imperial corporations all the way to a remote fishing village in northern Korea.

Losing all hope, Hyŏngsam fantasizes about the possibility of joining his friend Shimura in Manchuria. However, even Hyŏngsam's friendship with Shimura is unsustainable because only Shimura as a Japanese national can be drafted to go to war in Manchuria. When the story first appeared in 1936, Koreans were not yet mobilized for the Japanese military.[41] The story ends with Hyŏngsam weakly climbing the stairs of a Shinto shrine where he runs into Shimura's old mother on her way to offer prayers. At first she refuses his help, but when a torrent of rain pours down suddenly, she takes his offer to carry her down, and holding on to him tightly, says, "I'm sorry."[42]

"Changsan Cape" is complex and refuses easy interpretations. I would like to think about this difficulty of the text itself by way of focusing on the spatial and temporal gaps in readings triggered in two different contexts of its consumption: when it was first introduced to Japanese readers during the context of the Korea Boom and then, after decades of being "lost" (its existence only known to Korean scholars by its title published in a journal), its reintroduction to Korean audiences to take its place in Kang's canonical corpus. The story first appeared in the *Osaka mainichi regional edition*, then it was republished in the metropolitan proletariat journal *Bungaku annai*, and then again appeared in a collection of Korean short stories, *Chōsen bungaku senshū* (Selections of Korean literature), coedited by Korean and Japanese writers including Chang Hyŏkchu. In the short span of years during the late-colonial period, the text was reproduced three times.

The attention the text received as an integral element of the Korea Boom contrasts sharply with its fate in the postliberation period in which it virtually disappeared from both the Japanese and Korean literary fields. The dramatic vicissitudes of the text, marked by its mediated relationship with its readers through multiple levels of translation, from the colonial period to the present, is one of the most important factors to be considered in our attempt to read and access the text.

"Changsan Cape" appeared in repeated renditions in Japanese translation in the Japanese-language mass media of the 1930s before it appeared in Korean translation in the late 1980s in the Korean literary field. The geopolitical changes between these years mark the pages of the work. The question of which language was the original and which was the translation is indeterminate. When it first appeared in the *Osaka mainichi*, there was no mention that the text was in fact a translation. All the selections in the series of the "Collection of Korean Women Writers" in which this story appeared (as discussed in chapter 8), as well as the entire Korea cultural series, were introduced without mention of any translators; this gave the readers of the *Osaka mainichi* the impression that these texts were written in Japanese originally.

However, all of the other stories in the "Collection of Korean Women Writers" were indeed confirmed translations from the Korean. Among them, only Kang's "original" Korean text has yet to be found; but there are a couple of other clues that lead us to assume that it was a translation. As mentioned before, Kang Kyŏngae's limited access to colonial education and the metropolitan center makes it doubtful that her Japanese was good enough to write literary works in Japanese. When the story was published in *Selections of Korean Literature*, Chang Hyŏkchu discusses, in his brief introduction, the circumstances of the necessity of translating Korean stories and regrets that in the case of Kang's story, the translator's name is not known. In a letter to Chang Hyŏkchu, [Kang] writes that she can read Japanese, and her Korean-language stories are interspersed with Japanese words and short phrases, reflecting the linguistic habits of the time; but the ability to write literary works in a nonnative language takes extensive effort, of which Kang's background as a peasant migrant shows no evidence.[43]

It is worth noting that the editor of Kang's collected works briefly introduces Chang Hyŏkchu while citing the letters exchanged between Kang and Chang on the pages of the journal *Sin Tonga* as follows: "With the publication of 'Chosŏn ŭi chisikch'ŭng e hosoham' [Chōsen chishikijin ni uttau] in Japanese in the journal *Bungei* (February 1939) [Chang], without doubt, began his act of collaboration through his writing. He became a Japanese national after the Korean war" (Yi Sanggyŏng ed., *Kang Kyŏngae chŏnjip*, 762). This editorial remark in effect draws a line between Chang the collaborator and Kang the nationalist resistance writer. There is no attempt to tease out the complexity of this exchange in which Kang invites Chang to come to Manchuria to find "a mountain of resources to write about." It is worth noting that Chang's stories about Korean migrants in Manchuria are considered "collaborationist" whereas Kang's are read as the realistic depiction of Korean peasants struggling against hardship in the Manchurian frontier. I would argue that neither can be neatly categorized under the rubric of "collaboration" and "resistance," but rather embody the complexities of late-colonial Korean experiences in the empire.

The absence of the translator and the indeterminacy of the act of translation are significant in helping us to see what gets elided at the level of the text's consumption, in the gap from the colonial to the postcolonial. In the colonial context, the absence of the possibility of the translated act gives the false appearance of natural and direct access to "Korean authenticity" which the Korea Boom in general, and the *Osaka mainichi* Korean culture specials in particular, were trying to curate in toto for Japanese readers. It also extends the image of a harmonious imagined community of the empire connected through a presumably shared imperial language that was being promoted by various means on the pages of the *Osaka mainichi*. This image of the harmonious imagined community—introducing Korean writers writing in Japanese—elides any trace of the labor of translation that has been invested in the process. Even those who may have been writing directly in Japanese themselves or were translating their own works into Japanese were performing acts of translation in the broader sense as minor writers in the empire, and this labor of the colonized in the effort to communicate in the empire is not only devalued but erased here. The image of colonial subjects effortlessly writing in or speaking the imperial language takes such acts as natural and self-evident, negating the violence of imperial censorship and propaganda policies of assimilation out of which such translations were demanded as necessary in the first place.

The popularity of "Changsan Cape" in the context of the Korea Boom thus consumed to satisfy the demands for authentic colonial kitsch raises disturbing questions about the way it was being read by Japanese readers. Whatever the intentions of the author may have been, it was first presented to Japanese readers on the pages of the *Osaka mainichi* next to the headline "Transport Corps Connecting Japan-Korea-Manchuria: Department of Railways Urges Completion"[44] and as part of the Korea Boom in the expanding empire; and in these circumstances of its consumption, it is difficult to sustain the postcolonial reading of the text as "strong resistance to empire" at the time of its earlier emergence. In fact, the moments in the text in which Hyŏngsam nostalgically desires the space of Manchuria and dreams of joining his friend Shimura in its battlefields cannot but hit a disturbing chord in light of the increasing assimilation of Korea into the empire's expansionist policies and invasions into China and Manchuria. Hyŏngsam's fantasy of a different temporal and spatial context than the one in which he dwells, in which there will no longer be disharmony among the various ethnic groups in the empire, is open to the postcolonial nationalist reading of subversive resistance to the uneven actuality of empire. But on the other hand, it is ironically just as available to a contending reading of mimicking the slogans of harmonious cooperation in the empire, such as the slogans *Naisen ittai* or *Gozoku kyōwa* mobilized to garner the support of imperial subjects for wartime expansions.

The ambivalence of the text and the possibility of two mutually oppositional readings along the binary of resistance versus collaboration seem to be the very crux of the significance of this late-colonial-period story. The unbridgeable gaps in the consuming audiences and their contending demands point to the utter inadequacy of such mutually exclusive binaries in our attempts to make sense of the text. This ambivalence of the minor text (whether written or translated into the major language), as I have tried to show throughout the book, raises complex questions about the difficulties of the late-colonial experience in Korea that refuse easy answers.

The virtual disappearance of the text after the spotlight it received in the late-colonial period mirrors the fate common to minor literature produced under similar circumstances elsewhere as we have discussed throughout the book. The conditions of censorship and propaganda served to define the context of the production and consumption of these texts before the focus of the imperial gaze was replaced by the scrutiny of the nationalist one; and the same texts celebrated in one context were later relegated to silence as shameful evidence of a "dark period" better to be forgotten.

Japanese-language texts by colonial Koreans produced for imperial readers were buried under postcolonial conditions of propaganda and censorship for decades before they were accessible—and even then they became accessible only in stages and with limits (see chapter 2).[45] In South Korea, it was not until the 1990s and well into the twenty-first century that some of the Japanese-language texts began to be engaged in earnest, but they have remained on the margins of popular discourses. In Japan, the writers were known within the resident-Korean (zainichi) communities, but when they began to gain mainstream attention, they were often disparaged as the "trendiness" of ethnic-minority writings. The paradigm of postcolonial studies through which some of these texts were being consumed for the first time was also precariously positioned in relation to mainstream discourses on national literature in Japan and Korea. (The location of postcolonial studies in the region will be further elaborated in chapter 10.) The unstable positions of these texts between obscurity and "trendiness" testify to their ongoing marginality from the colonial to the postcolonial periods.

Postcolonial Regime of Colonial Realism

Throughout the book I have discussed the contradictions underlying the imperial demand for the authentic representation of the Other which accompanied the erasure of the Other's full humanity or complexities of experiences. Here, I would like to focus on a similar logic of selective blindness undergirding postcolonial nationalist demands placed upon the same colonial texts: to represent authentic "colonial reality" which narrowly meant either unequivocal resistance to colonial powers or the sufferings of the colonized under colonial exploitation. What is ironic is that in the wide gap between the colonial and the postcolonial consumptions of these texts, an uncanny echo appears in the similar logic followed by the demands for colonial authenticity in the Korea Boom, and the opposing postcolonial demands for colonial realism in the same texts.

When "Changsan Cape" was discovered by Korean scholars in 1989, it was quickly translated back into Korean to be introduced to Korean readers. The introduction accompanying the translation perpetuates the assumption which began during the colonial period that the text was first written in Japanese by eliding the question of an "originary" translation, making it appear that the translation published in 1989 was the first Korean-language version of the text. It is necessary to keep in mind that we have access only to the text that Kang herself wrote through the Japanese translation and then through the Korean translation of this Japanese version. Such a multiply mediated access to the text hints at the gap that lies between our experience of reading the text and the difficulty of accessing colonial reality naturally and "as is" through our reading. The burden of the regime of realism, which dictates how colonial literature comes to gain value in the postcolonial era and how the boundaries of the national canon are determined, is likewise placed upon "Changsan Cape" with no reflexivity about our own limited access to the text's complex realities.

However, postcolonial assessment of the text is telling. On the one hand, the text is considered somewhat lacking by such standards of the regime of realism: "The actualization of the theme of solidarity of the international proletariat class is relegated to a flashback of the camaraderie of the laborers Hyŏngsam and Shimura, and the concrete incident became something similar to human sympathy between Shimura's mother and Hyŏngsam, and therefore, the story fails to become a model text."[46] In fact, critics lament the fact that Kang's texts, particularly those penned in the late-colonial period, begin to lose the strong purpose (of tendency literature) and expose "weakness" by being overwhelmed by "human sympathy" rather than focusing on concrete descriptions of "reality." Despite the unfortunate melodrama of the text that hindered its realistic *effect*, the critic continues confidently: "We can gain a clear sense of what Kang Kyŏngae as a colonial writer wanted to convey to her Japanese readers, and how she felt about ethnic issues. She was powerfully revolting against the prejudice and the contempt of the Japanese toward the Korean people."[47] Thus, we see that the text is lauded for its clear depiction and critique of the racism of the Japanese toward the Koreans. The *colonial reality* that is desired in such critiques of Kang's texts is equated with how well the perspectives and plights of the Korean victims have been depicted. The fact that these same texts by Kang, lauded for such colonial reality, depict Chinese and Japanese characters (if they appear at all) in racialist stereotypes rarely warrants mention. Such double standards of the national literary canon that demand the text to be true to colonial reality—but only so far as it follows set expectations of what this colonial reality seems to be—are ironically similar to the imperialist desires for colonial authenticity for which the same texts were called upon in the first place. A disavowed continuity exists from the logic of the nation and that of empire when it comes to patrolling what is included and excluded at their borders; likewise, there are continuities from the colonial to the postcolonial eras that are yet to be acknowledged. The next chapter will examine some of these paradoxes that are ongoing in the region today.

TEN

PARADOX OF POSTCOLONIALITY

This book has examined a few case studies of what I have been calling shared but disavowed histories between Korea and Japan. The focus has been on contentious cultural memories of transcolonial encounters that speak to a broader postcolonial impasse going beyond the two nation-states of Japan and Korea. Perhaps in the absence of a neat closure or ending to these troubled legacies, it may be fitting to return to where we began the book to consider how these stories of colonial disavowal are impacting our shared global legacies into the present.

I recently had the opportunity to visit the Meiji Gakuin University in Tokyo to peruse the December 1909 issue of the coterie magazine *Shirogane gakuhō* in which Yi Kwangsu's Japanese-language story "Aika" was first published while he was a "Korean exchange student" there. As we introduced in this book's opening, this subsequently forgotten story told of the unrequited homoerotic desire of a Korean student for his elusive Japanese classmate, which textually in form and content, and metatextually from the site of production to that of consumption, embodied unspeakable entanglements at the scene of the colonial contact zone. The story's subsequent forgetting in both Korea and Japan despite Yi Kwangu's importance in the cultural exchange between the two also reflects the disavowed nature of their contested colonial pasts.

On the occasion of the university's celebration of the 150th anniversary of its founding, a group of scholars affiliated with the school initiated a symposium titled "Who Is Yi Kwangsu?" The eponymous question of the symposium hints at the long-forgotten status of this alumnus who had been demoted immediately after Japan's traumatic loss of empire from his once-prominent position as an imperial subject at the forefront of Japan's territorial expansions. This forgotten status stands out when compared with the fate of an older alumnus of the school, Shimazaki Tōson (graduating class of 1894), whose central place in the modern Japanese literary canon is undisputed today.

The commemorative publication of the symposium noted the unprecedented nature of such an event hosted in a Japanese university to discuss the significance of an alumnus from one of Japan's former colonies. It is important that the question, Who is Yi Kwangsu? is beginning to be posed in Japan, although rather belatedly and still limited to scholarly dialogues.

While change is starting to happen in some areas, Japan still has a long way to go to acknowledge the vibrant cultural impact and exchange from its colonies during the formative period of its modern history. Studies of Japan's modernity still focus primarily on the interaction between Japan and the West, at the expense of consideration of its inter-Asian relations.[1] A case in point is the unrecognized plight of its postcolonial minority populations such as ethnic Koreans whose legacies go back to the colonial past and continue to plague contemporary Japanese society.

Korea, too, is selectively myopic regarding its troubling colonial past and its relation to its modern history. For example, while Yi Kwangsu's contributions to its modern literary history are undeniable, his writings that embody contested aspects of the colonial encounter or that are deemed traitorous or collaborationist to the nation, especially those penned in the Japanese language, have been long excised from Yi's official collection of "Complete Works" as well as from the modern national literary canon at large.

I will close this book by considering such lingering significance symbolized by both Japan's and Korea's belated postcolonial encounters with Yi Kwangsu's "Aika" and other cultural exchanges from their shared colonial past. I will argue that this is a symptom of the *still* deeply divided nature of memories of the colonial past between Korea and Japan in particular, and in the Asia-Pacific more broadly.

Postcolonial Nostalgia

A selective myopia or the refusal to acknowledge significant swaths of a once-entwined colonial past appears to be a widespread phenomenon of divided memories in the postcolonial aftermath. This problem is certainly not limited to bilateral relations between Korea and Japan. In the case of Europe, for example, many of the colonies were reluctantly relinquished, and only with tremendous pressures from long-fought decolonial movements within the colonies as well as from the impasse of violent rivalries among other imperial powers. Furthermore, when independence was finally granted reluctantly, many after drawn-out wars and other forms of extreme violence, the handover was made palatable to the begrudging imperial powers by couching it as their benevolent bequeathing of liberty to their colonized subjects. There was a notable refusal to acknowledge defeat by the imperial powers in the face of revolutionary oppositions or their own impotent incapacity to sustain empire by old methods of brute force while quarreling among themselves—culminating in the infamy of two world wars. The prominence of films that portray the colonial past in a romantically nostalgic and melancholic light many decades after the loss of empire signifies the stubborn inability to reckon with the responsibilities of having violently imposed colonial subjection on the majority of the world's peoples in the dubious name of civilizing them (!). For example, David Lean's *Passage to India* (1984), Brigitte Roüen's *Outremer* (1990), and Régis Wargnier's *Indochine* (1991) are merely a few of the most prominent. In his important work, *Postmodernism*, Fredric Jameson has roundly criticized the ahistoricity of such "nostalgia films" and their desperate desire to appropriate the past through merely stylistic connotations devoid of actual historical content.[2]

Wars were also too often sanitized of the fact of their imperial underpinnings. The familiar memory of World War II as the "good war," in which Allied powers are seen to have fought heroically against the evils of Fascism and Nazism, elides Western Europe's own imperialist rivalries buttressed by racist ideologies of white supremacy and scrambling for territories that in fact triggered the war. The official end of the war may have settled some of these imperial rivalries for the time being, but not the question of how to acknowledge and reckon with the mass-scale violence inflicted around the world in the name of the so-called civilizational mission of empire. Related to this common affliction of selective memory, Eric Santner, in *Stranded Objects*, argued that in the case of Germany, which is often seen as standing in opposition to an amnesiac Japan, for example, in its more repentant attitude toward wartime crimes, it was in fact through collectively scapegoating the Nazi regime that the rest of society was allowed to escape the stigma of its own complicity in the imperial wars and the Holocaust. Furthermore, a focus on the horrors of the Holocaust stands in stark contrast to a lack of accounting for sufferings caused beyond the borders of Europe. In this sense, Germany and Japan may have more in common in terms of selective memories of their wartime and colonial pasts than is commonly acknowledged.

Imperial Triangulations

In East Asia, there were yet other ways that imperial entanglements were obscured. For example, the history of imperial relations in the region has worked by underplaying the Manichean divide between the self and Other that neatly defined and organized Europe's colonial ideology, although not in actual practice. East Asia's imperial relations have long been about more than two players negotiating various and shifting degrees of relative proximity and distance. For example, in the Sinocentric world order, long before the onset of modernity, imperial relations in the region entailed often nuanced but no less hierarchical and repressive regimes along a spectrum between the poles of dominance and submission. For centuries, regional hierarchies were understood in terms of concentric circles of influence and association based on shifting logistics of proximity and distance (cultural, linguistic, ethno-racial, spatial, etc.) rather than a fixed binary opposition between the colonizer and the colonized that was ideologically constructed in Eurocentric cognitive mappings of the imperial encounter—mappings that were often predicated on historical circumstances of distances real and imagined across oceanic expanses.

In the modern era, arguably by the eighteenth and certainly by the nineteenth century, with the rising prominence of variously contending Western imperial powers forcing their way into Asia, internally vexed relations became yet again multipronged albeit in starkly different configurations—with long-extant regional relations thrown into flux in the face of competing empires, both internal and external to the region. For example, Kirk Larsen's *Tradition, Treaties, and Trade* examines such shifts in the case of the Qing empire. The region's internal relations, which were always *at least* triangulated among contiguous neighbors of deeply entwined histories, had erased their nonetheless imperial logic (through the civilizational rhetoric of Sinocentrism (Chunghwa [Middle Kingdom]; Tianxia [All under Heaven]). These complexities became further muddled with the influx, this time in the name of yet another civilizational discourse, of the Western *mission civilisatrice* undergirded by the new hegemonic discourse of modernity. This new civilizing mission was buttressed by religion, capital, and guns, and many more agents backed by good intentions, oxymorons, and euphemisms to brutally enforce their provincial values, standards, regulations, and hierarchies in the name of a universal civilization.

In the case of Korea, such entanglements came to the fore when the decline of the Sinocentric regional order, for example, entailed desperate strategies of "using barbarians against barbarians" by the last king, Kojong, in the face of overwhelming and simultaneous threats from Russia, France, Japan, the United States, and others.[3] Thus, Korea's precarious place within the previously extant ecosystem of internal conflicts and diplomatic checks and balances of the Sinocentric world order was overdetermined and concealed yet again with the competition among multiple Euro-American empires in the region.

Korea's place between empires, as Andre Schmid has so aptly characterized for the turn of the nineteenth century,[4] entails continued imbrications of a semicolonial status that also coexisted with formal colonization in different degrees from the past to the present. The mass media imperial phenomenon of the Korea Boom that has been examined throughout the book, for example, was a cultural trend that arose out of and mirrored the confusion of broader geopolitical transformations of multiple imperial involvements in the region as the hegemonic role was then being taken for the time being by Japan (with a nod from the United States). This cultural trend embodied contradictory yet necessarily coexisting imperial logics of assimilation and differentiation familiar from various global imperial contexts, as well as more local changes toward an entirely unprecedented logic of imperialization of colonial Korea. This constantly shifting position between the global and the local redefined Korea's place in the region in complex ways during this era. Its precarious location of culture was unfolding in the midst of global, regional, and local restructurings, vis-à-vis not only metropolitan Japan but also in relation to China and Manchuria and to areas in Southeast Asia, as the Japanese empire was infiltrating the Rest of Asia, in collusion with and competition against Western empires.

Intimate Empire has argued that such entanglements were difficult to untangle even at the time they were unfolding, and were further muddled by later postcolonial erasures that too often projected and reinforced simple binary oppositions such as that of resistance and collaboration. This postcolonial cognitive mapping that simplified and organized the understanding of the colonial past ironically reproduced the very Manichean logic of empire in its critique of it. Such divided logics further add to our utter failure to illuminate actual imbrications at the scene of transcolonial encounters through postcolonial critique. The imposition of a postcolonial binary further undermined the agency and subjectivity of the colonized by reducing them to cartoonish mythical and propaganda figures (heroes and villains), further rhetorically committing the same violence of repeating the colonial logic of reducing the colonized to a place of objectified and dehumanized Otherness.

This book has traced the resulting conundrum of the colonial cultural producer perched between two different but uncannily parallel scenes that vacillated between inclusion and exclusion, between recognition and alienation, from the colonial to the postcolonial. In the wartime imperial discourse, the rhetoric of "collaboration," "volunteerism," and "cooperation" strategically erased the actual conditions of violence, coercion, censorship, and conscription that had actively produced such "collaborations" (*Naisen ittai*, Japan and Korea, One Body); in some sense this erasure was repeated in the equally impossible retroactive demands for unequivocal resistance in the postcolonial judgment of these producers who then had to violently suppress a whole range of their experiences from their pasts as if they had never existed.

The prominence and recognition bequeathed by the metropole (seemingly benevolently) to colonial cultural producers (such as *Kaizō* and the Akutagawa Literary Prize), and the rise of colonial collections, roundtables, coproductions, and other forms of transcolonial translations, show well the lure of mutuality that coexisted with the underlining violence and censorship behind such collaborations. The problem of recognition, as well as the vacillation between desire and coercion, that the imperial language symbolized for the colonial modern subject has been at the forefront of this conundrum.

Considering these complex historical and geopolitical embroilments of the times, we now see that cultural productions that may appear to be innocuous in fact embodied deeply political significations for the past to the present. For example, it was no mere coincidence that, within the rigid hierarchy of empire and despite imperial rhetoric otherwise, the issue of the journal *Kaizō* announcing Chang Hyŏkchu's celebrated debut into the Japanese Bundan also happened to mark the commemoration of the Manchurian Incident (1931), and the establishment of the puppet regime of Manchukuo (1932) which raised the need to further mobilize colonial Korea for such expansions. It was also no coincidence that even in the absence of a first-place winner, Chang's story "Gakidō" could only be recognized with a "second prize," mirroring Korea's favored but nonetheless secondary status in the imperial hierarchy, in which the "first place" was implicitly reserved for Japan.

Chang Hyŏkchu's debut into the metropolitan Bundan, as well as the series of Korea collections in the *Osaka mainichi local edition* examined in chapter 8, marked just a few significant yet subsequently forgotten milestones of the muddy imbrications of cultures across transcolonial borderlines which this book has examined. In subsequent years, this imperial consuming desire for colonial culture increased proportionately with Japan's expanding imperial polices into China and Manchuria and beyond with Korea's constantly shifting role as the decade dragged on.

All this came to the fore in the imperial consumption of translated colonial literature as chihō bungaku (regional or local literature), which exemplified contradictions facing colonial writers. As discussed in chapter 8, the notion of chihō within the Japanese main islands was already filled with ambivalence, both representing pristine pastness and authentic *Japaneseness* at a time when Japan was taking the self-appointed role as Asia's leader, owing to its speedy advancement toward modernity as defined by Western standards. Whatever the chihō came to signify, it was always defined as an Other within a binary opposition: the past to the future, tradition to modernity, country to city, the familiar to the unfamiliar, Japan to the foreign, and perhaps even the sense of comfort or calm to anxiety and uncertainty at a time when the world itself was seen to be in transition and in crisis. It is not surprising that another nostalgic signifier for chihō was "hometown" (*furusato*).

The image of *chihō* was both reified as pastness and sublimated into signi-fying a repository of Japaneseness, and as Japan continued to promote itself as the technologically advanced and modern leader of Asia in order to subsume it, the image of chihō shifted to the gaichi (colonial hinterlands), and an equiva-lence was established between the colonies and the local countryside of Japan; what was once deemed external to the main islands was being incorporated into its peripheries. The extension of the discourse of locality (*chihō bunka* [local, regional culture] and *chihō bungaku* [local, regional literature]) into the colonies actively incorporated the discussion on the position of colonial culture and literature, and this discourse of chihō translated into the colonial context in contradictory ways.

It included both the desire to promote colonial culture and literature in the empire with Japanese cultural figures actively reaching out to help. This was often done with them touring around the peripheries of the Naichi (Japan) as well as the gaichi, taking part in roundtables with participants from the chihō to help them develop their culture. On the other hand, the discourse also included the desire to preserve the authenticity of the chihō, in all its pristine pastness, which should be introduced to the metropole *as is*. The simultaneous (dual) gestures of assimilation and differentiation of Korean literature into chihō bungaku, including the recruitment and recognition of colonial culture producers and participants in creating this new genre of Japanese literature at the time Korea was supposed to be seamlessly incorporated into the imperial body as imperial subjects, signified multiple contradictions: on the level of production as well as that of consumption, with disconcerting ramifications (complicating the questions of agency, complicity, participation, victim, and perpetrator) beyond the literary and cultural spheres. To this day, these effects remain difficult to unravel, even decades after the collapse of the Japanese empire. The question of the agency and subjectivity of abjected colonial populations such as the comfort women and conscripted soldiers from the colonies is still neither adequately understood nor reckoned with.

Disavowing Empire

The colonial discourse of locality (chihō), as an apparent impulse to subsume the colonies seamlessly into the imperial body politic, and presumably away from colonial status, thus exemplifies a broader predicament that has impeded our understanding of the workings of empires, their agents, and their postcolonial legacies in East Asia. The remaining task of untangling imperial relations in the region, already complicated by the simultaneous comingling of multiple partners in varying positions of unevenness and hierarchical relations, is further challenged by the fact that imperialism in the region was accompanied by its disavowal from the outset. Certainly, all empires work on the logic of disavowal to varying degrees; however, the so-called late-developing empires such as Russia, the United States, Japan, and China, in fact, were predicated from their inception on the very denial of colonialism (or brute territorial aggrandizement). In fact, these empires were formed in the very name of anticolonialism, in their nonetheless imperial ambitions. In order to be viable in a shifting global climate, these latecomers to the imperial banquet had little choice but to distinguish themselves from older, more established European counterparts who were in decline. Therefore, they tried to differentiate themselves from older, more straightforward types of colonial domination, but were faced with the added predicament of desiring to acquire colonial possessions at a time when decolonizing movements and satiated imperial contests among other imperial powers were rendering conditions less and less favorable for blatant imperial plunder.

The United States of America, for example, had recently declared self-determinacy as a key paradigm in global relations (Atlantic Charter and Woodrow Wilson's Fourteen Points). The fact that this right was never meant to extend to the colonized did not prevent them from translating and deploying the very rhetoric of self-determinacy against their colonial masters in their demands for sovereignty and critique of such hypocrisy. Takashi Fujitani, in an important study comparing the United States and Japanese wartime empires from the perspectives of segregated minority soldiers in the imperial armed forces, *Race for Empire: Koreans as Japanese and Japanese as Americans during World War II*, designates such hypocrisies as the "polite racism" of inclusion. This work makes the important and unexpected comparison between the United States and Japan to show commonalities shared by these two late empires in wartime, which are still often seen only in oppositional Manichean terms. As Fujitani clearly demonstrates, these two empires have much more in common than previously acknowledged in nation-centered histories.

In the case of Japan, the denial of colonialism was already in effect even at the height of its imperial expansions.[5] The famous case of the puppet regime of Manchukuo propped up as a spectacle, with an aura of an independent nation-state, is but one well-known example.[6] It is less well known that as the cooperation of the colonized became more and more necessary in the over-extended wartime empire, the official rhetoric avoided the characterization of even already extant colonies such as Korea as "colonies."[7]

The important volume on Cold War U.S. military expansions *Over There: Living with the U.S. Military Empire from World War Two to the Present*, edited by Maria Höhn and Seungsook Moon, discusses the challenge of dispersing past assumptions characterizing the United States as a "phantom empire," especially in the face of undeniable and all-too-visible massive military industrial complexes throughout the globe. Amy Kaplan and Donald E. Pease's *Cultures of United States Imperialism* was another groundbreaking scholarly collaboration deploying a concerted critique by scholars from various fields on the long absence of imperialism within the discipline of American studies despite its own forgotten imperial origins. (See also Melani McAlister's *Epic Encounters*, Christina Klein's *Cold War Orientalism*, and Michael H. Hunt and Stephen I. Levine's *Arc of Empire*, for important contributions.)

Anne McClintock, in *Imperial Leather*, has written about the U.S. disavowal of its own history of imperialism in relation to the problem of postcoloniality as follows: "Since the 1940s, the U.S. imperialism-without-colonies has taken a number of distinct forms (military, political, economic and cultural), some concealed, some half-concealed. The power of the U.S. finance capital, research, consumer goods, and media information around the world can exert a coercive power as great as any colonial gunboat. It is precisely the greater subtlety, innovation and variety of these forms of imperialism that make the historical rupture implied by the term postcolonial especially unwarranted."[8]

When *Was* Postcoloniality in Asia?

Such pitfalls of postcoloniality at large are multiple and have been cogently critiqued from no shortage of experiences from Europe's empires. For example, scholars have pointed to postcoloniality's vague semantics, its Eurocentric origins and characteristics, and dubious or impotent politics, as some of the problems inherent in the discourse itself. As for semantics, it is confusing whether postcoloniality refers literally to the temporal aftermath of official colonization and whether it applies to both the former colonized and colonizer societies or to a broader global condition at large. If it refers to a general global condition in the aftermath of colonialism, how do we account for various differences and temporalities in experiences and histories? When was the postcolonial period for Australia, Hong Kong, or Taiwan, for example? Is the postcolonial experience of colonial settlers like the French *pieds noirs* and Japanese settlers in Korea comparable or commensurate under the same category of postcoloniality as the experience of the colonized in Algeria or in Korea? What is gained and lost through establishing such equivalences across divides?

The term "post" semantically further obfuscates actually ongoing legacies of colonialism as well as continuities in similar structures of domination by other means. If the term pertains to a critical impulse that arose in the era of late capitalism along with its counterpart postmodernity, then how do we account for, and does it apply to, myriad decolonial or anticolonial movements that began long before the concept of postcoloniality attained canonicity in academic circles, and that had in fact helped usher in the end of official colonialisms? The questions become even further muddled because historically, the end of coloniality was never as clearly delineated as liberation narratives would have us believe. The question of when postcoloniality arrived in Algeria and colonial Indochina, where decades of long drawn-out wars against multiple empires were waged, for example, is not easy to answer.

The Eurocentric origins and core of postcolonial discourse is another point of contention. Some have pointed out the Eurocentric origins of postcolonial discourse itself as well as its rise to influence in the former metropolitan centers of Europe and the United States that gave it legitimacy (couched in the aura of high theory) as an academic discourse. The Subaltern Studies group's intimate links to Marxist discourses of British historians (for example, E. P. Thompson and others of history-from-below movements) and the privileging of Eurocentric knowledge productions by the postcolonial "triumvirate" (Spivak, Bhabha and Said) from post-structuralism to European literary canonical texts have also been questioned. Unfortunately, postcolonial discourse has been largely about the descendants of former colonial subjects "writing back" to the former metropolitan centers, in privileged imperial languages (primarily English, and to a lesser degree, in French), rather than about linking different areas of colonial legacies in productive engagements about materially shared but discursively and historically divided predicaments.

Furthermore, it was only quite recently that scholars have been looking more specifically at the colonial experiences that have had constitutive roles in producing metropolitan discourses such as post-structuralism.[9] Although Derrida's colonial origins as an Algerian Jew is well known, it is interesting to note how his oeuvre shifts anxiously between deconstructing universalism and perpetuating it, and his writings that specifically reference his own colonial origins are deeply ambivalent between these two poles. His *Monolingualism of the Other*, for example, which begins with his own personal experience of linguistic alienation in the colonial context, starts with a potentially powerful critique of colonial alienation made from the center of post-structuralist theory and ends dubiously with musings about the universal alienation through language of all mankind, therefore losing the potency of a critique of imperialism in the name of universalism. Julia Kristeva, another pied noir from occupied Algeria, whose concept of the abject we have found so useful to approximate the impossible position of the bilingual translator Kim Saryang/Kin Shiryō in chapter 5, reveals in her otherwise powerful book, *Strangers to Ourselves*, deeply biased assumptions about how the abject situation of foreigners in contemporary France must be worse than elsewhere: "Nowhere is one *more* a foreigner than in France. . . . When your otherness becomes a cultural exception—if, for instance, you are recognized as a great scientist or a great artist—the entire nation will appropriate your performance, will assimilate it along with its own better accomplishments, and give you recognition better than elsewhere. This will not happen without a twinkling of the eye directed at your oddity, so un-French, but it will all be carried off with great panache and splendor."[10]

Perhaps this limited perspective arises because it is her own personal pain that has been so keenly felt in France. But after having overheard echoes of an exact parallel situation from another time and another place throughout this book, we are left confounded by and deeply suspicious of such presumed Eurocentric exceptionalism in the name of critiquing Eurocentrism. In a book based on her own most intimate personal experiences of being marginal in France, it is through a curious vacillation between Francophobia and Francophilia through which Kristeva rhetorically exceptionalizes France of the territorial hexagon as *the* world standard. I am afraid similar vacillations are more common than we'd like, even in richly provocative works such as Pascale Casanova's *World Republic of Letters*, which purports to take a broader and more inclusive perspective toward world literature. This ironic rhetorical move in fact unwittingly refuses a wider relevance of her theoretical musings and potential for building solidarity with others around the world who share similar predicaments. Structural similarities of Kristeva's context to other contexts such as the one we have been examining of late-colonial Korea in the Japanese empire are simply undeniable. However, postcolonial theory has time and again revealed selective blindness via a curiously Eurocentric lens in its quest to dismantle Eurocentrism.

My purpose here in focusing on these myriad blind spots is not to point an accusatory finger outward at others, but to show just how difficult it is for all of *us* situated in metropolitan centers, even those with the best of intensions, to fall prey to dominant assumptions *despite* ourselves. *Intimate Empire* itself is positioned ambivalently in relation to prior postcolonial discourses. While it relies on, and is in fact enabled by and indebted to, much of the invaluable strides made in postcolonial studies within the last few decades, its attempt at a genuine dialogical engagement continues to be frustrated by some of the stark pitfalls inherent in postcolonial theory today. The provincial Eurocentric impulse undergirding postcolonial studies at large despite its purported raison d'être of debunking Eurocentrism is at the heart of the paradox of postcolonial discourse which still has not been fully accounted for or understood. This blind spot may emerge from various reasons, including the manifest desire to achieve universalist aspirations and recognition from the metropolitan center or to mediate the legitimation of marginal discourses on a global or world stage; it seems so prevalent in those who are acutely self-conscious of their own marginality (even while speaking from privileged positions in ivory towers).

Postcolonial discourse from the time of its emergence has predominately privileged the Anglophone experience (in the English language) and then to a lesser degree, Francophone histories; and it is in urgent need of provincialization, as many have pointed out (Chakrabarty, *Provincializing Europe*). Francophone studies and the newly and rapidly emerging Sinophone studies are significantly expanding the terrain of the dialogue, but some of these conversations are also wrought in their own ambivalent desires and will to power toward universalist recognition competing with a more critical impulse. All postcolonial discourses, whether Anglophone, Francophone, or Sinophone, (and of even more recent vintage Japanophone), embody deeply ambivalent relationships to the metropole (defined relationally to each particular context) and its language (for example standardized English, French, Chinese, Japanese), which they simultaneously seem to be trying to debunk, decenter, and deconstruct, while unwittingly privileging, centering, and strengthening them.

Many have pointed out the problematic relationship of postcolonial discourse to knowledge production and power more broadly through the irony of the fact that postcolonial discourse (as has gained traction primarily in academic realms) has been primarily based on Eurocentric and first world origins, borrowing methodologies and language and themes from, for example, post-structuralism, and applying them to other contexts. It bears repeating that these contexts were primarily the former colonies of Britain, and to lesser extent that of France. In other words postcolonial discourses universalized its translatability to wider global contexts based on an astonishingly limited perspective and case studies.

The above concerns directly lead to the critique of postcolonial discourse's precarious relationship to politics on the ground. This critique ranges from questioning both political agendas as well as efficacy. For example, there is so much nostalgia for colonial pasts even within postcolonial writings that seriously put into doubt its claims toward criticality in relation to hegemonic power dynamics. Furthermore, it does not help matters that those who have had the most vocal influence are all perched comfortably in metropolitan (primarily U.S.) ivory tower institutions of academic privilege, undergirding and legitimating their very location of enunciation.

Gayatri Spivak, for example, famously became ruffled when interrogated by "native intellectuals" from India about her privileged "return on the wings of progress back to India to speak about Indian conditions."[11] In this same article, Arif Dirlik only half facetiously answers Ella Shohat's prior provocation "when exactly was the postcolonial?" (herself asking about the actual legacies of coloniality that still persist globally), stating, "when postcolonial intellectuals 'arrived in' and garnered recognition from the Euro-American academic establishments."[12] This withering critique also echoes what Rey Chow has cogently diagnosed in *On Diaspora*: the power imbalance and native-informant and translator roles played by diasporic intellectuals for metropolitan establishments. These self-reflexive critiques by those whom others might identify as postcolonial diasporic intellectuals (though they themselves may or may not choose to see themselves this way) seem to be an important intervention toward transforming postcolonial studies from within.

Paradox of the Cold War and the Post–Cold War

In East Asia, there are multiple reasons why "postcoloniality" as a concept or postcolonial theory as a paradigm came belatedly. Rather than assuming that this is a native lag resulting from theoretical immaturity in the region (an anxiety expressed both inside and outside the region), we might do better to keep in mind the inherent paradoxes (including the Eurocentrism at its core) embedded within postcolonial discourse as some of the underlying reasons behind this belated encounter. Kwŏn Myŏnga, a feminist scholar and activist in South Korea, speaks to a local situation, in which postcolonial theory arrived around the late 1990s; however, it did not come as a critical paradigm with wide popular and political appeal, but was limited to a minority discourse in academia whose privileged access to Euro-American theory as a new standard produced internal divides rather than a productive means toward bridging impasses in transnational dialogues across uneven and systemic geopolitical divides. (For similar critiques, see Dirlik and Michael Hardt and Antonio Negri.) Kwŏn critiques Korea's postcolonial scholarship's primary focus on the colonial past as producing an inability, in practice, to bridge studies of historical pasts to neocolonial continuities in contemporary society.

Furthermore, the inherent pitfalls of postcolonial discourse were overdetermined by yet other structural barriers within the region. The belated and deferred nature of postcoloniality is a symptom of the ongoing problem of the paradox of colonial modernity shared across the colonial and postcolonial divides of Korea and Japan in their persistent anxieties about late development, both real and perceived. This sense of belatedness, what Harootunian calls "untimeliness"[13] continued and was aggravated by the imposition of yet another external standard of value of yet another world order, that of Cold War geopolitics, to which both the former colonizer and the former colonized now had to catch up and whose basic structure of global alignment still remains intact in the region.

In fact, the deferral of postcoloniality as a discourse to analyze actual conditions in the region was a direct symptom of the very neocolonial structures of the Cold War that in effect barred a true reckoning with the region's colonial pasts. With Japan's defeat in the Pacific War, it was relegated back into the waiting room of history (from which it had barely escaped not long ago as the sole nonwhite imperial power). It was then forced to relinquish its sovereignty and that of its colonies to the victors who descended simultaneously as occupation military forces in the societies of the former colonizer and the former colonized alike.

Thus the end of the colonial relationship between Japan and the Koreas (the latter pluralized by a swift and arbitrary division by the emerging Cold War powers)[14] would result in an uneasy alignment of the former colonized and the former colonizers in mirrored relations as occupied territories and eventually as "client states" (albeit on different rungs in the hierarchy) of the newly arising regional and world order, relegated to await their fates "in due course." This was an unprecedented logic of a unilateral victor's judgment of the United States that meted out the "justice" of occupation to both the former colonizer and the former colonial subjects of Japan, in the name of democracy and development.

Empire by Other Means

In the Asia-Pacific, postcoloniality was inaugurated simultaneously with and overshadowed by the paradigm of Cold War, which was also framed as a "post-war,"[15] both inadequate if not ironic frameworks in a region marred by violent and unending proxy wars of the new imperial powers. This new world order instilled another Manichean opposition to an Other (this time in the name of another color line, that of Red Communism)[16] and a developmentalist drive in the name of self-defense. This new paradigm or world order instilled new divisions on top of already extant ones inherited from the immediate past of colonial and wartime contests. It is no coincidence that the predicament of the paradox of postcoloniality has uncanny similarities with the conundrum of colonial modernity that has been examined throughout the book.

The barred condition of colonial modernity and the denial of the fundamental fact of the colonial underpinnings of modernity then continued in different configurations in the so-called postcolonial era. The condition of being synchronous yet having been denied the recognition of this synchronicity lies at the very heart of the paradoxical conundrum of colonial modernity with which this book has engaged. Likewise, the structural continuities from the colonial to the postcolonial in the "new world order" have also been elided, further exacerbating our ability to recognize the problem diachronically from the past to the present.

The debates on colonial modernity emerged simultaneously with the debates on postcoloniality and triggered mixed responses in East Asia. The transnational discourse on colonial modernity that was spearheaded in U.S.

academia incited a heated debate and deep anxieties in East Asia. In Korea, for example, there have been ceaseless responses since, ranging along a spectrum from defensively critical to open and engaging, as well as from various disciplines: history, literature, film studies, and so forth.

In the discipline of history, for example, it triggered debates about whether colonial modernity closely resembles the colonial modernization discourses of imperialist apologists, the yoke of which postcolonial nationalists have struggled so long to overcome, or whether it undermines the genealogies of "internal development" that were carefully built as decolonial struggles to overcome the aforementioned colonizing discourses. There were also criticisms that this was an elitist discourse that failed to take into consideration the perspectives of the subalterns, although the original colonial modernity issue of *positions* was supposed to have received inspiration from the Subaltern Studies group themselves.

Furthermore, the difficulty of untangling imperial relations also arises from the uncanny ideological repetitions seen, albeit in differing configurations, from the Sinocentric world order of tributary relations to the imposition of Western empires via "civilizing missions" and unequal treaty systems, and from the rise of the Japanese empire (and the rhetoric of mutuality and coprosperity) all the way to Cold War U.S.-Soviet "occupations" and "client statism." The challenge consists in the coexistence of similarities and differences in each subsequent system of rule that was supposedly overcoming prior systems of domination.

In the case of Korea, there was no time in its history in which actual domination did not come in the name of "sovereignty" and "liberation" promised either presently or "in due course"—often in the name of "freedom" from a past hegemon from which it was supposedly being liberated by the new force. For example, many visitors to Seoul misrecognize the landmark Independence Gate (Tongnimmun) as commemorating liberation from Japanese colonization, but in fact, it marked Korea's earlier "independence" from the Sinocentric order that paved the road for Japan to freely colonize Korea after Korea become Japan's "protectorate." In such a case where the negotiation for the end of one system of dominance occurred in conjunction with the beginning of another, it is difficult or well-neigh impossible to determine where one system starts and ends, and in fact, whether and when coloniality started or ended. This predicament of postcoloniality is linked to the paradox of the Cold War and the post–Cold War in a region where unending wars force us to reconsider the challenges of such periodizations of beginnings and endings, as Heonik Kwon reminds us in *The Other Cold War*.

The troubling disavowal of empire continues into the so-called postcolonial and the so-called post–Cold War era of the present. Newly formed divisions by Cold War logic inaugurated a new order in the name of liberation from imperial subjection that linger into the post–Cold War where Cold War occupations and territorial partitions stubbornly persist. Such disavowals are at the core of the ongoing paradox of postcoloniality and continue to challenge our ability to understand the postcolonial condition in the region and across the Asia-Pacific. In the end, we are still wrestling with shared but divided legacies of colonialism into the present that include, but are not limited to, issues of unresolved historical and ethical reckoning of past atrocities, the rights and livelihood of ethnic minority and migrant communities, uneven flows of capital and labor, and ongoing tensions arising from the Cold War structure whose tenacious legacies still occupy us today when empire persists by other means and in ever new forms.

Chapter 1. Colonial Modernity and the Conundrum of Representation

1. Edward Said describes the "voyage-in" thus: "[It is a] powerful impingement, that is the work of intellectuals from the colonial or peripheral regions who wrote in an imperial language." *Culture and Imperialism*, 243. See chapter 3: "Resistance and Opposition," particularly section 6, "Voyage In and the Emergence of Opposition," 239–61. Said is mindful of the moments of resistance and opposition to imperialism produced from its margins. While my focus is on a wide range of complex affects, not necessarily unequivocally resistant or oppositional, at work in the colonial interaction, I hope to open up a space through the critical encounter in which to read these affects oppositionally in order to critique imperial logic.

2. Many personal and place names are rendered simultaneously in Japanese and Korean readings in this book because the Sino-Korean/Japanese characters may be read as either/or. Unless marked by glosses by the author, their indeterminacy in the majority of written texts is significant. The name is glossed as Bunkichi in "Aika" but even in such cases, echoes of plural reading possibilities coexist.

3. The English translation by John Wittier Treat appears as part of a welcome retrospective on Yi Kwangsu. I have relied on Treat's masterful translation here with some minor modifications. Yi Kwangsu, "Maybe Love (Ai ka)," in *Azalea*. This passage is from 321–22. For the Korean translation, see Yi Kwangsu, "Saranginga," translated by Kim Yunsik, in *Munhak sasang*, 442–46.

4. I discuss intimate textual and metatextual intercourse or interconnections throughout the book. By metatextual intercourse, I am referring to the text's intimate relationship to extratextual elements beyond the narrative content such as the language and form in which the story was written as well as broader transnational historical contexts and social circumstances within which the text was produced and consumed.

5. The story was published under Yi's given name, Yi Pogyŏng, in the student coterie journal *Shirogane gakuhō* of Meiji Gakuin the year before Korea's annexation by Japan. Yi, "Aika," 35–41. I discuss the significance of what I call the "colonized-I-novel" in chapter 3.

6. See Kim, *Yi Kwangsu wa kŭ ŭi sidae*. See also Treat's translation, "Maybe Love (Ai ka)," for an excellent rendering into English and for emphasizing this important link. Other themes that will become canonical to modern Korean literature are the anguish of youth as the paradigmatic modern subject; absence of the love object (both allegorically and literally); and the unacknowledged but prevalent connection to Japan and Japanese, in form and content.

7. Throughout the book, I refer to the contentiously shared legacies of Korea and Japan's colonial relations as "postcolonial." The concept of the postcolonial is itself contested and paradoxical as pointed out by many. I will defer to chapter 10 a more theoretical engagement with the problems of the postcolonial in East Asia and elsewhere, and here use this term to signify both a temporal aftermath, following the colonial era (post-1945 in this case) as well as the contending responses to the colonial conditions and ongoing legacies in Korea and Japan.

8. "Saranginga," translated by Kim Yunsik, in *Munhak sasang*, 442–46.

9. Kurokawa, ed., "Gaichi," *no Nihongo bungakusen*, vol. 3, 21–26.

10. Evans, *An Introductory Dictionary of Lacanian Psychoanalysis*, 43–44; Laplanche and Pontalis, *The Language of Psycho-Analysis*, 118–21.

11. For a pioneering study on the context of Taiwan, see Ching, *Becoming "Japanese."*

12. How do these experiences relate to the erasure of the fates of the so-called comfort women and conscripted soldiers who were mobilized to die for the empire? Writers like Yi Kwangsu were at the forefront of mobilizing soldiers. See Driscoll, *Absolute Erotic, Absolute Grotesque*, Fujitani, *Race for Empire*, and Kawashima, *The Proletariat Gamble*, for nuanced studies about these historical aporias.

13. Also known as the Mukden Incident. On September 18, 1931, the Japanese army staged a bombing of a small area on the South Manchurian Railway near Mukden, and then blamed the Chinese as a pretext to invade northern China. A puppet regime of Manchukuo was subsequently established and, after censure from the global community, Japan withdrew from the League of Nations.

14. Komagome, "Colonial Modernity for an Elite Taiwanese, Lim Bo-Seng."

15. The Korean-language translation of Shin and Robinson's aforementioned book is titled *Korea's Colonial Modernity: Beyond Internal Development and Colonial Modernization*. Also see Chŏng Yŏnnae, *Hanguk kŭndae wa singminji kŭndaehwa nonjaeng*.

16. Jameson, *Singular Modernity*; Appadurai, *Modernity at Large*; Ching, *Becoming "Japanese"*; Spivak, *Other Asias*; Mignolo, *Darker Side of Western Modernity*; Yun, *Singminji kŭndae ŭi p'aerŏdoksŭ*.

17. See Lewis, *Cambridge Introduction to Modernism*, 1–34.

18. Hall, "The West and the Rest"; Sakai, "Modernity and Its Critique" and "You Asians."

19. Japan's ambivalent status in relation to other imperial powers as the sole non-Western imperial power is rendered as semi-imperial, akin to the ambivalent semicolonial status of some colonies in between multiple imperial powers.

20. For a cogent critique, see Harootunian, "'Modernity' and the Claims of Untimeliness," 367–82.
21. Said, "Representing the Colonized," 200, 293–316, 313.
22. Said, "Representing the Colonized," 313.
23. Said, "Representing the Colonized," 315.
24. My aim here is not to impose so-called Western theory on a different world experience in uncritical ways. Yet given the hegemony of theories of modernity which emerge from the Western experience—and the hegemony of Western theory generally—it is as impossible for postcolonial thinkers today to evade these terms and conditions as it was for the colonial subjects with whose thoughts this chapter engages. Rather than reinvent the wheel, however, I seek to retool these theories by putting other global experiences in conversation with and in contention with them—a process that inevitably exposes their limitations and occasional hubris.
25. See, for example, Rey Chow, "Things, Common/Places, Passages of the Port City: On Hong Kong and Hong Kong Author Leung Ping-kwan" on postcolonial Hong Kong.

Chapter 2. Translating Korean Literature

1. Some scholars stress the significance of the year 1937, as it marked Japan's invasion of China and the implementation of new policies of war mobilization under the Konoe Home Ministry (the first Konoe cabinet was established in June 1937). Others prefer the year 1938, which marked the launch of Governor General Minami Jirō's (1874–1955) increasingly harsh assimilation policies; while others again favor the period from 1939 to the early 1940s, when censorship of Korean-language media intensified, and Japanese-language texts by Koreans rapidly increased in volume.
2. Gaichi, literally means outer territories. It can also be translated as colony, hinterlands, and so forth.
3. Caprio, *Japanese Assimilation Policies in Colonial Korea*; Yi Yŏn-suk, *Kokugo to iu shisō*.
4. For Korea, see Paek, *Chosŏn sinmunhak sajosa*, 398–99; Im, *Ch'inil munhak non*; Chŏng, "Yi Kwangsu, Kim Saryang no Nihongo Chōsengo shōsetsu"; Chŏng, *Hanguk kŭndae ŭi singminji ch'ehŏm kwa ijung ŏnŏ munhak*; Kim Yunsik, *Ilche malgi Hangguk chakka ŭi Ilbonŏ kŭlssŭgi non*; Lee Kyoung-Hoon [Yi Kyŏnghun], *Yi Kwangsu ŭi ch'inil munhak yŏngu*; Kim, Chul [Kim Ch'ŏl], *Kungmunhak ŭl nŏmŏsŏ*; Kim Chaeyong, *Hyŏmnyŏk kwa chŏhang*; Yun Taesŏk, "1940 nyŏndae 'kungmin munhak' yŏngu"; and Yun Taesŏk, *Singminji kungmin munhak non*.

    For Japan, see Im Chŏnhye, *Nihon ni okeru Chōsenjin no bungaku no rekishi*; and An Usik, *Hyōden Kin Shiryō*. See also Isogai Jirō and Kuroko Kazuo, eds., *Zainichi bungaku zenshū*. Some recent literary histories have also begun to deal with resident Korean literature in substantial ways: see, for example, Inoue Hisashi and Komori Yōichi, eds., *Zadankai Shōwa bungakushi*. Other works that have contributed significantly to the issue are Hayashi Kōji, *Zainichi Chōsenjin Nihongo bungakuron*; Ōmura Masuo and Hotei Toshihiro, eds., *Kindai Chōsen Nihongo sakuhinshū 1901–1938*; Shirakawa Yutaka, "Chang Hyŏkchu yŏngu"; Shirakawa, *Shokuminchiki Chōsen no sakka to Nihon*; and Nam Pujin, *Bungaku no shokuminchishugi*.

5. Personal conversation, August 23, 2007.

6. Ri Myŏngho, ed., *Kim Saryang chakp'umchip*.

7. See Paek Ch'ŏl, *Chosŏn sinmunhak sajosa*, 398–99.

8. See Im Chongguk, *Ch'inil munhak non*.

9. The privileging of the imperial language even in the postcolonial reckoning is not isolated to Japan. I shall return to this broader problem in chapter 10.

10. He underscores three main and interrelated disavowals: that of proletariat resistance and imperial-language writings from the colonial era and works by "authors who went north" (*wŏlbuk chakka*). See *Literature and Film in Cold War South Korea*.

11. Kim and Kwak, *Kim Saryang chakp'um kwa yŏngu*, vol. 4.

12. Illegal or unacknowledged imports, however, have nonetheless entered, even appearing as ubiquitous television shows, albeit with the Japanese language dubbed over. It was a common experience until recently for South Korean citizens to visit Japan and realize for the first time that beloved childhood animations were Japanese in origin.

13. Talk at Duke University "Amnesic Fissures" (March 26, 2009); and Han, *Sasang kwa sŏngch'al*. Other significant recent contributions include the important anthology *Hŭndŭllinŭn ŏnŏdŭl* edited by Im, Hyŏng-t'aek et al. Serk-Bae Suh writes about the plight of the postwar poet Kim Suyŏng's secret diaries in the Japanese language "Tanil ŏnŏ sahoe rŭl hyanghae."

14. "Foreign Husband" in Wender, *Into the Light*.

15. Shirakawa, *Chōsen kindai no chinichiha sakka kutō no kiseki*, translated into Korean as *Hanguk kŭndae chiil chakka wa kŭ munhak yŏngu*.

16. Cho Kwanja, "Shinnichi nashonarizumu no keisei to hatan."

17. See for example, Chŏng, "Yi Kwangsu, Kim Saryang no Nihongo Chōsengo shōsetsu"; Chŏng, *Hanguk kŭndae ŭi singminji ch'ehŏm kwa ijung ŏnŏ munhak*; Kim Yunsik, *Ilche malgi Hangguk chakka ŭi Ilbonŏ kŭlssŭgi non*; Lee Kyoung-Hoon [Yi Kyŏnghun], *Yi Kwangsu ŭi ch'inil munhak yŏngu*; Kim Ch'ŏl, *Kungmunhak ŭl nŏmŏsŏ*; Kim Chaeyong, *Hyŏmnyŏk kwa chŏhang*; Yun Taesŏk, "1940 nyŏndae 'kungmin munhak' yŏngu"; Yun Taesŏk, *Singminji kungmin munhak non*; and Hwang, *Pŏllae wa cheguk*.

18. See Im Chŏnhye, *Nihon ni okeru Chōsenjin no bungaku no rekishi*; and An, *Hyōden Kim Saryang*.

19. See Isogai and Kuroko, eds., *Zainichi bungaku zenshū*.

20. See, for example, Inoue and Komori, eds., *Zadankai Shōwa bungakushi*.

21. Hayashi, *Zainichi Chōsenjin Nihongo bungakuron*; Ōmura and Hotei, eds., *Kindai Chōsen Nihongo sakuhinshū*; Shirakawa, "Chang Hyŏkchu yŏngu"; Shirakawa, *Shokuminchiki Chōsen no sakka to Nihon*; and Nam Pujin, *Bungaku no shokuminchishugi*.

22. For example, in an article published in 1933, Aono Suekichi (1890–1961) links the general state of anxiety (*fuan*) in Japanese society to the uncertain historical context after the Manchurian Incident. See Aono, "Honnen bundan no sōkatsuteki kannsatsu," 2–12. See also Lippit, *Topographies of Japanese Modernism*; and Harootunian, *Overcome by Modernity*. For Korea, see Ch'a Sŭnggi, "1930 nyŏndae huban chŏnt'ongnon yŏngu"; and Kim Yerim, *1930 nyŏndae huban kŭndae insik ŭi t'ŭl kwa miŭisik*. For conditions in Europe, see Hobsbawm, *Age of Empire*.

23. See Edward Said about the commonness of the voyage-in to the metropolitan centers from the colonies. *Culture and Imperialism*, 239–61.

24. "Aika" [Love?] was published under Yi Kwangsu's courtesy name Yi Pogyŏng in the student coterie journal *Shirogane gakuhō* in December 1909. It was introduced to Korean readers in translation by Kim Yunsik under the title "Sarang in ga," published in the journal *Munhak sasang* in February 1981. The long-deferred and linguistically mediated encounter by Korean readers with these well-nigh forgotten Japanese-language texts testifies to the ongoing marginal condition of these works.

25. *Kim Tongin chŏnjip* 6:19; quoted in Kim Yunsik, ed., *Yi Kwangsu wa kŭ ŭi sidae* 1:609.

26. See Hotei, "Ilche malgi ilbonŏ sosŏl yŏngu"; and Yun Taesŏk, "1940 nyŏndae 'kungmin munhak' yŏngu."

27. See Ōmura Masuo and Hotei Toshihiro, eds., *Kindai Chōsen Nihongo sakuhinshū 1901–1938*, vols. 1–5.

28. An exiled Korean government was set up in Shanghai in 1919.

29. Rosaldo, "Imperialist Nostalgia," 108; see also Norindr, *Phantasmatic Indochina*.

30. The discourses on Chosŏn munhak and Chōsen bungaku were not defined by the ethno-national identity of the enunciating subjects, since these identities were often fluid in the context of empire. In a broad sense, I distinguish the discourses according to the language communities they were primarily addressing, which often corresponded to the language in which they were conducted. It is important to realize, however, that any such distinctions were regularly blurred, especially in the late-colonial period when assimilation policies resulted in a mixing of linguistic communities, with many colonized Koreans partaking in the imperialist discourse alongside the colonizers. Indeed, the various ways in which the two discourses converge and diverge attest to the complex interactions that took place at the contact zones.

31. "Japan" itself was being defined in relation to its colonies, as Naichi (inlands, metropole, or Japan) or as *teikoku* (empire), for example. Many of these terms manifest various meanings in the translated encounter between the metropole and colony. See Oguma, *Nihonjin no kyōkai*.

32. "Chosŏn munhak ŭi chŏngi irok'e kyujŏng haryŏ handa," *Samch'ŏlli* 8:8 (June 1936): 82–98. Hereafter, references to this article will be in parenthetical citations.

33. *Yŏlha ilgi* [Travelogues in Rehe] (1870), by Pak Chiwŏn (courtesy name, Yŏnam; 1737–1805); *Samguk yusa* [The memorabilia of three kingdoms] (1281), by Master Iryŏn (1206–1289).

34. Rabindranath Tagore (1861–1941), J. M. Singe (1871–1901), Isabella Augusta Gregory (1852–1935), and William Butler Yeats (1865–1939).

35. *Kuunmong* [Dream of nine clouds, 1687] and *Sassi namjŏng ki* [Lady Sa's southward journey, date unknown] were fictional works by Kim Manjung (1637–1692). *Dream of Nine Clouds* exists in both Korean and classical Chinese versions, and the work is set in Ming China. *Lady Sa's Southward Journey* was written in Korean and set in Ming China, and it was also translated into classical Chinese.

36. Yi Kwangsu and Chang Hyŏkchu, in particular, occupied positions at the forefront of the discourse on the shifting position of Korean literature. Their Japanese-language writings pushed the limits of the boundaries of "national literature" in the

Japanese empire at the time. Perhaps the desire for clear boundaries was that much more intense for those who were perched anxiously on the borderlines. Oblique evidence for this can be found in the fact that Yi T'aejun, who wrote in Japanese himself, repeatedly tried to distance himself from other writers who wrote in the language of the colonizers.

37. The use of the derogatory name "China" to refer to China, instead of Chungguk (Middle Kingdom), is significant at this historical juncture. Relatedly, Stefan Tanaka has noted the significance of the use of the term "Shina" to refer to China in the Japanese empire. See Tanaka, *Japan's Orient*, 228–62.

38. In another survey published in the same journal, the key question posed relates to how Korean literature measures up to the standards of world literature. Answers range from questioning the very assumption of a "world standard" to theorizing Korea's uncertain position in the global context. See "Chosŏn munhak ŭi segyejŏk sujungwan," *Samch'ŏlli* 4:8 (April 1936): 308–26.

39. Chang Hyŏkchu, "Gakidō," 1–39.

40. See Hirotsu Kazuo, "Bungei shihyō," 5. Quoted in Nakane Takayuki, *"Chōsen" hyōsho no bunkashi*, 212.

41. Chang Hyŏkchu, "Boku no bungaku," 11–12.

42. Kim T'aejun, "Sosŏl ŭi chŏngŭi," 61–63. Sosŏl is a genre of Korean vernacular fiction. The question of whether the sosŏl (*shōsetsu* in Japanese, and *xiaoshuo* in Chinese) in East Asia is comparable to the Western novel continues to confound critics.

43. See Miyoshi, *Off Center*, for ways the anxieties of translation still persists.

44. See Hwang, "Nobŭl, ch'ŏngnyŏn, cheguk," 263–97.

45. Im Hwa began writing in the mid-1930s and continued his endeavors into the early 1940s, when his serialized literary history of Chosŏn munhak was curtailed by Japanese censorship.

46. Im and Han, eds., *Im Hwa sinmunhaksa*, 18.

47. I discuss the spatial hierarchies constructed between center and periphery/region (*chibang/chihō*) in the context of the Japanese empire elsewhere. See Kwon, "Translated Encounters and Empire," 180–241.

48. Yi Kwangsu, "Chosŏn munhak ŭi kaenyŏm," 31–34.

49. Yi Kwangsu, "Chosŏn sosŏlsa," 77–79.

50. Im and Han, eds., *Im Hwa sinmunhaksa*, 77.

51. Harry Harootunian notes that Japanese philosophers perceived their modern predicament as "untimely" and "belated." Intellectuals in colonial Korea felt this untimeliness even more keenly because they were playing catch-up with two different empires. See "'Modernity' and the Claims of Untimeliness." For a cognate discussion in another context, see Chow, *Woman and Chinese Modernity*.

52. The logic of transplantation that Im Hwa and others follow is predicated on problematic assumptions of "purity," "one's own," and so on. Yet critiquing these myopic predilections of the colonized in their "jealous exilic conditions" demands much more than a casual dismissal. Edward Said has discussed the ironic turn inward and the xenophobic tendencies of those who have been forcibly displaced in his essay "Reflections on Exile," in *Reflections on Exile and Other Essays*. The essay refers

to the Jewish-Palestinian conflicts, and the complexity of their victim/victimizer dynamic.

Chapter 3. A Minor Writer

1. Kim Saryang, "Letter to Mother," 104. "Letter to Mother" was written in Japanese and published in the journal *Bungei shuto* in 1940. We do not know whether it was an actual letter Kim wrote to his mother or if it was performatively written just for the Japanese mass media. The indeterminacy of its "authenticity" raises important questions about the minor writing act.

2. I will discuss other necessary points of departure here from Deleuze and Guattari's definitions. However, I retain the term "minor" in order to begin a dialogue across acknowledged differences. They offer us a shared vocabulary although the definitions require translation and adaptation over vast experiences. See Deleuze and Guattari, *Kafka*, in particular, chapter 3. See also Edward Said about the way "colonized" and "third world" subjectivities have come to be seen as synonymous from the colonial to the postcolonial periods, "Representing the Colonized," 293–316.

3. Kim was writing about his Korean-language story *Nakcho* (Setting sun) which appeared in serialization in 1940–1941. Postcard from Kim Saryang to Ch'oe Chŏnghŭi, reprinted in Kim Yŏngsik, ed., *Chakko munin 48-in ŭi yukp'il sŏhanjip* (Collected letters of 48 deceased writers), 120–21.

4. A similar anxiety is expressed in Derrida's *Monolingualism of the Other.*

5. Historians commonly divide imperial policies in colonial Korea into three eras: 1) The military era, 1910–1919; 2) the cultural policy era, 1920–1937; and 3) the total war era, 1937–1945. The period I focus on here is the last, when assimilation policies were becoming more rigorous in order to mobilize colonial subjects for war. The slogan of *Naisen ittai* (Japan and Korea, One Body) was introduced by Governor General Minami Jirō in a gruesome metaphor of hearts, flesh, and blood mixing together: "If you hold hands, you will separate again. If you mix water and oil, they will become a mixed substance in form, but that will not do. Body, heart, blood, and flesh must all become one." Greetings of the Governor General at the Meeting for the Role of the Korean League in National Spiritual Mobilization, 30 May 1939.

6. The "Korea Boom" was a part of the larger phenomenon of imperial fetishism of colonial possessions throughout the expanding empire. I will discuss this further in chapter 5.

7. The question of what constitutes a "national language" in the colony is fraught. For colonial language policies in Korea, see Im Chongguk, *Ch'inil munhak non*. For a comparative study on the policies throughout the Japanese empire, see Yi Yŏngsuk, *"Kokugo" to iu shisō* [The ideology of "national language"], especially chapters 11 and 12 for the Korean case specifically. For important interventions in English, see Robinson, *Cultural Nationalism in Colonial Korea 1920–1925*; and Caprio, *Japanese Assimilation Policies in Colonial Korea 1910–1945*. See Kleeman, *Under an Imperial Sun*, especially chapter 6 for comparative perspectives.

8. There have been numerous studies on the significance of this prize in and beyond Japan. For a recent study in English on the direct contribution of the prize in the

formation of the idea of a modern Japanese literary canon, see Mack, *Manufacturing Modern Japanese Literature*, especially chapter 3.

9. Furthermore, Kawamura's concerns are limited to "Japanese" writers and with "Japanese literature," and he never falters in his assumption of their selfsameness, even in the context of the shifting borders of empire. My chapter questions such assumptions of selfsameness of the nation and its narration both in the metropolitan center and in the colonial peripheries. See Kawamura, *Manshū hōkai* [The collapse of Manchuria], 140–50.

10. Chang Hyŏkchu, another colonial Korean writer, debuted into the Japanese Bundan in 1932 for the second-prize story "Realm of Hungry Ghosts" [Gakidō]. Writers from the other colonies were ambivalently watching these imperial recognitions with both admiration and concern.

11. *Akutagawashō zenshū* [Collected works of the Akutagawa prize], vol. 2, 394.

12. These comments can be found in *Bungei shunjū* 18:4 (March 1940): 348–56.

13. *Akutagawashō zenshū*, vol. 2, 397.

14. *Bungei shunjū* 18:4 (August 1940): 350.

15. Two winners, Ishikawa Jun and Tomizawa Ushio, were awarded simultaneously in 1936. In the first half of 1939, both Handa Yoshiyuki and Hase Ken received the Akutagawa Prize.

16. *Akutagawashō zenshū*, vol. 2, 396.

17. Imperialist discourses in Japan from the Meiji era have continually been fixated on what was called the "Korea problem" (*Chōsen mondai*). Andre Schmid considers the utter lack of engagement in the postcolonial aftermath with the role of the colonies in modern Japanese history to be a symptom of yet another "Korea problem." See Schmid, "Colonialism and the 'Korea Problem' in the Historiography of Modern Japan," 951–76.

18. "Letter to Mother," 106.

19. Edward Mack convincingly argues that there is room to interpret the story "Koshamainki," for example, as subversive toward or critical of imperialism. See *Manufacturing Modern Japanese Literature*. Let me point out the significant absence of any references to such possibilities embodied in the work in the judges' commentaries. "Poacher" in fact is arguably also set in a colonial context, albeit that of an internal colony within Japan proper (Hokkaidō). This fact is mentioned only in passing (if at all) and the rest of the comments are overwhelmingly focused on the "literariness" or the form of its writing. For example, judges focus on the story's vivid description to its sympathetic characterization and character development and its exceptional use of the Japanese language. A double-edged political unconscious of selective remembering and forgetting may be at work here: selectively highlighting Japan's new colonies like Korea occurred while naturalizing the backdrop of Hokkaidō as Japan proper and thus forgetting its colonial origins. For cogent analyses on selective imperial forgetfulness, see Lippit, *Topographies of Japanese Modernism*, Murai, *Nantō ideorogi no hassei*, Ōguma, *Tan'itsu minzoku shinwa no kigen*.

20. See Sakai, "Modernity and Its Critique" on the ongoing complicity between universalism and particularism.

21. *Jihenka no bungaku* [Literature in times of crisis], reprinted in *Kindai bungei hyōron sōsho*, vol. 22, 127–28.

22. *Jihenka no bungaku* [Literature in times of crisis], reprinted in *Kindai bungei hyōron sōsho*, vol. 22, 130.

23. Naoki Sakai's study of universalism versus particularism is applicable here as well. When we examine the Japanese I-novel's wavering history between Japanese essentialism (particularity) and equivalence with the West (universality), the colonial Other remains a constant blind spot in the binary. Also see Fredric Jameson's comment on metropolitan blind spots in *Singular Modernity* for an example from the Euro-American context.

24. "Letter to Mother."

25. Suzuki, *Narrating the Self*, 65.

26. Suzuki, *Narrating the Self*, 65.

27. The quote is from Kobayashi, *Literature of the Lost Home*, 53. As Suzuki argues, "At the same time, Kobayashi here seems to imply that the Japanese intellectuals and writers now shared contemporary European concerns as well as the potential of their European counterparts" (Suzuki, *Narrating the Self*, 58). For other insightful analyses of Kobayashi in English, see Anderer's introduction to the translated volume, *Literature of the Lost Home* and Lippit, *Topographies of Japanese Modernism*.

28. Jameson, "Third-World Literature in the Era of Multinational Capitalism," 65–88.

29. Jameson, "Third-World Literature in the Era of Multinational Capitalism," 77. Good intentions aside, mere sympathies of the metropolitan critic may not be what the minor writer wants. As Frantz Fanon writes, "The man who adores the Negro is just as 'sick' as the man who abominates him" because he assumes a category of radical difference as an object to be loved or hated as he wills and defines (Fanon, *Black Skin, White Masks*, 8).

30. Perhaps most famously in Ahmad, "Jameson's Rhetoric of Otherness and the 'National Allegory.'"

31. Some readers may be startled to see myself referred to as a metropolitan critic. The position of the metropolitan subject, like that of the subaltern, is not a fixed identity but a relational one. Here I am self-consciously referring to the voyage-in of post-colonial scholars into the heart of metropolitan universities, where we sometimes find ourselves unwittingly repeating the very structures we were theoretically said to oppose. I will return to the paradox of the postcolonial in chapter 10.

32. An uncanny haunting in Japan's postwar literary field which harks back directly to the 1940 competition of the Akutagawa Literary Prize is worth considering further in relation to the dialectic of postcolonial memory and forgetting. After the collapse of the Japanese empire, postcolonial writers from the (former) colonies garner periodic waves of attention through metropolitan prizes such as the Akutagawa Prize. In 1971, for example, Ri Kaisei (b. 1935), a postcolonial zainichi Korean writer and Higashi Mineo (b. 1938), an Okinawan writer are simultaneously awarded the Akutagawa Prize. In the author's comments published with his winning story, Ri recalls the 1940 competition and says that he feels he is belatedly accepting the prize on behalf of Kim Saryang himself (*Bungei shunjū* 15.3 March 1971, 319). It is no coincidence that the 1971 recognition occurred in tandem with ambivalent govern-

ment policies regarding postcolonial remnants of internal Others. For example, the Normalization Treaty with South Korea in 1965 and the subsequent "Repatriation Movement" encouraged the "return home" of Korean minorities in Japan to North Korea throughout the decade. The complexities of the "Return to Japan" movements in American-occupied Okinawa culminated in Okinawa's "return to Japan" in 1972 while still retaining the majority of U.S. military bases on the islands. Trendy waves of metropolitan consumption and recognition of minor and postcolonial writers must be contextualized in the ambivalent imbrication of Japan's "postwar" and "postcolonial" rise in the realigned regional order of the Asia-Pacific. I will return to this point in chapter 10.

Chapter 4. Into the Light

1. Kim Saryang, "Hikari no Naka ni" [Into the Light], 2–29, subsequent citations from the story will be in parenthetical page numbers.
2. Letter in private collection of Long Yingzong, quoted in Shimomura Sakujirō, *Bungaku de yomu Taiwan* [Reading Taiwan through literature], 210–12, hereafter cited with page number in parentheses.
3. *Bungei shuto*, July 1940.
4. Likewise, it is important to keep in mind the shared and unshared predicaments of colonized subjects from different contexts. For analysis of the colonial formations of and postcolonial responses to Taiwanese imperial literature (*kōmin bungaku*), see Ching, *Becoming "Japanese"* and Ching, "'Give Me Japan and Nothing Else!'" 763–88.
5. A similar anxiety can be detected in the afterword to his first short-story collection, also entitled *Into the Light*, in which he describes the circumstances of his writing: "Soon after I wrote 'Into the Light' I became known to the world. It was the spring after graduating from university while staying in Keijō [colonial Seoul], in a small *ondol* room, filled with tense agitation, I wrote it in one breath" (346).
6. Judith Butler's work on performative identities informs my reading. See *Gender Trouble* and *Bodies That Matter*, particularly chapters 5 and 6 on crossings and passings at work in various identification processes.
7. This word is written in katakana script, marking its foreignness.
8. There were exceptions even in the European context such as the role of England in Ireland, Scotland, and Wales, and the issue of "passing" is a major anxiety-producing social phenomenon in all racialized contexts.
9. Unfortunately, such abjection of Haruo is not limited only to the textual level. Later, a North Korean critic laments that this story's limitation in that it is not about the plight of the Korean people, but about a "mixed-blood" child, Haruo. Chang Hyŏngjun, "Chakka Kim Saryang kwa kŭ ŭi munhak" [Writer Kim Saryang and his literature], 6–7.
10. In the original text, the two characters here have been censored out by imperial censors. Based on the context, it might be the word *teikō* (to rebel or to resist).
11. Subject formations mediated through the specular gaze of the Other have been discussed in the psychoanalytic formulations of Jaques Lacan. See "The Mirror Stage as Formative of the I Function, as Revealed in Psychoanalytic Experience."
12. In the preface to the Korean translation of Kim Saryang's biography, the author,

An Usik, a zainichi Korean critic, writes that when he first read "Into the Light," he could readily identify with the characters because the setting of the story was his own childhood neighborhood. See An, *Kim Saryang Hyōden* [Critical biography of Kim Saryang], 14.

13. I am informed by Lacan's theory of decentered subjectivity which focuses on the violent clash of the self/other binary of the imaginary realm, but I "misappropriate" the formulation into the social realm of encountering the Other which seems to mirror the situation described in Kim's text. Perhaps closer to the future suggested here is something described in Luce Irigaray's interventions on Lacanian conception of the ethical relationship with the Other on an interpersonal level, in terms of intimacy. Butler's nuanced reading is worth quoting here: "In Irigaray's most systematic reading of the history of ethical philosophy, *Éthique de la différence sexuelle*, she argues that ethical relations ought to be based on relations of closeness, proximity, and intimacy that reconfigure conventional notions of reciprocity and respect. Traditional conceptions of reciprocity exchange such relations of intimacy for those characterized by violent erasure, substitutability, and appropriation" (*Bodies That Matter*, 46). See Irigaray, *Ethique de la différence sexuelle*. For the ways critics have productively "misappropriated" Lacan's theory of the registers and transgressed the imaginary other/Symbolic Other divide for political ends, see Van Pelt, "Otherness."

Chapter 5. Colonial Abject

1. On the spiritual fervor that accompanied the war mobilization, see Keene, "Japanese Writers and the Greater East Asia War," 209–25.
2. Kim Chaeyong, *Hyŏmnyŏk kwa chŏhang*, 282.
3. Kokumin bungaku literally means national literature; however in the context of mobilization of imperial subjects in colonial Korea, it is more accurate to translate it as imperial literature.
4. Im Chongguk, *Ch'inil munhak non*, 45–76.
5. Kim Saryang himself was an active translator of Korean literature into Japanese at the time.
6. Kim Yunsik, *Hanil kŭndae munhak ŭi kwallyŏn yangsang sillon* [New perspectives on the relationship between Korean and Japanese modern literatures], 70.
7. Kristeva, "Approaching Abjection," 4.
8. Kristeva's theory of abjection is linked to the Lacanian mirror stage (six to eighteen months) when a sense of identity is first formulated and language is acquired through the imposition of the symbolic Law (as represented by the Father), which severs the heretofore harmonious world of the child (as represented by the Mother). Diverging from Lacan, Kristeva argues that before this primal repression (of the desire to cling to the mother), which ultimately links a sense of loss with language and desire, there occurs a movement of the subject (child) toward rejecting/expelling the mother. Since all this presumably happens in the unconscious, the abjection of the mother is in effect the abjection of an aspect of the self that is perceived as intolerant by the child. It is an act wrought with ambivalence and conflict since the child must reject that which offers it security as well as stifles it.

The abject in relation to the physical body includes those spaces/orifices that are construed as neither inside nor out. The bodily fluids and waste that emerge such as milk, blood, urine, and feces induce a repulsion because they represent the "breaking down of a world that has erased its borders: fainting away" (Kristeva, "Approaching Abjection," 4). The corpse is considered the penultimate abject since it crosses the ultimate border between life and death. The elaborate rituals (e.g., food taboos, toilet etiquette, mourning rituals) that keep societies in order reveal the universal revulsion towards such borderline yet necessary aspects of life (Kristeva, "Approaching Abjection," 2–4).

9. Douglas, *Purity and Danger*, 94.

10. Kristeva, "Approaching Abjection," 4.

11. Kristeva, "Approaching Abjection," 17.

12. Douglas, *Purity and Danger*, 94.

13. Kristeva, "Approaching Abjection," 4.

14. Kristeva, "Approaching Abjection," 17.

15. *Kim Saryang zenshū*, vol. 4, 21–34.

16. It is worth noting that this criticism is republished in Japanese in the colonial Korean popular journal *Samch'ŏlli*, at a time when the pages of this and other publications were increasingly turning Japanese. An example of a "failed translation," the article was published in Japanese with only a different title, "The Problem of the Korean Language." This failed translation in the colonial Korean context — in which the complex issues of colonial translations were merely recast as the problem of the Korean language — reveals another failed encounter in the empire.

17. "*Chōsen bunka tsūshin*" (Dispatches on Korean culture), 27. Subsequent references to this essay will be in parenthetical page numbers within the text.

18. Interestingly, Kim Saryang attempts to negotiate and play with this impasse by writing at times, two or more versions of the same story, in both Korean and Japanese. Significant differences exist among these auto-translations that deserve closer examination.

19. Antonio Gramsci discusses two main types of intellectuals: those whose work sustains the status quo, and those whose work challenges it. In particular, what he calls the "organic intellectuals" work toward countercultural production, by new means of collective action toward overcoming the plight of the marginalized and excluded. Gramsci, *Selections from the Prison Notebooks*, 5–14.

20. I am using this term as used in ethnology, and I am in agreement with Gayatri Chakravorty Spivak when she appropriates the problematic concept "as a name for threat mark of expulsion from the name of Man," thus as a site of slippage from within dominant discourses. Spivak, *Critique of Postcolonial Reason*, 6.

21. The terms *moga* and *mobo* first appeared in Japan in 1926, and soon after in Korea. Kon, *Kogengaku nyūmon* [Introduction to modernology].

22. See Modern Girl Around the World Research Group, ed., *The Modern Girl around the World*.

23. Kim Saryang, "Tenma," 352–84.

24. What I call the "(colonized) modern boy" is a translation of the term *mo(yo) bo*, which was used by a colonial writer, taking the Japanese neologism *mobo* or "modern boy" and grafting it to the term *yobo*, a derogatory term used by the Japa-

nese to refer to Koreans during the colonial period. It was a term of self-parody that shows ironic self-consciousness toward colonial mimicry of the quintessential emblem of Western modernity, the dandy of the city. Implicit in the self-deprecating comic term is the keen recognition of the doubly mediated or translated nature of Korea's modern experience vis-à-vis modern Japan's own complex relations in the new global chronotope.

25. I have used the doubled pronunciations of Genryū/ Hyŏllyong's name in Japanese and Korean readings to emphasize his doubled identities. The characters of his name could be read either way.

26. With official colonization of Korea in 1910, the name of the capital city of Korea, called Hanyang or Seoul, which means "capital city," was changed to Keijō by the Governor General. The boroughs and streets of the city were also marked as Japanese by Japanese-style names at this time.

27. For the biographical details of Kim's life, see An, *Hyōden Kim Saryang* [A critical biography of Kim Saryang].

28. Hutcheon, *Theory of Parody*, xii, 37. Subsequent references will be in parenthetical page numbers in the text.

29. Other critics have pointed out the similarities of the character to the Korean writer/critic Kim Munchip, who wrote many texts in Japanese and is considered to have ingratiated himself to the Japanese Bundan by espousing the assimilation of colonial literature into Japanese national literature. The most obvious similarity is that Kim Munchip changed his name to Oe Ryūnosuke, mimicking the Japanese writer Akutagawa Ryūnosuke. In the last scene Genryū/Hyŏllyong refers to himself as "Gennokami Ryūnosuke." As is well known, Koreans were required to take on Japanese-style names during the latter part of the colonial period as part of the move to mobilize the colony as loyal subjects of the imperial war machine. In his critical essay "Chōsen bunka tsūshin," Kim Saryang reveals his ambivalence toward a Japanese critic who assumes that the story is autobiographical. My point here is that the textual characters' resemblance to actual figures and the debates triggered by this riddle reveal the curious nature of this story crossing boundaries of biography/autobiography, reality and fiction, and the ultimate indeterminacy of the identity of the characters. See Nam, *Kindai bungaku no "Chōsen" taiken* [Korean experience in modern literature].

30. See, for example, the reading in Kim Chaeyong, *Hyŏmnyŏk kwa chŏhang*.

31. Frantz Fanon, in *Black Skin, White Masks*, writes that ambivalence is "inherent in the colonial situation" (83) and Homi Bhabha discusses ambivalence as a potential site of resistance by threatening the colonizer's need to differentiate the colonized. If resistance can be read in the character Genryū/Hyŏllyong, I would say it occurs at the site of the reader critiquing the context in which such characters emerged rather than at the site of the character himself, the embodiment of colonial ambivalence. Bhabha, chapter 4, "Of Mimicry and Man," in *The Location of Culture*.

32. The Japanese settled in the southern part of Seoul; the northern part was inhabited by Koreans. A different section of the city, in central Seoul, called Chung-gu (Central district), was designated the "foreigners" district and was settled primarily by Westerners. It is interesting that the "foreign" area is distinguished from the Japa-

nese section, the assumption presumably being that the Japanese, as the colonizers and thus owners of the land, were not foreign.

33. Kim, "Tenma," 354.
34. For details of the Western-style constructions of these buildings, see Kungnip hyôndae misulgwan, ed., *Hanguk kônch'uk 100-nyôn* [One-hundred years of Korean architecture].
35. Freud, "Uncanny," 219–40.
36. On Honbura, see Lee Kyoung-Hoon [Yi Kyônghun], "Mitsukoshi, kûndae ûi shyowindou—munhak kwa p'ungsok 1," 107–47. On *Ginbura*, see Kon Wajiro, *Kogengaku nyūmon*. Interestingly, the image of Honmachi, including the Mitsukoshi Department Store, depicted in a promotional movie commissioned by the Chōsen Governor General such as the film "Keijō" (1943) shows harmonious intermingling of Koreans and Japanese as they enjoy browsing and buying the commodities.
37. As indicated in the text, traveling to Manchuria was a popular trend during the time. Like all fads (such as the "Korea Boom"), this one didn't just happen out of the blue. After the "Manchurian Incident" of 1931, the war with China was full-blown by 1937 ("Pegasus" was published in 1940), and the Japanese imperial state made calculated efforts to transplant people into these newly acquired territories. For details of the concerted efforts of Japanese government and business interests in Manchuria, see Young, *Japan's Total Empire*; Kim, "Tenma," 356.
38. Kim, "Tenma," 356.
39. An interesting aside, one police report recorded in the Governor General's *Guide to Keijō* mentions the frustrations felt in the impossibility of chasing down Korean criminals once they dodged into these impenetrable mazes of alleyways. *Sinpan Keijō annai* [New guide to Keijō]. Edited by Chōsen Sōtokufu [Governor General of Korea].
40. Kim, "Tenma," 357.
41. Kim, "Tenma," 357.
42. Naichi is also translated as inland. The ironic nomenclature that defines Japan as Naichi reveals the social production of space at work. The claim to "interiority" of Japan through imperial logic defies geographical realities since the Japanese archipelago occupies the outermost position vis-à-vis the Asian continent.
43. Two stories penned in the colony at this time can be read in a similar vein: Pak T'aewŏn's *Sosŏlga Kubossi ûi iril* [A day in the life of the writer Kubo], in which the writer is depicted as sickly, impotent, and infantile in his monotonous and aimless wanderings in the colonial city, as well as Yi Sang's "Nalgae" (Wings), in which the protagonist in the colonial city meets a tragic end; his refusal to partake in the capitalist relations of commodity fetishism and the ideology of temporal progress shown in his regression to infantile status alienated from all forms of social and economic exchange lead him to the story's end where he stands atop the roof garden of the Mitsukoshi department store, ready to jump off, desperately calling for man-made wings to sprout. These stories reveal the exclusionary contradictions of capitalist imperial logic as manifest in the colony.
44. The Chosŏn [Chōsen, J] Hotel was also built by the Japanese, following Western architectural motifs, suggestive of the doubly transplanted nature of Korean moder-

nity in the colonized context; it was an exclusive hotel, serving primarily Japanese and foreign guests, and some privileged Koreans.

45. See An, *Hyōden Kim Saryang*.

46. Yi Sŏnok makes an interesting argument that many women writers considered to be "pro-Japanese" found a way out of repressive households and found new politicized identities by writing and promoting the Japanese imperial cause.

47. Kim, "Tenma," 359.

48. Yi Sŏnok, "P'yŏngdŭng e taehan yuhok: yŏsŏng chisigin kwa ch'inil ŭi naechŏk nolli."

49. Kim, "Tenma," 359.

50. The binary between imperialist and nationalist perspectives was not clearly divided along the ethnic identities as there were Koreans who supported imperial policies and Japanese who opposed them. However, the point is that power dynamics between the colonizers and the colonized were intact even as assimilation was being espoused purportedly to overcome such divisions.

51. For details, see Sin Hyŏnggi, *Haebang chikhu ŭi munhak undong non* [On immediate postliberation literary movements].

52. "Munhakcha ŭi chagi pip'an" [Writers' self-reflection].

53. "Munhakcha ŭi chagi pip'an" [Writers' self-reflection].

54. It may be worth noting that Yi T'aejun's own "pro-Japanese text" has been uncovered since. See Hotei Toshihiro, "Ilche malgi Ilbonŏ sosŏl yŏngu" [Japanese-language fiction from the late-colonial period]. I point this out not to condemn Yi along the same logic of his own criticism of Kim but to note just how impossible it is to draw lines between "purity" and "impurity" based on vanishing traces of the past. The point here is not necessarily to "uncover the truth," but to linger on the effects of the violence that arise from its burial or denial, both on the personal and institutional levels, when considering Korea's colonial past. I am not advocating a turn away from issues of responsibility or culpability from the discourse, but rather wish to complicate the discussion away from the discourse of scapegoating.

55. Kim, "Tenma," 383–84.

Chapter 6. Performing Colonial Kitsch

1. Quoted from *Literary Review* (November 1934) in Kleeman, *Under an Imperial Sun*, 160.

2. Huang Yuan, ed., *Shanling: Chaoxian Taiwan duanpian xiaoshuo ji* [Mountain spirits: Korean and Taiwanese short story collection]. Translated by Hu Fung. Shanghai: Wenhua shenghuo chubanshe, 1936.

3. A parallel dichotomy in the case of colonial Taiwanese literature between "nativist" and "imperial-subject literature" is introduced and complicated in Kleeman, *Under an Imperial Sun*, chapters 7 and 8.

4. The event was widely covered and reviewed in major journals and dailies in Japan and Korea such as *Keijō nippō, Asahi shinbun, Teatoro, Bungaku, Teikoku daigaku shinbun, Engeki gahō, Chogwang, Samch'ŏlli, Chosŏn ilbo,* and *Maeil sinbo,* among others. For a detailed account of the various performances see Shirakawa, *Shokuminchi Chōsen no sakka to Nihon*. See also Paek, "Minjokchŏk chŏnt'ong kwa

tongyangjŏk chŏnt'ong." On the "Korea Boom" (popularity of colonial Korean culture) in Japan in general, see Im Chŏnhye, *Nihon ni okeru Chōsenjin no bungaku no rekishi*; and Nakane Takayuki, *"Chōsen" hyōshōno bunkashi*. In English, see Atkins, *Primitive Selves*.

5. There are various versions extant, over one hundred "traditional" versions, and numberless modern retellings. It is also known as *Ch'unhyang ka* 春香歌 [The song of Ch'unhyang] in the song narrative version. For the purposes here, I will refer to the urtext as *Ch'unhyang* in italics.

6. It is significant that not until 1995, some sixty years after the end of empire, did a Japanese scholar of colonial Korea first puzzle together the event's significance from scattered archival materials in Japan and Korea. It was only in the late 1990s that more active scholarly exchanges became possible between the former colony and metropole. Likewise, the stark contrast between the attention the performance received throughout the empire and its long-forgotten status is symptomatic of the contentious condition of the postcolonial relationship in the region. See Paek, "Minjokchŏk chŏnt'ong kwa tongyangjŏk chŏnt'ong."

7. For example, a quarter-page advertisement in the *Maeil sinbo* on October 22, 1938, announced the performance as the "handshake of the art of *Naisen ittai*" (*Naesŏn ilch'e yesul ŭi aksu*).

8. Rosaldo, "Imperialist Nostalgia," 107–22. For a similar phenomenon in another imperial context, see Norindr, *Phantasmatic Indochina*.

9. Duara, *Rescuing History from the Nation*; Saaler and Koschmann, eds., *Pan-Asianism in Modern Japanese History*.

10. For example, even Fukuzawa Yukichi, before his famous declaration of "Escape the East and Enter the West," espoused a unity with Asia. See Tanaka, *Japan's Orient*, Ōguma, *Tan'itsu minzoku shinwa no kigen* and *Nihonjin no kyōkai*; Duus, *Abacus and the Sword*; Chŏng, "Singminji hubangi Hanguk munhak e nat'anan tongyang non yŏngu"; Ch'a, "1930 nyŏndae huban chŏnt'ong non yŏngu." In Japan, such debates were often couched in the binary oppositions of the East versus the West. See Harootunian, *Overcome by Modernity*. The call was for the Eastern or "yellow" brothers to stand together to defend their traditions or "spiritual survival" in the face of Western or "white" imperialism. See Dower, *War without Mercy*, 1986. For the false dichotomy between the West and the Rest, see Hanawa and Sakai, eds., *Traces 1*.

11. On competing universals, see Liu, *Tokens of Exchange*, introduction.

12. See Hwang Chongyŏn, "1930 nyŏndae kojŏn puhŭng undong ŭi munhaksajŏk ŭiŭi," 217–60; Ch'a Sŭnggi, "1930 nyŏndae huban chŏnt'ongnon yŏngu"; Chŏng Chonghyŏn, "Singminji hubangi (1937–1945) Hanguk munhak e nat'anan tongyang non yŏngu"; Cho Kwanja, "Nitchū sensōki no 'Chōsengaku' to 'koten fukkō'—shokuminchi no 'chi' o tou," 59–81.

13. Nostalgia, according to the OED, is defined as follows: "Nostalgia (n.): 1) Acute longing for familiar surroundings, esp. regarded as a medical condition; homesickness. 2) Sentimental longing for or regretful memory of a period of the past, esp. one in an individual's own lifetime; (also) sentimental imagining or evocation of a period of the past."

14. Boym, *Future of Nostalgia*, xiii.
15. Late colonialism (1930s–1940s) refers to the last decade of the colonial relationship between Japan and Korea. This was a period of fluctuation in the rise and fall of Japan's wartime empire, coeval with the broader global condition of economic and political crises, culminating in the imperialist clash of World War II (and economic crisis), and finally leading to the demise of familiar forms of colonialism and toward a new world order divided along Cold War loyalties. This time is often described as a time of "crisis," "transition" or upheaval throughout the world, and my focus is on the coevalness of world events as well as on the effect of the global in the local in the context of colonial Korea.
16. See Sŏl Sŏnggyŏng, *Ch'unhyang chŏn ŭi pimil*, for a recent attempt to solve the puzzle of *Ch'unhyang*.
17. For example, in *Hanguk munhak ch'ongsŏ* (Series on Korean literature), Yi Sangt'aek writes, "As is well-known, *The Tale of Ch'unhyang* is the representative work of [Korea's] classical literature which is still appreciated by the people" (37). Richard Rutt, in the introduction to his English language translation, writes, "Ch'unhyang ka" (The song of Ch'unhyang) is Korea's favorite story. No one knows when it was first told or who told it, but every Korean alive knows both the plot and the characters intimately. The tale had been told thousands of times: in Korean and Chinese, in verse and in prose, as opera, drama, film, and musical comedy; in cartoons, and in elegant embroidery on screens and scrolls. It has become part of Korea's folk heritage" (238). Sŏl Sŏnggyŏng writes, "The national classic *Ch'unhyang chŏn*, for 360 years, has been revived in diverse artistic forms and has propelled scholarship," in *Ch'unhyang chŏn ŭi pimil*, 4.
18. Stephen Vlastos's comment that traditions are chosen rather than inherited is significant here in showing the deliberate choice of privileging *Ch'unhyang* in this transition to the modern. Vlastos, *Mirror of Modernity*.
19. Lee, *Contemporary Korean Cinema*; Baek Moon-im, *Ch'unhyang ŭi ttaldŭl*; Lee, "The Road to Ch'unhyang."
20. Vlastos argues that both views are ahistorical and work to reinstate the binaries of premodern/modern and stasis/change that have been linked to the Western concept of modernity, thus failing to "problematize the historicity of tradition . . . [and] the normative status and repetitive practice of invented traditions [which] powerfully naturalize them." Vlastos, *Mirror of Modernity*, 2–3.
21. Hobsbawm, *Invention of Tradition*; and Vlastos, *Mirror of Modernity*.
22. Vlastos writes, "In Edward Shils's formulation, tradition is 'far more than the statistically frequent reoccurrence over a succession of generations of similar beliefs, practices, institutions, and works.' The core of tradition is strongly normative; the intention (and the effect) is to reproduce patterns of culture. Shils writes, 'It is this normative transmission which links the generations of the dead with the generations of the living.' In this conception, rather than representing culture left behind in the transition to modernity, tradition is what modernity *requires* to prevent society from flying apart" (Vlastos, *Mirror of Modernity*, 2, emphasis in the original).
23. Vlastos writes, "The double meaning of 'invention': signifies both imagination and

contrivance, creation and deception. Every tradition trades between these two poles" (Vlastos, *Mirror of Modernity*, 6).

24. See Hwang Jong-yŏn, "1930 nyŏndae kojŏn puhŭng undong ŭi munhaksajŏk ŭiŭi" and Ch'a Sŭnggi, "1930 nyŏndae huban chŏnt'ongnon yŏngu."

25. "Korea Boom" is a phrase that originally referred to Japan's new economic policies in the colonies, but it spread into other cultural realms. In his afterword to Vlastos's *Mirror of Modernity*, Dipesh Chakrabarty discusses the difference between Japan's experience of inventing its traditions and that of the colonized non-West. Japan actually had control over how its traditions would be defined, however essentialist it may be; but colonized subjects found their traditions invented and exoticized by the colonizers. I would suggest that Japan was not free from being exoticized either by imperial others or even by itself. See "Revisiting the Tradition/Modernity Binary," in Vlastos, ed., *Mirror of Modernity*, 286–97.

26. For a similar consumer trend objectifying Manchuria, see Young, *Japan's Total Empire*. For a focused study on literary consumption of the colonies, see Kawamura Minato *Manshū hōkai*. In film, see Baskett, "The Attractive Empire" and *Attractive Empire*.

27. See for one example, Brandt, "Objects of Desire," 711–40; and *Kingdom of Beauty*.

28. The movement for "Japan-ization" or kōminka (making imperial subjects).

29. See Baskett, *Attractive Empire*. See also Robertson, *Takarazuka*.

30. Tanaka, *Japan's Orient*.

31. Akita Ujaku, "Kokyō e kaeru Shunkōden: yūgō shita futatsu no bunka no kōryū [*Ch'unhyang chōn*'s homecoming: The exchange of two unified cultures]." *Keijō nippō*, October 9, 1938.

32. Chang Hyŏkchu. "Shunkōden." *Shinchō* 35:3 (August 1938), reprinted as *Shunkōden* (Shinchōsha, 1938, 1941).

33. See Young, *Colonial Desire*, and Bhabha, *The Location of Culture*, especially chapter 6, "Signs Taken for Wonders," which deals with the notions of ambivalence and hybridity in colonial contexts.

34. For colonized writers of Chang's generation, many of whom over time became more well versed in Japanese than in Korean, the concept of a "mother tongue" is complex and defies easy categorization.

35. Said, *Culture and Imperialism*.

36. Later literary histories in Korea exclude him as a "pro-Japanese" collaborator for his writings during the latter part of the Pacific War. It is undeniable that Chang did write in support of the Japanese war effort, but as one of the colonized, his relationships to Japan and Korea have been wrought with ambivalence and cannot be understood simply along the binary of pro- or anti-Japanese. More research needs to be done to examine the complexity of his position and writings during a period that was tumultuous and traumatic, both historically and personally.

37. Murayama Tomoyoshi, "Shunkōden no Chikuji jōen ni tsuite," *Chōsen oyobi Manshū* 364 (March 1938): 60.

38. Murayama Tomoyoshi, "Chōsen to no kōryū," *Asahi shinbun*, September 15, 1938.

39. Murayama Tomoyoshi, "Shunkōden no Chikuji jōen ni tsuite," 59.

40. Yu Ch'ijin, "*Ch'unhyang chŏn* ŭi Tonggyŏng sangyŏng kwa kŭ pŏnan kakpon ŭi pip'yŏng 1, 2, 3," *Chosŏn ilbo*, February 24–26, 1938. Emphasis is mine.

41. Murayama Tomoyoshi, "*Shunkōden* yodan" [Musings on Shunkōden], *Keijō nippō*, May 31, 1938; Yu Ch'ijin, "*Shunkōden* o miru—Shinkyō gekidan torai no igi" [Viewing *Ch'unhyang chŏn*—the significance of the crossover of the Shinkyō Troupe], *Keijō nippō*, October 27, 1938; Murayama Tomoyoshi, "Chōsen to no kōryū," *Asahi shinbun*, September 15, 1938.

42. The script is substantially altered, cutting down Chang's six acts and fifteen scenes to five acts and eleven scenes by Murayama. Murayama Tomoyoshi, "*Shunkōden* no Chikuji jōen ni tsuite," 60.

43. Murayama Tomoyoshi, "*Shunkōden* yodan: Keijō demo jōen shitai," *Keijō nippō*, May 31, 1938.

44. "I thought that my version was used merely as a reference, but in act six, the scene of the coming of the Secret Inspector was exactly the same as my own, that I thought I was on the Kukyŏnjwa stage." Yu Ch'ijin, "*Ch'unhyang chŏn* o miru—Shinkyō Gekidan torai no igi," *Keijō nippō*, October 27, 1938, quoted in Shirakawa, *Shokuminchiki Chōsen no sakka to Nihon*, 103. Shirakawa interprets this as a rivalry between two colonized writers—Yu and Chang—but what seems significant here is the power imbalance between the dramatist Murayama and the native informants he consulted. See Shirakawa, *Shokuminchiki Chōsen no sakka to Nihon*, 103. For other references to Murayama's "editing" hand, see Murayama Tomoyoshi, "*Shunkōden* yodan" [Musings on Shunkōden], *Keijō nippō*, May 31, 1938; and Yu Ch'ijin, "*Shunkōden* o miru—Shinkyō gekidan torai no igi," [Viewing *Ch'unhyang chŏn*—the significance of the crossover of the Shinkyō troupe], *Keijō nippō*, October 27, 1938.

45. Murayama Tomoyoshi, "Chōsen no inshō: Kangsŏ, Kyŏngju, Namwŏn, nado," *Chōsen oyobi Manshū* 368 (July 1938): 53.

46. There were some naysayers, but these were put down as just a few "professional critics" who didn't know better. See Akita Ujaku's categorical dismissal of any negative press in Japan, *Keijō nippō*, October 9, 1938.

47. Murayama Tomoyoshi, "*Shunkōden* yodan: Keijō demo jōen shitai," *Keijō nippō*, May 31, 1938.

48. Murayama Tomoyoshi, "*Shunkōden* yodan: Keijō demo jōen shitai," *Keijō nippō*, May 31, 1938.

49. Author unknown. "Eigaka sareru *Shunkōden*-jō," *Keijō nippō*, June 9, 1938.

50. Murayama Tomoyoshi et al., "Eigaka sareru *Shunkōden* zadankai" [The making of the movie, *Shunkōden*, roundtable discussion], *Keijō nippō*, June 9, 1938.

51. In her book *Takarazuka*, Jennifer Robertson analyzes a parallel movement of what she coins "cross-ethnicking" to describe this essentialist performing of the role of an ethnic Other. Her sustained work on similar phenomena in *Takarazuka* lends support to a wider phenomenon of the use of theater as a technology of imperialism (Robertson, *Takarazuka: Sexual Politics and Popular Culture in Modern Japan*, especially chapter 3).

52. Author unknown. "Eigaka sareru *Shunkōden*, chū," *Keijō nippō*, June 10, 1938.

53. This seems to be a common myopia of Japanese leftists who, in the name of solidar-

ity with colonized Koreans, often missed seeing the uneven colonial relationship that they themselves were occupying.

54. Noguchi, "Izoku no otto (Foreign husband)." Such scenes of colonial surveillance are ubiquitous in colonial Korean literature. See for example, Yŏm Sangsŏp's "On the Eve of the Uprising."

55. See Chang Hyŏkchu, "Chōsen no chishikijin ni uttau," 225–39, and various responses. This text is seen as showing Chang's "pro-Japanese" tendencies. It is in fact quite complex, not merely a tirade by Chang on Koreans. In fact, he himself is implicated as a target in this piece, complicating the simple binary between the subjectivity of the colonizer (Japan) and the colonized (which Chang embodied). The piece deserves a nuanced reading which will be deferred for later.

56. *Pip'an* (December 1938).

57. *Pip'an* (December 1938). There is an unmistakable echo here of the modern versus traditional women debates going on at that time in which the modern woman, who was perceived to be too liberated, or Westernized, was reprimanded in the media. Similar phenomena occurred in Japan and China as well.

58. See Schmid, *Korea between Empires.*

59. Japan did structure its empire on a distinctively hierarchical scale, with Korea often seen as second son or third son, depending on how the "internal colonies" such as Okinawa and Hokkaido were defined. See Christy, "Making Imperial Subjects in Okinawa."

60. Bhabha, *The Location of Culture*, especially chapter 4, "Of Mimicry and Man." The critics' anxiety in their insistence on "authenticity" is revealed ironically by moments when they use code switching to Japanese freely during the conversation. They make ample references to Japanese cultural productions of the past and present, revealing that they are quite well read in metropolitan texts. The natural infusion of their casual conversational language with Japanese words exposes the hybrid colonial linguistic condition that renders ironic these critics' demand for pure authenticity in Chang.

61. Rey Chow in *Woman and Chinese Modernity* makes a cogent assessment of this situation. Also see Schmid, *Korea between Empires*; and Duara, *Rescuing History from the Nation.*

62. The woman as an allegory of the nation is a common motif. Countless colonial-period novels depict the victimization of women (often through sexual assault that "taints" them); these novels are commonly read as "national allegories" of the colonial "shame." Also relevant is the so-called comfort-women issue in which nationalist contests between Korea and Japan have been fought over the bodies of these women. See Kim and Choi, eds., *Dangerous Women.*

Chapter 7. Overhearing Transcolonial Roundtables

1. What I mean by "overhearing" has multiple significations. One, I use it in the sense of eavesdropping, implying simultaneously a privileged and a limited access to a dialogue, as well as "overhearing" in the sense of "to hear again," connoting both a temporal and spatial distance (hearing something from a place and time beyond the actual event) as well as a repetitive act of hearing again and again. The "over"

of overhearing also implies the overdetermined nature of any dialogue with a text, particularly a text passed down through colonial legacies. See the section "Overhearing the Roundtable" below for further explication of this reading methodology.

2. Yamazaki Yoshimitsu, "Modanizumu no gensetsuyōshi toshite no 'zadankai'— *Shinchō* 'gappyōkai' kara *Bungei shunjū* no 'zadankai' e" ["Roundtable" as a phenomenon of modernism—from the "collective reviews" of *Shinchō* to the "roundtables" of *Bungei shunjū*], 45–57.

3. For example, in a chapter "Conversation and Conference" in *Off Center*, Masao Miyoshi links the prominence of such "conversations" in contemporary Japan to the decline of a written discourse and a viable critical discourse in Japan (219). Throughout this short chapter, Miyoshi seems to waver between broad generalizations on Japanese culture, linking the prevalence of the roundtable to a uniquely Japanese penchant for orality over writing, only to qualify these comments by skillfully remarking that this type of commodified "conversationalism" is not in fact unique to Japan. Miyoshi's book, written for an English-speaking audience, seems to perpetuate stereotypical images such as assumptions of the tendency for Japanese toward group consensus. Miyoshi, *Off Center*, 217–31.

4. Yamazaki, "Modanizumu no gensetsu yōshitoshite no 'zadankai,'" 55–56.

5. Yamazaki, "Modanizumu no gensetsu yōshitoshite no 'zadankai,'" 55–56.

6. *Shinchō* (August 1923). Quoted in Yamazaki, "Modanizumu no gensetsu yōshitoshite no 'zadankai,'" 52.

7. Sakai, et. al, "Zadankai," 232–53.

8. Interestingly, Miyoshi made this same assessment in an earlier attempt to locate the rise of the zadankai format in the particularities of postwar Japanese society, generally taking a positive perspective toward the zadankai of the prewar period. *Off Center*, 217–31.

9. In fact, perhaps it is symptomatic of colonial modernity that the zadankai of vexing encounters between the colonizers and the colonized disappeared from the public radar in the postcolonial period almost as quickly and expediently as they had emerged in the colonial period.

10. Likewise, the fact that these roundtables have been overlooked in later discussions of the roundtables in Japan seems symptomatic not only of their exclusion from the postliberation discursive space (in Korea and Japan), but also of the ever-widening gap between postcolonial readers and the text of the colonial past. An exceptional article that discusses the issue of roundtables in the Japanese empire is Matsuda Toshihiko, "Sōryokusenki no shokuminchi Chōsen ni okeru keisatsu gyōsei," 195–223. In recent years, there has been an important rise in critical scholarship on transcolonial roundtables. See, for example, Sin Jiyŏng, *Pujae ŭi sidae* and Yi Wŏndong, *Singmin chibae tamnon kwa* Kungmin munhak chwadamhoe. The belatedness of this critical encounter some seventy-years later is worth noting here. A translated collection of roundtables from the journal *Kokumin bungaku* is another welcome contribution. See Mun Kyŏngyŏn, et. al, eds., *Chwadamhoe ro ignŭn* Kungmin munhak.

11. Sakai, et. al, "Zadankai: Bunka no seijisei," 235.

12. Sakai, et.al, "Zadankai: Bunka no seijisei," 236.

13. Aczel, "Understanding as Over-hearing," 604.
14. Aczel, "Understanding as Over-hearing," 597.
15. Aczel, "Understanding as Over-hearing," 597.
16. Aczel, "Understanding as Over-hearing," 597.
17. Aczel, "Understanding as Over-hearing," 607.
18. "Zadankai: Chōsen bundan no saishuppatsu o kataru" [Roundtable: Discussing the new start of the Korean literary field], *Kokumin bungaku* (November 1941); "Zadankai: NichiBei kaisen to tōyō no shōrai" [Roundtable: Beginning of war between Japan and America and the future of the orient], *Kokumin bungaku* (January 1942); "Zadankai: bungei dōin o kataru" [Roundtable: Discussing cultural mobilization], *Kokumin bungaku* (January 1942); "Zadankai: daitōa bunkaken no kōsō" [Roundtable: The concept of a greater East Asian cultural sphere], *Kokumin bungaku* (February 1942); "Zadankai: Hantō kirisutokyō no kaikaku o kataru" [Roundtable: Discussing the reform of Korean Christianity], *Kokumin bungaku* (March 1942); "Zadankai: gunjin to sakka chōhei no kangeki o kataru" [Roundtable: Discussing the gratitude of conscripted soldiers and writers], *Kokumin bungaku* (July 1942); "Zadankai: hoppōken bunka o kataru" [Roundtable: Discussing cultural field of the north], *Kokumin bungaku* (October 1942); "Zadankai: kokumin bungaku no ichinen o kataru" [Roundtable: Discussing one-year of imperial literature], *Kokumin bungaku* (November 1942); "Zadankai: ashita e Chōsen eiga" [Roundtable: Tomorrow's Korean cinema], *Kokumin bungaku* (December 1942); "Zadankai: shin-Hantō bungaku e no yōbō" [The demand for new Korean literature], *Kokumin bungaku* (March 1943); "Zadankai: kimukyōiku ni naru made" [Roundtable: Until the establishment of mandatory education], *Kokumin bungaku* (April 1943); "Zadankai: nōson bunka no tameni—idō gekidan, idō eiga" [Roundtable: For the sake of the culture of the countryside—traveling theater and traveling cinema], *Kokumin bungaku* (May 1943); "Zadankai: sensō to bungaku" [Roundtable: War and literature], *Kokumin bungaku* (May 1943); "Zadankai: kokumin bungaku no hōkō" [Roundtable: The direction of imperial literature], *Kokumin bungaku* (August 1943); "Zadankai: sōryokusen undō no shin kōsō" [New concept of the total war movement], *Kokumin bungaku* (December 1944).
19. Some examples include "Bunka o tazunete: sansakka o fukumu zadankai" [Searching for culture: A roundtable around three writers], *Keijō nippō* (June–July 1939); "Bunjin no tachiba kara Kikuchi Kan-si o chūsin ni Hantō no bungei o kataru zadankai" [From the perspective of a cultural figure, focused on Mr. Kikuchi Kan, a roundtable discussing Korean culture], *Keijō nippō* (August 1940); "Hantō bunka o kataru zadankai" [A roundtable discussing Korean culture], *Asahi shinbun* (August 1943); "Atarashii Hantō bundan no kōsō" [The concept of a new Korean literary field], *Ryokki* (April 1942); "Mite kita kaigun seikatsu o kataru" [Discussing the lifestyles of naval forces after returning from observation], *Kokumin sōryoku* (October 1943). See Ōmura and Hotei, eds., *Kindai Chōsen bungaku Nihongo sakuhinshū 1939–1945*, vol. 3.
20. In *Keimu ihō*, a colonial police monthly, beginning around 1937, we can see serials on "Jikyoku zadankai shiryō" [Data on roundtables in these times] and from 1938, articles appear assessing the effectiveness of roundtables staged for propaganda

purposes: for example, "Jikyoku zadankai jisshi jōkyō" [The condition of implementation of roundtables in these times] (February 1938); "Jikyoku zadankai jisshi
no jōkyō ni tsuite" [On the condition of implementation of roundtables in these
times] (February 1939); and "Jikyoku zadankai jisshi jōkyō" [The condition of
implementation of roundtables in these times] (March 1939).

21. The roundtable was published in *Keijō nippō* in six installments between November
29 and December 8, 1938. It was republished in the January 1939 edition of *Bungakukai*.

22. *Bungakukai* (January 1939): 271–72.

23. For an overview of *Naisen ittai* and the various contending responses by Koreans
see Miyata Setsuko, "'Naisen ittai' no kōzō nitchū senka Chōsen shihai seisaku
ni tsuite no ichikōsatsu," in Yanagisawa and Okabe, eds., *Tenbō Nihon rekishi
teikokushugi to shokuminchi*. Also, Ch'oe Chinsŏk, "Nitchū sensōki Chōsen chishikijin no Naisen ittai ron."

24. This ruse is evident in the utter failure of the postcolonial Japanese government to
take responsibility for or even acknowledge colonial subjects it had once actively
and often forcibly mobilized. See, for example, the situation of the so-called
comfort women and also the plight of forced laborers and conscripted soldiers.
(See Utsumi Aiko, *Sengo hoshō kara kangaeru Nihon to Ajia*, among others.)

25. Fujitani, *Race for Empire*.

26. "Chōsen bunka no shōrai to genzai" (*Keijō nippō*, November 29, 1938) and "Chōsen
bunka no shōrai" (*Bungakukai*, January 1939).

27. In fact, from our multiply distant positions to the actual event itself as "overhear-
ers," we are not privileged to such information.

28. *Keijō nippō* 1 (November 29, 1938). Hereafter citations from *Keijō nippō* include
installment number, month, date, and year. The irony of the fact that these critics
who admit that they know nothing about the Korean cultural field are gathered
here in the powerful position to discuss its future seems to go unnoticed. Such
admittance of ignorance by Japanese participants, often seemingly safely packaged
in a joke, seems to be a popular trope in these types of zadankai, perhaps such
apparently humble attitudes smoothing the way to their later pronouncements on
Korean culture soon to follow. For example, a zadankai serialized in the *Keijō nippō*
from June to July 1939 entitled "Bunka o tazunete: sansakka o fukumu zadankai"
was assembled on the occasion of the visit to Korea by three Japanese writers,
none of whom are much familiar with Korea. One of the writers admits jokingly,
"All I know are ondol, [flute-heated stone flooring] songs [*uta*], and *kisaeng*
[female entertainers like geisha] (*Laughter*)" (*Keijō nippō*, July 1939. Reprinted in
Ōmura and Hotei, eds., *Kindai Chōsen Nihongo sakuhinshū 1901–1938*, 379–88. The
quotation is from p. 382). This does not prevent the writers from freely discussing
a wide spectrum of topics with varying degrees of levity and seriousness, in just
as wide a spectrum of blindness and insight, from folksongs to famous scenery to
the future of the Korean language. Here again, each installment is punctuated by a
catchy title highlighting the issues at hand, giving an appearance that a meaningful
discussion might be occurring among the participants on these various subjects.
When we read the content, however, we find merely a smorgasbord of subjects

touched upon like a cocktail party discussion. It is worth noting that the issue of whether Korean writers should be writing in Korean or Japanese ends vaguely, with everyone seemingly commiserating together on the need for Korean publishers to travel all the way to Osaka to buy paper because of the shortage in the colony (*Keijō nippō*, June–July 1939).

29. *Keijō nippō* 1 (November 29, 1938).
30. *Keijō nippō* 1 (November 29, 1938). In the *Bungakukai* version, "Laughter" is added after this comment, perhaps an attempt at making tolerable an otherwise too-depressing situation.
31. *Keijō nippō* 5 (December 7, 1938).
32. *Keijō nippō* 3 (December 2, 1938).
33. *Bungakukai* (January 1939), 274.
34. *Keijō nippō* 1 (November 29, 1938).
35. *Keijō nippō* 4 (December 6, 1938). The shock of this direct question seems to have rendered Akita momentarily hard of hearing (perhaps suggesting his conundrum when confronted with the direct question that could expose all the contradictions of the roundtable: Akita: "What was that? I didn't quite hear" (*Keijō nippō* 4 [December 6, 1938]). This awkward moment is conveniently excised in the *Bungakukai* version.
36. *Keijō nippō* 4 (December 6, 1938).
37. *Keijō nippō* 4 (December 6, 1938).
38. *Keijō nippō* 4 (December 6, 1938).
39. *Keijō nippō* 4 (December 6, 1938).
40. *Bungakukai* (January 1939), 275.
41. Hayashi, "You don't need to be so stubborn" (*Sō koshitsu shinakutomo yoroshi-inoda*), *Bungakukai*, 277. Note that Hayashi uses the informal speech commonly used to address children or other inferior interlocutors.
42. *Keijō nippō* 4 (December 6, 1938). One can almost taste the frustration behind his sarcastic remark.
43. What Murayama calls *Ch'unhyang chŏn's* essence (*esupuri*), *Bungakukai*, 275.
44. *Keijō nippō* 3 (December 2, 1938); *Bungakukai*, 275.
45. *Keijō nippō* 3 (December 1, 1938).
46. In the *Bungakukai* version, this chauvinistic comment has been changed from "all women" to the gender-neutral "all people" (*manjin*), *Bungakukai* 275.
47. Kwŏn Podŭrae, *Yŏnae ŭi sidae* [The age of romance].
48. The coexistence of the simultaneous critique of and nostalgic desire for the colony as a backward remnant of the colonizers' own lost past is a common contradiction found in colonizers' discourses of varying contexts.
49. This bar itself can be read as ironically alluding to the uncrossable (untranslatable) distance between the colonizers and the colonized, and in turn the failure of *Naisen ittai*. It also alludes to the impossibility of return for Chang, the migrant writer who has contaminated himself by writing primarily in Japanese for the Japanese literary field.
50. Choi Kyeong-Hee argues that there occurred a shift from an external censorship during the early colonial period as visibly marked on the censored pages through

ink-outs, *fuseji's*, and so on, toward a disciplined condition of self-censorship in the latter colonial period. (Paper presented at the Chōsen bunka kenkyūkai, Waseda daigaku, 2006.)

51. If the Koreans did indeed applaud eagerly here as represented by the *Bungakukai* version, after the reading strategy we have followed here, in this context, one can imagine that the meaning behind the applause cannot be reduced to a simple reading as unequivocal "pro-Japanese" sentiments. However, in the face of censored texts, it is difficult to access the complex psychology and politics that may have been at work here.

52. *Bungakukai* (January 1939), 279.

53. *Bungakukai* (January 1939), 279.

54. *Bungakukai* (January 1939), 279.

55. *Bungakukai* (January 1939), 279. What I have bracketed here appears only in the *Keijō nippō*.

56. *Bungakukai* (January 1939), 279.

57. *Bungakukai* (Janurary 1939), 279.

58. *Bungakukai* (January 1939), 279.

59. *Bungakukai* (January 1939), 279.

Chapter 8. Turning Local

1. *Kimera: Manshukoku no shōzō* [Chimera, a portrait of Manchukuo].

2. For the debates on "overcoming modernity" in Japan, see Hiromatsu Wataru, *Kindai no chōkoku ron* and Calichman, ed., *Overcoming Modernity*. For the way these debates impacted colonial Korea, see, for example, Kim Ch'ŏl, "Tonghwa hokŭn ch'ogŭk" and *Kungmin iranŭn noyae*.

3. I shall translate this term only when I am privileging one definition over the rest, but otherwise shall leave it untranslated to evoke simultaneously these varied meanings.

4. Fujitani in *Race for Empire* calls this a shift from vulgar racism to polite racism; Anne McClintock in *Imperial Leather* refers to American empire as "imperialism-without-colonies." See also Kaplan and Pease, ed., *Cultures of U.S. Imperialism* about the historical absence of empire in American studies.

5. On the maintenance of colonial difference, see also Mignolo, 2002.

6. Schmid, *Korea between Empires*.

7. Yi Kwangsu wrote in his "Na ŭi kobaek" (My confession): "The Manchurian Incident was a big setback for the nationalist movement in Korea. The fall of Manchuria into the hands of Japan meant that the base of our independence movement was stolen from us (p. 268 of "My Confession," quoted in Kim Yunsik, ed., *Yi Kwangsu wa kŭ ŭi sidae*, vol. 2, 188). For an extended study of the decadence and despair pervasive in late 1930s Korea, see Kim Yerim, *1930 nyŏndae huban kŭndae insik ŭi t'ŭl kwa miŭsik* (Modern episteme and aesthetic consciousness in the late 1930s).

8. For details on the "Korea Boom," see Pak Ch'unil, *Kindai Nihon bungaku ni okeru Chosenzō*. Also Watanabe Kazutami, *Tasha to shite no Chōsen*. For parallel images of colony and chihō as spatial imaginaries in Japan, see Nakane Takayuki, *"Chōsen" hyōshōno bunkashi*.

9. In *Imagined Communities*, Benedict Anderson argues that the advent of print capitalism and the dissemination of a shared language through the mass market worked as "a device for the presentation of simultaneity in 'homogeneous, empty time'" (25) and a sense of belonging in a particular "language field" (44). His examples are the mass-produced books and newspapers, the daily ritual of reading the latter which he calls a "mass ceremony": "Each communicant is well aware that the ceremony he performs is being replicated simultaneously by thousands (or millions) of others of whose existence he is confident, yet of whose identity he has not the slightest notion. Furthermore, this ceremony is incessantly repeated at daily or half-day intervals throughout the calendar. What more vivid figure for the secular, historically clocked, imagined community can be envisioned?" (35).

   Anderson makes the explicit link between nationalism and imperialism in chapter six, "Official Nationalism and Imperialism," and offers Japan as a case in point although not without revealing the limits of his historical knowledge. For example, he continues on a logic of Japanese particularity based on the assumption of a "unique antiquity of the imperial house" and the myth of "centuries of Japanese isolation," even though he admits in a footnote that he has been informed of the controversy over the possibility of a Korean origin of the imperial line (93–99).

10. For example, "A new heaven and earth for the expansions of our Korean brethren into Greater Manchuria: sending 2 million in the coming 10 years, establishing big businesses by Korean officials and people (*Dai Manshū no heigen ni dōhō kaitaku no shintenchi: mukau jūkanenkan ni okuru nihyakumanjin: hankan, hanmin no taikaisha o setchi*)," *Osaka mainichi Chōsen-ban*, December 1, 1934.

11. "Regions" (margins) and "centers" were constantly shifting depending on one's point of reference. Japan was a "region" in relation to the metropolitan West, but the metropolitan "center" vis-à-vis its own colonies. Such fluctuating relations reveal the instability of such constructed hierarchies.

12. In an insert on June 24, 1934, a list of all the chihō editions appears. They are Osaka (two editions), Kyōto (two editions), Shiga, Hyōgo, Kōbe, Hanshin, Wakayama (two editions), Nara, Mie, Gifu, Mikawa, Nagoya, Fukui, Ishiwawa, Toyama, Kagawa, Ehime, Kochi, Okayama, Hiroshima (two editions), Tottori, Shimane, Yamaguchi, Kita-Kyūshū, Fukuoka, Ōita, Saga, Nagasaki, Kumamoto, Miyazaki, Kagoshima/Okinawa, Chōsen (two editions), Taiwan, and Manshū.

13. Hashimoto Mitsuru, "Chihō: Yanagita Kunio's Japan" in *Mirror of Modernity*, 133–34, for Yanagita Kunio's invention of chihō as the repository of pure Japaneseness. See also, Kishida Kunio, "Chihō bunka no shinkensetsu," and the dialogue between Kishida and Kim Saryang in "Chosŏn munhak munje e taehaesŏ," 26–35.

14. References to Korea's "future" became increasingly synonymous with *Naisen ittai* as the decade wore on.

15. Scholars have speculated about the "coincidence" of this foundational date with the March 1 Independence Movement of 1919 in Korea. It is worth pointing out that there were some Koreans writing in Japanese in the Japanese Bundan before Chang, but the overwhelming attention they began to receive around this time was unprecedented.

16. Chang Hyŏkchu, "Gakidō," 1–39.

17. There was no "first place" winner but two "second place" nominations for what was the fifth annual literary competition for *Kaizō*. Metropolitan critical responses to Chang Hyŏkchu's nomination significantly mirror the response to Kim Saryang's nomination for the Akutagawa Prize in 1940, revealing that, for the metropolitan Bundan, colonized writers knocking at its doors were the source of an ongoing conundrum throughout the decade. As Nakane in "Chōsen" hyōshōno bunkashi" has pointed out, the institution of the literary prize initiating ingénues into the Bundan was a new phenomenon at this time with the Akutagawa Prize and Naoki Prize established in the mid-1930s after the Kaizō literary prize. It may be worth reiterating here the point I made in chapter 3 of the significant role played by the colonized writer at the foundational moment in the making of the modern Japanese literary canon.
18. Park, *Two Dreams in One Bed*.
19. Jun Uchida, *Brokers of Empire*.
20. *Manchuria under Japanese Domination*, 10. Originally published as *Kimera*.
21. See Nakane, *"Chōsen" hyōshōno bunkashi*, 34–144.
22. The contemporary phenomenon of the "Korea Wave" (Hallyu K, Kanryū J) and the popularity of a dehistoricized image of "Korea" stand in stark contrast to the controversies surrounding unresolved historical issues such as the prime minister's Yasukuni Shrine visits, history textbooks, the "comfort women" legacy, and territorial disputes over the island rocks, Tokto/Takeshima. On the other hand, tensions between the Democratic People's Republic of Korea (DPRK) and Japan over nuclear weapons, long-range missiles, and the kidnappings of Japanese citizens have been regular fare in the Japanese evening news since 2001.
23. For a close examination of the contradictions between the various imperial slogans, see Tanaka Ryūichi, "Tairitsu to tōgō no 'Senman' kankei," 106–32.
24. For example, Miki Kiyoshi attempted to espouse the notion of the Tōa Kyōdōtai while warning against Japanese imperialism, but his philosophy was finally subsumed under imperialist logic. See Miki Kiyoshi, *Tōa kyōdōtai no tetsugaku*; and Uchida Hiroshi, ed., *Miki Kiyoshi tōa kyōdotai ronshū*. In English, a good overview of the history of Pan-Asian ideology of Japan can be found in Saaler and Koschmann, eds., *Pan-Asianism in Modern Japanese History*, especially the chapter "Pan-Asianism in Modern Japanese History: Overcoming the Nation, Creating a Region, Forging an Empire," by Sven Saaler.
25. See Mizuno Naoki on the name-change policies that included the remainder of the original Korean identity to be retained in the clan records. For example, "Tonghwa wa ch'aihwa: Ilbon ŭi singminji chibae wa 'ch'angssi kaemyŏng,'" 69–82. Also on the issue of name change policies, see Miyata Setsuko, Kim Yongdal, and Yang T'aeho, eds. *Sōshikaimei*; and Kim Yongdal, *Sōshikaimei no kenkyū*.
26. This was the day when the first installment of Kang Kyŏngae's "Chōzangan J; Changsankot, K" appeared. Changsankot is an area at the tip of the Korean peninsula jutting out into the Yellow Sea, in Changyon kun of Hwanghae Province. The story, hereafter "Changsan Bay," which will be examined in chapter 9, appeared in the *Osaka mainichi, Korea local edition*.
27. Fagōru, the advertisement claims, was invented by the collaborative efforts of

doctors from the Tokyo Imperial University and was effective not only for the treatment of tuberculosis but also for the prevention of infections. The image of a scientific, modern, and vigorous Japan was often advertised throughout the empire via the promotion of health and beauty products manufactured in the metropole.

28. It may be worth emphasizing here that I am not making the claim that there was indeed widespread acceptance of the notion of an "imagined community" that seeped into all aspects of the empire—from the official to the popular level. In fact, when we keep in mind that Japanese-language imperial newspapers were being read by only a minority throughout the colonies, namely the colonized elites and Japanese colonial settler communities for the most part, one must question just how pervasive the notion of an "imagined community" infiltrated the everyday experiences of the general population living in the empire. An attempt to theorize any overarching sense of the shared experience of an "imagined community" on the scale of empire would require much more complex examinations than I have room for here, and it is not my purpose to make general pronouncements about the effectiveness of imperial ideologies on any grand scale. What I would like to highlight here for the purposes of my own project is the significance of such an *image* of an "imagined community" that was being circulated in the mass media throughout the empire at this time. It is also important to point out that such an image of a putative imperial community linked by the imperial language was accompanied by violent imperial assimilation policies aimed at the censorship of vernacular languages and customs, and by the repression of vernacular cultural productions and assemblies of the colonized. In the case of colonial Korea, the few vernacular newspapers that did remain in circulation in the face of severe censorship laws were, for the most part, mirror versions of what was being circulated in the Japanese-language dailies, with recycled headlines, photographs, and advertisements. Although the 1930s were also considered a dynamic era of emerging cultural productions including new popular journals, "diversity" of productions was allowed only within permitted boundaries of severe censorship laws; and when considering the fact that many journals were "sibling" versions of extant newspapers, "diversity" in this era often meant repetition of the same, though in a different guise. This book focuses on the ironic simultaneity of the emptiness yet pervasiveness of such an image of a harmonious "imagined community" in light of the violent repressions of difference and conflict upon which such an image was constructed.

29. *Osaka mainichi Chōsen chihō-ban,* June 6, 1936.

30. *Osaka mainichi Tottori chihō-ban,* June 6, 1936.

31. *Osaka mainichi Manshū chihō-ban,* June 6, 1936.

32. *Osaka mainichi Manshū chihō-ban,* June 6, 1936.

33. The caption reads "Zen (ōrū) Nippon o tsunagu Ajinomoto hōshijin" (Ajinomoto line-up servicing *all* of Japan), *Osaka mainichi,* January 3, 1935. Ajinomoto was one of the most recognizable metropolitan commodities across the Japanese empire. Advertisements appeared in major journals and dailies of the colonies, catered to specific markets. For example, the advertisements that appeared in Korean women's journals featured women in Korean traditional dress and bilingual copy to assure

the transmission of the message for colonial women with limited access to the imperial education system.

34. *Osaka mainichi*, April 9, 1936.

35. On April 10, 1936, the headline reads "Opening Today the Brilliant Japan Expo" (*kyō aku kagayaku Nipponhaku*) listing the major exhibitions including "the Pan-Asian exhibit" (*han-taiheiyōkan*), "science exhibit" (*kagakukan*), "technology exhibit" (*kikaikan*), "national products exhibit" (*kokusankan*), "imperial army exhibit" (*kōgunkan*) and "Manchuria exhibit" (*Manshūkan*). *Osaka mainichi*, April 10, 1936.

36. For example, on April 11, 1936, a photograph of a dancing kisaeng troupe displayed before a large crowd is highlighted with the caption "Popular attraction at the great Japan expo" (*kagayaku Nipponhaku ninkimono*). *Osaka mainichi*, April 11, 1936.

37. See, for example, "Chōsenkan ni hikaru isai 'hakkei hasshō'; tairiku kibun minagiru Manshūkan" (Exotic 'eight scenic landscapes' shining in the Korea exhibit; Manchuria exhibit overflowing with continental feeling). *Osaka mainichi*, April 20, 1936.

38. The Japanese began to acquire Western exhibitionary skills in the late 1860s. For a study of the Japanese participation in international fairs in the United States, see Harris, "All the World a Melting Pot?" 24–54. For Japan's participation in international expositions, see Conant, "Refractions of the Rising Sun." See also Christ, "Sole Guardians of the Art Inheritance of Asia," 675–709.

39. See Araki Rīchirō, *Osaka mainichi shinbun gojūnen*, 437–39, 448–53, for the paper's expressed commitment to imperial expansions after the Manchurian Incident. See also Ono Hideo, *Osaka mainichi shinbunshasha*, 98–99, for the opening of the "Western local" branches of the paper into the colonies.

40. *Keijō nippō* 4 (December 6, 1938).

41. *Osaka mainichi Chōsen-ban*, June 11, 1934.

42. *On Longing*, ix. Subsequent citations are inserted parenthetically in the text.

43. *Osaka mainichi Chōsen-ban*, April 13, 1936.

44. *Keijō nippō* 4 (December 6, 1938).

45. Similarly, Stewart hints at the colonialist gesture of the "narrative of the collection" when considering acquisitions from other cultures: "The logic behind the blithe gesture toward decontextualization in museum acquisitions . . . [is] a gesture which results in the treasures of one culture being stored and displayed in the museums of another" (*On Longing*, 162). It is unfortunate that she does not pursue this thread of inquiry any further than this highly suggestive yet passing comment.

46. Stewart distinguishes between the logic of the souvenir and the collection and discusses kitsch as "souvenirs of an era" representing a collective identity, as opposed to the souvenir that represents individual histories. However, her discussion of "exotic souvenirs" as kitsch seems to segue into our discussion of the colonial collection as kitsch, opening up a space to discuss parallel logic underlying kitsch and the collection (*On Longing*, 166–67).

Chapter 9. Forgetting Manchurian Memories

1. Kim Inhwan, Kim Chaeyong, et al., eds. *Kang Kyŏngae t'ansaeng 100 chunyŏn kinyŏm*, cover copy.

2. Yi Sanggyŏng distinguishes Kang, whose access to literature was said to have been through the classics of Korean literature such as *Ch'unhyang chŏn*, from those writers such as Yi Kwangsu and Kim Tongin who learned modern literature as exchange students in Japan, mediated through the Japanese language (Yi Sanggyŏng, *Kang Kyŏngae*, 19).

3. Yi Sanggyŏng, *Kang Kyŏngae*, 18. Subsequent citations will be parenthetically included within the text.

4. The episode is told by Yang Chudong himself: "This stout and assertive girl came to me in the dark night, 'Mister, please teach me English! And poetry, and literature too. I'm a third year student in Junior High but I still do not know anything. But I have plenty of literary talent, so please educate me!'" (quoted in Yi Sanggyŏng, *Kang Kyŏngae*, 35).

5. Kim Saryang, "Chōsen bunka tsūshin."

6. In an essay Kim Yongjae, a Korean poet who studied abroad in Japan and wrote extensively in Japanese, writes about the difficulties of writing in Japanese. "Hantō bundan to kokugo no mondai," 124–30.

7. It was common for women writers to gain more attention as fodder for gossip than for their writings at the time. Yi Sangyŏng, *Kang Kyŏngae*.

8. Peasants, women, and the countryside were common tropes of cultural authenticity, even in Japan. See Duara, *Sovereignty and Authenticity*, 131–69, 171–77, 209–43.

9. Chŏng Chonghyŏn, "Singminji hubangi (1937–1945) Hanguk munhak e nat'anan tongyangnon yŏngu" especially, chapter 3; Watanabe Naoki, "Manchuria and the Agrarian-Proletariat Literature of Colonial Korea."

10. Kim Inhwan, Kim Cheyong et al., eds., *Kang Kyŏngae sidae wa munhak*, 7.

11. In recent years, there have been scholarly battles fought over memories of this region between nationalist historians in Korea and China.

12. Park, *Two Dreams in One Bed*.

13. Han Sŏkchŏng [Han Suk Jung] has called Manchuria a "black box" of Korean history. See *Manjuguk kŏnguk ŭi chaehaesŏk*.

14. Along with displaced peasants, there were still many others in the bunch of migrants, ranging from outlaws, opportunists, and even runaway kisaeng, whose stories fill the pages of the days' mass media. *Keijō nippō*, *Chosŏn ilbo*, *Chogwang*, and *Samch'ŏlli*, for example, are scattered with such stories from the mid-1930s on.

15. The Wanbaoshan Incident is just one of the most famous of many clashes between Koreans and Chinese that was manipulated to serve Japanese imperial propaganda. See Pak Yŏngsŏk, *Manbosan sakŏn yŏngu*; Park, *Two Dreams in One Bed*; Kim Chul [Kim Ch'ŏl], "Mollak hanŭn sinsaeng."

16. *Sin kajŏng* (May–October 1934).

17. *Yŏsŏng* (November 1937).

18. Motherhood is an important trope in Kang's corpus. It is significant that the protagonist remains nameless; in fact, she is the only character in the story who is not named. Only known as So-and-So's Mother, this follows the common convention in Korean society in which women's identities are often mediated through their familial relationships. Such a mediated identity here alludes to her subaltern status

on multiple levels, not only on the level of the private family structure but also in the "imperial family" of the Japanese empire.

19. Chōsen sōtokufu, ed., *Chōsen Sōtokufu shisei nenpō*.
20. Yŏnbyŏn taehakkyo Chosŏn munhak yŏnguso, ed., Kang Kyŏngae, 390–91. Subsequent references will be provided parenthetically in the text.
21. The x's mark the censor's ink strokes.
22. Ōmura Masuo, "Kang Kyŏngae *Ingan munje* p'anbon pigyo."
23. A scholar recently used chemical methods to decode most of what lay behind the inked-out parts, and as suspected, the North Korean version had "rewritten" a much more nationalist and pro-communist version than what actually lay beneath the ink. See Han Mansu, "Kang Kyŏngae 'sogŭm ŭi 'putch'il pokcha' pogwŏn kwa Pukhan 'pogwŏn ŭi pigyo," in Kim Inhwan, ed. *Kang Kyŏngae sidae wa munhak*, 28–48.
24. Kang Kyŏngae, *Ingan munje*.
25. *Ingan Munje*, Kang's most canonical book, for example, was repeatedly altered in South Korea. See Ōmura Masuo, "Kang Kyŏngae *Ingan munje* p'anbon pigyo."
26. Yŏnbyŏn taehakkyo Chosŏn munhak yŏnguso, ed., *Kang Kyŏngae*, 222.
27. For previous discussions on the significance of the "impaired body" in colonial Korean literature, see Choi, "Impaired Body as Colonial Trope," 431–58.
28. This loss of control of the self becomes evident in the text in several places where words fail her, and she is literally rendered speechless. The inability to speak of subaltern characters is a common motif in Kang's texts.
29. Chinese shop owner Mr. Chin is described in animalistic terms: "His bloodshot eyes were swimming with beastliness, and his heaving breath fumed with the stench of dog" (Yŏnbyŏn taehakkyo Chosŏn munhak yŏnguso, ed., *Kang Kyŏngae*, 225); "Mr. Chin's yellow hands were peeling fruit and from his forehead to his cheeks big beads of oily sweat oozed down" (Yŏnbyŏn taehakkyo Chosŏn munhak yŏnguso, ed., *Kang Kyŏngae*, 226). Such degrading and dehumanizing images of the Chinese abound in Kang Kyŏngae's works. While pointing out the presence of such racism in her works, I would like to also point to the multiple layers of power imbalance enabled by the racist hierarchy of the imperial situation. Rather than showing the "harmony of the five races," as imperial ideology would purport, this hierarchy reveals the disharmony, violence, racism, and discrimination that were rampant in this context of unevenness. Such cross-cultural encounters expose the mutual disrespect and violence against one another on multiple levels.
30. Kurahara Masanao, *Nihon no ahensen*.
31. Jennings, "The Forgotten Plague," 795–815.
32. *Chōsen Sōtokufu shisei nenpō*. For recent scholarship, see Kingsberg, *Moral Nation* and Jennings, *Opium Nation*.
33. See the works of Kim Saryang, such as "Chijimi," 259–69; "Kyōshū," 286–313; and "Mushi." Also, Yokomitsu Riichi, "Pale Captain," in *"Love" and Other Storeis of Yokomitsu Riichi*, 99–108, as well as various short stories by Hyŏn Kyŏngjun, for example. The discussion of the issue of opium and morphine addiction as a pervasive trope of colonial Korean literature must be postponed for later.

34. According to Kurahara, Koreans, unlike the Chinese, did not have a past tradition of smoking opium. Kurahara, *Nihon no ahensen*.

35. "She recalled how she started to fear and suspect her husband after he started smoking opium, how defeated he was after losing his job; he tried to commit suicide, and then when he began hanging around Cheil, with opium hanging from his mouth, how he would scream and cry" (Yŏnbyŏn taehakkyo Chosŏn munhak yŏnguso, ed., *Kang Kyŏngae*, 223).

36. Yi Sanggyŏng, "Introduction," 327.

37. "From the sea spread out before him, he didn't have the tools to catch one minnow. Since Mt. Chang was taken over by Mitsui, they couldn't even touch one pine straw." *Osaka mainichi Chōsen-ban* 5 (June 10, 1936).

38. *Osaka mainichi Chōsen-ban* 1 (June 6, 1936).

39. *Osaka mainichi Chōsen-ban* 1 (June 6, 1936).

40. *Osaka mainichi Chōsen-ban* 1 (June 6, 1936).

41. This would happen in 1938 with the establishment of volunteer corps followed by conscription in 1942.

42. *Osaka mainichi Chōsen-ban* 5 (June 10, 1936).

43. "Chang Hyŏkchu sŏnsaeng ege."

44. "Naisenman o tsunagu yusōjin—kansei o isogu tetsudōkyoku."

45. See, for example, Im Chongguk, *Ch'inil munhak non*; Im Chŏnhye, *Nihon ni okeru Chōsenjin no bungaku no rekishi-1945 nen made*; Hayashi Kōji, *Zainichi Chōsenjin Nihongo bungakuron*; and Ōmura Masuo and Hotei Toshihiro, eds., *Chōsen bungaku kankei Nihongo bunken mokuroku 1882–1945*.

46. Yi Sanggyŏng, "Introduction," 328.

47. Yi Sanggyŏng, "Introduction," 328.

Chapter 10. Paradox of Postcoloniality

1. Kuan-Tsing Chen makes the important point that inter-Asian relations have been disregarded in Asia while privileging the relationship with the West. See *Inter-Asia Cultural Studies* and *Asia as Method*. In recent years, there has been a welcome rise in efforts to engender inter- and intra-Asian dialogues in order to move beyond past blind spots resulting from limiting comparisons to the metropole/colony binary.

2. See especially chapter 1, "The Cultural Logic of Late Capitalism."

3. See Duus, *Abacus and the Sword*, and Uchida, *Brokers of Empire*.

4. *Korea between Empires*.

5. Mizuno, "Senjiki no shokuminchi shihai to 'Naigaichi kōsei ichigenka'"; Komagome, *Shokuminchi teikoku Nihon no bunka tōgō*; Fujitani, *Race for Empire*; Duara, *Sovereignty and Authenticity*.

6. Duara, *Sovereignty and Authenticity* and Han Suk Jung, *Manjuguk kŏnguk ŭi chaehaesŏk*.

7. Mizuno, "Senjiki no shokuminchi shihai to 'Naigaichi kōsei ichigenka'"; Fujitani, *Race for Empire*.

8. McClintock, *Imperial Leather*, 13.

9. See, for example, Ahluwalia, *Out of Africa*; and Wise, *Derrida, Africa, and the Middle East*.

10. *Strangers to Ourselves*, 38–40.

11. Quoted in Dirlik, "Postcolonial Aura," 328–56.

12. Dirlik, "Postcolonial Aura," 329.

13. Harootunian, "'Modernity' and the Claims of Untimeliness."

14. See Cumings, *Korea's Place in the Sun*.

15. The designation "postwar" signifies a different temporality from the perspective of Korea and that of Japan. In Japan, postwar signifies the aftermath of the Pacific War, the defeat in that war, and the immediate occupation by the U.S. military. According to official historiography, the postwar ended in Japan proper in 1952, when U.S. occupation of the Japanese main islands was largely transferred to Okinawa. In Okinawa, however, the postwar condition is said to be ongoing, since its occupation status under the dual auspices of Japan and the United States still continues. The postcolonial condition of Okinawa was itself taboo until the mid-1990s. In Korea, "postwar" designates the aftermath of the Korean War, not the Pacific War. This view stems from a nationalist perspective in which the Pacific War is not considered a "Korean" war.

16. Kwon, *Other Cold War*.

(Korean-language sources, unless otherwise noted, are published in Seoul; Japanese-language sources, unless otherwise noted, are published in Tokyo).

Primary Sources in Japanese and Korean
NEWSPAPERS AND JOURNALS IN JAPANESE

Asahi shinbun (Asahi newspaper)
Bungaku (Literature)
Bungakukai (Literary world)
Bungei (Literary arts)
Bungei shunjū (Literary spring and autumn)
Bungei shuto (Metropolitan arts)
Chisei (Intellect)
Chōsen oyobi Manshū (Korea and Manchuria)
Chōsen sōtokufu shisei nenpō (Korean Governor General annual administrative report).
    Ed. Chōsen Sōtokufu.
Kaizō (Reconstruction)
Keijō nippō (Seoul daily)
Keimu ihō (Imperial police administration)
Kōdō (Action)
Kokumin bungaku (Imperial literature)
Kokumin sōryoku (Imperial power)
Modan Nippon (Modern Japan)
Osaka manichi shinbun chihō-ban (Manshū, Chōsen, Tottori, Taiwan, etc.)
    (Osaka daily news regional editions, Manchuria, Korea, Tottori, Taiwan, etc.)
Ryokki (Olive banner)
Shinchō (New tides)

Shin jidai (New era)
Shirogane gakuhō (Shirogane campus bulletin)
Sinpan Keijō annai (New guide to Keijō). Ed. Chōsen Sōtokufu (Governor General of Korea), 1936.
Teatoro (Theater)
Teikoku daigaku shinbun (Imperial university newspaper)

NEWSPAPERS AND JOURNALS IN KOREAN:

Chogwang (Morning light)
Chosŏn ilbo (Choson daily)
Immun p'yŏngnon (Humanities criticism)
Inmin yesul (Peoples arts)
Maeil sinbo (Daily news)
Pip'an (Criticism)
Sahoe kongnon (Public discourse)
Samch'ŏlli (Three thousand leagues)
Sin kajŏng (New home)
Yŏsŏng (Woman)

Secondary Sources

Aczel, Richard. "Understanding as Over-hearing: Towards a Dialogics of Voice." *New Literary History* 32 (2001): 597–617.

Ahluwalia, D. P. S. *Out of Africa: Post-Structuralism's Colonial Roots*. Abingdon, UK: Routledge, 2010.

Ahmad, Aijaz. "Jameson's Rhetoric of Otherness and the 'National Allegory.'" In *In Theory: Classes, Nations, Literatures*. London: Verso, 1992.

Akita Ujaku. "Kokyō e kaeru *Shunkōden*: yūgō shita futatsu no bunka no kōryū" [*Ch'unhyang chŏn*'s homecoming: The exchange of two unified cultures]. *Keijō nippō* October 9, 1938.

Akita, Ujaku, and Chang Hyŏkchu et al., eds. *Chōsen bungaku senshū* [Selections of Korean literature]. Vol. 1. Akatsuka shobō, 1941.

Akutagawashō zenshū [Complete works of the Akutagawa Prize]. Vol. 2. Bungei shunjū, 1982–2002.

Anderson, Benedict. *Imagined Communities: Reflections on the Origin and Spread of Nationalism*. London: Verso, 1983, 1991.

An Usik [An Ushoku]. *Hyōden Kin Shiryō*. [Critical biography of Kim Saryang]. Tokyo: Iwanami shoten, 1972.

———. *p'yŏngjŏn Kim Saryang* [Critical biography of Kim Saryang]. Translated by Sim Wŏnsŏp. Munhak kwa chisŏngsa, 2000.

Aono Suekichi. "Honnen bundan no sōkatsuteki kannsatsu" [Overview of this year's literary field.] *Kōdō* 1:3 (December 1933): 2–12.

Appadurai, Arjun. *Modernity at Large: Cultural Dimensions of Globalization*. Minneapolis: University of Minnesota Press, 1996.

Araki Rīchirō. *Osaka mainichi shinbun gojūnen* [Fifty years of Osaka mainichi]. Osaka: Osaka mainichi shinbunsha, 1932.

Atkins, E. Taylor. *Primitive Selves: Koreana in the Japanese Colonial Gaze, 1910–1945*. Berkeley: University of California Press, 2010.

Baek Moon-im [Paek Munim]. *Ch'unhyang ŭi ttaldŭl: Hanguk yŏsŏng ŭi pantchoktchari kyepohak* [Daughters of Ch'unhyang: A stunted genealogy of Korean women]. Ch'aek sesang, 2001.

Barlow, Tani E., ed. *Formations of Colonial Modernity in East Asia*. Durham, NC: Duke University Press, 1997.

Baskett, Michael. "The Attractive Empire: Colonial Asia in Japanese Imperial Film Culture, 1931–1953." PhD diss., University of California, Los Angeles, 2000.

———. *Attractive Empire: Transnational Film Culture in Imperial Japan*. Honolulu: University of Hawai'i Press, 2008.

Bhabha, Homi. *The Location of Culture*. London: Routledge, 1994.

Bourdieu, Pierre. *The Field of Cultural Production: Essays on Art and Literature*. Cambridge, UK: Polity Press, 1993.

Boym, Svetlana. *The Future of Nostalgia*. New York: Basic Books, 2001.

Brandt, Kim. *Kingdom of Beauty: Mingei and the Politics of Folk Art in Imperial Japan*. Durham, NC: Duke University Press, 2007.

———. "Objects of Desire: Japanese Collectors and Colonial Korea." *positions* 8:3 (Winter 2000): 711–40.

Butler, Judith. *Bodies That Matter: On the Discursive Limits of "Sex."* New York: Routledge, 1993.

———. *Gender Trouble: Feminism and the Subversion of Identity*. New York: Routledge, 1990.

Calichman, Richard F., ed. *Overcoming Modernity: Cultural Identity in Wartime Japan*. New York: Columbia University Press, 2008.

Caprio, Mark E. *Japanese Assimilation Policies in Colonial Korea, 1910–1945*. Seattle: University of Washington Press, 2009.

Casanova, Pascale. *The World Republic of Letters*. Cambridge, MA: Harvard University Press, 2004.

Ch'a Sŭnggi. "1930 nyŏndae huban chŏnt'ongnon yŏngu: sigan-konggan ŭisik ŭl chungsim ŭro." PhD diss., Yŏnse taehakkyo, 2003.

Chakrabarty, Dipesh. *Provincializing Europe: Postcolonial Thought and Historical Difference*. Princeton, NJ: Princeton University Press, 2008.

Chang Hyŏkchu [Chō Kakuchū]. "Boku no bungaku." *Bungei shuto* 1:1 (January 1933): 11–12.

———. "Chōsen no chishikijin ni uttau [An appeal to Korean intellectuals.]" *Bungei* (February 1939): 225–39.

———. "Gakidō." *Kaizō* 14:4 (April 1932): 1–39.

Chang Hyŏngjun. "Chakka Kim Saryang kwa kŭ ŭi munhak" [Writer Kim Saryang and his literature]. In *Kim Saryang chakp'umchip* [Selections of Kim Saryang's works], edited by Ri Myŏngho, 1–22. P'yŏngyang: Munye ch'ulp'ansa, 1987.

Chen, Kuan-Tsing. *Asia as Method: Toward Deimperialization*. Durham, NC: Duke University Press, 2010.

Ching, Leo. *Becoming "Japanese": Colonial Taiwan and the Politics of Identity Formations*. Berkeley: University of California Press, 2001

————. "'Give Me Japan and Nothing Else!': Postcoloniality, Identity, and the Traces of Colonialism." *South Atlantic Quarterly* 99:4 (2000): 763–88.

Cho Kwanja. "Nitchū sensōki no 'Chōsengaku' to 'koten fukkō—shokuminchi no 'chi' o tou" [Sino-Japanese wartime "koreanology" and "classics revival"—questioning colonial "knowledge"]. *Shisō* (March 2003): 59–81.

————. "Shinnichi nashonarizumu no keisei to hatan: Yi Kwangsu, minzoku hangyakusha toiu shinkyū o koete [Rise and fall of ch'inil nationalism: overcoming the national traitor label]." *Gendai shisō* 29.16 (December 2001): 222–43.

Ch'oe Chinsŏk. "Nitchū sennsōki Chōsen chishikijin no naisen ittai ron." *Quadrante* 7 (March 2005).

Choi, Kyeong-Hee. "Impaired Body as Colonial Trope: Kang Kyŏngae's 'Underground Village.'" *Public Culture* 13:3: 431–58.

————. Paper presented at the Chōsen bunka kenkyūkai, Waseda daigaku, Tokyo, Japan, March 2006.

Chŏng Chonghyŏn. "Singminji hubangi (1937–1945) Hanguk munhak e nat'anan tongyangnon yŏngu." PhD diss.,Tongguk taehakkyo, 2005.

Chŏng Paeksu. *Hanguk kŭndae ŭi singminji ch'ehŏm kwa ijung ŏnŏ munhak* [Modern Korea's colonial experience and bilingual literature]. Asea Munhwasa, 2000.

————. "Yi Kwangsu, Kim Saryang no Nihongo Chōsengo shōsetsu: shokuminchiki Chōsenjin sakka no nigengo bungaku no arikata" [The Japanese- and Korean-language fiction of Yi Kwangsu and Kim Saryang: The bilingual writings of colonial Korean writers]. PhD diss., Tokyo daigaku, 1998.

Chŏn Sanguk. "Panggakpon *Ch'unhyang chŏn* ŭi sŏngnip kwa pyŏnmo e taehan yŏngu" [On the rise and transformations of woodblock prints of *Ch'unhyang chŏn*]. PhD diss., Yŏnse taehakkyo, 2006.

Chŏng Yŏnnae. *Hanguk kŭndae wa singminji kŭndaehwa nonjaeng* [Korea's modernity and the debates on colonial modernization]. P'urŭn yŏksa, 2011.

"Chosŏn munhak munje e taehaesŏ: Ikch'anhoe munhwa pujang Kishida Kunio, Kim Saryang yangssi ŭi taedam." *Chogwang* 7:4 (April 1941): 26–35.

Chow, Rey. "Things, Common/Places, Passages of the Port City: On Hong Kong and Hong Kong Author Leung Ping-kwan," 207–26. In *Sinophone Studies: A Critical Reader.* Edited by Shu-mei Shih, Chien-hsih Tsai, and Brian Bernard. Columbia University Press, 2013.

————. *Woman and Chinese Modernity: The Politics of Reading between West and East.* Minneapolis: University of Minnesota Press, 1991.

————. *Writing Diaspora Tactics of Intervention in Contemporary Cultural Studies.* Bloomington: Indiana University Press, 1993.

Christ, Carol Ann. "The Sole Guardians of the Art Inheritance of Asia: Japan and China at the 1904 St. Louis World's Fair." *positions: east asia cultures critique* 8:3 (2000): 675–709.

Christy, Alan. "Making Imperial Subjects in Okinawa." In *Formations of Colonial Modernity*, edited by Tani E. Barlow. Durham, NC: Duke University Press, 1997.

Clapp, Priscilla, Akira Iriye, and Joint Committee on Japanese Studies. *Mutual Images: Essays in American-Japanese Relations.* Cambridge, MA: Harvard University Press, 1975.

Conant, Ellen P. "Refractions of the Rising Sun: Japan's Participation in International

Exhibitions, 1862–1910." In *Japan and Britain: an Aesthetic Dialogue, 1850–1930,* edited by Tomoko Sato and Toshio Watanabe. London: Lund Humphries, 1991.

Cumings, Bruce. *Korea's Place in the Sun: A Modern History.* New York: W. W. Norton, 2005.

Dainotto, Roberto M. *Europe in Theory.* Durham, NC: Duke University Press, 2007.

Deleuze, Gilles, and Félix Guattari. *Kafka: Toward a Minor Literature.* Minneapolis: University of Minnesota Press, 1986.

Derrida, Jacques. *Monolingualism of the Other, or the Prosthesis of Origin.* Stanford, CA: Stanford University Press, 1998.

———. "Passages—from Traumatism to Promise." In *Derrida, Points:* Interviews, 1974–1994. Translated by Peggy Kamuf et al., 386–87. Stanford, CA: Stanford University Press, 1995.

Dirlik, Arif. *Global Modernity: Modernity in the Age of Global Capitalism.* Boulder, CO: Paradigm Publishers, 2007.

———. "The Postcolonial Aura: Third World Criticism in the Age of Global Capitalism." *Critical Inquiry* 20.2 (Winter 1994): 328–56.

Douglas, Mary. *Purity and Danger: An Analysis of Concepts of Pollution and Taboo.* New York: Praeger, 1966.

Dower, John W. *War without Mercy: Race and Power in the Pacific War.* New York: Pantheon Books, 1986.

Driscoll, Mark. *Absolute Erotic, Absolute Grotesque: The Living, Dead, and Undead in Japan's Imperialism, 1895–1945.* Durham, NC: Duke University Press, 2010.

Duara, Prasenjit. *Rescuing History from the Nation: Questioning Narratives of Modern China.* Chicago: University of Chicago Press, 1996.

———. *Sovereignty and Authenticity: Manchukuo and the East Asian Modern.* Lanham, MD: Rowman and Littlefield, 2003.

Duus, Peter. *The Abacus and the Sword: The Japanese Penetration of Korea, 1895–1910.* Berkeley: University of California Press, 1998.

Eagleton, Terry, Field Day Theatre Company, Fredric Jameson, and Edward W. Said. *Nationalism, Colonialism, and Literature.* Minneapolis: University of Minnesota Press, 1990.

Evans, Dylan. *An Introductory Dictionary of Lacanian Psychoanalysis.* London: Routledge, 1996.

Fabian, Johannes. *Time and the Other: How Anthropology Makes Its Object.* New York: Columbia University Press, 1983.

Fanon, Frantz. *Black Skin, White Masks.* Translated by Charles Lam Markmann. New York: Grove Press, 1967.

Freud, Sigmund. "The Uncanny." In *The Standard Edition of the Complete Psychological Works of Sigmund Freud.* Edited and translated by James Strachey. Vol. 17 (1919). London: Hogarth Press, 1957.

Freud, Sigmund, Anna Freud, and James Strachey. *The Standard Edition of the Complete Psychological Works of Sigmund Freud.* London: Hogarth Press / Institute of Psychoanalysis, 1953.

Fujitani, Takashi. *Race for Empire: Koreans as Japanese and Japanese as Americans during World War II.* Berkeley: University of California Press, 2011.

Gramsci, Antonio, Quintin Hoare, and Geoffrey Nowell-Smith. *Selections from the Prison Notebooks of Antonio Gramsci*. New York: International Publishers, 1972.

Hall, Stuart. "The West and the Rest: Discourse and Power." In *Formations of Modernity*. Edited by Stuart Hall and Bram Gieben. Oxford: Polity in association with Open University, 1992.

Hanawa, Yukiko, and Naoki Sakai. *Traces 1: Specters of the West and the Politics of Translation*. Ithaca, NY: Cornell University, distributed by Hong Kong University Press, 2001.

Hanscom, Christopher. "A Question of Representation: Korean Modernist Fiction of the 1930s." PhD diss., UCLA, 2006.

———. *The Real Modern: Literary Modernism and the Crisis of Representation in Colonial Korea*. Cambridge, MA: Harvard University Asia Center, distributed by Harvard University Press, 2013.

Han Suk Jung [Han Sŏkchŏng]. *Manjuguk kŏnguk ŭi chaehaesŏk: koeroeguk ŭi kukka hyokwa, 1932–1935*. [Reinterpreting the establishment of Manchukoku: The state-effect of the puppet state]. Tonga taehakkyo ch'ulp'anbu, 1999, 2007.

Han Su-yŏng. *Sasang kwa sŏngch'al: Han'guk kŭndae munhak ŭi ŏnŏ, chuch'e, ideollogi* [Ideology and introspection: Language, subject and ideology in Korean modern literature]. Somyŏng ch'ulp'an, 2011.

Hardt, Michael and Antonio Negri. *Empire*. Cambridge, MA: Harvard University Press, 2000.

Harootunian, Harry D. "'Modernity' and the Claims of Untimeliness," *Postcolonial Studies* 13.4 (December 2010): 367–82.

———. *Overcome by Modernity: History, Culture, and Community in Interwar Japan*. Princeton, NJ: Princeton University Press, 2000.

Harris, Neil. "All the World a Melting Pot? Japan at American Fairs, 1876–904." In *Mutual Images: Essays in American-Japanese Relations*, edited by Akira Iriye. Cambridge, MA: Harvard University Press, 1975.

Hashimoto Mitsuru. "Chihō: Yanagita Kunio's Japan." In Stephen Vlastos ed. *Mirror of Modernity: Invented Traditions of Modern Japan*. Berkeley: University of California Press, 1998: 133–34.

Hatano Setsuko. *Mujŏng ŭl ingŭnda: Mujŏng ŭi pit kwa kŭrimja* [Reading Mujŏng]. Somyŏng ch'ulp'an, 2008.

———. "Yi Kwangsu no Nihongo sōsaku to Nihon bundan." *Chōsen gakuhō* (April 2012).

Hayashi Kōji. *Zainichi Chōsenjin Nihongo bungakuron* [Japanese language literature by resident Koreans]. Shinkansha, 1991.

Hiromatsu Wataru. *Kindai chōkoku ron: Shōwa shisōshi e no ichishigaku* [On overcoming modernity: A perspective on Shōwa history of thought]. Kōdansha, 1989.

Hobsbawm, E. J. *The Age of Empire, 1875–1914*. New York: Pantheon Books, 1987.

Hobsbawm, E. J., and T. O. Ranger. *The Invention of Tradition*. Cambridge: Cambridge University Press, 1992.

Höhn, Maria, and Seungsook Moon. *Over There: Living with the U.S. Military Empire from World War Two to the Present*. Durham, NC: Duke University Press, 2010.

Hotei Toshihiro. "Ch'ogi Pukhan mundan sŏngnip kwajŏng e taehan yŏngu—Kim

Saryang ŭl chungsim ŭro" [On the establishment of early post-liberation North Korean literary field—focusing on Kim Saryang]. PhD diss., Sŏul taehakkyo, 2007.

———. "Ilche malgi Ilbonŏ sosŏl yŏngu" [On Japanese-language writings of the late-colonial period]. Master's thesis, Sŏul taehakkyo, 1996.

Huang Yuan, ed. *Shanling: Chaoxian Taiwan duanpian xiaoshuo ji* [Mountain spirits: Korean and Taiwanese short story collection]. Translated by Hu Fung. Shanghai: Wenhua shenghuo chubanshe, 1936.

Hughes, Theodore H. *Literature and Film in Cold War South Korea: Freedom's Frontier.* New York: Columbia University Press, 2012.

Hunt, Michael H., and Steven I. Levine. *Arc of Empire: America's Wars in Asia from the Philippines to Vietnam.* Chapel Hill: University of North Carolina Press, 2012.

Hutcheon, Linda. *A Theory of Parody: The Teachings of Twentieth-Century Art Forms.* Urbana: University of Illinois Press, 2000.

Hwang Hoduk. *Pŏllae wa cheguk: singminji mal munhak ŭi ŏnŏ: saengmyŏng chŏngch'i, t'ek'ŭnolloji* [Animal and imperium: Language, biopolitics, and techne]. Sae mulkyŏl, 2011.

Hwang Jong-yon [Hwang, Chongyŏn]. "Munhak iranŭn yŏgŏ: 'Munhak iran hao' hogŭn Hanguk kŭndae munhak non ŭi sŏngnip e kwanhan koch'al" [The translingual practice of literature: "What is literature" and the establishment of modern literary theory]. *Tongak ŏmunnonjip* 32.12 (December 1997): 457–80.

———. "1930 nyŏndae kojŏn puhŭng undong ŭi munhaksajŏk ŭiŭi" [Significance in literary history of the classics revival movements of the 1930s]. *Hanguk munhak yŏngu* 11.12 (November 1988): 217–60.

———. "Nobŭl, ch'ŏngnyŏn, cheguk: Hanguk kŭndae sosŏl ŭi t'onggukkagan sijak" [Novel, youth, empire: The transnational beginnings of the modern Korean novel]. *Sanghŏ hakpo* 14.2 (February 2005): 263–97.

Im Chongguk. *Ch'inil munhak non* [On pro-Japanese literature]. P'yŏnghwa ch'ulp'ansa, 1963.

Im Chŏnhye. *Nihon ni okeru Chōsenjin no bungaku no rekishi—1945 nen made* [The history of literature by Koreans in Japan—until 1945]. Hōsei daigaku shuppankyoku, 1994.

Im Hyŏng-t'aek, and Taedong Munhwa Yŏn'guwŏn. *Hŭndŭllinŭn ŏnŏdŭl: Ŏnŏ ŭi kŭndae wa kungmin kukka.* Sŏnggyun'gwan taehakkyo ch'ulp'anbu, 2008.

Im Kyuch'an and Han Chinil, eds. *Im Hwa Sinmunhaksa* [Im Hwa history of new Korean literature]. Hangilsa, 1993.

Inoue Hisashi and Komori Yōichi, eds. *Zadankai Shōwa Bungakushi.* Vol. 5. Tokyo: Shūeisha, 2003–2004.

Irigaray, Luce. *Ethique de la différence sexuelle.* Paris: Editions de Minuit, 1984.

Isogai Jirō and Kuroko Kazuo, eds. *Zainichi bungaku zenshū* [Complete works of resident-Korean literature]. 18 vols. Bensei shuppan, 2006.

Itagaki Naoko. *Jihenka no bungaku* [Literature under the crisis]. Reprinted in vol. 22 of *Kindai bungei hyōron sōsho.* Nihon tosho senta, 1992.

Jameson, Fredric. *Postmodernism, or, the Cultural Logic of Late Capitalism.* Durham, NC: Duke University Press, 1990.

————. *A Singular Modernity: Essay on the Ontology of the Present*. London: Verso, 2002.

————. "Third-World Literature in the Era of Multinational Capitalism." *Social Text* 0:15 (Autumn 1986): 65–88.

Jennings, John M. "The Forgotten Plague: Opium and Narcotics in Korea under Japanese Rule 1910–1945." *Modern Asian Studies* 29:4 (October 1994): 795–815.

————. *The Opium Empire: Japanese Imperialism and Drug Trafficking in Asia, 1895–1945*. Westport, CT: Praeger, 1997.

Kang Kyŏngae. "Chang Hyŏkchu sŏnsaeng ege." *Sin Tonga* (July 1935).

————. *Ingan munje*. Pyongyang: Munye ch'ulp'ansa, 1986.

Kaplan, Amy, and Donald E. Pease. *Cultures of United States Imperialism*. Durham, NC: Duke University Press, 1993.

Kawamura Minato. *Manshū hōkai: Daitōa bungaku to sakkatachi* [The collapse of Manchuria: Greater East Asia and its writers]. Bungei shunjū, 1997.

Kawashima, Ken C. *The Proletarian Gamble: Korean Workers in Interwar Japan*. Durham, NC: Duke University Press, 2009.

Keene, Donald. "Japanese Writers and the Greater East Asia War." *Journal of Asian Studies* 23:2 (February 1964): 209–25.

Kleeman, Faye. *Under an Imperial Sun: Japanese Colonial Literature of Taiwan and the South*. Honolulu: University of Hawaii Press, 2003.

Kim Chaeyong. *Hyŏmnyŏk kwa chŏhang* [Resistance and collaboration]. Somyŏng ch'ulp'an, 2003.

Kim, Chul [Kim Ch'ŏl]. *"Kungmin" iranŭn noyae: Hanguk munhak ŭi kiŏk kwa manggak*. [A slave called "national subject": Memory and forgetting in Korean literature]. Samin, 2005.

Kim, Chul [Kim Ch'ŏl]. *Kungmunhak ŭl nŏmŏsŏ* [Beyond national literature]. Kukhak charyowŏn, 2000.

————. "Mollak hanŭn sinsaeng: 'Manju' ŭi kkum kwa 'nonggun' ŭi odok" [Collapsing of "new life" and mis-reading "nonggun"]. *Sanghŏ hakpo* 9 (2002).

————. "Tonghwa hokŭn ch'ogŭk: Singminji Chosŏn esŏŭi kŭndae ch'ogŭk non" [Assimilation or overcoming: Overcoming modernity in colonial Korea]. *Tongbang hakchi* (2009).

Kim, Chul [Kim Ch'ŏl], and Sin Hyŏnggi, eds. *Munhak sok ŭi p'asisŭm* [Fascism in literature]. Samin 2001.

Kim, Elaine H, and Chungmoo Choi. *Dangerous Women: Gender and Korean Nationalism*. New York: Routledge, 1998.

Kim Inhwan, Kim Cheyong et al., eds. *Kang Kyŏngae t'ansaeng 100 chunyŏn kinyŏm, nambuk kongdong nonmunjip, Kang Kyŏngae sidae wa munhak* [South and North Korean collaborative collection in celebration of the centennial of Kang Kyŏngae's birth, Kang Kyŏngae, her times, and her literature]. Raendŏm hausŭ, 2006.

Kim Saryang. "Chijimi." *Samch'ŏlli* (April 1941): 259–69.

————. "Chōsen bunka tsūshin" [Dispatches on Korean culture]. *Genchi hōkō* (July 1943). Reprinted in Kim Saryang Zenshū Henshū iinkai, ed., *Kim Saryang zenshū*, vol. 4 Kawade shobō shinsha, 1973: 21–34.

————. *Hikari no naka ni* [Into the light]. Koyama shoten, 1940.

————. *Kokyō* [Hometown]. Kōchō shorin, 1942.

————. "Kyōshū" [Nostalgia]. *Bungei shunjū* (July 1941): 286–313.

————. "Letter to Mother." In Kim Saryang Zenshū Henshū iinkai, ed., *Kim Saryang zenshū*, vol. 4. Kawade shobō shinsha, 1973.

————. "Mushi" [Bug]. *Shinchō* (July 1941).

————. "Tenma" [Pegasus]. *Bungei shunjū* (June 1940): 352–84.

Kim Saryang sakuhinshū [Selected works of Kim Saryang]. Edited by Kim Talsu. Tokyo: Rironsha, 1972.

Kim Saryang Zenshū Henshū Iinkai, ed. *Kim Saryang zenshū* [Complete works of Kim Saryang]. 4 vols. Kawade shobō shinsha, 1973.

Kim T'aejun. "Sosŏl ŭi chŏngŭi."[Defining the sosŏl]. *Sahoe kongnon* 1:1 (May 1935): 61–63. *Kim Tongin chŏnjip* [Complete works of Kim Tongin]. Vol. 6. Samjungdang, 1976.

Kim Yerim. *1930 nyŏndae huban kŭndae insik ŭi t'ŭl kwa miŭsik* [Modern episteme and aesthetic consciousness of the late 1930s]. Somyŏng ch'ulp'an, 2004.

Kim Yongdal. *Sōshikaimei no kenkyū* [On colonial name change policies]. Miraisha, 1997.

Kim Yongjae. "Hantō bundan to kokugo no mondai." *Ryokki* (March 1942): 124–30.

Kim Yŏngsik, ed. *Chakko munin 48-in ŭi yukp'il sŏhanjip P'ain Kim Tonghwan 100— chunyŏn kinyŏm.* [Collection of letters of 48 deceased writers compiled on the centennial of P'ain Kim Tonghwan's birth]. Minnyŏn, 2001.

Kim Yunsik. *Hanguk kŭndae munye pipy'ŏngsa yŏngu* [On modern Korean literary criticism]. Ilchisa, 1973.

————. *Hanil kŭndae munhak ŭi kwallyŏn yangsang sillon* [New perspectives on the relationship between Korean and Japanese modern literatures]. Sŏul taehakkyo ch'ulp'anbu, 2001.

————. *Ilche malgi Hangguk chakka ŭi Ilbonŏ kŭlssŭgi non* [Late-colonial period Japanese-language writings of Koreans]. Sŏul taehakkyo ch'ulp'anbu, 2003.

————. *Yi Kwangsu wa kŭ ŭi sidae* [Yi Kwangsu and his times]. Rev. ed. 3 vols. Sol ch'ulp'ansa, 1999.

Kingsberg, Miriam. *Moral Nation: Modern Japan and Narcotics in Global History.* Berkeley: University of California Press, 2014.

Kishida Kunio, "Chihō bunka no shinkensetsu." *Chisei* (July 1941).

Klein, Christina. *Cold War Orientalism: Asia in the Middlebrow Imagination, 1945–1961.* Berkeley: University of California Press, 2003.

Kobayashi, Hideo, and Paul Anderer. *Literature of the Lost Home: Kobayashi Hideo— Literary Criticism, 1924–1939.* Edited and translated and with an introduction by Paul Anderer. Stanford, CA: Stanford University Press, 1995.

Komagome Takeshi. *Shokuminchi teikoku Nihon no bunka tōgō.* Iwanami shoten, 1996.

————. "Colonial Modernity for an Elite Taiwanese Lim Bo-Seng: The Labyrinth of Cosmopolitanism," 141–59. In *Taiwan under Japanese Colonial Rule, 1895–1945: History, Culture, Memory.* Edited by Liao Ping-wei and David Der-wei Wang. New York: Columbia University Press, 2006.

Kon Wajiro. *Kogengaku nyūmon* [Introduction to modernology]. Chikuma bunkō, 1997.

Kristeva, Julia. "Approaching Abjection." In *Powers of Horror: An Essay on Abjection.* Translated by Leon S. Roudiez. New York: Columbia University Press, 1982.

———. *Powers of Horror: An Essay on Abjection.* New York: Columbia University Press, 1982.

———. *Strangers to Ourselves.* New York: Columbia University Press, 1991.

Kungnip hyŏndae misulgwan [National museum of contemporary art], ed. *Hanguk kŏnch'uk 100-nyŏn* [One hundred years of Korean architecture]. P'ia, 1999.

Kurahara Masano. *Nihon no ahensen: kakusareta kokka hanzai* [Japan's opium war: Hidden national crimes. Kyōei shōbo, 1996.

Kurokawa, Sō. *"Gaichi" no Nihongo bungakusen*, 3 vols. Shinjuku shobō, 1996.

Kwak Hyoungduck [Kwak Hyŏngduk], and Kim Chaeyong, eds. *Kim Saryang chakp'um kwa yŏngu.* 4 vols. Yŏngnak, 2008–2014.

Kwon, Heonik. *The Other Cold War.* New York: Columbia University Press, 2010.

Kwŏn Myŏnga. *Singminji ihu rŭl sayu hada: T'alsingminhwa wa chaesingminhwa ŭi kyŏnggye* [Imagining the post-colony: Boundary between postcolonization and recolonization]. Ch'aek sesang, 2009.

———. *Yŏksajŏk p'asijŭm: Cheguk ŭi p'ant'asi wa chendŏ chŏngch'i* [Historical fascism: Imperial fantasy and gender politics]. Ch'aek sesang, 2005.

Kwon, Nayoung Aimee. "Translated Encounters and Empire: Colonial Korea and the Literature of Exile." PhD diss., UCLA, 2007.

Kwŏn Podŭrae. *Yŏnae ŭi sidae* [The age of romance]. Hyŏnsil munhwa yŏngu, 2003.

Lacan Jaques. "The Mirror Stage as Formative of the I Function, as Revealed in Psychoanalytic Experience." In *Ecrits: A Selection.* New York: W. W. Norton, 1977.

Laplanche, J. and J. B. Pontalis, eds. *The Language of Psycho-Analysis.* Translated by Donald Nicholson-Smith. New York: W. W. Norton, 1973.

Larsen, Kirk W. *Tradition, Treaties, and Trade: Qing Imperialism and Chōson Korea, 1850–1910.* Boston: Harvard University Asia Center, 2011.

Lee, Hyangjin. *Contemporary Korean Cinema: Identity Culture and Politics.* Manchester, UK: Manchester University Press, distributed exclusively in the United States by Palgrave, 2000.

Lee, Leo Ou-fan. *Shanghai Modern:The Flowering of a New Urban Culture in China, 1930–1945.* Cambridge, MA: Harvard University Press, 1999.

Lee, Peter H. "The Road to Ch'unhyang: A Reading of the *Song of the Chaste Wife Ch'unhyang." Azalea* 3: 257–376.

Lewis, Pericles. *The Cambridge Introduction to Modernism.* Cambridge: Cambridge University Press, 2007.

Liao Ping-wei and David Der-wei Wang, eds. *Taiwan under Japanese Colonial Rule, 1895–1945: History, Culture, Memory.* New York: Columbia University Press, 2006.

Lippit, Seiji M. *Topographies of Japanese Modernism.* New York: Columbia University Press, 2002.

Liu, Lydia, ed. *Tokens of Exchange: The Problem of Translation in Global Circulation.* Durham, NC: Duke University Press, 1999.

———. *Translingual Practice: Literature, National Culture, and Translated Modernity— China 1900–1937.* Stanford, CA: Stanford University Press, 1997.

Mack, Edward Thomas. *Manufacturing Modern Japanese Literature: Publishing, Prizes, and the Ascription of Literary Value.* Durham, NC: Duke University Press, 2010.

Matsuda Toshihiko. "Sōryokusenki no shokuminchi Chōsen ni okeru keisatsu gyōsei—keisatsukan ni yoru 'jikyoku zadankai' o jiku ni." *Nihonshi kenkyū* 452 (April 2000).

McAlister, Melani. *Epic Encounters: Culture, Media, and U.S. Interests in the Middle East, 1945–2000.* Berkeley: University of California Press, 2001.

McClintock, Anne. *Imperial Leather: Race, Gender, and Sexuality in the Colonial Conquest.* New York: Routledge, 1995.

Mignolo, Walter. *The Darker Side of Western Modernity: Global Futures, Decolonial Options.* Durham, NC: Duke University Press, 2011.

————. "The Geopolitics of Knowledge and The Colonial Difference." *The South Atlantic Quarterly* 101.1 (Winter 2002): 57–96.

Miki Kiyoshi. *Tōa kyōdōtai no tetsugaku: sekaishi tachiba to kindai higashi Ajia. Miki Kiyoshi hihyō senshū.* Shoshi shinsui, 2007.

Miyata Setsuko, Kim Yongdal, and Yang T'aeho, eds. *Sōshi kaimei* [Imperial name-change policies]. Akashi shoten, 1992.

Miyoshi, Masao. *Off Center: Power and Culture Relations between Japan and the United States.* Cambridge, MA: Harvard University Press, 1991.

Mizuno Naoki. "Senjiki no shokuminchi shihai to 'Naigaichi kōsei ichigenka.'" *Jinbun gakuhō* 79:77–102.

————. *Sōshi kaimei: Nihon no Chōsen shihai no naka de* [Imperial name-change policies: Inside Japan's occupation of colonial Korea]. Iwanami shoten, 2008.

————. "Tonghwa wa ch'aihwa: Ilbon ŭi singminji chibae wa 'ch'angssi kaemyŏng.'" In *Ilche Singminji sigi saero ilki.* Hyean, 2007.

Modern Girl Around the World Research Group, ed., *The Modern Girl around the World: Consumption, Modernity, and Globalization.* Durham, NC: Duke University Press, 2008.

Mufti, Aamir. "The Aura of Authenticity." *Social Text* 18:3 (2000).

"Munhakcha ŭi chagi pip'an" [Writers' self-reflection]. *Inmin yesul* 2 (October 1946): 39–48.

Mun Kyŏngyŏn, et. al., eds. *Chwadamhoe ro ignŭn Kungmin munhak* [Reading *Kungmin munhak* through roundtables]. Somyŏng ch'ulp'an, 2010.

Murai Osamu. *Nantō ideorogī no hassei: Yanagita Kunio to shokiminchishugi.* [Genesis of south seas ideology: Yanagita Kunio and colonialism]. Ōta shuppan, 1995.

Nakane Takayuki. *"Chōsen" hyōshōno bunkashi: kindai Nihon to tasha wo meguru chi no shokuminchika* [Cultural anthropology of the image of Korea: The colonization of knowledge of the other]. Shinyōsha, 2004.

Nam Pujin. *Bungaku no shokuminchishugi* [Literature and imperialism]. Sekaishisōsha, 2006.

————. *Kindai bungaku no "Chōsen" taiken* [Korean experience in modern literature]. Bensei shuppan, 2001.

Noguchi, Minoru. "Izoku no otto" (Foreign husband). *Sinchō* 55.5 (May 1958): 164–82

————. "Izoku no otto" (Foreign husband). Translated by Nayoung Aimee Kwon. In

Melissa Wender, ed. *Into the Light: An Anthology of Literature by Koreans in Japan.* Honolulu: University of Hawaii Press, 2010: 66–91.

Norindr, Panivong. *Phantasmatic Indochina: French Colonial Ideology in Architecture, Film, and Literature.* Durham, NC: Duke University Press, 1996.

Ōguma Eiji. *Nihonjin no kyōkai: Okinawa, Taiwan, Chōsen shokuminchi shihai kara fukki undō made* [Boundaries of the Japanese: From colonial rule in Okinawa, Taiwan, Korea until decolonization]. Shinyōsha, 1998.

————. *Tan'itsu minzoku shinwa no kigen: "Nihonjin" no jigazō no keifu* [The myth of the homogeneous nation: Genealogy of the Japanese self-image]. Shinyōsha, 1995.

Ōmura Masuo, "Kang Kyŏngae *Ingan munje* p'anbon pigyo" [Comparison of various versions of *Ingan munje*]. Paper presented at Waseda University Chōsen bunka kenkyūkai, 2006.

Ōmura Masuo and Hotei Toshihiro, eds. *Kindai Chōsen bungaku Nihongo sakuhinshū 1939–1945.* Vol 3. Ryokuin shobō, 2002.

————, eds. *Kindai Chōsen Nihongo sakuhinshū 1901–1938* [Compilation of modern Korean Japanese-language works]. 5 vols. Ryokuin shobō, 2004.

Ono Hideo. *Osaka manichi shinbunshashi* [History of the Osaka manichi shinbun]. Osaka: Osaka mainichi shinbunsha, 1925.

Paek Ch'ŏl. *Chosŏn sinmunhak sajosa* [Historical tendencies of modern Korean literary thought]. Paegyangsa, 1947.

Paek Hyŏnmi. "Minjokchŏk chŏnt'ong kwa tongyangjŏk chŏnt'ong—1930nyŏndae huban Kyŏngsŏng kwa Tonggyŏng esŏ ŭi "Ch'unhyang chŏn" kongyŏn ŭl chungsim ŭro." [National tradition and East Asian Tradition—on the performance of "Ch'unhyang chŏn" in late-1930s Kyŏngsŏng and Tokyo.] *Hyŏndae munhak iron yŏngu* 23: 213–45.

Pak Ch'unil, *Kindai Nihon bungaku ni okeru Chosenzō* [The image of Korea in modern Japanese literature]. Miraisha, 1969, 1985.

Pak Yŏngsŏk. *Manbosan sakŏn yŏngu: Ilcheha taeryuk ch'imnyak chŏngch'aek ŭi ilhwan ŭrosŏ* [Wanbaoshan incident as an aspect of imperial Japan's policies of continental infiltration]. Asea munhwasa, 1978.

Park, Hyun Ok. *Two Dreams in One Bed: Empire, Social Life, and the Origins of the North Korean Revolution in Manchuria.* Durham, NC: Duke University Press, 2005.

Pratt, Mary Louise. *Imperial Eyes: Travel Writing and Transculturation.* London: Routledge, 1992.

Rhys, Jean, Charlotte Brontë, and Judith L. Raiskin. *Wide Sargasso Sea.* New York: W. W. Norton, 1999.

Robertson, Jennifer Ellen. *Takarazuka: Sexual Politics and Popular Culture in Modern Japan.* Berkeley: University of California Press, 1998.

Robinson, Michael Edson. *Cultural Nationalism in Colonial Korea, 1920–1925.* Seattle: University of Washington Press, 1988.

Rosaldo, Renato. "Imperialist Nostalgia." *Representation* 26 (Spring 1989): 107–22.

Rutt, Richard, and Kim Chong-Un. *Virtuous Women: Three Classic Korean Novels.* Seoul: The Royal Asiatic Society, Korea Branch, 1979.

Saaler, Sven, and J. Victor Koschmann, eds. *Pan-Asianism in Modern Japanese History: Colonialism, Regionalism and Borders.* London: Routledge, 2007.

Said, Edward. *Culture and Imperialism*. New York: Knopf, 1993.
———. *Orientalism*. New York: Vintage Books, 1978.
———. *Reflections on Exile and Other Essays*. Cambridge, MA: Harvard University Press, 2000.
———. "Representing the Colonized: Anthropology's Interlocutors." In *Reflections on Exile and Other Essays*. Cambridge, MA: Harvard University Press, 2000.
———. "Traveling Theory Reconsidered." In *Reflections on Exile and Other Essays*. Cambridge, MA: Harvard University Press, 2000.
Sakai, Naoki. "Modernity and Its Critique: The Problem of Universalism and Particularism." In *Postmodernism and Japan*, edited by Masao Miyoshi and H. D. Harootunian. Durham, NC: Duke University Press, 1989.
———. *Translation and Subjectivity: on "Japan" and Cultural Nationalism*. Minneapolis: University of Minnesota Press, 1997.
———. "You Asians: On the Historical Role of the West and Asia Binary." *South Atlantic Quarterly* 99: 4 (Fall 2000): 789–817.
Sakai, Naoki, et al. "Zadankai: bunka no seijisei" [Roundtable: Politics of culture]. *Sekai* 573 (October 1992): 232–53.
Santner, Eric L. *Stranded Objects: Mourning, Memory, and Film in Postwar Germany*. Ithaca, NY: Cornell University Press, 1990.
Sato, Tomoko, and Toshio Watanabe, eds. *Japan and Britain: An Aesthetic Dialogue 1850–1930*. London: Lund Humphries in association with the Barbican Art Gallery, 1991.
Schmid, Andre. "Colonialism and the 'Korea Problem' in the Historiography of Modern Japan," *Journal of Asian Studies* 59.4 (November 2000): 951–76.
———. *Korea between Empires, 1895–1919*. New York: Columbia University Press, 2002.
Scott, Christopher. "Invisible Men: The Zainichi Presence in Postwar Japanese Culture." Phd diss., Stanford University, 2006.
Shih, Shu-mei. *The Lure of the Modern: Writing Modernism in Semicolonial China, 1917–1937*. Berkeley: University of California Press, 2001.
Shih, Shu-mei, Chien-hsin Tsai, and Brian Bernards. *Sinophone Studies: A Critical Reader*. New York: Columbia University Press, 2013.
Shils, Edward. *Tradition*. Chicago: University of Chicago Press, 1981.
Shimomura Sakujirō. *Bungaku de yomu Taiwan: shihaisha, gengo, sakkatachi* [Reading Taiwan through literature: Dominance, language and writers]. Tahata shoten, 1994.
Shin, Gi-Wook, and Michael Robinson, eds. *Colonial Modernity in Korea*. Cambridge, MA: Harvard University Press, 1999.
———. *Han'guk ŭi singminji kŭndaesŏng : Naejaejŏk palchŏnnon kwa singminji kŭndaehwaron ŭl nŏmosŏ* [Korea's colonial modernity: Beyond internal development and colonial modernization]. Samin, 2006.
Shirakawa Yutaka. "Chang Hyŏkchu yŏngu." PhD diss., Tongguk taehakkyo, 1989.
———. *Chōsen kindai no chinichiha sakka kutō no kiseki: Yomu Sansopu, Chan Hyokuchu to sono bungaku*. Bensei shuppan, 2008.
———. *Han'guk kŭndae chiil chakka wa kŭ munhak yŏngu*. Kip'ŭn saem, 2010.
———. "Saga Kōtō Gakkō jidai no Kin Shiryō." *Chōsen gakuhō* 147 (April 1993): 127–152.

———. *Shokuminchiki Chōsen no sakka to Nihon* [Colonial Korean writers and Japan]. Okayama: Daigaku kyōiku shuppan, 1995.

Sin Hyŏnggi. *Haebang chikhu ŭi munhak undong non* [On immediate postliberation literary movements]. Hwada, 1988.

Sin Jiyŏng. *Pujae ŭi sidae: kŭndae kyemonggi mit singminjigi Chosŏn ŭi yŏnsŏl chwadamhoe* [Age of absence: Korea's modern enlightenment and colonial period speeches and roundtables]. Somyŏng ch'ulp'an, 2012.

Sŏl Sŏnggyŏng. Ch'unhyang chŏn *ŭi pimil* [The mystery of the tale of Ch'unhyang]. Sŏul taehakkyo ch'ulp'anbu, 2001.

Spivak, Gayatri Chakravorty. *A Critique of Postcolonial Reason: Toward a History of the Vanishing Present.* Cambridge, MA: Harvard University Press, 1999.

———. "Can the Subaltern Speak?" In *Marxism and the Interpretation of Culture.* C. Nelson and L. Grossberg, eds. Basingstoke: Macmillan Education, 1988: 271–313.

———. *Other Asias.* Malden, M.A.: Blackwell Publishing, 2008.

Stewart, Susan. *On Longing: Narratives of the Miniature, the Gigantic, the Souvenir, the Collection.* Durham, NC: Duke University Press, 1993.

Suh, Serk-Bae. "Tanil ŏnŏ sahoe rŭl hyanghae." *Hanguk munhak yŏngu* 29 (December 2005): 185–219.

———. *Treacherous Translation.* Berkeley: University of California Press, 2013.

Suzuki, Tomi. *Narrating the Self: Fictions of Japanese Modernity.* Stanford, CA: Stanford University Press, 1996.

Takahashi Azusa. "Kim Saryang no nigengo sakuhin ni okeru hyōgen no sai o meguru kōsatsu: "Ryūchijō de atta otoko" (Chōsengo), "Q Hakushaku (Nihongo) o chūshin ni." *Gengo chiiki bunka kenkyū* vol. 20 (January 2014): 291–308.

Tanaka Ryūichi. "Tairitsu to tōgō no 'Senman' kankei—'naisen ittai' 'gozoku kyōwa' 'senman ichinyo' no shosō" [Conflict and unity in Korea-Manchuria relations: Various aspects of "Japan-Korea as one body," "harmony of five races," "harmony of Korea and Manchuria"]. *Hisutoria* 152 (1996): 106–32.

Tanaka, Stefan. *Japan's Orient: Rendering Pasts into History.* Berkeley: University of California Press, 1993.

Thornber, Karen. *Empire of Texts in Motion: Chinese, Korean, and Taiwanese Transculturations of Japanese Literature.* Cambridge, MA: Harvard University Press, 2009.

Tyler, William Jefferson. *Modanizumu: Modernist Fiction from Japan, 1913–1938.* Honolulu: University of Hawaii Press, 2008.

Uchida Hiroshi, ed. *Miki Kiyoshi Tōa kyōdotai ronshū* [Miki Kiyoshi, Collection on East Asian coprosperity sphere]. Kobushi shobō, 2007.

Uchida, Jun, and Harvard University Asia Center. *Brokers of Empire: Japanese Settler Colonialism in Korea, 1876–1945.* Cambridge, MA: Harvard University Asia Center, distributed by Harvard University Press, 2011.

Utsumi Aiko, *Sengo hoshō kara kangaeru Nihon to Ajia* [Japan and Asia from the perspective of postwar reparations]. Yamakawa shuppansha, 2002.

Van Pelt, Tamise. "Otherness." *Postmodern Culture* 10:2 (January 2000).

Vlastos, Stephen, ed. *Mirror of Modernity: Invented Traditions of Modern Japan.* Berkeley: University of California Press, 1998.

Watanabe Kazutami. *Tasha to shite no Chōsen: bungakuteki kosatsu* [Korea as other: A literary examination]. Iwanami shoten, 2003.

Watanabe Naoki. "Chang Hyŏkchu no Chōhen shōsetsu *Kaikon* (1943) ni tsuite." *Hanguk munhak ŭi yŏngu* vol. 36 (October 2008).

———. "Manchuria and the Agrarian-Proletariat Literature of Colonial Korea," paper presented at the annual meeting of the Association for Asian Studies, Boston, MA, March 22–25, 2007.

Watanabe Naoki, Hwang Hoduk, and Kim Ungyo, eds. *Chŏnjaeng hanŭn sinmin, singminji ŭi kungmin munhwa: Singminji mal Chosŏn ŭi tamnon kwa p'yosang.* [Behind the lines: Culture in late-colonial Korea]. Somyŏng ch'ulp'an, 2010.

———. "Singminji Chosŏn esŏ "Manju" tamnon kwa chŏngch'ijŏk muŭisik: munhak p'yŏngnonga Im Hwa ŭi 1940 nyŏndae chŏnban ŭi nonŭi rŭl chungsim ŭro."

Weisenfeld, Gennifer. M AVO: *Japanese Artists and the Avant-Garde 1905–1931.* Berkeley: University of California Press, 2002.

Wender, Melissa, ed. *Into the Light: Anthology of Literature by Koreans in Japan.* Honolulu: University of Hawaii Press, 2011.

Wise, Christopher. *Derrida, Africa, and the Middle East.* New York: Palgrave Macmillan, 2009.

Yamamuro Shin'ichi. *Kimera: Manshūkoku no shōzō* [Kimera: A portrait of Manchukoku]. Chūō kōronsha, 1993.

———. *Manchuria under Japanese Domination.* Philadelphia: University of Pennsylvania Press, 2006.

Yamamuro, Shin'ichi, and Joshua A. Fogel. *Manchuria under Japanese Domination.* Philadelphia: University of Pennsylvania Press, 2006.

Yamazaki Yoshimitsu. "Modanizumu no gensetsuyōshi toshite no 'zadankai'—*Shinchō* 'gappyōkai' kara *Bungei shunjū* no 'zadankai' e." *Kokugo to kokubungaku* (December 2006): 45–57.

Yanagisawa Asobu and Okabe Makio, eds. *Tenbō Nihon rekishi teikokushugi to Shokuminchi.* Vol. 20. Tokyōdō shuppan, 2001.

Yi Haeryŏng. "Chosŏnŏ pangŏn ŭi p'yosangdŭl: Hanguk kŭndae sosŏl kŭ ŏnŏ ŭi injongjuŭi e taehayŏ." In *Hŭndŭllinŭn ŏnŏdŭl: Ŏnŏ ŭi kŭndae wa kungmin kukka.* Edited by Im Hyŏng-t'aek and Taedong Munhwa Yŏn'guwŏn Sŏnggyun'gwan taehakkyo ch'ulp'anbu, 2008.

———. "Maybe Love (Ai ka)." Translated by John Wittier Treat. *Azalea: Journal of Korean Literature & Culture* 4 (2011): 321–27.

———. "Saranginga." Translated by Kim Yunsik. *Munhak sasang* (February 1981): 442–46.

Yi Kyŏnghun [Lee Kyoung-Hoon]. "Mitsukoshi, kŭndae ŭi shyowindou-munhak kwa p'ungsok 1" [Mitsukoshi, modern show-window and customs 1]. *Hanguk kŭndae munhak kwa Ilbon munhak.* Kukhak charyowŏn, 2001.

———. *Yi Kwangsu ŭi ch'inil munhak yŏngu.* [On the pro-Japanese literature of Yi Kwangsu]. T'aehaksa, 1998.

Yi Sanggyŏng, ed. *Kang Kyŏngae chŏnjip* [Complete works of Kang Kyŏngae]. Somyŏng ch'ulp'an, 1999.

————. "Introduction" to Kang Kyŏngae's "Changsangot." Translated by Kim Sŏkhŭi. *Hanguk munhak* (December 1989): 327–29.

————. *Kang Kyŏngae: munhak esŏ ŭi sŏng kwa kyegŭp* [Kang Kyŏngae: Sexuality and class in literature]. Kŏnguk taehakkyo ch'ulp'anbu, 1997.

Yi Sangt'aek, ed. *Hanguk munhak ch'ongsŏ 2: Kojŏn sosŏl* [Series on Korean literature 2: Classical fiction]. Haenam, 1997.

Yi Sŏnok. "P'yŏndŭng e taehan yuhok: yŏsŏng chisigin kwa ch'inil ŭi naechŏk nolli" [Seduction of equality: Women intellectuals and the rationalization of collaboration]. *Silch'ŏn munhak* vol. 67 (Spring 2002): 254–69.

Yi Wŏndong, *Singmin chibae tamnon kwa* Kungmin munhak *chwadamhoe* [Discourse of colonial occupation and Roundtables in *Kungmin munhak*]." Yŏngnak, 2009.

Yi Yŏn-suk. *"Kokugo" to iu shisō: kindai Nihon no gengo ninshiki* [The ideology of "national language": modern Japan's linguistic consciousness]. Iwanami shoten, 1996.

Yōichi Komori. *Posutokoroniaru* [Postcolonial]. Iwanami shoten, 2001.

Yokomitsu Riichi. *Love and Other Stories of Yokomitsu Riichi*. Translated by Dennis Keene. University of Tokyo Press, 1974.

Yŏm Sangsŏp. "On the Eve of the Uprising." In *On the Eve of the Uprising and Other Stories from Colonial Korea*. Edited and translated by Sunyoung Park in collaboration with Jefferson J. A. Gatrall. Ithaca, NY: Cornell East Asia Series, 2010.

Yŏnbyŏn taehakkyo Chosŏn munhak yŏnguso, ed., *Kang Kyŏngae*. Pogosa, 2006.

Yonetani Masafumi. *Ajia/Nihon* [Asia/Japan]. Iwanami shoten, 2006.

Young, Louise. *Japan's Total Empire: Manchuria and the Culture of Wartime Imperialism*. Berkeley: University of California Press, 1998.

Young, Robert J. C. *Colonial Desire: Hybridity in Theory, Culture, and Race*. London: Routledge, 1995.

Yun Haedong. *Singminji kŭndae ŭi p'aerŏdoksŭ* [Paradox of colonial modernity]. Hyumŏnisŭt'ŭ, 2007.

————. *Singminji ŭi hoesaek chidae* [Colonial gray zone]. Yŏksa pip'yŏngsa, 2003.

Yun Haedong, Ch'ŏn Chŏnghwa, et al., eds. *Kŭndae rŭl tasi illŏnda* [Rereading the modern]. 2 vols. Yŏksa pip'yŏngsa, 2007.

Yun Taesŏk. "1940 nyŏndae 'kungmin munhak' yŏngu" [On 1940s discourse on "imperial literature"]. PhD diss., Sŏul taehakkyo, 2006.

————. *Singminji kungmin munhak non* [Colonial-era discourse on "imperial literature"]. Yŏngnak, 2006.

Note: Italicized numbers indicate a figure; n indicates an endnote

abjection: the notion of, 83–84, 223–24n8; as the perpetual position of bilingual colonized writers and translators, 84–90; as the perpetual position of colonized Korea itself, 140–41, 158, 202; as the perpetual position of imperial colonial literature, 71, 177; as portrayed by characters in "Into the Light," 71–73, 222n9; as portrayed by characters in "Pegasus," 88–98; as a symbol of cultural purity to Korean postcolonial nationalists, 177

Aczel, Richard, 137–38

agency, 12, 155–56, 199–200, 201–2

"Aika" ("Love?"), 1–3, 5–7, 21, 27, 195, 213–14nn3–6, 217n24

Akita Ujaku, 129, 145–46, 231n45, 236n35

Akutagawa Literary Prize: the assessments of nominees (1940), 49–53; the awarding of, 220n15, 221–22n32, 239n17; and the imperial Japanese sociopolitical agenda, 47–49, 52, 53–54, 57–58, 76, 200; and the Korea Boom, 81–82; the nomination of Kim Saryang for his "Into the Light," 41, 50–52, 53–54, 81–82, 88, 99; the nomination of zainichi authors for, 25; the significance of, 47

allegory, 58, 74, 232n62

assimilation: the Akutagawa Literary Prize as a tool to promote colonial, 52, 53, 76; censorship as a tool for forcing Korean cultural, 35, 108, 122–23, 162, 176, 217n30, 240n28; as a conundrum for Korean cultural producers, 27–28, 59–60, 77, 105–6, 114, 201–2, 205; and differentiation as complementary policies of empire, 8, 45, 46, 75–76; the failure of allegedly successful colonial, 103–4, 113, 123, 128, 138–39, 171; imperial Japanese policies of, 6, 17, 28, 108–9, 156, 159, 162–63, 215n1, 227n50; the Korea Boom as a tool for colonial, 109, 131, 162–63; Korean attempts to retain cultural identity despite imperial, 37, 85, 105; the of Korea exacerbated by Japanese expansion into Manchuria, 7, 27, 138, 157–59, 191, 199; racism and loss of identity as byproducts of imperial, 71, 75–78; and the rhetoric of *Naisen ittai*, 7–8, 15, 76, 92–93, 219n5

audience: and the challenge of promoting transcolonial cultural understanding, 36–37, 86, 101; the misrepresentation of translated works to the metropolitan, 15, 53–54, 148, 173, 189, 191; and the roundtable format, 132, 134, 136, 137; satisfying as a primary goal of imperial culture curators,

chihō bunka (local culture), 201–2

China: the disavowal of its imperial activities by, 202; and Japanese imperial triangulation strategies, 40, 155–56, 174, 178, 198–202; Japan's incursions into, 18, 31, 45, 61, 214n13, 215n1, 218n37; Japan's 1937 invasion of, 80, 191, 226n37; Japan's use of Korea and Koreans for its expansion into, 27, 140, 157–60, 182, 185, 199; Korea as a crossroad between Japan and, 88, 139–40, 154, 201

ch'inil ("intimacy" or "collusion"), 8, 15, 22, 23, 24, 100

Chōsen būmū. See Korea Boom

Chōsen bungaku: the imperial appropriation of as consumer kitsch, 18, 28, 35, 37, 189; as the Japanese counterpart to Chōsŏn munhak, 35, 217n30; the popularity of in the imperial metropole, 28, 35, 37. See also Chosŏn munhak; Korean literature

Chosŏn dynasty, 33, 126, 143–44

Chosŏn munhak (Korean literature): Chōsen bungaku as the Japanese counterpart to, 35; discourses concerning among colonized nationalists, 18, 28, 34–35, 37–40, 217n30, 218n38, 218n45. See also Chōsen bungaku; Korean literature

Ch'unhyang: the alterations to by Murayama Tomoyoshi, 102–3, 114–24, 231n44; the original Korean tale, 101–2, 107–8, 229n17; the response among Japanese critics to the theatrical performance of, 118–19, 148; the response among Korean critics to the theatrical performance of, 125–28, 148; the reworking of the into Korea Boom kitsch, 103–6, 108–9, 123, 128, 228n7; the roundtable discussions concerning the performance of, 125–29, 139; the theatrical Japanese adaptation of the, 101–2, 112–15, 118–24, 228n6; the transcolonial traveling performance of, 102, 118, 119, 125; the translation and script by Chang Hyŏkchu, 112–15, 124, 127–28, 129–30, 149–50; versions of the, 228n5, 229n18

chwadamhoe (K). See roundtable discussions

Cold War, 40, 174, 203, 208–11, 229n15

collaboration: accusations against Chang Hyŏkchu of imperial, 23, 25, 100, 113–14, 128–30, 190, 230n36; accusations against Yi Kwangsu of imperial, 1, 7, 100, 196; accusations of as a conundrum for colonized bilingual writers, 7, 8; the case of the theatrical production of the Ch'unhyang, 103, 104, 128–30, 139; as failed interaction between colonizer and colonized, 131–32, 200; Im Chongguk's study of among colonized Korean cultural producers, 19–20; the literature of, 8, 15, 19–20; Pan-Asianism disguised as, 155, 157; postcolonial reassessment of colonial, 26, 175–78, 184, 187, 190, 200; as a postcolonial stigma implying traitorous behavior, 20, 22, 23; the resistance-collaboration binary as an oversimplified construct, 157–58, 174–75, 177–78, 186–87, 191–92, 199–200; transcolonial, 15–16; versus resistance, 8, 101, 174–75, 175–78, 190–91, 199. See also Korean writers; resistance

collection: as an assertion of control over a culture, 167–68; the museum as a symbol of stagnation, 148, 166, 168, 171, 241n45

collective reviews (gappyōkai), 132, 133–34, 233n2

collectivity: art as an expression of, 13, 130; colonial culture producers positioned as "exceptional representatives" of, 54; colonial culture producers positioned as representative of a universal, 36, 46–47, 56–58, 74–75, 177; imperial objectification of the colonized as, 13, 56–57, 69, 74, 87, 169–70, 241n46; the souvenir as representative of, 173, 241–46

colonial encounter: the assumptions of the colonizer, 15, 113, 139, 144–51, 156, 168–69, 173; the blindness inherent to the colonizer, 14–16, 58, 77, 170–71, 192, 235–36n28; the confusion of the individual with the collective populace, 13, 36, 46–47, 54, 169; Edward Said on the, 13–15; the forefront position of cultural producers in the, 8, 15, 86, 93–94, 118, 138–39; the hierarchical and repressive qualities of the, 15–16, 86, 89, 106, 138, 240n28, 243n29; the hopes of the colonized, 8, 15, 87–88,

colonial encounter (*continued*)
113, 200, 227n54; the influence of the on the cultural production of the colonized, 13, 83–86, 169–71, 218–19n52, 224n19; the inherently coercive nature of the, 8, 191, 200, 240n28; Kim Saryang's "Aika" as a statement regarding the, 2–5; Kim Saryang's "Into the Light" as a study of the psychological damage inherent to the, 59, 67, 69, 75; the physically violent nature of the, 71, 141, 162, 197–98, 200, 209; the postcolonial aftereffects of the, 10, 16, 132, 136–38, 195–96, 199–200; the psychologically violent nature of the, 12–15, 33, 67, 70, 171, 200, 223n13; the roundtable as a staged, 131–32, 138–39; the sociopolitical role of colonial kitsch in the, 28, 30, 87, 159–60, 171, 241n46
colonialism: the hierarchical logic inherent to, 34, 74–75, 93; imperialists' denials of their, 202, 203, 211; the lingering influence of, 204, 211; the Manichean logic underlying, 70, 105
coloniality, 9, 12, 77, 204, 207, 210
colonial kitsch: as a devaluation and exoticization of a colonized culture, 37, 104, 106, 156, 172–73; Korean literature as an object of, 28, 30, 37, 103, 166, 191; as a product of the colonizer, 15, 28–29, 106, 108–9, 130, 159–60. *See also* nostalgia; tradition
colonial modernity, 9–10, 208–10, 233n9
colonized subjects: the accusations of imperial collaboration made against some, 8, 15–16, 128–30, 217n30, 230n36, 232n55, 236n49; the aspirations for imperial equality among, 15, 93–94, 96, 140–41, 240n28; the blurring of colonizer and, 64–75, 97, 128; cast as a solely collective entity by the colonizer, 54–56, 76, 86; the challenges of modernity faced by, 40, 92; the challenge to of accurately presenting their cultural heritage, 36, 86–88, 104, 106–7, 113–14, 149–50; the colonized I-novel, 54–58, 59; the conundrum of representation faced by cultural producers, 10–15, 75–76, 89–90, 113–14, 222n4; imperial hierarchical behavior toward, 48–49, 61, 96, 121–22, 141–43, 145–47,

152–53; "Into the Light" as a study of the psychological damage suffered by, 64–75; Japanese assimilation-differentiation policies toward, 6–7, 45–46, 108–9, 145–47, 151–52, 225n31, 239n17; Japanese-language literature produced by, 18, 84–85, 145–46, 170–72, 230n34; "minor" writers among Japan's, 44–45, 54, 76–77, 83–84, 87, 155–56; the objectification of by colonizers, 166–70, 172–73, 199–200; the participation of in transcolonial roundtables, 131–32, 138–39, 145–53; the plight of bilingual writers, 14–15, 42, 45, 52–53, 60–61, 78–79, 98; the postcolonial disregard for the cultural achievements of, 7–9, 192–93, 233n9; the postcolonial reanalysis of the cultural productions of, 24–25, 31, 132, 174–75; the sense of belatedness and lacking among colonizers as well as among, 12–15, 39–40, 208–9, 230n25; as victims and as perpetrators of racism, 64–75, 93, 106, 126–27, 218–19n52; war mobilization as an influence on imperial policies toward, 45, 104–5, 140–41, 155, 157–58, 203
colonizer: the assumption of entitlement by the, 92, 225–26n32; the assumption of knowledge by the, 93, 148–49, 173; the blindness inherent to the, 14–16; the blurring of with the colonized in "Into the Light," 65–74; the damaging effects of the hierarchical assumptions of the, 75, 198; the damaging effects of the racist attitudes of the, 65–76, 97; the disavowal of the past shared with the colonized by the, 7, 10, 128, 233n9; the forced enculturation of colonial subjects by the, 113, 145, 158, 162, 171, 215n1; the influence of war preparations on the Japanese, 17, 27, 45, 80, 88, 108–9, 159–60; the inherent and unbreachable divide between colonized and, 7, 98, 147, 236n49; Japan's assumption of cultural superiority to its colonies, 54, 166–67, 230n25, 236n48; Japan's coercion of colonized writers to produce for Japanese consumers, 54, 87–88, 155–56, 217n30, 232n55; Japan's dual position as non-Western Other and also as, 12, 15,

40, 208–9; the power relationship of the
with its colonies, 97, 104, 106, 130, 145–47,
152–53, 227n50; transcolonial cultural
encounters between colonized and, 15–16,
131–32, 138–39; the violence of the toward
the colonized, 8; the Western or European, 11. *See also* Japanese empire
comfort women, 80, 202, 214n12, 232n62,
235n24, 239n22
communists and communism, 151, 177, 180,
183, 209, 243n23
conscription, 200, 202, 214n12, 234n18,
235n24, 244n41
consumer. *See* metropolitan consumers
contact zones: colonial literary production
from, 8, 18, 30, 155, 156; the complexity of
cultural interactions at, 6, 11, 45, 75, 195,
217n30; roundtables staged in, 136, 138
conundrum of representation, 10–11, 14–15,
18, 34, 76–78, 87, 159
cultural production: the constraints placed
on colonized writers and artists, 10, 16,
29–30, 83–86, 169–73, 240n28; imperial
coercion of colonial, 7, 103, 139, 144–51,
155–56, 162–63, 214n12; Kawamura Minato on colonial, 25, 47–48, 53, 229n09;
as problematic to nationalist delinea-
tions, 28

Deleuze, Gilles, 44, 58, 219n2
Derrida, Jacques, 6, 12, 137, 205, 219n4
differentiation: as a complement to imperial
Japanese identification policies, 7, 76,
88, 158, 163, 225n31; as a complement to
imperial Japanese assimilation policies, 8,
45, 75, 109, 131, 157–59, 199; as conundrum
for Korean colonials, 46, 71, 72, 74, 162–
63, 201–2
discrimination: as a complement to Japan's
imperial assimilation policy, 7, 45, 88, 93,
185, 188, 243n29; as studied in "Into the
Light," 67–69, 71, 75

education: the acquisition of as a challenge
to colonized women, 176–77, 189, 242n4;
the Japanese enculturation of Korean
colonial intellectuals, 7, 21, 77, 113, 157–58,
176

ethnography: Korean writers cast as self-
ethnographers, 15, 82–84, 88, 90, 155; as
part of the conundrum of the colonized
writer, 114, 156, 157. *See also* native informants
Eurocentrism, 11, 14, 39–40, 198, 204–8,
221n23
exclusion: the influence of on colonial
Korean literature, 25, 44, 48; and Japanese
ambivalence toward colonized Koreans,
52, 78, 175, 226n43
exoticization: of colonial culture as imperial
nostalgia, 28–29, 109, 166, 172, 241n37,
241n46; and the conversion of cultural
creations into mass-produced kitsch, 28,
37, 104, 108; as an element of the imperial
Korea Boom, 45, 101, 160, 163; and
imperial ideas of "Koreanness," 36–37,
87, 109, 128, 165, 230n25; the impressment
of colonized writers to serve imperial
consumers, 54, 82–83, 87–88, 130, 131, 159,
163; as a means of devaluing and differentiating a colonized culture, 28, 52, 88, 92,
106, 126, 160

Fanon, Frantz, 6, 221n29, 225n31
France, 38, 51, 95, 199, 204–7
Furukawa, 151–52

gaichi (hinterlands; *oeji*, K): gaichi bungaku
(colonial or hinterland literature), 30;
Japan's postwar loss of, 17; Korea's colonial status as both chihō and, 157, 201;
portrayed as proof of Japan's imperial
success, 158–59, 163, 165; versus Naichi
(Japanese mainland), 92, 158, 201, 215n2,
217n31, 226n42
Great Britain, 34, 38, 143, 204, 207, 222n8
Guattari, Félix, 44, 58, 219n2

Harootunian, Harry D., 134–36, 208, 218n51,
228n10
Hayashi Fusao, 139–42, 145–48, 151–52, 154–
55, 236n41
hierarchy: the concentric circle as the con-
ceptual basis for imperial regional, 12, 74,
158, 198, 218n47, 232n59, 238n11; gendered,
122, 148, 185–86; the global pattern of

hierarchy (*continued*)
value based on ideas of cultural, 18, 45, 126, 143, 198–99, 202, 209; the imperial as a construct based on power, 94; Korean acceptance of ideas of global cultural, 32–33, 34, 126; the permanent position of colonial inferiority in the imperial, 9, 15, 49, 53, 58, 61; the plight of the bilingual writer in an imperial, 86, 94, 123; racial discrimination as inherent to the imperial, 7, 45, 74–75, 185, 188, 243n29; the unstable imperial in Manchuria, 155–57, 200; the use of Father and Mother analogies in an imperial, 73, 74, 75
Honmachi, Korea, 90–91
Hutcheon, Linda, 89

identity: abjection and loss of self-, 223–24n8; the fragmentation of self- as a product of colonial racism, 59, 66, 67–74, 83–84, 93, 97; imperial name-changing policies as a redefinition of colonial, 239n25; the narrating I of the I-novel, 59, 65–66; the overshadowing of individual by colonial collectivity, 168–69, 238n9, 241n46; self- as a challenge for bilingual colonized writers, 46–47; social relationships as a means of conferring, 221n31, 242–43n18; the study of in "Into the Light," 59, 65–74, 75–76; the study of self- in "Pegasus," 89–93, 97, 225n29; Westernization and modernization as challenges to Japanese self-, 55–56
ilche malgi. *See* late-colonial period
Im Chongguk, 19, 20, 219n7
Im Chŏnhye, 23, 25, 227–28n4
Im Hwa: on Korean national literature, 33–34, 38–39, 148, 166, 171, 218n45; on the plight of the bilingual colonial writer, 34, 39–40, 142, 145–46, 149–50, 218–19n52
imperial language: the forced use of by colonized Korean writers, 5, 10–16, 18, 35–37, 40, 200, 213n1; as an impediment to Korean cultural expression, 10, 12, 15, 18, 46, 54, 59; Japanese motivations underlying the use of, 15, 60, 145, 163, 173, 190, 214n28; kokugo, 145; the postcolonial suppression of in Korea, 22, 24, 216nn9–10; and the

problem of Korean-Japanese written translation, 11, 15, 77, 170, 191, 205; the use of the as a deterrent to communication, 36–37, 42–43, 54, 59–60, 176
individuality: art as an expression of, 13; imperial construing of colonized as representative of a universality, 56, 57–58, 69, 171–73; imperial disregard for the of the colonial subject, 54, 82, 86, 168–71; as used in the I-novel, 56
I-novel, 5, 41, 54–57, 59, 76–77, 214n5, 221n23
intellectuals: the conflict between native and postcolonial, 207; the conundrum of colonized Korean, 37, 42, 124, 126–27, 141, 213n1, 218n52; diasporic, 207; Gramsci on organic versus status quo, 87, 224n19; imperial Japanese, 221n27; the involvement of in recovering zainichi literature, 23, 25–26, 99, 192, 215–16n4, 221n32, 222–23n12; Korean and the problem of belatedness, 218n51; the Korean disparagement of colonial Korean writers, 8, 19, 113, 202, 221–22n32; the training of colonized Korean, 7, 23, 26–27, 76, 94, 113, 176–77
intermarriage as studied in "Into the Light," 57, 68–69, 222n9
intimacy. *See* collaboration
"Into the Light": the actions of Yi and Yi's mother in, 68–71; the ghetto setting of, 57, 68, 72–73; Kim Saryang's ambivalence toward, 54–55, 61, 222n5; the literary context of, 59–61, 78–79; misconstrued as an I-novel, 55, 56, 59, 61, 76–77; the nomination of for the Akutagawa Literary Prize, 41, 50–51, 56–57; the plight of Haruo's mother in, 68–69, 73, 74; the plight of Minami/Nam in, 65–74, 77–78; the portrayal of damaged individuals in, 65, 73–74, 78; racism in, 64–71, 74–75; the shattered and schizophrenic characters in, 57, 61–62, 70–71, 76; the situation of Hauro's father in, 69, 71, 73–75; the story and characters of, 61, 65–78, 222–23n12; as a study of the falsehood of colonial harmony, 73–75; Yamada Haruo's racist behavior in, 65–71, 73
Itagaki Naoko, 35, 53–54

Jameson, Frederic: on modernity and colonial blind spots, 9, 197, 221n23; on the novel as national allegory, 57–58; on the roundtable format, 135, 136

"Japan and Korea, One Body" slogan. *See Naisen ittai*

Japanese cultural producers: candidates for the Akutagawa Prize, 49–54; cast as imperial liaisons, 80, 88, 139–40, 142, 145–47, 154, 201; Japanese critics, 35–36, 129, 145–46, 148–49, 231n45, 236n35

Japanese empire: the abrupt collapse of the, 6, 17, 174; assumptions regarding the cultural backwardness of its colonies, 32, 54, 143, 167, 201; the contradictory policies of concerning opium, 184–86; and the false "Rest"-West dichotomy, 6, 11, 27, 53, 105, 158, 199; the Father-Mother colonial binary, 73, 75; the late colonial period of the, 229n15; the Pan-Asian assertions of the, 6, 118, 155, 159, 162, 239n24; the self-assertion of the as the leader of Asia, 104–5, 201; travel in the, 41–42, 109, 119, 163, 165, 226n37, 235–36n28. *See also* colonizer

Japanese imperialism: the Akutagawa Literary Prize and, 47–48, 53; assertions regarding the unification and oneness of Asia, 162, 226n37, 239n24; censorship as a tool of, 18, 84–87, 136, 143–47, 151–52, 162–63, 240n28; and the Korean migration to Manchuria, 162, 178, 226n37, 242n15; Korean resistance to, 175, 177, 178; policies regarding colonial Korea, 219n5; the response of some female writers to, 227n46; the subsuming of colonized literatures and cultures as an element of, 81–82, 108, 109, 140–41, 144–46

Japanese language: assumptions regarding the equivalency of the Korean language and the, 35, 169–70, 189; the case of the *Ch'unhyang*, 101, 103–4, 112–13, 122–23, 128, 149–51; the censorship of the Korean language to promote the, 7, 17, 49, 80, 162, 170; Chang Hyŏkchu's banned writings, 35, 39, 99, 113–14, 128, 160; and the conundrum of the bilingual colonial writer, 32, 39, 43–46, 77, 113–14, 192, 217–18n36; the empire-wide circulation

of newspapers, 156, 158, 167, 171, 240n28; the forced use of the to promote colonial homogenization, 46, 122–24, 145, 158, 162, 171, 215n1; imperial name-change policies, 108, 225n26, 225n29, 239n25; imperial pressures on colonized Korean writers to write in, 17, 18–19, 27–28, 227n54, 242n2; as the intermediary language between its colonized peoples and the West, 27; Japanese-language literature, 26–27; Kim Saryang on the disadvantages of Korean writers writing in the, 84–87; Kim Saryang's controversial writings in the, 21–22, 27, 41; Korean postcolonial nationalist biases against the, 22, 85, 175–76, 187, 196, 216n12; the mass consumption of Korean-authored works in the, 35, 163, 166–67; "minor" literature by Korean authors written in the, 44, 176–77, 220n19; the postcolonial reanalysis of colonial Korean writings in the, 21–25, 192, 195, 217n24; the preeminence of the Japanese audience over colonial cultural producers, 15, 145–46, 167–68, 171

Japaneseness, 68–69, 75, 120, 159, 201, 238n13

Kabuki, 103, 118–20, 128, 143, 166

Kang Kyŏngae: "Changsan Cape[or Bay]," 169, 178, 187–89, 192–93, 239n26; the Manchurian frontier writings of, 175, 177–78; "Opium," 178, 184–85, 243–44nn33–35; the peasant background of, 173, 175–77, 189–90, 242n2; racism and stereotyping depicted in the works of, 182, 187–89, 193, 243n29; "Salt," 178–82; the thirst for education of, 176–77, 189, 240–41n33, 242n4; the works of in Korea's literary canon, 174–77, 179, 182–84, 187; the works of misconstrued by Japanese censors, 179, 182; the works of misconstrued by Korean nationalists, 177–78, 182–83, 187, 189, 193, 243n23, 243n25; the works of serialized during the Korea Boom, 175, 178, 189–92, 239n26; the writing perspective of, 175, 177–78, 180–82, 242–43n18, 243n28; the writings of in the context of the resistance-collaboration binary, 175–78, 184, 190–93

87; the as a source of anxiety for bilingual Korean writers, 77, 85–86; metropolitan assumptions regarding knowledge of the, 122, 145–48, 235–36n28; as one defining element of Korean literature, 31–32; the *Samch'ŏlli* survey regarding Korean language and literature, 31–33

Korean literature: the *Ch'unhyang*, 101–2, 107–8, 124, 228n5, 229nn17–18; the contributions of Yi Kwangsu to, 1–2, 5, 27, 32–35, 39; the effects of imperial censorship on the development of, 18, 35; Im Hwa on, 33–34, 38–39; imperial Japanese assumptions regarding Chōsen bungaku, 35–36, 53–54, 142–43; the incorporation of into Japanese imperial culture, 27–39, 156, 159, 167, 201–2; Japanese postcolonial study of, 26; Kim Saryang on, 84–85, 223n5; nationalist colonial discourses defining the nature of, 18, 28, 31–35, 37; as an object of colonial kitsch, 28, 30, 35–37, 80–82, 104, 156, 167–68; the plight of the bilingual Korean writer of, 27–28, 32–33, 35–37, 40, 84–85, 88–89, 217–18n36; postcolonial discourses defining the nature of, 26, 189–90, 214n6; postcolonial disparagement of bilingual Korean writers, 21–22, 99, 113, 124; postcolonial reanalysis of bilingual, 23–24, 25, 215–16n4; postcolonial study of *zainichi*, 23–26, 99, 179, 243n27, 243n33; the reanalysis by Kim Yunsik of bilingual, 21; the representation of translated as original to imperial audiences, 35, 40, 53–54, 156, 189–90; the *Samch'ŏlli* survey (1936) debating the nature of, 31–32, 34, 39; *sosŏl* versus the Western novel, 37–38, 39; Western influences on perceptions of, 37–40, 218n38; written by Korean colonials in Japanese, 18–19. *See also* literary canon

Koreanness: as an arbitrary Japanese construct, 29, 92, 104, 119–20, 121, 122, 165; as a dilemma of image presentation for Korean writers, 36–37, 87, 163; and racism in imperial Japan, 68–69, 71

Korean War, 21, 190, 245n15

Korean writers: agency as a paradox for colonized, 12, 155–56, 199–200, 202; cast as self-ethnographers, 15, 82–84, 88, 90, 114, 155–57; the charges of imperial collusion against colonial, 7, 8, 34; the Korean disparagement of colonial, 8, 19, 22, 113, 202, 221–22n32. *See also* bilingualism; collaboration; translators

Kristeva, Julia, 83–84, 205–6, 223–24n8

Kume Masao, 47, 49–51, 52

Lacan, Jacques, 6, 222n11, 223–24n8, 223n13

late-colonial period (*ilche malgi*): the chronological parameters of the, 17–18; the coincidence of the Korea Boom and the Manchurian Migration Boom during the, 160, 174, 190; Korean literary production during the, 20, 99, 159, 177, 189–93, 217n30, 227n54

"Letter to Mother" (*Haha e no tegame*), 41–42, 54, 219n1

literary canon: authors and works included in the Korean national, 5, 25, 28, 107, 175, 177, 182–83; bias and longevity as factors that configure a, 143, 174–75, 193–94; the case of Chang Hyŏkchu, 128, 239n17; the case of Kang Kyŏngae, 174–77, 179, 182–83, 187, 189, 193–94; the case of Yi Kwangsu, 196, 239n17, 243n25; colonial bilingual authors included in the Korean national, 23–25, 27, 175–77; imperial conversion of works in the Korean into colonial kitsch, 30, 76, 104; imperial exclusion of colonial works from the Japanese, 48–52, 76–78, 239n17; the influence of the world literary market on the imperial Japanese, 51, 52; the Japanese I-novel, 5; the role of the Akutagawa Literary Prize in establishing the Japanese, 47, 49–52, 219–20n8; the traits of imperial metropolitan canonical texts, 14, 50–51. *See also* Korean literature

Long Yingzong (Ryū Eisō), 60–61

Manchukuo puppet regime, 157, 160–61, 200, 203, 214n13

Manchuria: the circulation of Japanese language newspapers in, 156, 159, 163, 241n39; the comparable plights of Korean and Manchurian colonial writers, 45–46,

Manchuria (*continued*)

53–54, 99; expansion of the Japanese empire into via Korea, 18, 140, 154–55, 157–63; as a frontier of the Japanese empire, 156, 158, 159–60, 174, 179, 190–91; the geopolitical triangulation of the region, 174, 191, 199, 201; Korea as a nexus for imperial travel to, 88, 90, 92, 139–40, 154, 226n37; the Korean migration into as part of Japanese expansion, 100, 158–62, 178, 182, 191, 238n10; as the location of colonial resistance fighters, 177–78, 191; the "Manchuria craze" and the objectification of, 154, 230n26, 241n35, 241n37; as the setting for Kang's frontier writings, 174–75, 177–78, 179–88, 190

Manchurian Incident (1931): as a hallmark in Japanese geopolitics, 80, 155, 157, 160, 214n13, 226n37, 241n39; as a hallmark in Japanese history, 17, 132, 216n22; as a hallmark in Japanese policy changes toward the Korean populace, 7, 27, 156, 157, 159–60, 200; as a setback for Korean nationalists, 237n7

mass media: the degradation of the in imperial Japan, 135–36; as an imperial tool for the incorporating its colonies, 157–60, 162–65, 170–71, 199, 215n1, 240n28; imperial censorship and the, 152–53, 189; the influence of the imperial on colonial cultural production, 15, 139, 144, 169–70, 219n1; the influence of the on the popularity of the roundtable in Japan, 132–34

melancholy: among colonized culture producers, 60–61, 108; the use of among Korean writers, 1, 65, 79, 93, 97

metropole: the insularity of cultural critics in the, 86, 92, 112–13; and the Korea Boom, 80–81, 85, 108–9; the oscillations of colonized writers to and from the, 43, 77, 83–84, 87, 94, 114; the popularity of Chōsen bungaku (Korean literature) in the, 28, 35–37; as a primary communication point for colonial writers, 86–87, 113–14, 149, 200; the uncertain status of colonized writers in the, 43, 45, 60, 97; the uneasy cultural relationship between colony and, 100, 106, 138, 156–59, 172–73, 201, 217n31

metropolitan consumers: as the impetus underlying the "Korea Boom," 45, 101, 104, 108, 131, 159; the influence of on the Korean writers, 36, 156

migration, 100, 157–58, 160, 162, 177, 178, 182

Minami Jirō, Governor General, 141, 215n1, 219n5

minor writers and literature: colonial Korean, 19, 25, 39, 40; the concepts of, 44, 219n2; Japanese ambivalence toward, 52–53, 221–22n32; the linguistic conundrum of colonized Korean, 45–46, 77, 190–92; the multiple implications of chihō bungaku, 30; the plight of in imperial Japan, 42–47, 54–55, 60–61, 87–88, 98, 219n1; and the racism of metropolitan critics, 58, 74–77, 221n29

modernity: the adaptation of Western symbols as physical statements of, 90–91, 95, 224–25n24; and "belatedness," 12–13, 18, 34, 39–40, 92–93, 208, 218n51; the *Ch'unhyang* as a focal point of the imperial debate concerning, 107, 126, 128, 149, 226n18; colonial as a conundrum for colonizer and colonized, 8–9, 13, 128, 159, 196, 198–99, 209–10; colonial as a subject of study, 8–9, 209–10; colonial defined, 10; and coloniality, 9, 12, 77, 204, 207, 210; the development of the I-novel as a response to, 41, 55–56; and the dichotomy of developed versus developing, 9, 208, 209; the dislocating effects of imported, 39–40; as a globally shared condition, 9, 14–15; Japan's Overcoming Modernity debates, 105, 109, 136, 237n2; Japan's struggles toward, 57, 105, 109, 201; as a state of impasse for the colonized subject, 10–11, 233n9; as a symbol of female liberation, 95; versus tradition, 229n20, 229n22, 230n25; the Western, Eurocentric concept of, 11, 214n4, 226n20

Mukden Incident. *See* Manchurian Incident (1931)

Mundan, 83, 84, 96

Murayama Tomoyoshi: the attitudes of regarding Korean culture, 115–22, 143, 144–46, 148, 166; criticisms of, 122, 125–28, 231n46; the motivations of in staging a theatrical version of the *Ch'unhyang chŏn* by, 102–3, 112–15, 118–19, 122–24, 231n44; the relationship of to Chang Hyŏkchu, 114–15, 124, 127–28

Naichi, 92, 158, 163, 165, 201, 217n31, 226n42
Naisen ittai ("Japan and Korea, One Body") slogan: as Japan's call for Asian unity against the West, 6, 162; and the metaphor of marriage, 92; the misleading and self-contradictory character of, 122, 123, 140–41, 151–52, 235n23, 236n49; the overlap of with ideas of *ch'inil* ("intimacy" or "collusion"), 8, 15, 100, 200, 228n7; as a summary of Japan's absorption of Korea, 7–8, 139–41, 154, 158, 191, 219n5, 238n14
name-change policies, 108, 225n26, 225n29, 239n25
nationalists: the biases of Korean against Korean bilingual writers, 85, 130, 174–75, 190–92; as creators of a nonexistent postcolonial history of Korea, 22, 182–84, 187–88, 191–94, 210, 242n11, 243n23; the defense of Korean culture and traditions by against imperial incursions, 105, 108, 109, 128, 130, 237n7; the ethnic biases of colonized Korean, 126–27; Korean cultural idols as constructs of, 175–78
native informants: imperial assumptions regarding the place of Korean, 58, 82–83, 86–87, 142; the plight of Chang Hyŏkchu in working on the *Ch'unhyang chŏn*, 101, 114, 115, 122, 124, 231n44; the plight of colonial Korean writers functioning as, 15, 96, 143, 168, 207. *See also* ethnography; translators
newspapers: the empire-wide circulation of Japanese-language, 156, 158, 163; as a means of both assimilating and exoticizing Korea, 159, 163, 166–68, 171, 188–90
Noguchi Minoru. *See* Chang Hyŏkchu
North Korea, 19, 176, 183, 221–22n32, 222n9, 243n23
nostalgia: the Japanese creation of colonial kitsch to promote, 108, 166; as a Japanese tool to deflect Korean concerns about their future, 148, 159, 166; and the Korean

desire for nationhood, 106, 108–9, 177; the of an imperial culture for what it has destroyed, 28–29, 104, 105–6; as a point of conflict between colonizer and colonized, 106, 108, 129–30, 191, 201, 236n48; postcolonial, 196–98, 207; as a product of personal loss, 106, 228n13. *See also* colonial kitsch
novel: the as national allegory, 57–58, 74, 76, 232n62; the colonized I-novel, 54–58; the influence of the Western concept of the on Asian writers, 37–38, 55–56; the I-novel format, 5, 55; the Japanese I-novel, 41, 55, 77, 221n23; the Korean *sosŏl* and the Western, 37–39, 218n42; Yi Kwangsu's *Mujŏng* (*The Heartless*), 5, 7

Okinawa, 156, 158–59, 163, 221–22n32, 232n59, 238n12, 245n15
"Opium" (Mayak), 178, 184–86, 243–44nn33–35
Osaka mainichi: the attempts by to collect and control Korean culture, 166–68, 171; the circulation of, 158, 163; coverage of the "Brilliant Japan" Great Exposition in, 165, 241nn35–38; as a facilitator of Japanese mass consumption, 167, 169, 200–201, 240–41n33; the Korean Culture Specials series of, 159, 166–71, 188–90; the misrepresentations of Korean writers by, 167–70, 189; as a perpetrator of Japan's imagined imperial community, 158–59, 163–66, 190–91, 238n10, 241n39; the serialization of "Changsan Cape" in, 188–90, 191, 239n26
Otherness: as a by-product of colonialism and modernity, 109, 201, 209, 221n23, 221–22n32; the conundrum of translating the Self into Other, 10, 13, 40, 93, 222n11; as a creation of Western universalism, 13–15; cross-ethnicking, 231n51; the Manichean aspects of, 70, 91, 198, 199, 203, 209; as means of enforcing an imperial sociopolitical hierarchy, 52–53, 75, 78, 120, 131, 166, 192; perceptions of as the basis for racism, 66, 69–73, 156, 198, 200, 223n13; the sense of as experienced by colonized subjects, 11–13, 76, 84, 89–90, 205

overhearing: the definition of, 132, 232–33n1; as a postcolonial position, 137–38, 152–53, 235n27; reading versus hearing, 136–37, 137–38, 139; the transcolonial roundtable, 136–39

Pan-Asianism, 6, 118, 155, 159, 162, 239n24
p'ansori, 103, 118
parody: Hutcheon on, 89; self- in "Pegasus," 88, 93, 95, 98, 224–25n24
passing: the social phenomenon of, 57, 113, 222n6, 222n8; as studied in "Into the Light," 66, 68, 69, 73, 78
"Pegasus": the ambitions of Genryū/Hyŏllyong, the tragic-comical hero of, 88, 91–93, 95–97, 225n25, 225n29; the character Mun So-ok as the colonial modern girl in, 94–95; the colonial modern (mo-yobo) boy in, 89, 93, 94, 97, 224–25n24; the exposure of the emptiness of imperial promises and colonial hopes in, 92–94, 95–97; the Japanese Bundan in, 88, 90, 92–94, 96; the Korean Mundan in, 96; metropolitan misinterpretations of, 86; the overlap of fiction with reality in, 93–95, 96, 97–98; the plot of, 89–93, 97; racism and segregation in, 90, 92–93; as a self-reflective parody, 88–89, 93, 96–97, 98; the setting of in the Honmachi district of Keijō (Seoul), 90–91, 92; as a study of the conundrum of the bilingual writer, 88–89, 94, 96–98
postcolonialism: the concept of postcoloniality, 204, 208; Korean and Japanese disavowals of their shared past, 6, 9, 10, 13–14, 16, 156, 195; the paradox of, 10, 40, 203, 209–11; postcolonial discourse, 204–9; postcolonial myopia, 183, 196–97, 231–32n53
postwar: geopolitics, 40, 135, 136, 209, 221–22n32, 245n15; literature, 221–22n32, 233n8
propaganda: the mobilization of culture and cultural producers to support imperial, 18, 80, 151, 165, 171; the of assimilation, 154, 158, 176, 191–92, 219n5, 238n14; the promotion of Japanese language use to support imperial, 7–8, 27–28, 191, 192; roundtables as ideal media for dispersing

imperial, 133, 134, 136, 139–41, 234–35n20; war-related, 28, 242n15

racial discrimination. *See* discrimination
racial passing. *See* passing
racism: the blind spots inherent to Eurocentric analysis, 11, 13–14; "Changsan Cape" as a study of, 187–88; colonized culture producers as victims of, 16, 22, 46; and the empire's "Korean problem," 51–52; the ethnic divide sensed by Bunkichi/Mungil in "Aika," 3, 5; ethnic ghettos and slums, 25, 57, 72, 73, 74, 77; as a failure to distinguish the individual from the collective, 69; the historical animosities between colonizer and colonized, 97, 185, 188, 193, 237n4, 243n29; imperial gendering as, 120–22; "Into the Light" as a study of the spectrum of psychological damage resulting from, 64–71, 74–75; in "Pegasus," 91–93, 97–98; the permanent status of inferiority attributed to colonized Koreans, 47–54, 156, 158, 198; the psychological violence inherent to, 67–68, 75; the psychosocial blindness suffered by victims of, 69–70, 74–75, 93; segregation, 75, 90, 93; selective forgetfulness, 220n19; the singling out of "exceptional representatives," 53–54; stereotyping, 36, 121–22, 182, 193, 233n3
representation: the conundrum of, 10–15, 17, 27, 34, 155–56, 159, 170–71; the crisis of, 10, 11, 78; Korean literary depiction of the conundrum of, 59–60, 76–78, 87–88
resistance: Kang Kyŏgae's works in the context of the resistance-collaboration binary, 175–76, 179, 183–84, 190–92; Korean nationalist constructs of anti-Japanese, 178, 179, 183–84, 216n10; the resistance-collaboration binary as an inaccurate and simplistic postcolonial construct, 157–58, 174–75, 177–78, 186–87, 191–92, 199–200; versus collaboration, 8, 20, 101. *See also* collaboration
"Rest" and West dichotomy, 6, 11, 27, 53, 105, 158, 199
Rosaldo, Renato, 28, 104
roundtable discussions: The discussion of

Korean critics regarding Murayama's *Ch'unhyang*, 125–28; as an experience of hearing or overhearing rather than of reading, 136–38, 232–33n1; the "Future of Korea" as imperial misrepresentation and propaganda, 143–44, 145, 146, 147, 148–49, 151–52; the "Future of Korea" disagreement in participants' perceptions, 142–53, 166, 171–72; the "Future of Korea" discussion (October 1938), 138–53, 235n21; the "Future of Korea" discussion on Korean language censorship, 151–52; the "Future of Korea" Korean versus Japanese published versions, 141–42, 147, 149, 152–53, 236n35; as an ideal medium for dispensing propaganda, 133–34, 139–40, 200, 201–2; the imperial popularization of the format, 132–34, 136, 139, 234–35nn18–19; the 1992 scholarly discussion of, 134–36, 233n3; the positioning of audiences observing, 137; as promotional advertisements, 112, 119; of the theatrical performance of the *Ch'unhyang*, 120, 125, 139, 148–49; theatrical performances staged as, 15, 96, 125, 131–32; as tools for shaping the evolution of colonial Korean culture, 234–35n18–20; transcolonial, 131, 138–40, 143, 152–53, 154, 233n10; Yamazaki Yoshimitsu on, 132–33

Russia, 96, 157, 162, 199, 202, 210

Said, Edward: the concept of the "voyage-in" of the colonized, 1, 213n1, 217n23; on the myopia of Eurocentrism, 11, 13–15, 218–19n52, 219n2

"Salt" (Sogŭm), 178, 179–82

Samch'ŏlli journal surveys, 31–35, 39, 218n38

Satō Haruo, 41, 47, 54–55, 56–57, 76

schizophrenia, 57, 61, 70, 76, 109

Schmid, Andre, 157, 199, 220n17

Seoul, 155, 176, 210, 222n5, 225n26, 225–26n32. *See also* Keijō

sexuality: female chastity in the *Ch'unhyang chŏn*, 102, 148; unrequited homoerotic desire in "Aika," 1, 6, 27, 195

Shinkyō Theater Troupe, 102–3, 112, 119–20, 231n41, 231n44

smuggling, 179–81

sosŏl, 37–39, 218n42

subaltern status, 44, 58, 182, 210, 221n31, 242–43n18, 243n28. *See also* third world

subjectivity: the conundrum of colonized representation, 12, 76–77, 232n55; the fragmentation of, 61, 65, 70–71, 72–73, 75–76, 223n13; imperial emphasis on the collective of colonized subjects, 54, 171, 199–200; relational and self-identity, 65, 71–72; versus agency, 12–13, 54, 202

Taiwan: imperial influence in via Japanese-language newspapers, 156, 159, 163, 165, 238n12; imperial Japan's "One Body" policy in, 6; the plight of native cultural producers in Japanese colonial, 24, 46, 60, 71, 99–100, 222n4, 227n3

technology: the imperial acquisition of as proof of modernity, 165–66, 201, 241n35; the influence of Western literary and scientific, 27, 37, 40, 105, 147, 241n38; the of knowledge production, 58; as a tool for promoting imperial expansion, 28, 109, 144, 156, 157–59, 163–64

"Tenma". *See* "Pegasus"

third world, 57–58, 219n2. *See also* subaltern status

Tokyo: the cultural center of imperial Japan, 112, 115, 118, 149, 150, 155, 158; the location of the imperial university, 1, 76, 95, 239–40n27; the seat of the Bundan, 41, 42, 96; the slums of as the setting for "Into the Light," 57, 65, 73

tradition: as the basis for cultural development, 166, 229nn22–23; the case of the *Ch'unhyang*, 114–30, 148, 229n18, 232n57; colonial Korean efforts to preserve, 105–6, 107–8; employed as an imperial device for suppressing Korean culture, 166; imperial Japanese inventions of, 55–56, 230n25; imperial Japan's construct of a shared "Asian," 104–5, 106, 108–9, 228n10; imperial Japan's "Overcoming Modernity" discourse, 105, 109, 136, 237n2; imperial Japan's "Revival of Traditions" discourse, 105, 108; "Korea Boom" corruptions versus Korean national, 29, 103–4, 106, 108–9, 114, 130; the multiple

tradition (*continued*)
concepts of, 107–8, 229n20, 229n22; the significance of the *Ch'unhyang* to Korean national, 107, 128. *See also* colonial kitsch

traitors: colonial Korean writers cast as by postcolonial nationalists, 1–2, 7, 85–88, 100, 113, 127–28, 196; the conundrum of "traitorous collaboration," 7, 20, 22, 25, 84, 89–90, 96–97

translation: the changes to and layers of translation of "Changsan Cape," 189–93; of the colonial Self into the imperial Self as a conundrum, 12–13, 14–15, 40; by colonized Koreans labeled as traitorous, 1–2, 7, 85–88, 100, 113, 127–28, 196; and the definition of national literary canons, 31–33; as a focal point of postcolonial aversions, 11, 15; imperial assumptions of language equivalency, 35, 53–54, 147–50, 169–70; imperial concealment of the fact of, 35, 40, 156–57, 169–70, 189–93; imperial devaluation of the inordinate labor required for, 15, 50–51, 81–83, 145–46, 170, 190–91; into English of Yi Kwangsu's "Aika" by John Wittier Treat, 213n3, 214n6; into Korean of "Aika" by Kim Yunsik, 217n24; Japanese consumption of Korean literature in Japanese, 53–54, 82–83, 147–50, 191–93, 200; Japanese misreadings of translated Korean authors, 86, 104, 147; Kim Saryang on the disadvantages of, 84–87, 224n18; "Letter to Mother" as epitomizing the conundrum of, 41–43; the loss of ideas and meaning through, 27, 84–87, 145–50, 170, 219n2, 224n16, 224–25n24; as a means of devouring another culture, 33, 84–85, 143–48, 173, 200; as the medium for training colonized writers, 39; the multiple versions of the *Ch'unhyang*, 122–24, 149–50, 229n17; rewriting and multiple levels of, 147, 149–50, 189, 192–93; as a tool for replacing Korean with Japanese, 33, 45–46, 145, 147

translators: colonial Korean labeled as traitors by postcolonial nationalists, 127–28, 149; imperial assumptions regarding the duties and place of colonial, 58, 82–84, 96, 122–23, 189–91, 207; and the imperial

Korea Boom, 45–46, 81, 101; the plight of colonial writers functioning as, 15, 16, 45–46, 85–88, 113–14, 127; the self-parody of in "Pegasus," 88–89. *See also* Korean writers; native informants

triangulation, 40, 155–56, 174, 178, 198–202

United States, 157, 199, 202–3, 204, 209, 241n38, 245n15

universality: of the standards of the Western novel, 37–38, 51–52, 56–57; universalism versus particularism, 51, 53, 205, 220n20, 221n23; the of modernity as a global ideal, 39–40, 104, 105, 198–99; the Western and Eurocentric assumption of representing human, 10–15, 205, 206–7

vernacular language and literature, 18, 37, 39, 107, 218n42, 240n28

Vlastos, Stephen, 229n18, 229n20, 229–30nn22–23

war: imperial assimilation policies as a war-influenced strategy, 45, 108–9, 138, 225n29; imperial mobilization of colonial Korea for participation in, 17, 24, 27, 140, 219n5; imperial mobilization of cultural producers as propaganda tools to support the, 80, 88, 151, 160, 223n1, 230n36; Japanese use of Pan Asianism to stir anti-West sentiments, 155, 162, 228n10; Japan's military expansion into Manchuria and China via Korea, 31, 80, 157, 160, 215n1, 226n37; as an opportunity for women writers to achieve independence, 95; World War II, 27, 28, 197, 203, 208, 229n15, 245n15

Western imperialism: as an additional threat to colonized Korea, 10, 17, 34, 40, 105; in Asia, 69, 214n19; Japanese imperialism construed as a response to, 6, 53, 104, 155, 162; and modernity, 10

women: as chattel, 184; "comfort," 80, 202, 214n12, 232n62, 235n24, 239n22; familial relationships as the basis for the identity of, 242–43n18; the limited access to education of Korean, 176–77, 189, 240–41n33, 242n4; Podŏk's Mother (character), 184, 187; Pongyŏm's Mother (character),

179–83; traditional versus modern Westernized, 232n57

Yamazaki Yoshimitsu, 132–33, 233n2
Yang Chudong, 176, 242n4
Yi Kungu, 32–35
Yi Kwangsu: "Aika" ("Love?"), 1–3, 5–7, 27, 195, 213–14nn3–6, 217n24; as the father of modern Korean literature, 1, 2, 5, 27; as Kayama Mitsurō, 2; on language and literature, 32, 39, 217–18n36; the writings of in the context of the resistance-collaboration binary, 2, 7, 23–24, 195–96, 214n12; as Yi Pogyŏng, 1, 214n5, 217n24
Yi Pogyŏng. *See* Yi Kwangsu

zadankai (J). *See* roundtable discussions
zainichi (Korean resident in Japan) literature, 23, 25–26, 99, 192, 215–16n4, 221n32, 222–23n12